ACES FALLING

By the same author:

The Somme
Bloody April: Slaughter in the Skies over Arras, 1917
Somme Success: the RFC and the Battle of the Somme

With Nigel Steel
Tumult in the Clouds
Defeat at Gallipoli
Passchendaele
Jutland 1916

ACES FALLING

WAR ABOVE THE TRENCHES, 1918

PETER HART

Weidenfeld & Nicolson
LONDON

First published in Great Britain in 2007
by Weidenfeld & Nicolson

3 5 7 9 10 8 6 4 2

A CIP catalogue record for this book
is available from the British Library.

ISBN: 978 0 297 84653 6

Typeset by Input Data Services Ltd, Frome

Printed in Great Britain by Butler and Tanner Ltd, Frome and London

Weidenfeld & Nicolson

The Orion Publishing Group Ltd
Orion House
5 Upper Saint Martin's Lane
London, WC2H 9EA

The Orion Publishing Group's policy is to use papers that are natural, renewable and recyclable products and made from wood grown in sustainable forests. The logging and manufacturing processes are expected to conform to the environmental regulations of the country of origin.

www.orionbooks.co.uk

I would like to dedicate this book
to two ordinary boys

EDGAR TAYLOR
Born Camas Meadows, Idaho, US
Born: 9 January 1897
Died: 24 August 1918

&

JACK WILKINSON
Born Kirkby Overblow, Yorkshire, GB
Born: 10 January 1898
Died: August 1981

Contents

List of Illustrations

Section 2

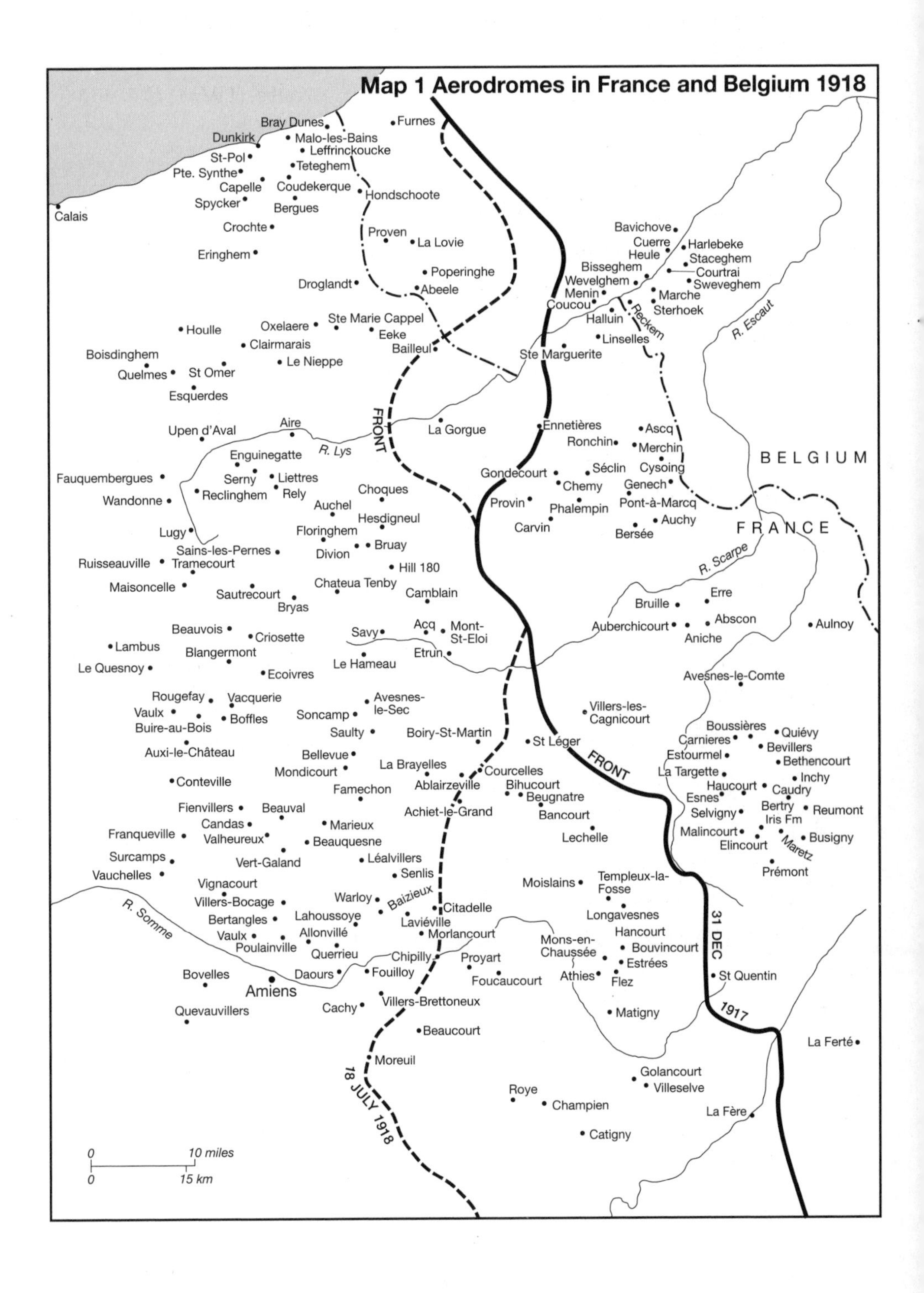

Map 1 Aerodromes in France and Belgium 1918
Bray Dunes
Furnes
Dunkirk
Malo-les-Bains
Leffrinckoucke
St-Pol
Teteghem
Pte. Synthe
Capelle
Coudekerque
Hondschoote
Spycker
Bergues
Calais
Crochte
Proven
La Lovie
Eringhem
Poperinghe
Droglandt
Abeele
Houlle
Oxelaere
Ste Marie Cappel
Eeke
Clairmarais
Bailleul
Boisdinghem
Le Nieppe
Quelmes
St Omer
Esquerdes
FRONT
Aire
Upen d'Aval
La Gorgue
R. Lys
Enguinegatte
Fauquembergues
Serny
Liettres
Choques
Wandonne
Reclinghem
Rely
Auchel
Hesdigneul
Lugy
Floringhem
Sains-les-Pernes
Bruay
Divion
Ruisseauville
Tramecourt
Hill 180
Maisoncelle
Chateua Tenby
Sautrecourt
Camblain
Bryas
Beauvois
Criosette
Savy
Acq
Mont-St-Eloi
Lambus
Blangermont
Etrun
Le Quesnoy
Le Hameau
Ecoivres
Rougefay
Vacquerie
Avesnes-le-Sec
Vaulx
Boffles
Soncamp
Buire-au-Bois
Saulty
Boiry-St-Martin
Auxi-le-Château
Bellevue
La Brayelles
Mondicourt
Courcelles
Conteville
Ablairzeville
Famechon
Fienvillers
Beauval
Achiet-le-Grand
Candas
Marieux
Franqueville
Valheureux
Beauquesne
Surcamps
Léalvillers
Vert-Galand
Vauchelles
Senlis
Vignacourt
Warloy
Baizieux
Villers-Bocage
Citadelle
R. Somme
Bertangles
Lahoussoye
Laviéville
Vaulx
Allonvillé
Morlancourt
Poulainville
Querrieu
Chipilly
Proyart
Bovelles
Daours
Fouilloy
Foucaucourt
Amiens
Cachy
Villers-Brettoneux
Quevauvillers
Beaucourt
Moreuil
18 JULY 1918
Bavichove
Cuerre
Harlebeke
Heule
Staceghem
Bisseghem
Courtrai
Wevelghem
Sweveghem
Menin
Marche
Coucou
Sterhoek
Halluin
Reckem
Linselles
R. Escaut
Ste Marguerite
Ennetières
Ascq
Ronchin
Merchin
BELGIUM
Gondecourt
Séclin
Cysoing
Chemy
Genech
Provin
Phalempin
Pont-à-Marcq
Carvin
Auchy
Bersée
FRANCE
R. Scarpe
Erre
Bruille
Abscon
Auberchicourt
Aulnoy
Aniche
Avesnes-le-Comte
Villers-les-Cagnicourt
Boussières
Quiévy
St Léger
Carnieres
Bevillers
Estourmel
FRONT
Bethencourt
La Targette
Inchy
Haucourt
Caudry
Bihucourt
Esnes
Beugnatre
Bertry
Reumont
Bancourt
Selvigny
Iris Fm
Malincourt
Busigny
Lechelle
Elincourt
Maretz
Prémont
Moislains
Templeux-la-Fosse
Longavesnes
31 DEC
Hancourt
Mons-en-Chaussée
Bouvincourt
Estrées
Athies
Flez
St Quentin
1917
Matigny
La Ferté
Golancourt
Roye
Villeselve
Champien
La Fère
Catigny
0
10 miles
0
15 km

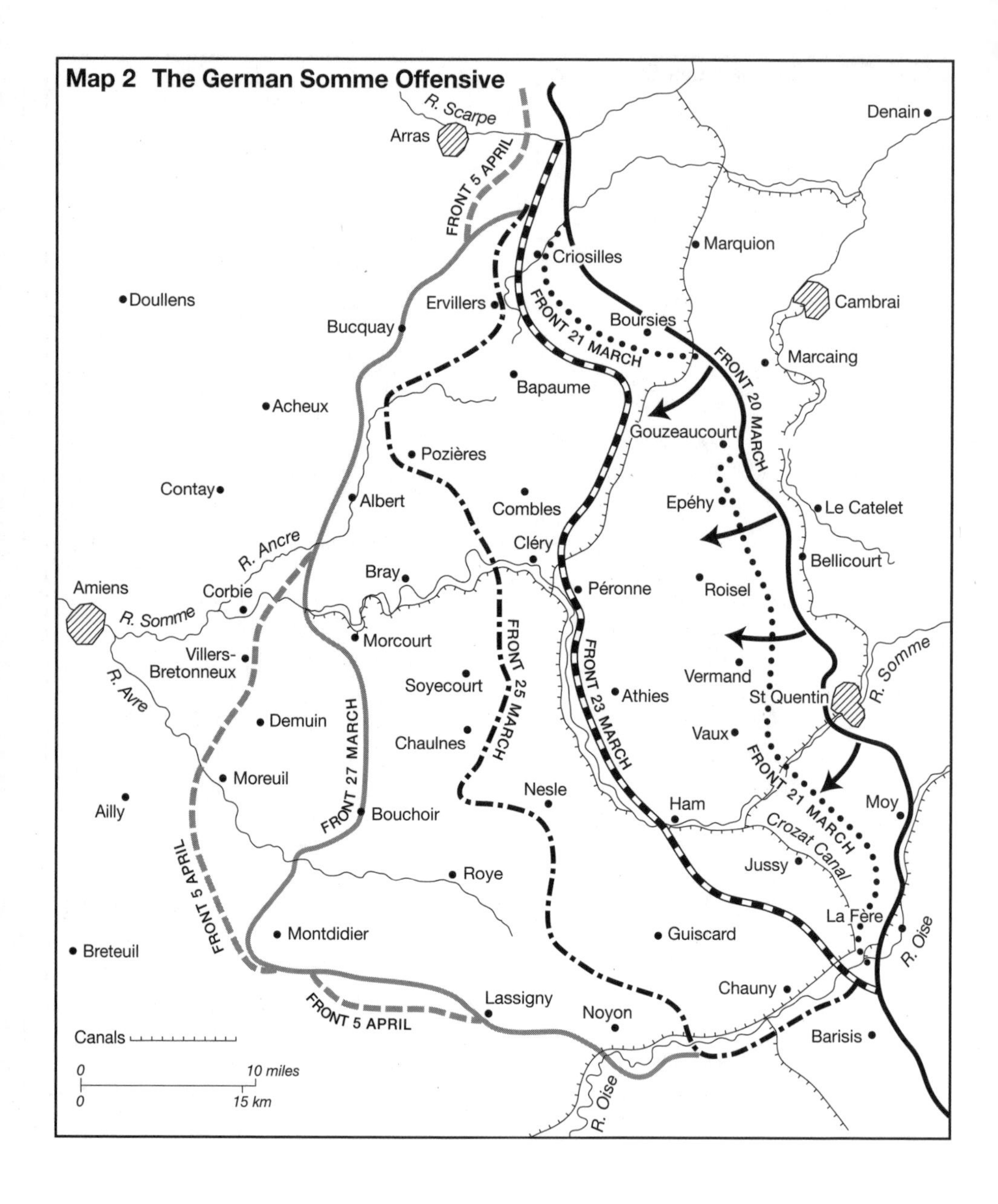
Map 2 The German Somme Offensive
R. Scarpe
Arras
Denain
FRONT 5 APRIL
Marquion
Criosilles
Cambrai
Doullens
Ervillers
Boursies
Bucquay
FRONT 21 MARCH
Marcaing
FRONT 20 MARCH
Bapaume
Acheux
Gouzeaucourt
Pozières
Contay
Albert
Combles
Epéhy
Le Catelet
Cléry
R. Ancre
Bellicourt
Bray
Amiens
Corbie
Péronne
Roisel
R. Somme
Morcourt
FRONT 25 MARCH
Villers-
Bretonneux
Vermand
R. Somme
R. Avre
Soyecourt
Athies
St Quentin
Demuin
FRONT 27 MARCH
Chaulnes
Vaux
FRONT 23 MARCH
Moreuil
FRONT 21 MARCH
Nesle
Moy
Ailly
Bouchoir
Ham
Crozat Canal
FRONT 5 APRIL
Jussy
Roye
La Fère
R. Oise
Montdidier
Guiscard
Breteuil
Chauny
Lassigny
Noyon
FRONT 5 APRIL
Barisis
Canals
0
10 miles
0
15 km
R. Oise

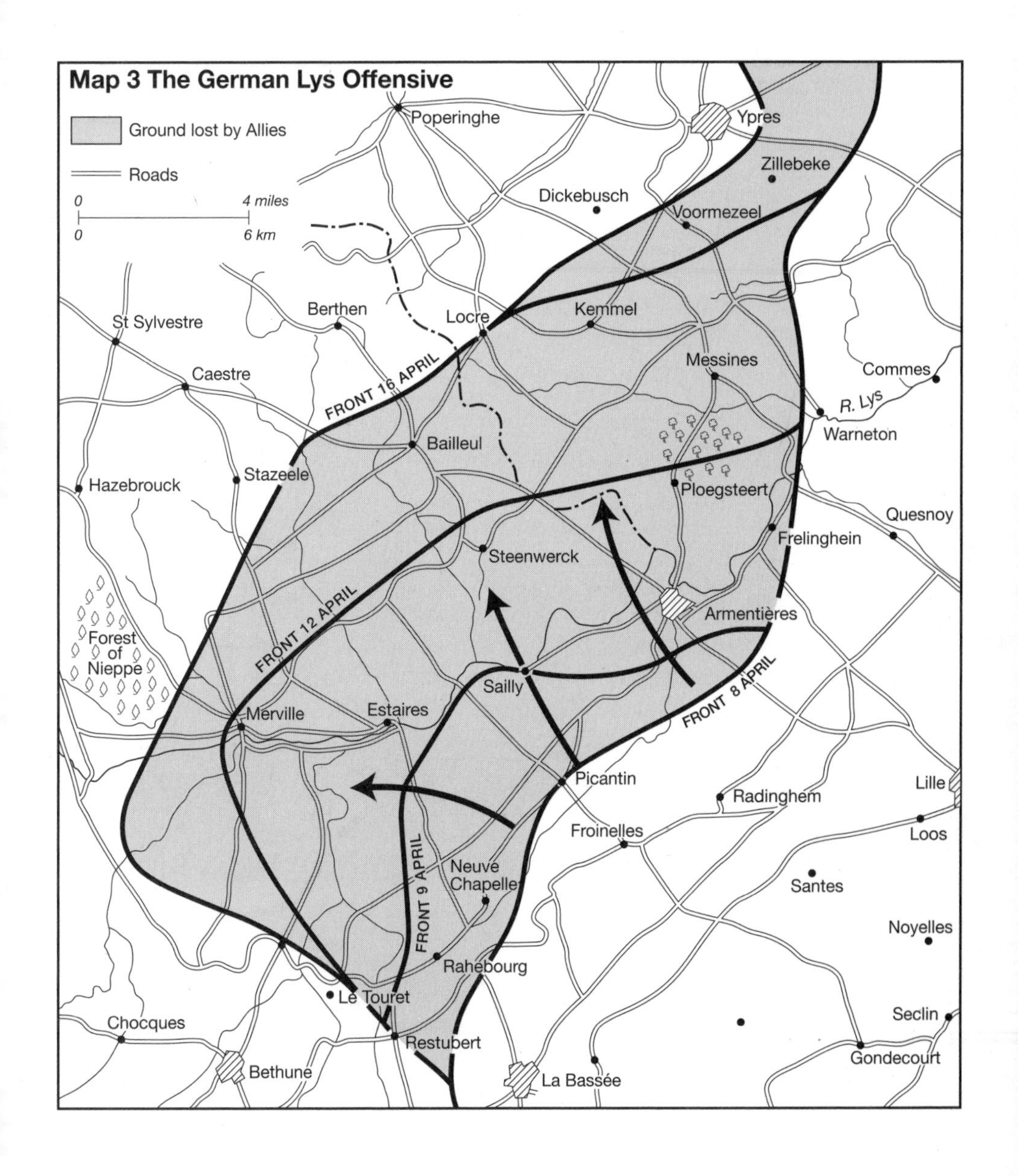
Map 3 The German Lys Offensive
Ground lost by Allies
Roads
0
4 miles
0
6 km
Poperinghe
Ypres
Zillebeke
Dickebusch
Voormezeel
Locre
Kemmel
Berthen
St Sylvestre
Caestre
Messines
Commes
R. Lys
Warneton
FRONT 16 APRIL
Bailleul
Stazeele
Hazebrouck
Ploegsteert
Quesnoy
Frelinghein
Steenwerck
Armentières
FRONT 12 APRIL
Forest of Nieppe
Sailly
FRONT 8 APRIL
Merville
Estaires
Picantin
Radinghem
Lille
Froinelles
Loos
FRONT 9 APRIL
Neuve Chapelle
Santes
Noyelles
Rahebourg
Le Touret
Seclin
Chocques
Restubert
Gondecourt
Bethune
La Bassée

Preface

The year of 1918 contained more air fighting than the rest of the Great War put together. Everything was on a stupendous scale: the dogfights between masses of highly coloured scouts swirling across the sky; the countless artillery observation and photographic reconnaissance missions; the raking low-level ground attacks that brought an extra terror into the lives of the long-suffering infantry. Perhaps the most ominous portent for the future was the increasing threat posed by bombing raids. These had begun to cause significant damage, not only to tactical objectives but also to strategic targets in cities deep behind the lines. War was reaching out to embrace civilians ever more firmly in its grasp. At the start of the hostilities, when the military deployment of the aeroplane was in its infancy, the generals and their airmen may have dreamed of what could be achieved, but the technological reality of their low-powered aircraft constantly thwarted them. But by 1918 it was no longer a question of what aircraft *might* achieve in conflict – they were already doing it. War in the air had reached an impressive maturity of both purpose and achievement by the last year of the Great War.

Yet, although there was an increasing recognition of the aerial dimension in military calculations 1918, also marked the end of the apparent primacy of the individual scout aces. The phenomenon of the ace scout pilot has dominated all perceptions of the Great War in the air. The myth of their chivalric aerial jousting and incredible feats of 'derring-do' have long been the staple of the popular view of the air war. Historians, too, have been obsessed with analysing all their 'victory' claims and minutely documenting all their victims. Who were these young men who have so captured the imagination? Crudely put, they flew fast scout aircraft whose role was to attack the enemy's two-seaters and at the same time to defend their own from their opposite numbers. The work of these photographic reconnaissance and artillery observation crews in their slow and steady two-seater aircraft was the real *raison d'être* of the air war. But their hard graft has been largely unrecognized and it was inevitable that the individual exploits of the scout pilots who preyed on them would be far more widely celebrated. The scout pilots' success could be far more easily and dramatically measured simply by counting the numbers of aircraft they claimed to have shot down. Each air force established its own rules for the acceptance of 'victories' and it became generally agreed that once a pilot had reached five victories then he could be considered an ace. In 1915 this was a considerable score as the skies were almost empty and the opportunities were correspondingly limited. But in 1916 as the number of aircraft dramatically increased some pilots began to push their scores ever upwards to dizzy heights. Every country had their early aces: the Germans had Oswald Boelcke and Max Immelmann; the British had Lanoe Hawker and Albert Ball; the French Roland Garros and Georges Guynemer.

It was the Germans who first saw the rich propaganda possibilities of the aces. The manly virtues of their entire nation could be embodied in a few heroic individuals; individuals whose achievements could be shouted from the rooftops and used as an inspirational force, not only within the German Air Service, but right across the whole of Imperial Germany. The French were of a like mind, but the British position was far more ambiguous. They preferred to maintain the illusion that they were all part of a team with no 'star turns'. Yet there were inevitable leaks to the relentless popular press who were desperate to celebrate their own British heroes. Thus while lip-service was paid to the policy of anonymity, their exploits were frequently emblazoned across the press as medal citations were written up and photos taken at every opportunity when the aces attended their medal investitures. Typical of this was the recognition and adulation poured over the high-scoring Captain Albert Ball on his return to England for a rest in October 1916.

The eye-catching exploits of men such as Ball and Boelcke offered hope that even in the Great War, where slaughter was mechanized on an industrial scale, an individual hero *could* make a real difference. The great aces seemed to transcend the grey homogeneity of modern warfare. Their public image was one of 'knights of the air', although if these were truly paragons of virtue then they inhabited a strange new world where ideas of chivalry sat uneasily alongside the grim reality of their ruthless killing to order.

Many of the best known aces had come to prominence in 1917, as they set out on the trail of broken aircraft and men that marked their passage from novice to practised killer. Some had learned quickly, naturals who seemed born to kill by instinct. Others had floundered until suddenly something seemed to click into place and a journeyman pilot was reborn almost overnight as a deadly ace. Once they had attained their five victories, most carefully counted and celebrated each and every one of their victims as their stepping stones to greatness in the imaginary league table that came to obsess many of them. The aces matched themselves against their peers in a never-ending game of leapfrog disrupted by the ramifications of leave, home postings, wounds and of course the inevitable fatalities among the aces themselves. This competition manifested itself at all levels. One example was to be found in the ranks of 22 Squadron where there were two competing aces: Lieutenants William Harvey and John Gurdon. Their rivalry was friendly, but all the same very real.

> My deadly rival (ha-ha), a very stout fellow named Gurdon, had the bad luck to get his observer fatally wounded in a big scrap the other day as well as himself. He is in hospital at present for a week with a bullet through the arm. So I am taking the chance to catch him up in the matter of Huns. The two today make us level once more.[1] *Lieutenant William Harvey, 22 Squadron*

The question of these victory totals – the siren call of which led many of them to their deaths – is controversial in the extreme. There is no doubt that the British pilots' tally of claims far outnumbered the casualties that can be readily identified among the German Air Service. As the British were fighting an offensive war, patrolling and fighting well over the German lines, it was always going to be difficult to resolve victory claims.

There was of course a downside to the adulation freely showered by the press on the aces. They were held up as glowing examples to their countries; as symbols of a nation's manhood. How then to explain when they were killed? As the early aces met their ends it was often amid a deliberately media-created blur which obfuscated exactly what had happened. Above all it was essential to avoid admitting that they had simply met a better, or luckier man. Thus when Guynemer died French schoolchildren were reportedly told that he had flown 'too high' and been taken by the angels. Albert Ball's death remained a mystery for years with added Arthurian connotations that he had flown into a cloud, only one day to return. Max Immelmann died in a mysterious accident when he shot his own propeller off, though the RFC claimed their men had done the shooting. Few aces seemed to die straightforward deaths in the years leading up to 1918.

It must have seemed to their contemporaries that the best known aces had made some kind of Faustian pact. They were heroes who blazed across the sky, but heroes all the same who seemed destined one day to have to pay the price for their amazing luck, their dazzling skills and their fame. Although they had apparently mastered their grim trade, many were increasingly afflicted by combat fatigue: the accumulated stresses of living a life where a single mistake could mean certain death. With the onset of the New Year in 1918, many of the very greatest of the surviving aces were clearly beginning to struggle. The losses of their friends and equals had shown them that all the skill and caution in the world would never be enough to guarantee safe passage in a bullet-strewn sky. Any fool could bring them down with a lucky hit. Many were further consumed with dark inner fears of being caught, as were so many of their victims, in a burning aircraft, facing the ultimate 'choice' of an agonizing immolation or a last hopeless leap into oblivion. An aura of doomed youth still clings strongly to the images that have survived of many of the aces. Looking at their photographs the natural effects of overwhelming tiredness and stress are transmuted in our imagination into the 'thousand-yard stare' of legend.

Unfortunately, just when many of the leading protagonists of the air war were desperately in need of a lengthy rest, the pace of the war on the ground reached a savage crescendo that dwarfed anything that had gone before. Whatever the romantic view of the war in the air, the reality remained that the air forces of both sides were still in thrall to the manifold needs of the ground forces. Even the greatest of the aces was as grist to the all-consuming mill; not even they could be spared from the Armageddon that was the Western Front in 1918. New priorities were increasingly forcing their way onto the agenda of all the air forces. Hundreds of scout aircraft would fly low over the battlefield, spraying machine-gun bullets on the fleeting targets of opportunity. Advancing troops, machine-gun posts, gun batteries, columns of marching men or supply columns were all fair game and low-level ground strafing could kill far more men in minutes than the most deadly ace could manage in a year. Bombing spread its wings to cover not only the battlefield itself, but reached back to encompass the airfields and billets of the pilots. By day or by night it was far easier to decimate a scout squadron by raiding their airfield than to shoot them down in 'fair' combat. The scope of the air war spread from the heights of 23,000 feet right down to ground level; it reached from the front lines back to the industrial heartlands and it was increasingly a 24-hour, 7-day-week affair. It was unrelenting in every sense on the protagonists. Gradually swamped by the scale of the fighting, the aces on both sides would fight on come what may in the cause of their countries. And in the last great battles of that awful year most of them would die – aces falling one by one.

Few of these aces now linger in the popular memory, though one has attained a strange immortality – the great Manfred von Richthofen. It is deeply ironic that the German 'ace of aces' should be remembered largely thanks to the efforts of a cartoon dog and an infuriatingly catchy tune – 'Snoopy Vs the Red Baron' – rather than any sensible appraisal of his many abilities. But the men Richthofen taught, led and inspired should not be forgotten: his brother Lothar von Richthofen, the iron man Rudolf Berthold, the deadly Ernst Udet and Erich Löwenhardt are just a few examples, but there were many, many more.

The doomed British heroes are led by the incomparable James McCudden, the supreme individual British ace with fifty-seven claimed victories before he was killed in an absurd flying accident during a routine take-off on 9 July 1918. The finest British patrol leader was surely Edward Mannock, the 'British Richthofen' who claimed about fifty victories before being shot down by ground fire while dallying over his latest 'kill' alongside a young protégé on 26 July 1918. But they were not alone: there was George McElroy, now forgotten, who changed gear after a slow start to claim a startling forty-nine victories between September 1917 and his death in action on 31 July 1918; the 'dead shot' Australian Robert Little who achieved some forty-seven successes before he was shot down fighting a Gotha night bomber on 27 May 1918; while his countryman Roderic Dallas claimed some thirty-nine victories before he met his death taking on three Fokker Dr.Is on 1 June 1918.

Of course not all the aces died. Many were just *hors de combat* and survived thanks to the very wounds that crippled them. Some battered warriors never found any kind of peace, but continued to battle on, in the case of Rudolf Berthold, fighting anybody and everybody rampaging across Germany at the head of his Freikorps, until he was himself callously butchered by Communists in 1920. Perhaps a man only has so much luck and these men went to the well once too often. Several of them managed to kill themselves in flying accidents shortly after the war. So died the South African Captain Anthony Beauchamp-Proctor in 1921, spinning into the ground while practising for an aerobatics display. Lothar von Richthofen perished piloting a Hollywood siren in his passenger aircraft in 1922. The great French ace Charles Nungesser disappeared in a ludicrously ill-considered attempt to fly the Atlantic in 1927. Samuel Kinkead was killed, in a sense looking to the next war and pushing back the frontiers of aerial technology, while attempting to break the world air speed record in the Supermarine S5 progenitor of the Spitfire in 1928. Canadian William Barker lasted a little longer until his barnstorming career as an entrepreneur and aerial showman culminated in a fatal air crash in 1930.

A few lived to enjoy their old age and some of the old warriors even served in one capacity or another in the Second World War, including Raymond Collishaw, William Bishop, 'Grid' Caldwell, Cecil Lewis, Gwilym Lewis and Ernst Udet. Yet whatever their fate the aces would never again attain the giddy heights that they had achieved as young men. One ace was certainly marked out for worldwide opprobrium when as a Nazi war leader Hermann Göring was for a while second only to Adolf Hitler himself.

Although this book charts the fall of a selection of the British, American and German aces (for space reasons alone the French contribution is sadly muted in these pages) it does so against the background of a growing appreciation of the *real* power that lay in the air for those who could grasp it. Aerial bombing and ground-attack strafing were where the future lay. It was a future where numbers, organization and technology would ultimately hold sway against any individual air ace, however luminously they might briefly shine. The lustre of the war in the air slowly faded until it became just another slaughterhouse in the all-encompassing mayhem that was the Great War.

Peter Hart, 2007

Chapter 1

Where Are We?

By 1918 the expansion of the Royal Flying Corps (RFC) had mirrored the expansion of its parent organization, the British Expeditionary Force (BEF). Since the outbreak of the Great War in August 1914 the role of the aircraft had developed from virtual fantasy to firm reality driven by the catalytic effect of war. The original simple reconnaissance functions had developed into the systematic photographic mapping of the entire German front line and hinterland. Experiments in observing the fall of artillery shells from the air had blossomed into a complex system of artillery observation that could control the gun batteries of an entire army corps to wreak destruction on sufficiently tempting targets. Early attempts to take any kind of weapon into the sky, starting with the rifle or even the pistol, had culminated in the development of fast, highly manoeuvrable scout fighters armed with twin machine guns. As to aerial bombing, it had advanced from a few determined individuals displaying their murderous intent by randomly lobbing *flechette* darts, hand grenades or adapted artillery shells out of their cockpits. Four years later well-drilled squadrons were dropping aimed bombs capable of inflicting serious damage on targets whether troop concentrations, the infra-structure of communications, munitions factories or just cities full of ordinary people.

After the successful incorporation of aircraft into the all-arms battle in 1915, the demand for the services of the RFC knew no bounds over the next three years. But the RFC was above all the handmaiden of the guns: aerial photographs allowed for the detection of significant targets; its artillery observation flights fine-tuned the accuracy of the guns; it had the power through its contact patrol flights to pierce the communication problems and general smoke of battle to report progress or bring down fire support when required.

It was a self-evident truth that the value of the guns and howitzers of the Royal Artillery was beyond measure. Indeed the British Army and its commanders had collectively learned a great deal during the traumatic Battle of the Somme in 1916. By the start of 1917 they knew that the preparations for any successful assault *demanded* a tremendous bombardment of artillery to smash the front-line defences and cow the surviving garrison troops. They knew that the German guns *had* to be faced down in a preliminary artillery duel to prevent them creating dreadful havoc once the British troops emerged from their trenches. It was now understood that those German batteries that had not been destroyed *had* to be neutralized, most commonly by the mass use of gas shells to drench the area with incapacitating noxious gases of varying lethality. When the assault went in the guns *had* to provide systematic creeping barrages ploughing forwards across the battlefield to suppress all serious opposition as the infantry struggled across No Man's Land. When a position had been taken a standing barrage of bursting shells *had to* be laid in front to ensure that any German counter-attack would be severely weakened before it got anywhere near the hastily consolidating infantry.

The primacy of the guns meant that the preliminary gunnery duel between the massed batteries of both sides was of crucial importance. As the Germans of necessity paid increasing attention to camouflaging their gun batteries from the RFC 'eyes in the sky', other methods were developed by the British to pinpoint their location. The blaze and noise of a gun's discharge could not be disguised and both flash spotting and sound ranging were routinely used to register the location of the German batteries. Yet these developments supplemented the work of the RFC rather than replaced it.

The Allied offensives of 1917 were designed to capitalize on the perceived damage done to the German Army in the previous year by the twin attritional battles of the Somme and Verdun, battles that had brought a hell on earth to their infantry and gunners. Yet the German Empire was no pushover. It had the resources to withstand an enormous amount of punishment. Its geographical diversity and the cooperation of neutrals enabled it, at least in part, to withstand the unceasing blockade from the Royal Navy that had been confirmed in its hegemony of the seas by the Battle of Jutland on 31 May 1916. The German Army was huge, millions of men marching under the Imperial colours. Hundreds of thousands had died, but each year another mass of recent schoolboys was ready for the call up to the colours. Many more must die before the Germans were ready to concede defeat.

The British Army had indeed learned a lot on the rolling hills of the Somme. Yet there was still much to learn, a lot of fine-tuning before the all-arms battle could be fully orchestrated. What seems obvious from the perspective of the twenty-first century was not always so crystal-clear in 1917. The British Commander-in-Chief Field Marshal Sir Douglas Haig was still firmly wedded to the idea of breaking through. He recognized the difficulties, but was repeatedly tempted to try to capitalize on the sheer effort and millions of shells needed to break through the German First Line system; he wanted to try to ride that wave of momentum right up to and over the German Second Line system. First at the Battle of Arras, then at Messines and throughout the Third Battle of Ypres he failed to realize that with the weapons systems then at his disposal the best tactical prospects lay in 'bite and hold'. This was the purest form of attrition where any gains in ground came a long way second to the systematic slaughter of German troops. The system recognized that the British field artillery was hamstrung by the limited 6,500-yard maximum range of their 18-pounders and 4½-inch howitzers. This meant that from their gun positions they could only reach about 2,500 yards into German lines and consequently they had to move forward before they could effectively bombard the German Second Line system.

Over the previous two years General Sir Henry Rawlinson and General Sir Hubert Plummer had hammered out the brutal tactics of 'bite and hold': first deluge the German defences and artillery with shells, advance under the cover of raking creeping barrages to a maximum depth of 2,000 yards, then dig in and slaughter the counter-attacking German troops. When the troops had fully consolidated their gains, then move forward the guns, replenish the ammunition supplies, bring in fresh troops and repeat *ad infinitum*. Berlin was a long way away at a mile a week, but success was defined by the efficiency of such methods in killing Germans at a far faster rate than the British were dying. The trouble was that 'bite and hold' demanded patience of the highest order and almost unlimited resources. Even when Plumer was grinding down the German defences on Gheluvelt Plateau and Passchendaele Ridge above Ypres, mistakes began to creep into the basic methodology. Short cuts led to inadequate bombardments, which in turn could lead to disasters mirroring the worst debacles of the Somme. And of course the Germans were never passive victims. They changed their defensive tactics to leave the forward zone lightly defended, mainly by machine-gun posts tucked out of harm's way in concrete bunkers or pillboxes; the Second Line system thus became the heart of the defence and the German counter-attack divisions stood ready to strike hard should the British expose themselves beyond the blanket cover of their field artillery.

The stage was now set for the next step in the development of British tactical theory. The 'headline news' was the attempt to exploit the massed use of tanks. First, they offered a certain method of crushing the German barbed wire without the necessity of a prolonged preliminary bombardment. Second, the tanks were useful against German strong-points or machine-gun posts. Third, they were seen as a method of breakthrough, driving on the attack to break through the German trench system. This last was probably not feasible given the low speed, mechanical unreliability and limited range of contemporary tanks.

The tanks may have caught the eye, but the real tactical advance was the seismic change in gunnery techniques achieved by the Royal Artillery. Every year of the war had brought more sophistication into the science of gunnery, but by late 1917 there had been a real step forward. Accuracy was massively improved, not this time by the efforts of the omnipresent RFC observers in the sky, but due to the pinpoint survey of the battlefields so that the maps really did reflect precisely what was there on the ground. Crucially, it was also at last fully grasped that gun barrels varied, not only in relation to each other, but also throughout their limited life span. They therefore needed to be 'calibrated' against a known standard, so that the errors from the norm could be determined and then built into the calculations for each gun. The variable effects of barometric pressure and wind speed on the flight of a shell were also understood and these meteorological observations were then routinely included in the gunners' calculations. This allowed the guns to open up in a barrage shooting 'by the map' with the appropriate corrections without the necessity of previously registering the guns.

All this innovation reintroduced the possibility of tactical surprise, which was brilliantly exploited at the Battle of Cambrai on 20 November 1917. The guns gathered in secret, registering from the map and not by firing the all too noticeable registering rounds that would have indicated their presence to the Germans. The guns opened with a mighty roar, smashing and neutralizing the Germans, the tanks rumbled forward, crushing the barbed wire, the infantry followed and until the lumbering tanks reached the nemesis of concealed German artillery batteries the way seemed open. In truth the British had been a little taken aback by the scale of their success. Their reserves had already been drained at Ypres and they could not capitalize; indeed they were themselves caught by a German counter-attack ten days later which premiered some of the mass bombardment and storm-trooper infiltration tactics that would be at the heart of their offensives in 1918. Both sides were learning how to use the weapons in ever more effective and deadly combinations.

Yet war is not only about attack. Over the winter the whole situation on the Western Front had changed beyond recognition as the collapse of Russia had released Germany from the trauma of fighting on two fronts at once. Most of its forces could now be concentrated on the Western Front for one last attempt to attain victory before the British naval blockade finally drained the German economy dry. By the spring of 1918 the Germans would have over 190 divisions massed on the 468 miles of the Western Front, while the British and French could only muster around 156. The likely outcome of the war had not really changed: the imminent arrival of the United States forces ensured that any advantage the Germans had on the Western Front would be but temporary. Although after eight months of war the Americans had taken up the burden only to the extent of just one division holding 6 miles of the front, there were hundreds of thousands more of them: all *nearly* trained, *nearly* ready for action. Nevertheless it was clear that the Russian collapse coupled with the dreadfully slow and mannered American mobilization gave Germany a brief window of opportunity in the spring and early summer of 1918. After that it would assuredly be too late.

The highest rung of the German High Command consisted of two men who many considered had risen to the level of *de facto* rulers of Germany. Field Marshal Paul von Hindenburg and General Erich Ludendorff had established their reputation with the crushing defeat of the Russians at the Battle of Tannenburg in August 1914. As a team they had replaced General Erich von Falkenhayn during August 1916, but their authority had grown to encompass much of civilian Germany. Neither was quite what they seemed: Hindenburg, a solid embodiment of the state made flesh, was brighter than he looked; while Ludendorff, the ice-cold brain, was prone to some degree of mental instability under stress.

The Germans were planning for breakthrough, for annihilation and for victory on the Western Front. They were not short of proposed plans. The first was for a massive assault in the Somme area to throw the British back and then, after leaving a protective flank guard against possible French intervention, to attack north, thereby 'rolling up' the British line. This option became known as Operation Michael. A second scheme, Operation George, envisioned a bold thrust to cut through the British lines in the river Lys sector near Armentières and then a race to the sea to cut the BEF from the succour of the Channel ports of Dunkirk and Calais. A third proposed taking on the French with twin attacks on either side of the Verdun salient to be known as Operations Castor and Pollux. Once Verdun had been 'pinched out' they presumed the French would be a spent force and the British could be targeted without fear of interruption. Other offensive plans included an envisioned attack in the Arras area – Operation Mars. After much discussion it was decided to target the British Army so Verdun was perforce ruled out. The question then was where to attack the British. After considerable vacillation the final choice was for Operation Michael. The strongly held Arras ridges were not a palatable option for a 'must-win' offensive and although planning continued it was relegated to a support role. The deciding factor was time: every month counted and it was apparent from the flooded terrain of the Lys valley that an attack could not be made before April, while the attack in the Somme area could be launched in March 1918. In Ludendorff's opinion the most important necessity was to achieve a breakthrough. Once they were through the British lines then the strategic objectives could be set according to the developing situation. His explanation exudes a certain smugness.

I was influenced by the time factor and by tactical considerations, first among them being the weakness of the enemy. Whether this weakness would continue I could not know. Tactics had to be considered before purely strategical objects, which it is futile to pursue unless tactical success is possible. A strategical plan which ignores the tactical factor is foredoomed to failure. Of this the Entente's attacks during the first three years of the war afford numerous examples.[1] ***General Erich Ludendorff, General Headquarters***

As the Germans plotted victory on the Western Front, back in Britain a group of politicians, led by the Prime Minister David Lloyd George, finally made their move to control Haig who in their view was wasting thousand upon thousands of British lives in futile assaults on the Western Front. It was Lloyd George's contention, backed by other 'Easterners', that the Allies should be concentrating their efforts on knocking Austria, Turkey or Bulgaria out of the war and thereby exposing the German 'underbelly'. To the 'Westerners' led by Haig and the Chief of Imperial General Staff Sir William Robertson such plans would mean throwing lives away in pointless side shows which, even if successful, would contribute nothing to the real deciding battle of the war on the Western Front. Yet Lloyd George and his cohorts remained unconvinced. After the relative failures of the BEF on the Western Front in 1917 they moved to retain in Britain a substantial proportion of the reinforcements that should have been restocking the depleted ranks of Haig's legions. To add further injury they ordered the despatch of more British divisions to bolster the Italian front.

As a result of this near suicidal policy, on the very eve of the German onslaught the British were forced to reshuffle and totally reorganize their chronically under-manned divisions, reducing the number of battalions in the constituent infantry brigades from four to three, and hence the number of battalions in a division to nine, which therefore matched the system employed in the French and German armies. This was not necessarily bad practice, but the timing for such a major reshuffle was dubious in the extreme. In this dramatic cull some 141 battalions disappeared. The remaining battalions would be brought up to full strength from the disbanded units.

The British and French commanders knew that the Germans would attack: the question was when and where. As Haig wisely commented later in the war, to the bemusement of the intellectually challenged ever since: 'How much easier it is to attack, than to stand and await an enemy's attack!'[2] The attacking general has the initiative, the enemy must respond to his moves; in defence you must guess how, where and when the blow will fall – no easy task and with awful consequences for failure. The British knew they must for once defend and of necessity they looked to the pragmatic system of defence in depth that the Germans had practised with considerable success during the Third Battle of Ypres in 1917. As a result, in December 1917 the General Headquarters of the BEF produced their *Memorandum on Defensive Measures*. In essence the bulk of the troops were held back, well away from the massed field artillery of the opposing force. The Forward Zone, based on the existing front line system, was intended merely to slow down the attacking troops, with a new emphasis on fortified strongpoints connected by fields of interconnecting machine-gun fire rather than linear trench systems. Pre-planned defensive barrages would crash down on any threatening incursion. Set back about 1 or 2 miles behind the Forward Zone was a more conventionally defended linear series of defences – the Battle Zone – that were out of range of the initial mass barrages from all but the very heaviest guns and howitzers. Behind this was the Rear Zone that was to be constructed about 4 to 8 miles further back.

Yet the British had little experience of defence; the last full-scale German offensive had been back at Ypres in April 1915, many lifetimes ago. There were several intractable problems that they were required to overcome before they could properly introduce a flexible system of defence. The first and most obvious was that their Forward Zone positions had been dictated by tactical considerations in the final throes of the last attack. They were often badly sited in valleys, overlooked by the Germans and with dreadful communications across the battlefield wastelands immediately behind them. There were salients that were simply indefensible. A series of tactical withdrawals might have seemed the answer, but for reasons of morale were almost inconceivable. The vulnerable bulges in the line left after the Third Battle of Ypres, and at Flesquières following the Battle of Cambrai, would have to be defended because how could they abandon the sacrificial ground that so many had died to capture just short months before? There were also the knock-on effects of the severe manpower shortage: exactly who would dig the new lines, construct the concrete pillboxes and lay the barbed wire? Did they actually have the time to get the new defences finished before the Germans attacked? Theoretically there was also a question as to whether the generals responsible had fully taken on board the concept of defence in depth. In many cases the idea of an elastic Forward Zone funnelling attacking troops between defended localities into machine-gun and artillery 'traps' seems to have been fatally compromised. Generals found it impossible to 'give up ground' and consequently placed up to a third of available troops in the Forward Zone, tethered well within the range of the German field artillery and vulnerable to being overrun.

The situation was complicated by the manifold alterations in the High Command at Home. David Lloyd George was an accomplished politician. Haig was as yet beyond his reach but CIGS General Sir William Robertson was a more feasible target. Lloyd George embroiled him in a dispute over his powers in relation to the Supreme War Council, casting his silken lines around the thrashing Robertson until he was forced into a corner and duly replaced by General Sir Henry Wilson. This could have been a serious blow to Haig as Wilson was not one of his foremost admirers and had a well-earned reputation for duplicity. Yet he was no incompetent and the press of events over the next few months meant that their relationship, while never warm, was functional. In a similar fashion the appointment of a new Minister of War, as Lord Milner replaced Lord Derby, did not really alter the overall situation. Lloyd George had intended this as the first steps in a root and branch renewal of command with the ultimate aim the toppling of Haig. In this he failed.

In the air war the situation had been transformed out of all recognition. The entire *raison d'être* of the Royal Flying Corps had been to facilitate the British offensives launched in 1915, 1916 and 1917. Its whole method as developed by the Commander of the RFC on the Western Front, Major General Hugh Trenchard, had been based on pushing the scouts deep behind the German lines and thereby allowing his reconnaissance and artillery observation aircraft free play over the German lines where their work truly counted. In a sense the Germans had acquiesced in this by adopting a defensive aerial strategy based on preserving their strength and generally harassing the superior numbers of RFC aircraft as best they could. Now in 1918 the Germans *had* to get their reconnaissance aircraft deep behind the British lines on a far more regular basis than had previously been their practice. Their scouts *had* to stop the RFC reconnaissance aircraft from crossing the lines to uncover the secrets of the German plans. Once the offensive began the German aircraft would be needed more than ever for artillery observation duties, infantry contact patrols and low-flying ground-strafing attacks on British infantry and artillery positions. The German Air Service could no longer remain on the aerial defensive; like the RFC during 'Bloody April' of 1917 they too were at the beck and call of the ground forces.

There was another serious problem facing the German Air Service. The tiny United States Army Air Corps may have seemed all but an irrelevance in the days following their declaration of war on Germany in April 1917, but it was soon apparent that its influence could be crucial if the war extended deep into 1918.

The United States had fifty-five airplanes at the time they declared war, and their aircraft industry was insignificant. Therefore, we did not have to reckon with the early appearance of American air units. It was likewise to be expected that the individual peculiarity of the Americans and their sources available for assistance did not promise that countless air units would be created to reinforce the France-British front, but rather that they would give the Entente their aid in furnishing material for building up their air resources. The number and type of American engineers, specialists and workmen was so significant that their influx in the aircraft operations in England and France must lead inevitably to a great increase in their production. It must also be expected that American factories, operating under the direction of British and French engineers, would be converted to the production of planes and motors. French and English flying schools were thoroughly able to train the large numbers of pupils that came pouring over from America and prepare them for work at the front.[3] *General Ernest Wilhelm von Hoeppner, German Air Service*

It was the responsibility of von Hoeppner to make sure that the German Air Service was fully equipped to meet this new challenge. After making his case and securing the essential support from Ludendorff and Hindenburg the 'American Programme' was drawn up. It was decided that they needed to have an extra forty Jagdstaffeln scout units and seventeen Flieger Abteilungen (A), the army cooperation units, which in turn would require more flying training and combat training schools. After four years of war this was not an easy matter and took immense effort and patient negotiations. They needed to double aircraft production to around 2,000 a week in a country where all the necessary raw materials, resources, machine tools and skilled workmen were in extremely short supply with numerous competing demands. The aviation industry desperately needed iron, steel, copper, nickel, zinc and aluminium but it faced legitimate competition from all sides of the war economy. At this late stage in the war Germany was in desperate need not just of aircraft but of submarines, warships of all kinds, artillery, mortars, machine guns, motor-transport, perhaps even the new tanks. Once manufactured, all this machinery of war needed fuel and oil if it was not to grind to an impotent halt. The German economy had been severely weakened by the pernicious long-term effects of the immovable Royal Navy blockade – the noose that slowly tightened around Germany's neck with every day that passed. Ironically the actual men needed to act as pilots, observers and ground crew for the expanded air force were not such a problem. Among the millions of mobilized men the 24,000 men required were a drop in the ocean.

Trenchard was well aware of both the increasing strength of the German Air Service and of the radical reversal in German and British priorities in the air war and as early as December 1917 he had prepared a pamphlet, *The Employment of the Royal Flying Corps in Defence.*

> The first and most important of the duties of the RFC in connection with defence is to watch for symptoms of attack and to use the utmost endeavours to obtain and transmit at once all information which may assist responsible Commanders to determine beforehand when and where an attack is coming and by what force. It is the duty of the Intelligence

Branch of the General Staff to keep the RFC constantly instructed as to the information which is required, and of the suspected areas of hostile concentration. Every detail observed should be reported. Points of apparent unimportance to an observer are often of great value in elucidating reports from other sources.[4] *Major General Hugh Trenchard, Headquarters, RFC*

The RFC was to look in particular for signs of construction of the communications and logistical infrastructure without which a major offensive was impossible: the railways and sidings, improvements to roads, the massive munitions dumps. Then there were the signs of German forces massing, the new aerodromes, the camps and the gun battery positions. Once an offensive was clearly imminent then the duty of the RFC was clear.

As soon as it has been established that preparations for an attack are in progress behind the enemy's line, the next duty of the RFC is to interfere with them. The means available are:
a) Cooperation with our artillery, the activity of which will probably be increased at this stage.
b) Extensive bombing attacks, to hinder the enemy's preparations, inflict casualties upon his troops and disturb their rest.[5] *Major General Hugh Trenchard, Headquarters, RFC*

The primacy of its role in ensuring that the fire of the Royal Artillery was effective would naturally continue once the German infantry came over the top. But the RFC would also be required to take its place alongside the infantry in the front line.

The means to be employed stated in their relative order of importance are:
a) Attacking the enemy's reinforcements a mile or two behind the assaulting line with low-flying aeroplanes.
b) Attacking the enemy's detraining and debussing points, transport on roads, artillery positions and reserves.
c) Sending low-flying machines, on account of their moral effect, to cooperate with the infantry in attacking the enemy's most advanced troops.[6] *Major General Hugh Trenchard, Headquarters, RFC*

For Trenchard, whatever the overall situation, there was one underlying principle that always endured: to carry out successfully their intended aims and objectives it was necessary for the RFC to maintain a never-ending offensive against all forms of German aviation.

> This can only be done by attacking and defeating the enemy's air forces. The action of the RFC must, therefore, always remain essentially offensive, even when the Army, during a period of preparation for offensive operations, is standing temporarily on the defensive.[7] *Major General Hugh Trenchard, Headquarters, RFC*

The pamphlet was issued on 16 January 1918, by which time Trenchard had left to take up the position of Chief of the Air Staff back in London. His replacement was Major General John Salmond. In practical terms the changeover had no impact on the RFC as Salmond was very much a 'Trenchard man' and had no intention of changing the priorities of the RFC. Whatever the German Air Service did, the RFC would attack, and keep on attacking. When push came to shove, ultimately even the greatest of the scout aces of both sides would find that they were expendable in the cause of their country.

Chapter 2

So Much to Learn

The demands made by the generals and their gunners from the RFC on the Western Front seemed to be never-ending. The logistics of producing so many highly trained flying personnel, which required numerous instructors and a steady supply of training aircraft, while at the same time maintaining the current commitments on the Western Front, were pretty complex. By late 1917 there were some 15,500 officers and nearly 100,000 other ranks of the RFC retained in the United Kingdom carrying out the roles of training, home defence and administration. It was estimated that they needed nearly 2,000 pilots to complete the establishment of the squadrons on the Western Front, with a further 11,500 needed to replace 'wastage' as pilots were killed, wounded, fell sick, or sent back for rest. More pilots were required for the Home Defence Squadrons to prevent German Zeppelin and Gotha bombing raids and the RFC had squadrons serving on all the other war zones. On the Western Front the average reconnaissance, artillery observation or bombing pilot lasted only sixteen weeks before he was killed, wounded or captured. Pilots with the scout squadrons lasted a mere ten weeks. The demands may have been huge but the British pilots and observers were hugely augmented, in both numbers and quality, by a continuing influx from the Empire, with the contribution of Canada and Australia being particularly important. It has been estimated that at one stage almost a quarter of airmen were Canadian.

The process of training new pilots and observers had become highly organized. The overall Training Division was divided into Northern, Eastern, Western and Southern Training Brigades, and additional training establishments were established in Egypt and Canada. Of necessity, the instructors were largely drawn from experienced personnel who had already served a tour of duty at the front and were back recharging their batteries. It had already been found that approximately 28 per cent of the pilots who commenced instruction failed to complete the course. The reasons varied: some were simply found incompatible with flying by reasons of incompetence; there was a high rate of sickness which probably indicated a temperamental unsuitability; and then there was the rather chilling number of young men who were badly injured or cut off in their prime in the frequent crash-landings. Whatever the reasons, for every four who started the training programme only three would emerge as qualified pilots.

Training observers had become equally important. Early in the war they had been recruited directly from the infantry and trained 'on the job' flying over the German lines. But the technical skills required by observers had steadily increased as the war became more scientific. They had to master the use of cameras and wireless; understand the complexities of the clock code in ranging gun batteries; and last, but certainly not least, they had to have a complete grasp of the Lewis gun or their career would soon be cut short by marauding German scouts. This was clearly not something that could be picked up casually and soon the observers were being properly trained. Whether they had been recruited from the army in France or were raw recruits, the prospective observers were sent for their initial training at the No. 1 School of Military Aeronautics at Reading.

> The course means pretty hard work as they cram a large amount into the month. This week we have been having, in the mornings, lectures on rigging with a certain amount of practical work such as pulling 'buses' to pieces and reassembling, and patching holes in planes. Also lectures on the instruments in the machine. Then in the afternoons we have been doing signalling practice, machine gun work and a lecture on various subjects. This work is somewhat harder, as you can imagine, to the large number who are new to flying than it is to me.[1] *Cadet John McDonald, No. 1 School of Military Aeronautics, Reading*

Many of their instructors had come back from the Western Front with a lot of hard-won personal experience, but not all of them had the ability to impart it to the cadets in front of them. They were often still fairly callow youths themselves with little natural authority in front of a classroom. Jack Wilkinson, who had been serving as an officer with 6th Battalion London Regiment, watched proceedings with some amusement.

> Work consisted of listening to lectures from observers who had been in France and now recounted their experiences to us with becoming modesty. These were very informal talks and we gathered that: (a) 'It was damned cold up there!' (b) The pilot's method of attracting his observer's attention was to hit him on the head, and, (c) 'It was damned cold up there!' It was only when someone started the ball rolling by asking questions that we got our 'instructor' (who had most likely bought his first razor yesterday) to open up and tell us if they did much Morse, how to recognise Hun machines – in which case he obligingly drew silhouettes on the blackboard, how many machines went out at a time, how long an observer's course in England could be made to last (very important this), how long a patrol lasted, and so on. But even when our curiosity had been satisfied, the lecturer usually rounded off his remarks by reminding us that, 'It was damned cold up there!'[2] *Lieutenant Jack Wilkinson, No. 1 School of Military Aeronautics, Reading*

When they reached the nitty-gritty of the course they all moved up into another gear. Artillery observation was crucial and a simple mock-up had been prepared to recreate for the pupils a typical 'shoot' over German lines. Everything possible was done to try to make it a reasonably realistic exercise.

> The floor of a large room was made into a relief map of a section of the line as it would appear to an observer in an aeroplane flying at an altitude of 2,000 feet. Tiny trenches were visible, and realism was obtained by the artist, who saw to it that as the eye moved away on either side of the front line so the countryside appeared more green and less shell-shocked. Concealed beneath the trench line and back areas were hundreds of small electric light bulbs, whose purpose we shall see in a moment. The class arranged itself in a balcony running round inside the four walls of the building, and each pupil was given a map of the ground below him. Slung up in the roof was part of an aeroplane fuselage, containing an observer's cockpit and Morse buzzing key, and in this we took turns to direct the

> 'shoot'. Signalling in Morse, the pupil would call up the battery with whom he was cooperating, and tell them to fire one round at the target – a piece of trench or a ruined house that was supposed to have been chosen the previous day. More often than not he would forget to let down his aerial wire before sending his first message, in which case he would be 'told about it' – but not until he had waited some moments, wondering why the devil the battery did not acknowledge! He was, of course, dumb until his aerial was hanging down. When the battery finally acknowledged receipt of the observer's signal, an electric bulb would flash – to show that the gun had fired – at the battery position. A few seconds elapsed – denoting the flight of the shell – and then another bulb would flash near the target. This was the shell bursting. From then on the observer signalled corrections, '30 yards, 5 o'clock', and so on – always with the understanding that the target was the centre of an imaginary clock face of which '12 o'clock' was due north. It was very fascinating to watch the imaginary shells creeping closer and closer to their objective, and, as soon as a direct hit had been obtained, the target was given a good drubbing. Even then the observer was not finished with his tribulations, for he would usually signify his intention to return to his aerodrome and, heaving a sigh of relief, begin to climb out of his cockpit. At once a joyful shout of, 'Aerial! Wind in your aerial!' would break out, and the luckless one had to climb back and wind in the aerial on the hand winch inside the 'office', as the cockpit was frequently called.[3] *Lieutenant Jack Wilkinson, No. 1 School of Military Aeronautics, Reading*

For the next stage in his training Wilkinson was moved to the School of Aerial Gunnery at Hythe where they were pleasantly accommodated in the Imperial Hotel that had been specially requisitioned for their use.

> For the first fortnight I was one of a party of six receiving instruction in the Lewis gun from a flight-sergeant. Although I had a fair knowledge of the principles of this gun, it became clear that I must work still harder at it, for my life, and that of my pilot, might easily depend on whether the Lewis were kept working. The conditions obtaining in air and ground fighting, too, were very different. As an infantry weapon, the Lewis gun was of service in attack or defence *in addition to* the rifle, bayonet or revolver. In an aeroplane,

the Lewis became of the utmost importance, for, if the observer's marksmanship were poor, or if he were careless in maintaining his gun in good condition or in rectifying stoppages, there was only a single fixed gun controlled by the pilot to fall back upon; this meant that the aeroplane itself had to be aimed at the enemy aircraft – not always convenient if one were making for home with a batch of Huns on one's tail! Again an infantry Lewis gunner could nearly always call on a pal to give him a hand with his gun, but an observer had to tackle the job alone, knowing full well that, if he had to remove any part of the gun to clear a stoppage, the said part would disappear overboard like a flash if he did not keep tight hold of it, or put it in a secure place – and secure places were scarce in the observer's 'office'. Morning, noon and night we worked on those Lewis guns. Soon with the aid of the point of a bullet, the only tool required, said 'Mr Lewis', we could actually strip and assemble the gun without having any bits left over! Then we became more ambitious and had bets as to who could completely strip and assemble it (correctly) in the shortest time. My temporary record of 4 minutes 25 seconds was soon eclipsed, and, for variation, we practised stripping and assembling the gun blindfold. This was much more amusing – for the spectators. From the lips of the competitor flowed a whispered commentary of the sequence of operations alternating with a spate of invective when things went wrong. We usually saw to it that they did go wrong by quietly transposing, say, the cocking handle and the bolt from their respective positions on the table while the competitors' groping fingers were wrestling with other parts of the gun![4] *Lieutenant Jack Wilkinson, School of Aerial Gunnery, Hythe*

Having completed their ground training the observers were then given a little taste of actual air experience in the form of a quick practice flight with an experienced pilot. Flying was not a common experience at this time and many were unquestionably nervous at the prospect.

We speculated on what would really happen on our first journey in the air. Rumour had it that one of the pilots took a delight in putting the wind up his passenger by flying low enough to run the wheels of his undercarriage along the tops of the Bessonneau hangars, and, what was more unpleasant still, he also expected the observer to show his pluck by climbing out of the front seat and walking out along the lower wing! We could hardly credit this last mad prank, but we were approaching a new medium where anything seemed possible.[5] *Lieutenant Jack Wilkinson, School of Aerial Gunnery, Hythe*

After the air experience flight the gunnery training took to the air in an effort to prepare the observer for the confusions endemic in aerial warfare.

Fighting with a camera gun was good fun. In appearance very like a Lewis gun we found that pulling back the cocking handle moved on the film and pressing the trigger made the exposure. When the negatives were developed the prints, by means of superimposed faint circles, showed the range at which the 'burst' had been fired, whether a hit had been scored, or how much error had been made. The film allowed for sixteen exposures, but, owing to lag in winding it on and off, we were lucky if as many as a dozen prints showed up. On one occasion it seemed as though I had a hundred and sixteen 'shots' to make, for it happened that, having taken five 'shots' I became violently airsick. Both we and the 'enemy' were stunting in order to make it more difficult for the opposing observer to take steady aim, and I suppose something inside me decided that it could not, or would not, stay put. Wearily I swung the camera gun round in its Scarff mounting, tried to draw a bead on the opposing aeroplane, and then a further attack of nausea seized me and I lay gasping over the side of the cockpit, gazing hopelessly at the swaying earth, the cock-eyed horizon, and the pale sun that matched my condition so damnably. 'How many more have you got to take?' the pilot called back. 'Oh, God, I dunno!' I croaked 'What?' he shouted. Then he looked round. A broad grin appeared below his goggles. 'Let's see – shepherd's pie for lunch, wasn't it?' he taunted me. But the worst was over, and I somehow managed to make the remainder of the exposures without the further loss of – shall we say – dignity![6] *Lieutenant Jack Wilkinson, School of Aerial Gunnery, Hythe*

There was more than one way of achieving total personal humiliation during these camera gun flights chauffeured by ruthlessly mischievous and totally unsympathetic pilots who saw them as fair game.

The first time I went up with this gun of course I didn't know anything – I didn't know which was ground and which was sky! The Canadian pilots were a bit of devils and the aeroplane went round like a drunken caterpillar. I looked round and I couldn't see aeroplanes anywhere. The pilot swore at me and pointed at the ground – I saw one on the ground so I took a photograph and gave it up! He screamed at me, 'Where do you want to go?' I said, 'I'd like to go to Hastings!' He said, 'All right!' We got to Hastings and he went right round the pier – I thought it looked nice so I took a photograph of it! I thought to myself, 'I've done myself now – I can't get this off.' We came back and landed. The squadron leader came racing over to the pilot ticking him off as apparently he wasn't allowed to go anywhere near Hastings and not thinking I pressed the trigger. The next day they read out that somebody got six aeroplanes, somebody got five and he said, 'Stand up, Cadet Andrews!' I stood up and he said, 'You've got one photograph of an aeroplane, very nice, one of Hastings Pier and one of the Squadron Leader – and he doesn't like it!'[7] *Cadet Howard Andrews, School of Aerial Gunnery, Hythe*

After they had passed the gunnery course the observers were ready for posting to the active service squadrons in France where they could compare theory and practice to their heart's content. Many would not last long.

The pilots had a similar basic education before they were launched into the air. Cadets entered the RFC Cadet Wings where for a couple of months they were taught the basic elements of soldiering; they then moved into one of the Schools of Military Aeronautics where their syllabus encompassed the theory of flight, the engines and rigging of aircraft, the basics of artillery cooperation, photographic reconnaissance, bombing and Morse code. At the end of the course most were granted their commission as second lieutenants in the RFC and sent to a training squadron where they actually learned to fly. Here those observers who had seemed suitable to retrain as pilots joined them and thus it was that Lieutenant Jack Wilkinson arrived at Northolt airfield. His first ever dual-control flight with a flying instructor was made under unusual circumstances in a Maurice Farman Shorthorn, an old 'pusher' that would have been familiar to pilots training in 1914.

Captain Tabernacle, the flight commander, spotted me late one afternoon as I mooned about outside the hangars. 'Here!' he called. 'Put a helmet on and climb in! Hurry up!' he rapped out. 'It'll be dark soon!' I fastened on a helmet and climbed in. Slowly the clumsy machine trundled across the aerodrome and bounced leisurely into the air. When the altimeter showed 200 feet we made a left turn, swung wide over the mess, turned left again and came charging in over the sheds. I felt a tap on my helmet. 'All right, take her down!' shouted Tabernacle. Take her down? My hat! But *how?* I pushed the joystick forward. 'That must be right!' I thought. The engine somehow ran faster than even I thought necessary, and the ground rushed upward. 'Close the throttle, you idiot!' yelled my instructor, suiting the action to the word and closing it for me. It was just as well he did, for I had only the haziest notion where the throttle was. With the engine ticking over and the wind whistling through the wires we dived straight for a patch of the aerodrome where I had decided to descend. 'No! No! *Glide*, dammit, not *dive!*' I yanked the joystick back. The nose rose steadily. 'Oh hell! Haven't you any sense of proportion? Leave her to me!' I released the controls and we made another circuit. 'Now,' said Tabernacle as we approached the aerodrome again. 'Listen! Throttle slowly back, stick slowly forward – a glide you see? *You* were trying to ram the ground, your way! Now I'm holding her just off the ground – take hold and let her settle – *no!*' The nose of the machine cocked up ever so slightly, and we sat down with an almighty crash. 'Oh, God!' We bounced once more; but this time the wheels ran along the ground. 'What the devil do you think you're playing at? How long 'dual' have you had?' 'None!' I answered meekly. 'Eh, what's that?' 'This is my first time up!' I explained. 'Oh *is* it!' Tabernacle was somewhat mollified and smiled. 'I quite thought you'd had an hour or two's dual with Pearman. Well that's how *not* to do it!'[8] *Lieutenant Jack Wilkinson, Northolt Airfield*

He was put on dual instruction with Peter Pearman who was not a calm individual in the air with his 'Huns', as the instructors called their pupils, being inclined to rage and storm at what he perceived to be dunder-headed buffoons.

Here we go again after about two and a half hours 'dual' instruction made up of ten-and twenty-minute flips. Pearman: 'For God's sake see that your nose is down – *down!* You bloody fool! When you make a turn! If you start spinning a "Rumpety" you'll never be quite the same again.

Now take her in and land her – hell's delight! You can't glide horizontally! Not for long anyway. Now you're going to scoop the roof off the B Flight's shed – I never did see such a fool! Glide, you idiot, *Glide!* Now hold her, *hold* her!' Crump! We bounce into the air again with the agility of a lobster. 'Oh my God!' Crump! We bounce again – harder this time, but not so high. 'Oh, you bloody cow!' Me or the Rumpety? Rumble-rumble-rumble. We have landed. 'Well that's what I call a damned fine three-piece landing – you, me and this blasted kite! How you get away with it I don't know! Take her off again!'[9] *Lieutenant Jack Wilkinson, Northolt Airfield*

Round and round they went, taking off, a quick circuit of the airfield and then the return to *terra firma*. It was a testing time for both novice pilot and instructor alike and some instructors already suffering from the effects of combat fatigue found it difficult to cope. Not all of them were officers, some were sergeant pilots, but the differences were subtle ones as far as the cadets were concerned.

Sergeant Saunders was good. He throttled down and shouted when he had to and sometimes he hit me over the crash helmet to emphasise a point, but he respected my (probationary) commission. I remember once when I nearly stalled the machine, the bang on the helmet and his furious, 'What the bloody hell do you think are doing – Sir?'[10] *Lieutenant Thomas Trail*

In the air, the engine was deafening but in the more modern training aircraft the instructors communicated their wishes through the use of a 'Gosport' speaking tube.

We had no telephone of the electric type, but simply a rubber tube with a mouthpiece hung round the neck of the instructor and earphones on the pupil! Oh no! The pupil had no mouthpiece. Custom had decreed that argument of the verbal type should be heavily loaded against the pupil in the air. When he shouted through the tube, 'Put on bank!' I could tell him as loud as I liked to go to anywhere that occurred to my fancy without being guilty of insubordination because he couldn't hear me! At Catterick there was a quite remarkable unanimity among the pupils as to a suitable destination for instructors![11] *Lieutenant William Grossart*

Gradually the pupils learned the mysteries of powered flight. Some of the techniques were obvious; some seemed counter-intuitive to the struggling beginner.

> I had a push-bike which makes a somewhat close analogy with flying terms. Try turning on a push-bike without putting on bank and you see what I mean! Baker spent quite a lot of eloquence in describing what my personal appearance would be like if I continued to turn with the use of the rudder alone. Banking is accomplished by means of a contraption called a joystick. By waggling it from side to side it gives what experts call lateral control. This is achieved by wires connected at its lower end which pass out of the fuselage and are fastened to bits of the wings at their tips, which the designer has thoughtfully cut out and hinged and are called the high-falutin' name of aileron. When you waggle the stick to the left the aileron on the left wing rises, while that on the right wing goes down. The air pressure then sends the left wing down and the right wing up. The exact opposite happens when you waggle the stick to the right. There are other strings attached to the lower end of the joystick for fore and aft control. When you pull the stick back it draws towards the vertical a piece of surface which the designer has hinged on behind the tail plane. This gadget is called the elevator. When it is drawn up by pulling the stick back, it presents a surface to the air current and this has the effect of depressing the tail plane and consequently bringing the nose of the machine up. By pushing the joystick forward the opposite happens and the machine descends. Then Baker began to concentrate on landings. 'These,' he said with a sigh at the prospect of much arduous work in front of him, 'were the most difficult and at the same time the most important of all evolutions.'[12] *Lieutenant William Grossart*

Landing was an essential skill as they couldn't stay up in the air for ever and it had to be mastered as quickly as possible. If they couldn't land safely then their prospects of long-term survival were remarkably poor!

> Anybody can fly, but the whole art is to learn to land, to get down on Mother Earth again! The knack of the landing is that when you come down, you've got your gliding height and your engine is off. An ideal landing is that you gradually pull your nose up as you lose flying speed, it stalls your airplane

and the perfect landing is to have the wheels and the tail-skid hit the ground together. That is the perfect landing, which happens once in twenty times. A bad landing is when you pull up your nose too early and you're not near enough the ground and your plane then drops. If it drops sufficiently badly your undercarriage is gone![13] *Cadet Laurie Field*

Their first solo flight was a real test of nerve and character. The 'soloist' carefully took off under the critical gaze of his instructor.

Gingerly I move forward the throttle and the machine gathered speed. We charged across the aerodrome making straight for a hedge that grew in size with alarming rapidity. Fascinated by the hedge, it took me some time – a fraction of a second in reality – for me to take in the fact that it was ages since I had heard the wheels running along the ground. Could it be? Yes – I was flying! Alone by gum! To hell with the hedge! Back with the stick, not too much though, and the hedge slipped beneath and out of sight. Let's try a turn to the left. I *must* turn some time, it occurred to me, if I didn't want to fly in a straight line for ever. Left bank and rudder. Whew a bit flat that one! Never mind, there's the mess on the left, two more turns will bring me behind the sheds, ready to land. Why two? Why not one long turn? Here goes! Blast! That was a nasty bump, felt as though somebody had kicked out behind. Still, there's old Pearman down there, cursing like hell, I'll bet! Throttle back – *glide* you bloody fool! Why, I must be talking to myself! Lower, lower, now hold her! Hold – Ah! Landed her by cripes! Who'd have thought it? I'd have called Trenchard 'Boom' to his face if he'd come along at that moment I was so cock a hoop![14] *Lieutenant Jack Wilkinson, Northolt Airfield*

Landing while flying solo was a matter of fine judgement that became easier the more experience the pilot gained. But the problem was gaining that experience without damaging either the aircraft or the pilot as Lieutenant Williams discovered on concluding his first solo flight.

For some time there had been an epidemic of first solos ending in smashed undercarriages, owing to the pilots 'flattening out' too soon. Lieutenant Dorman had taught me to do this when individual blades of grass could be distinguished. During my approach to the landing I kept saying to myself, 'I won't flatten out too soon! I won't flatten out too soon! I won't!' The result was that I left it a fraction of a second too late, partly due to coming in at rather too steep an angle and so at greater speed. This would make the exact time for flattening out more critical. Anyway, I dived nose first into the ground, which I hit with such force that the momentum fortunately broke the anchorage of the webbing strap with which I was held in and I took a dive through the air myself, over the wreckage of my machine, landing on my own nose! My machine had turned a complete somersault, and had, at the same time, twisted itself round so that the fore-end was upside down facing the wrong way and the tail half also facing the same way, was right side up! It felt as if my nose had been torn off, but investigation with my hand proved that it was still in place, though bleeding profusely. I picked myself up, but promptly fell down again due to my being dazed![15] *Lieutenant H. G. R. Williams, Duxford*

He had managed to write off a brand-new aeroplane that had only been delivered to the unit the week before. Indeed, in the subsequent enquiry into the accident the document listing the damaged parts had a wry note to the effect that it would have been quicker to list the undamaged parts! In the traditional fashion he was sent up again the same morning and this time successfully judged his landing. A lasting memento of his abortive first solo flight was a walking stick made from the propeller of the smashed machine. He had been incredibly lucky. Others were not: accidents were common and sometimes horrific.

Gliding in at a very steep angle, on the far side of the aerodrome, was a Sopwith Camel. For a fraction of a second it seemed as though the pilot would still be able to make some sort of a landing, but he was coming in much too fast to be able to land in the middle of the aerodrome. While we were wondering whether he would realise his mistake in time his machine suddenly made a half-roll, when about 200 feet up, and dived hard into the ground on its back. It did not catch fire. Two pupils, friends of the pilot, jumped on to the ambulance as it moved off. They were soon seen walking slowly back to the hangars, their faces the colour of cigar-ash. One of them seemed incapable of speech. The other, in response to our enquiries, muttered, 'Awful! Just a pool of blood!' And went behind the sheds where he was sick.[16] *Lieutenant Jack Wilkinson, Northolt Airfield*

If they survived, whether it be a minor prang or a real smash-up, it was the firm practice to send them straight back up in an attempt to ensure that they had no time to brood and could recover their confidence.

It was a recognised thing that, after a mild crash, the pilot of the crashed machine should be taken up at the earliest possible opportunity so that he would not have time to mope about it, or let it prey on his mind. Learning to fly has this in common with learning to drive a car – a gentle bump, early in the proceedings, often acts as an antidote to undue confidence and resultant carelessness.[17] *Lieutenant Jack Wilkinson, Northolt Airfield*

Flying an aircraft was a strange combination of technique, art form and inspiration. It was sometimes best not to think too much, but try to make the correct responses by instinct.

He asked me if I had ever ridden a horse. I said I had ridden with the cowboys and loved horses. And he said, 'Well, have you got to the point where you forgot that you were on a horse, is that right?' And I said, 'Yes, Sir!' And he said, 'Well, you have to get to the point where you forgot that you're in an aeroplane, and the aeroplane will do what you want it to, and you don't have to give it thought!'[18] *Lieutenant Ralph O'Neill, American Air Service*

When, by hook or by crook, they had learned the basics of flying, they were ready for the next stage in their training to get them used to the generic type of aircraft they would be flying in action. Lieutenant Jack Wilkinson was sent to 62 Training Squadron near Dover. Here he found they were flying the Avro Trainers which were intended to prepare them for their ultimate trade flying Sopwith Camels.

Accidents were still common as Wilkinson found out when he made one of the simplest mistakes during take-off: he tried to turn back towards the aerodrome. Pilots were told never to do this since it caused the aircraft to lose speed, stall and made a crash inevitable.

Unfortunately it was a natural reaction to try to turn back to 'safety' when things went wrong. So it was for Lieutenant Jack Wilkinson when his engine failed as he was taking off in his Avro. He was all too aware that he was heading straight for the cliffs with the cold sea below. This posed a difficult problem.

> We were just above the sheds when, to my amazement, the engine cut out completely. 'If the engine fails when taking off,' ran the instructions, '*never* turn back – land straight ahead.' 'Yes,' I thought, 'but straight ahead is the sea! Surely I've got enough speed to turn back and make some sort of a landing? It'll be down-wind, I know, but even that's been done at times.' I pushed the nose down as much as possible to keep flying speed and swung round, banking gently, to face the aerodrome again. I was sure I could bring it off! But, as the turn was completed and I moved the stick over to take off the bank, I felt the controls go slack! I was stalling – the worst of the many deadly sins when flying! Move the stick where I would, nothing happened, and, with the nose dropping in a good natured attempt to regain flying speed, we rushed at the ground. Now, although everything happened very quickly, to me it seemed as deliberate as a slow-motion picture. Just when I ought to have been scared out of my life I felt no fear at all. I was so supremely confident that I should regain flying speed before hitting the ground. Of course I *didn't* regain flying speed – why, that patch of ground, just there, was where we should hit. And hit it we did! I must have instinctively braced my left hand against the padded fairing in front of my face. There was a tearing, rending, 'C-r-r-r-unch!' A terrific jolt that jerked me violently against the safety belt, and then the Avro stood on its nose, finally flopping over on to its back! 'So that's what a crash feels like,' was my first thought as I hung head downwards in the safety belt. My second thought was, 'Will she catch fire?' Petrol was dripping down from the inverted petrol tank and as I could not reach the ignition switch I lifted the quick release catch of the belt and fell out on my head. 'How silly!' I reflected as I stood upright. 'Of course you fall on your head if you're upside down!'[19] *Lieutenant Jack Wilkinson, 62 (Training) Squadron*

By this time it had been realized that the pupils intended for scout work must understand the tactics and challenges of aerial combat. Special Schools of Aerial Fighting were established where the very best scout pilots could impart their accumulated knowledge to the pupils.

> McCudden gave a great talk this morning – sort of opened up a bit – and made it very clear that successful pilots are so only because they have worked like sin, studied every phase and detail of flying, machines, and the habits and haunts of the Hun. To hear him talk nonchalantly of doing in Germans at 20,000 feet and of studying all available material in order that he may know where to go and look for them convinces you that this is surely the greatest game God created. There's nothing like it.[20] *Lieutenant Bogart Rogers, School of Aerial Fighting, Ayr*

The advanced flying training was carried out at the School of Special Flying established and run at Gosport under Lieutenant Colonel Smith-Barry. Here the most promising flying instructors had their own flying polished to perfection and learned the new techniques at the heart of the Gosport method.

> The words 'danger and nerves' must not form part of the instructor's vocabulary. Nothing that a pupil may do in the air is dangerous, if he knows what he is doing and what the results will be. Almost all accidents are caused by ignorance, and if, instead of telling a pupil that a manoeuvre is dangerous, he is taught how to do it, his instinct of self-preservation will do the rest.[21] *Lieutenant Colonel Smith-Barry, School of Special Flying, Gosport*

Many of his pupils found the course a veritable revelation. Flying ceased to be a mystery and became an activity where cause and effect were understood and any flying manoeuvre within reason was both repeatable and teachable to those with the necessary degree of natural talent and coordination.

> The course of aerobatics is quite interesting, but I find it strange being in the role of pupil, after many hours in France and having been an instructor myself for some time. However I realise I have a lot to learn when it comes to advanced aerobatics. Today tried out loops, rolls and spins. The air simply full of machines busy stunting, often half a dozen at low heights

over the aerodrome doing all kinds of weird stunts.[22] *Captain Ewart Garland, School of Special Flying, Gosport*

Under the influence of Smith-Barry's theories, up and down the country there were pilots testing the nerve and tolerance of the local authorities by outrageously stunting at the lowest possible altitudes. There was an obvious risk but the pilots were young and simply didn't care what the civilians thought of their antics.

We used to go to Brighton and fly along the sea front very often below the level of the pier. Then we'd zoom up over the West Pier, down again, zoom up over the Palace Pier and down again. We'd swing round and fly inland looking as if we were going to fly in the windows of the hotels then we'd zoom up over the roofs. That gave us great amusement but the people of Brighton didn't like it very much![23] *Second Lieutenant Archibald Yuille*

As the pilots trained in Britain they were joined by pilots who had completed their initial flying training in Canada. Among these was a wave of American pilots who had volunteered to serve with the RFC rather than in their own putative Air Service. One such was Second Lieutenant Edgar Taylor, the son of immigrant Oldham cotton workers, who had been brought up in the wild open spaces of their homestead ranch in Camas Meadows, Fremont County, Idaho. Born on 9 January 1897, after an uneventful childhood he was sent during a period of illness to live with relatives in the more 'healthy' environs of Rhode Island. Meanwhile his older brother Alfred Taylor had enlisted in Canada and was soon serving with the RFC on the Western Front. Edgar Taylor was determined to follow in his brother's footsteps and after the US entered the war he enlisted as an airman in the US Navy in April 1917. He was quickly disillusioned with the complete absence of anything resembling flying training and secured a discharge so that he could enlist in the RFC in Canada, which he duly did on 30 August 1917. He went through the usual flying training programme near Toronto, where he became romantically entangled with a young teacher, Irene Pearson. He was also shocked by the news that his brother was a prisoner after being shot down over the German lines in September 1917. This made the war far more of a personal issue, especially as Alfred had initially been reported missing presumed dead. Edgar crossed the Atlantic in January 1918 and was immediately struck by his first experience of London on his twenty-first birthday. He found the city a very different proposition from anything he had seen before.

> This is sure some place. New York City isn't anything more than a backwoods town in comparison to this. But it is fast. The way the women act is shocking. I just can't tolerate them. They smoke continually. It made me homesick. Just to be out in Idaho again. That country attracts me more the further I wander from it, but if I have luck, I'm going back there. I am tired of the city. It is rotten and full of corruption.[24] *Second Lieutenant Edgar Taylor*

He was sent first to Stockbridge and then to Chichester on the south coast for his advanced flying training and introduction to service aircraft. In the final stages of their training, like Yuille just up the coast, they were encouraged to engage in stunt flying to test their skill and nerve. And stunt they most certainly did, often watched by their admiring contemporaries awaiting their turn. It was all a great game.

> Last night as the sun was getting low a large number of us stood on the ground and watched the antics of our pilots; all of them boys under 25. It seems to have an underlying fascination for everybody. My instructor is a very old pilot (24) as far as experience goes; yet he stood on the ground as keen and interested as the newcomers. We watched one chap in a Sopwith Pup. He would dive down until he was within a foot of the ground then he would loop and every time we would clap and cheer his dare-devilry. There is no restriction on how foolishly you risk your neck here. You must know your own limit. It is the daredevils that come back safe and sound from France. It's all in the game. Of course, though I stunt as much as anyone, I do it at a safe height. It's the low stuff that causes the funerals.[25] *Second Lieutenant Edgar Taylor*

Many of these keen new pilots would be flying two of the most famous British scout aircraft to see service on the Western Front: the Sopwith Camel and SE5a. These were not new designs; indeed they had first flown in the spring and early summer of 1917. But by 1918 all their teething problems had been eradicated, they had various modifications to increase their effectiveness and power and they were being supplied by the thousand to the RFC. The best known is probably the Sopwith Camel. This stubby little aircraft earned its universal nickname through the 'hump' created in the cowling by the twin Vickers machine guns that fired through the propeller. It was driven by a powerful rotary engine that allowed it to reach about 105mph.

> The Camel was a very tricky aeroplane to fly because of the right-hand torque with the fairly small wingspan and this very powerful engine. If you put your right wing down in a right-hand turn if you weren't very careful you spun down on the torque. It was so light that you were over and spinning before you knew where you were![26] *Second Lieutenant Archibald Yuille, 151 Squadron*

It was supremely agile once it was in a dogfight, able to turn fast, and perform violent acrobatics with just a feather touch. Like many of the best scouts it was always teetering on the edge of being out of control. The Camel killed many inexperienced pilots in accidents but it had a deadly surprise element in combat: if the pilot barely knew what was happening how could his opponent?

> I pulled the Camel up into a stall, then put on rudder and the machine just fell away sideways. The most sickening sensation. It fell towards the earth, one wing tip first on its side. Suddenly it whipped round, flicked round very quickly into this quick spin, round and round. I was thrown violently to one side of the cockpit with a fierce blast of wind on one cheek. Then you got used to that and tried to straighten everything and bring it out. In my case it usually wouldn't come out very quickly. You just had to put everything central and wait.[27] *Second Lieutenant Ronald Sykes, 9 Squadron, RNAS*

The other well-known British single-seater was the far more prosaically named SE5a. This was a sturdy well-built beast of an aeroplane that could withstand the bullets of the enemy or the stresses imposed by the ham-fisted flying of incompetent pilots. Its Wolseley Viper or Hispano-Suiza engine was reliable and gave it a top speed of about 127mph and it was armed with one fuselage-mounted Vickers machine gun and a Lewis gun on the top wing. The two guns were fired by the pilot operating a trigger on the joystick and were trained to intersect on a spot approximately 100 yards ahead. The Lewis gun could also be pulled back to fire upwards if an enemy was above. Major Sholto Douglas was of the opinion that the SE5 was the most successful of any of the single-seater fighters employed during the war.

> That will cause howls of anguish from the pilots who flew the Sopwith Camel; but it was a fact that the SE5 retained in a large measure its performance at high altitudes, which the Camel did not. And since the SE5 was very steady in a fast dive – which nine times out of ten was our way of making attacks – this was an additional advantage over the Camel. The faster we dived in the SE5 the steadier the aircraft became as a gun platform. The Camel, on the other hand, being an unstable machine, would vary in its angle of dive at high speed in spite of all the pilot's efforts to keep it steady; and because of its rotary engine there was also a good deal of vibration when diving fast, which made good shooting difficult.[28] *Major Sholto Douglas, 84 Squadron*

In essence the SE5 was better at diving to attack a German aircraft, before zooming back up to regain altitude. These characteristics made it ideally suited to cautious stalking tactics. The Camel was a formidable and slippery proposition once caught up in a dogfight thanks to its incredibly tight turning circle and overall manoeuvrability.

> On a Camel you could turn inside the turning circle of an Albatros or Pfalz. Life on a Camel was certainly safer than on an SE, for though you could not be sure of your man you could be reasonably sure of being able to get away if hard-pressed.[29] *Captain Harold Balfour, 43 Squadron*

But the SE5 pilots would argue that if flown properly they did not need to engage in a dogfight as they could and would kill their opponent in the first deadly pass.

By the time the new scout pilots had finished their training they were above all confident: in themselves, their machines and in their indestructibility in the face of anything the Germans could throw at them.

I feel confident I can look after myself. I can handle a machine in any position and I have made good marks in gunnery. I will not be on trench strafing but am on a fighting scout of the very best. I was up today: I rolled, looped, spun and did a hundred other stunts which will be useful in fighting in France.[30] *Second Lieutenant Edgar Taylor*

Whether British, American, Canadian, Australian or whatever, in a sense Edgar Taylor, as an ordinary young boy at war, speaks for all these young pilots when he tries to explain to his family what he was doing, so far from home, fighting for a country he had never even seen before.

It must be said England is a pretty place. Though as one wanders down the winding lanes and over the rolling hills of this place it is hard to realise the stress which this country has withstood for over three years. Old men and boys are all that are left here at present. Even thousands of women have gone to France to do their bit for old England. We may ask ourselves what is the world fighting for, conquest or self-defence? At times we may feel tired of it all, especially when we see our poor fellows maimed for life. What are we doing it for? Look all around us: see the quiet cities beneath us as we fly and then picture once peaceful Belgium. Belgium with farms, cities and homes like ours. What are they now; just ruins with her people exiled to slavery. Shall England be the same? We know what we fight for, we know the price we will pay, but it is worth it.[31] *Second Lieutenant Edgar Taylor*

Chapter 3
Aces Rising

The ace phenomenon truly began with the mercurial exploits of two young Germans flying the Fokker E.III in 1915. Leutnants Max Immelmann and Oswald Boelcke were the first to benefit from flying this innovative monoplane aircraft with its machine gun firing directly through the propeller using an interrupter gear, a development not then available to the RFC. The aircraft itself was nothing special, but there were huge benefits for the pilot who only had to aim the aircraft at his target rather than perform some complex deflection shooting. In a few months the two men effectively carved out the basic premises that would inform aerial fighting for the next forty years. Immelmann was finally killed in combat in June 1916, but Oswald Boelcke had just about enough time to pass on his experience to his young pilots when he returned to the front in command of Jasta 2 in September before, on 28 October, he was killed in an accidental mid-air collision. By then he had mentored the birth of a second generation of scout pilots of whom by far the most promising was a young Prussian minor aristocrat, Leutnant Manfred von Richthofen. Born on 2 May 1892, Richthofen had a privileged upbringing which inculcated in him the skills of a natural hunter. He was destined for the army, starting as an officer cadet at the tender age of just 11 years old, before he was finally commissioned into the cavalry in 1912. He saw active service in 1914, but in 1915 he transferred as an observer into the German Air Service. He was soon determined to train as a pilot and eventually joined Jasta 2 in September 1916. He scored his first victory on 17 September and thereafter began to score victories at a gradually accelerating rate for the rest of the year.

During the air battles of 1917 the German Air Service was forced to fight defensively, as did the German Army below it. They had to face the fact that they were badly outnumbered and they therefore used all their wiles to concentrate what forces they had to secure a temporary local tactical supremacy and then to avoid action when the advantage was lost to them. They simply could not afford losses of either aircraft or pilots. By now Richthofen was truly in his element. He had mastered and refined his craft until he seemed an invincible force as he sent aircraft after aircraft tumbling from the sky during the 'Bloody April' aerial fighting that formed the grim backdrop to the Battle of Arras. But his greatness lay not only in the number of victories he himself had achieved; it lay also in his inspirational influence. When he was appointed to command Jasta 11, Richthofen had not only adopted the methods espoused by Boelcke but also took on his role as mentor.

The Jasta was smaller than the British squadron of eighteen pilots and aircraft. Its normal strength consisted of between ten and twelve pilots and it was inevitable in the increasingly hostile and crowded skies of 1917 that they would begin cooperating together on an informal basis as required. Richthofen was promoted to Rittmeister and given command of the first permanent grouping of Jastas 4, 6, 10 and 11 known as Jagdgeschwader 1. So the 'Flying Circus' of legend was born in June 1917.

Yet almost immediately Richthofen was sharply reminded of his essential mortality. It all started with a deceptively simple encounter on 6 July 1917 when a flight of the obsolescent FE2ds was ambushed by Richthofen and a number of other pilots from Jagdgeschwader 1. In the scrap that followed two of the German Albatros scouts attacked head-on an FE2d piloted by Captain Donald Cunnell accompanied by his observer Second Lieutenant Albert Woodbridge, who would not forget the encounter that ensued.

> I recall there wasn't a thing on that machine that wasn't red, and God, how he could fly! I opened fire with the front Lewis and so did Cunnell with the side gun. Cunnell held the FE to her course, and so did the pilot of the all-red scout. Gad, with our combined speeds, we must have been approaching each other at somewhere around 250mph. Thank God my Lewis didn't jam. I kept a steady stream of lead pouring into the nose of that machine. He was firing also. I could see my tracers splashing along the barrels of his Spandaus and I knew the pilot was sitting right behind them. His lead came whistling past my head and ripping holes in my 'bathtub'. Then something

happened. We could hardly have been 20 yards apart when the Albatros pointed her nose down suddenly. Zip, and she passed under us. Cunnell banked and turned. We saw the all-red plane slip into a spin. It turned over and over and round and round. It was no manoeuvre. He was completely out of control. His motor was going full-on, so I figured I had at least wounded him.[1] *Second Lieutenant Albert Woodbridge, 20 Squadron*

In the turmoil of the dogfight that followed he did not see whether the red Albatros crashed. Indeed Woodbridge later insisted that he could not claim to have definitely been the man to have shot Richthofen down; but he has generally been given the credit and his story was undoubtedly slightly embroidered by other hands. Richthofen left his own account to record his hubristic defeat.

I watched as the observer, obviously excited, shot at me. I calmly let him fire, for his best marksmanship would not have helped at a distance of over 300 metres. One just does not score at that distance! Now he turned on me completely and I hoped to get behind him in the next turn to burn his hide. Suddenly I received a blow on my head! I was hit! For a moment my whole body was completely paralysed. My hands dropped to the side and my legs dangled in the fuselage. The worst part was that the blow on the head affected my optic nerve and I was completely blinded. The machine plunged down. For a moment it flashed through my mind that this is the way it looks just before death. I doubted if the wings could stand the strain, and I expected they would break off at any moment. I did not lose consciousness immediately. I fought to regain control of my arms and legs so that I could grasp the control stick. I managed to shut off the fuel and the ignition. But would that alone help me? I had moved my eyes around and taken my goggles off, but it was impossible to see even the sun. I was completely blinded. The seconds were an eternity to me. I continued to fall.[2] *Rittmeister Manfred von Richthofen, Jagdgeschwader 1*

At the very last minute he regained partial vision and managed to land safely just before fainting. It had been a close-run thing. His over-confidence in allowing himself to come under long-range fire from a 'puny' Lewis gun had nearly been the end of him. He had suffered a severe skull fracture from a glancing bullet and was rushed to hospital.

It appeared that his recovery was swift for he was back in the air by 16 August when he shot down his victim. Yet Richthofen was a changed man. Now bothered in the air by intermittent headaches, dizziness and nausea, he became far more conscious of his own mortality and consequently was a little more cautious in his tactics. His wound had not really healed and he was persuaded to take an extensive period of leave between early September and November of 1917. Whatever the reason his rate of kills fell sharply over the following months. He had shot down fifty-seven aircraft in the eleven months leading up to 6 July 1917, but would only shoot down another twenty-three victims in the nine months left of his career. There is no doubt that some of the after-effects of this brief encounter dogged Richthofen deep into 1918.

In the spring and summer of 1917 a new generation of German aces had emerged from behind Richthofen's substantial shadow. Leutnant Werner Voss was a consummate air fighter shooting down forty-eight aircraft before over-confidence or a simple misjudgement led him into a dogfight against far superior numbers in which he was finally downed on 23 September over Ypres. One of the other rising aces was Leutnant Lothar von Richthofen, the brother of Manfred, who scored rapidly, but using a far more aggressively direct manner, which consigned him to much more time than most on the sidelines recovering from various wounds. Many aces had excelled but then fallen by the wayside in 1917: Karl Emil Schäfer claimed thirty before he was killed in June 1917; Karl Allmenröder had thirty before he too was killed that month; while the deadly Kurt Wolff died aged only 22 years old in September having shot down thirty-three.

Nevertheless Manfred von Richthofen endured into 1918, still blessed with a supreme combination of all the qualities required in an ace. After his long leave he had recovered much of his former health and vitality. He still had the flying skills, the eyesight, the tactical awareness, the gunnery ability and the underpinning courage; but on top of these manifest virtues he was a superb teacher who tried to inculcate the same merits in all who served with him. When carefully selected replacement pilots joined his jagdgeschwader they were sent up on practice flights around the airfield for up to two weeks, polishing their flying skills, practising the simple manoeuvres they would need as part of a Jasta. When they flew for the first few times in action they would take their place in the formation but would drop out as soon as there was an engagement. Richthofen constantly watched the new men, determining their strengths and weaknesses, working out where best they fitted into the formation.

His attack tactics were simple, direct and deadly. He had made his reputation in shooting down the artillery observation and photographic reconnaissance machines that were handmaidens of the Royal Artillery, the greatest and most deadly enemy of the German Army. He stalked his prey mercilessly.

> I dive out of the sun at him taking into consideration the wind direction. Whoever reaches the enemy first has the privilege to shoot. The whole flight goes down with him. So-called 'cover' at great altitude is a cloak for cowardice. If the first attacker has gun trouble, then it is the turn of the second, or the third and so on; two must never fire at the same time.[3]
> *Rittmeister Manfred von Richthofen, Jagdgeschwader 1*

If he reached his target first, and as the formation leader he usually did, then there was rarely a need for anyone else to fire. To the end Richthofen remained a protégé of the great Oswald Boelcke.

> The subject 'aerial battle technique' can be explained with one sentence, namely, 'I approach the enemy from behind to within 50 metres, I aim carefully, fire and the enemy falls.' These were the words used in explanation by Boelcke when I asked him his trick. Now, I know that this is the whole secret of aerial victory. One does not need to be a clever pilot, or a crack shot, one only needs the courage to fly in close to the enemy before opening fire.[4] *Rittmeister Manfred von Richthofen, Jagdgeschwader 1*

His tactics against the ever multiplying formations of British scouts naturally employed the same principle. His men would dive from altitude aiming to hit their usually unsuspecting targets with maximum force from close range. The initial impact was everything. Richthofen himself, far from staying above the dirty work and seeking easy kills among the stragglers, was leading from the front and at the heart of the action.

The commander must not concentrate on stray enemy planes but should always attack the main body; stray fliers will be destroyed by the planes that follow. Until this time no one from the formation should pass the commander. Speed is to be regulated by throttling back and not by manoeuvre. But, from the moment the commander dives on an enemy squadron, each pilot should be intent on being the first to engage the enemy. The enemy squadron should be ripped apart by the impact of the first attack and through the absolute determination of each individual to get into battle.[5] *Rittmeister Manfred von Richthofen, Jagdgeschwader 1*

Once the initial impact had been made, Richthofen would usually zoom back up to hang above any dogfight that ensued, from which vantage point he would intervene to rescue any of his more inexperienced pilots who had got into difficulties. He then acted as a focus to reassemble his formation as soon as possible and assess the situation.

If such a battle is successful and has split up into individual combats, the Jagdgeschwader becomes dispersed. It is not easy to reassemble it, and in most cases it will be possible to find only individual separated aircraft. The commander must circle at the battle's centre or over a predetermined easily recognisable point. Individual pilots should now attach themselves directly to him. If he collects sufficient strength the hunt can be continued.[6] *Rittmeister Manfred von Richthofen, Jagdgeschwader 1*

Back at their airfield Richthofen always emphasized the value of proper debriefing, using it as an opportunity to deliver a practical tutorial in scout tactics.

It is important, and instructive, that a discussion be held immediately after each Jagdgeschwader flight. During this, everything should be discussed from take off to landing and whatever has happened during the flight should be talked through. Questions from individuals can be most useful in explaining things.[7] *Rittmeister Manfred von Richthofen, Jagdgeschwader 1*

One excuse that Richthofen took little heed of was that of problems with the machine guns. His attitude was robust and a lesson to all his men. There was no excuse.

It is the pilot and not the ordnance officer or the mechanic who is responsible for the faultless performance of his guns. Machine gun jams do not exist! If they do occur, it is the pilot whom I blame. The pilot should personally examine his ammunition and its loading into the belt to ensure that the length of each round is consistent with that of the others. He has to find time to do this during bad weather, or in good weather, at night. A machine gun that fires well is better than an engine that runs well. I pay considerably less attention to flying ability. I had shot down my first twenty whilst flying itself caused me the greatest trouble.[8] *Rittmeister Manfred von Richthofen, Jagdgeschwader 1*

The inference is all but spelt out. It is the guns and marksmanship that kill; all the flying ability in the world will not help if the pilot cannot hit his target when in the right position. There was one final bit of advice.

It is never wise to stick obstinately to an enemy you were unable to shoot down through bad shooting or his manoeuvrability when the fight takes place far across on his side of the front line and one faces a large number of opponents alone.[9] *Rittmeister Manfred von Richthofen, Jagdgeschwader 1*

One of the more distinguished pilots recruited to his Jagdgeschwader was Leutnant Ernst Udet who had already downed some twenty aircraft. Udet was born on 26 April 1896. He had served as a motorcyclist before training as a pilot in 1915. As was usual he served for a year with artillery observation aircraft, where he impressed his superiors enough to be given a chance as a scout pilot with Jasta 15 in September 1916. Here he scored six victories before transferring to Jasta 37 in June 1917. He had taken over command in November but was unable to resist the call to join Richthofen at Jagdgeschwader 1. On his arrival Udet was immediately impressed at the work ethic instilled by Richthofen – this was no privileged group of dilettantes.

Other Jastas live in castles or small villages, 15 or 20 miles behind the lines, but Richthofen's unit was housed in portable corrugated iron buildings, that could be taken down and re-erected in a few hours. It was seldom more than 15 miles behind the front line trenches. Whereas other Jastas took off two or three times a day, Richthofen and his men made five or more flights in the same period. In bad weather the others ceased flying, but Richthofen's machines were nearly always in the air. A few kilometres behind the front, often within reach of the enemy shells, we used to sit in flying kit, in deckchairs which had been placed in the middle of the aerodrome. Our machines stood close by with their engines running. As soon as a hostile aeroplane appeared on the horizon we took off.[10] *Leutnant Ernst Udet, Jasta 11, Jagdgeschwader 1*

By this time Richthofen had brought up a whole generation of German aces under his regime of comradeship tempered by strict discipline. His influence was increasingly pervasive right across the German Air Service on the Western Front. Perhaps his value as a teacher and symbol meant that he should have been withdrawn from the front line. But as the great German offensive loomed, at the moment of his country's greatest crisis, Manfred von Richthofen was not a man to stand on the sidelines.

I should consider myself a despicable creature if, now that I am loaded with fame and decorations, I should consent to live on as the pensioner of my own dignity and to preserve my valuable life for the nation, while every poor fellow in the trenches, who is doing his duty just as much as I am, has to stick it out.[11] *Rittmeister Manfred von Richthofen, Jagdgeschwader 1*

In this, as for so much else, he spoke for most of the truly great aces of both sides in the Great War.

THERE was no equivalent dominating figure flying on the British side of the trenches. In 1916, and for a brief moment on his short-lived return to the front in 1917, Captain Albert Ball had provided an example of supreme courage that inspired the whole of the RFC. But Ball took no heed of the nuances of a tactical situation; he simply went for his opponents using bull-headed tactics that at heart relied on incredible luck and were simply unsustainable in the longer term. Ball was duly killed on 7 May 1917. Of the other leading aces the most remarkable was the Canadian Captain William Bishop, who was born on 8 February 1894 in Ontario, Canada. He attended the Royal Military College and served with the Canadian Mounted Rifles on the outbreak of war.

He transferred as an observer to the RFC serving with 21 Squadron on the Western Front in 1915. After a crash he retrained as a pilot and returned to fly a Nieuport 17 with 60 Squadron in the spring of 1917. He began scoring victories straight away and within a couple of weeks had qualified as an ace. From then on his score mounted rapidly as Bishop adopted the increasingly unfashionable 'lone wolf' *modus operandi* that culminated in a daring attack on a German airfield for which he was awarded a Victoria Cross in June 1917. By the time he had returned to England in August 1917 he had run up a claimed total of forty-seven. Unfortunately there were rarely witnesses to his feats and a rough-hewed scepticism has set in which has never really been dissipated. As a result Bishop has become a controversial figure but in essence he was an irrelevance to the air war. He over-claimed, that seems evident, but then so did many others. The key point is surely that, other than the undoubted boost his claimed successes gave to Canadian and RFC morale, Bishop was not a tactical leader for the men who served alongside him. His was a lone war. When he did come to command 85 Squadron on his brief return to the front in 1918, the unit was almost rudderless as young, inexperienced pilots were given nothing to follow other than the example of his latest tales of wild success.

It was therefore unsurprising that in the absence of a truly dominant ace with the inclination and ability to share that experience, the RFC scout pilots simply pooled their knowledge to provide a collective tactical framework: during 1917 all the basics of aerial scout fighting were slowly standardized and disseminated through the RFC.

But by the start of 1918 one British scout pilot had begun to show some of the attributes of a 'British Richthofen', although his rise to prominence had been far more laboured. Captain Edward Mannock was born on 24 May 1887 and at 30 he was considerably older than the average pilot on either side. He was certainly not a natural ace and had great difficulty in recording his first successes. In many ways a nervous individual, plagued by inner doubts, he even came under suspicion of being a coward when his nerve seemed to have failed him on occasion during his first few missions over the front with 40 Squadron in April and May 1917. Yet Mannock had a deeply analytical mind; he was always thinking, always processing acquired information. Slowly he began to develop a system of aerial tactics based on diligent preparation of men and machines, a healthy dose of restraining caution, careful stalking of his prey and the primacy of a flight formation working together as a team. His impact on his men was amplified by his exuberant personality and generally larger-than-life character.

Mannock was the hero of the squadron at that time. He left the squadron with twenty-one victories and his victories were good. He came on to form having been older than most of us and a more mature man. He had given great, deep thought to the fighting and had re-orientated his mental attitudes which was necessary for a top fighter pilot. He had got his confidence and he had thought out the way he was going to tackle things. He became a very good friend of mine and I owed a lot to him that he was so friendly. I was unnecessarily reserved and he liked to give people nicknames – he called me 'Noisy'! He was a lot of fun.[12] *Captain Gwilym Lewis, 40 Squadron*

Mannock himself was often known as 'Mick' within the RFC in honour of his family's Irish background.

Among the men most influenced by Mannock was Lieutenant George McElroy. He had joined 40 Squadron back in August 1917, but he too was to prove a slow starter. McElroy soon became Mannock's first real protégé, learning from him the basic principles of air warfare.

Mick was able to spot McElroy's potential within hours of their meeting, for 'McIrish', as Mick named him, was very headstrong and would probably have been killed early on had it not been for Mick's tuition and patience. He was the first of Mick's pupils in the true sense. He took an interest in the lad from the first and coached him daily.[13] *Lieutenant William Douglas, 40 Squadron*

Once McElroy found his feet and started scoring victories in December 1917, he began to cut a veritable swath through the German ranks.

Unlike most great fighters he used frequently to open fire at comparatively long range, and being a wonderful shot, the fight was sometimes over before the victim had time to realise it had begun. He stood alone in this respect. He was such a remarkable shot in the air that he occasionally killed at long range. He was as crafty as a fox, and by opening fire early, made his intended victim think the attacker was a raw novice with the 'wind-up'. This affected the Hun's tactics and lulled him into a fancied security. The error was generally discovered when too late.[14] *Lieutenant F. Gilbert, 40 Squadron*

Mannock had become an influential flight commander with 40 Squadron when he was sent back to England for a period of home service in January 1918. A month later, while serving with a training squadron, he first met his future biographer Lieutenant Ira Jones who left his vivid impressions of Mannock's tactics in action from their subsequent service together with 74 Squadron. Underlying everything was a lightning flexibility of thought which enabled him to react and adapt to the ever changing situations encountered in the skies. His foremost aim was always to attack from the direction not expected by the enemy: usually from the east, out of the sun or bursting out of the clouds.

He not only mystified and surprised the enemy, but also the formations he led. Once over the lines, he would commence flying in a never-ending series of zigzags, never straight for more than a few seconds. Was it not by flying straight for long periods that formation leaders were caught napping?[15] *Lieutenant Ira Jones, 74 Squadron*

Mannock was popularly supposed by some, including Jones, to have defective vision in one eye, but this seems to have been a myth, or at least grossly exaggerated. Indeed Jones himself pays no uncertain tribute to Mannock's amazing air vision.

Suddenly his machine would rock violently, a signal that he was about to attack – but where were the enemy? His companions could not see them, although he was pointing in their direction. Another signal and his SE would dive to the attack. A quick half roll, and there beneath him would be the enemy formation flying serenely along; the enemy leader with his eyes no doubt glued to the west – the result a complete surprise attack.[16] *Lieutenant Ira Jones, 74 Squadron*

When they dived they would be flying and attacking as a formation, not as individuals. What they were doing was not new, certainly not to the German aces trained by Richthofen and before him Boelcke. But Mannock was particularly good at achieving complete surprise, which was more than half the battle given reasonable shooting accuracy. And Mannock was a crack shot.

> Mannock would take the leader if possible in order to give his pilots coming down behind him a better chance of an easy shot at someone before the enemy formation split up, and the dogfight began. Having commenced the fight with the tactical advantage of height in his favour, Mannock would adopt dive and zoom tactics in order to retain the initiative.[17] *Lieutenant Ira Jones, 74 Squadron*

An example of Mannock's crucial influence occurred when he was stationed at the same airfield as an Australian squadron.

> Funny thing about 4 Australian Flying Corps, was that they were not getting any Huns at the start and the Camel was so good up to 10,000 feet. Mick Mannock was asked to go across and give them a talk. This did the trick, for then on they got cracking and did well.[18] *Major Keith Caldwell, 74 Squadron*

One of those Australians who benefited immeasurably from Mannock's instruction and advice was Lieutenant Arthur Cobby.

> Mannock took upon himself the task of making all the pilots around him keen and aggressive. Several talks of his to the Australian pilots there were responsible for some fine aggressive shows against the enemy, and numerous combined affairs were successfully carried out. No matter how great the odds, Mannock always managed to extricate his patrol without losing machines.[19] *Lieutenant Arthur Cobby, 4 Squadron, Australian Flying Corps*

In all his teaching Mannock was a great believer in one simple maxim: 'Gentlemen, always above; seldom on the same level; never underneath.'[20] And he hammered home this message at every opportunity.

Anyone who came within his sphere of influence would be soon convinced.

> Go into the fight from above if possible. To illustrate my meaning clearly, take two armed men, each armed with a stout stick. One man is in a steep ditch, and the other on the bank above. The man in the ditch would be foolish to commence a fight with the other; whereas the man on the bank has the advantage of being able to commence a scrap if he so desires, or run away. The man below could not catch him, as he would lose time scrambling out of the ditch. This simple parallel governs the entire tactics of aerial fighting.[21] *Lieutenant Arthur Cobby, 4 Squadron, Australian Flying Corps*

Mannock was emphatically not the only man pushing forward these tactics, but his dramatic personal success and generally inspiring *persona* gave him a considerable influence. Gradually the overall doctrine practised and preached by Mannock and other key pilots spread through the whole of the RFC.

> It is all a case of keeping a good lookout to prevent surprise attack and using your brains. The days of dogfights where machines rush at one another and circle around each other, firing all the while, seem to be gone. It is now a case of getting higher than the Hun and using sun, wind direction, and the shape and position of the lines to secure a favourable quick dive at the Hun and, unless he is keeping a very sharp lookout, he is dead or going down in flames before he knows what has happened.[22] *Lieutenant William Harvey, 22 Squadron*

The other prime consideration was the necessity of preserving the formation come what may. Isolated aircraft were not only easy targets, vulnerable to being picked off by any passing German scout formation, but by their absence from the formation they also weakened the whole.

> I had to give strict orders that no pilot was on any account to leave the formation, even to take on what looked like an easy opportunity to shoot down an enemy aircraft. The initiative in any attack, I ruled, was to rest

wholly in the hands of the leader. If he dived to the attack, the whole squadron was to dive with him; and when he zoomed away after an attack, even if he had failed to shoot down the enemy machine that they were attacking, all his pilots were to zoom away with him, still keeping formation. Being the most experienced of all the pilots, the leader was the most capable of shooting down the enemy quickly and effectively; and with the squadron behind him and acting as a buffer against any attack from the rear he could afford to concentrate all his powers on the destruction of the enemy without having to peer all the time over his shoulder.[23] *Major Sholto Douglas, 84 Squadron*

The influence of thinking pilots like Edward Mannock and Sholto Douglas would gradually spread throughout the RFC; but there was another leading British ace making his presence painfully felt among the men of the German Air Service by the end of 1917.

Captain James McCudden was the ultimate 'professional' air fighter. Born on 28 March 1895 in Gillingham, he had made a career of the Royal Flying Corps even before the war. He had joined as a mechanic as early as 1913, having previously enlisted as a bugler into the Royal Engineers in 1910. He had served as an engine fitter with 3 Squadron on the Western Front in 1914, then he took to the air with them as an occasional observer in 1915, where he showed himself a steady man during the 'Fokker scourge'. After learning to fly back in England in 1916, he returned as a pilot, flying the FE2b with 20 Squadron, and then the single-seater DH2s with 29 Squadron. After a successful period learning his trade as a combat flyer and claiming the five victories necessary to be an ace, McCudden returned home for a stint as an instructor. Here he demonstrated some of his flying skills to his agog pupils.

McCudden was a brilliant pilot, absolutely outstanding. I saw him do the most hair-raising stunts round the aerodrome when he was demonstrating what a Pup could do. His favourite was to loop directly off the ground when he was taking off and continue looping! Once he looped thirteen times from take off and when he finished he was 500 feet high. A wonderful piece of flying. Or he would go up to about 1,000 feet, turn the machine upside down and just go round the airfield till the engine stopped – then he'd go on gliding. Next thing he'd roll it out, get the engine going again and away he'd go. He was absolutely marvellous – there wasn't a thing that he couldn't do with that machine.[24] *Second Lieutenant J. C. F. Hopkins, RFC*

Among his pupils was one Edward Mannock who certainly learned a great deal from his instructor.

McCudden returned to the fray as a flight commander with 56 Squadron in 1917. He was now the fully formed article: his natural flying talents and shooting ability augmented by an absolute attention to detail on the ground. He took every care to make sure that his engine was running smoothly, generating every possible ounce of power. His machine guns were checked and rechecked, he carefully aligned their sights and did everything possible to avoid the endemic gun jamming that plagued the British scouts. He drank little alcohol and took care to make sure that he himself was in good shape for the ordeals ahead.

Captain McCudden was punctilious to a degree. Always very smart on parade, he was a man who kept himself extraordinarily fit and was a very good pilot. But far more than that he was a shooting genius and I think it was for that reason that he kept himself so fit because he realised that the wonderful touch and eyesight that he possessed could only have their full use if he lived in training almost like a competitor for the King's Prize at Bisley.[25] *Equipment Officer Lieutenant Hubert Charles, 56 Squadron*

McCudden's shooting was spectacular through a combination of superb hand-eye coordination, rigorous scrutiny of his weapons and sheer hard work firing at practice targets. To those who watched him he appeared to have some kind of wondrous gift, but the gift had been earned and polished to perfection.

I've seen McCudden shoot at targets: we'd all go up and we'd fire at the target but McCudden would come down and he would tear the target to shreds. He had such a wonderful way of shooting; what it was no-one seemed to know. But he only had to fire a matter of 20 rounds and the machine seemed to fall to pieces. You might fly along and fire 200 bullets and the machine still goes floating on – not a bit of damage done![26] *Lieutenant Thomas Isbell, 41 Squadron*

There was no doubt that his eyesight was exceptional and that, combined with his long experience in the air, meant that he could almost always see his German prey well before they saw him. He would then stalk them across the skies until he could take advantage of his murderously accurate gunnery skills. His professional attitude was demonstrated in his hard, pragmatic approach to the whole business of aerial warfare. He had no time for any knight errantry in the skies.

My system was to always attack the Hun at his disadvantage if possible, and if I were attacked at my disadvantage I usually broke off the combat, for in my opinion the Hun in the air must be beaten at his own game, which is cunning. I think that the correct way to wage war is to down as many as possible of the enemy at the least risk, expense and casualties to one's own side.[27] *Captain James McCudden, 56 Squadron*

Men like Major Sholto Douglas welcomed the replacement of the 'berserker' tradition hitherto espoused and demonstrated by Captain Alan Ball. It became less a matter of demonstrating courage in the face of adversity and more a logical assessment of a tactical situation, which would then determine whether a flight commander took his pilots into action – or not.

I had to din into them that one must always strive to take the enemy at a disadvantage, and that, equally, one must not be taken at a disadvantage oneself. Quite often this meant deliberately refusing to accept the challenge, and cautiously retiring so as to get into a better position. The only exception to that rule that was permissible was if one saw other Allied aircraft, of any number, being overwhelmed by superior numbers of the enemy; and then, whatever the odds, one must accept battle.[28] *Major Sholto Douglas, 84 Squadron*

There is no doubt that as 1917 ended James McCudden had attained a state of near perfection in the interception of the German LVG and

Rumpler high-reconnaissance aircraft, mainly in the course of extra solo patrols on top of his routine patrols as a flight commander. This was exemplified by his fantastic success on 28 December. In a laconic combat report McCudden described what happened that morning.

> Left aerodrome at 10.15 to look for enemy aeroplanes west of the lines. At 11.10 I saw a Rumpler coming west over Boursies. I got into position at 75 yards, fired a short burst from both guns, when enemy aeroplane (EA) at once went into right-hand spiral dive and its right-hand wings fell off at about 17,000 feet, and the wreckage fell in our lines north of Velu Wood at 11.15. At 11.30 saw a Rumpler going north over Haplincourt at 17,000 feet. I secured a firing position and fired a good burst from both guns, when flames at once came from enemy aircraft's fuselage and he went down in a right-hand flat spin and crashed in our lines near Flers (as near as I could judge), as I remained at 17,000 feet, so as not to lose time by going down and having to climb up again. EA crashed about 11.35. I now saw an LVG being shelled by our anti-aircraft over Havrincourt at 16,000. AA fire did not stop until I was within range of EA. I obtained a good position at fairly long range and fired a burst with the object of making him dive, which he did. EA dived very steeply (about 200mph), starting at about 16,000 feet, and at about 9,000 feet I fired another burst into EA at 100 yards range, when flames issued from EA fuselage and then he broke up over Havrincourt Wood, the wreckage falling in our lines. The EA had been diving so fast that the hostile observer could not fire even if I gave him the chance. I climbed again at 12.15, at 18,000 feet I saw an LVG being shelled by our AA over Lagnicourt. EA dived down east and I caught up to him just east of the lines and fired a good burst from Lewis at 100 yards, when a small burst of flame came from EA but at once went out again. EA dived steeply, kicking his rudder from side-to-side, and I last saw gliding north-east over Marquion at 12.20 at 9,000 feet, under control.[29] *Captain James McCudden, 56 Squadron*

So much is plain, but in sharp contrast to many such claims of dramatic successes among RFC pilots, McCudden's claims were based on a reality that could be easily confirmed. His three victories have been traced as the Rumpler flown by Unteroffizier Munz and Leutnant Rücker, a second Rumpler with Leutnant Hans Mittag and

Unteroffizier Oskar Günert and an LVG crewed by Leutnants Walter Bergmann and Albert Weinrich. He did not claim the second LVG as he had been unable to complete the kill when his Vickers machine gun had jammed and he was forced to rely on his secondary and less powerful Lewis gun armament.

> Whilst the Hun was going down fast I noticed the observer frantically shouting and waving to the pilot over the left-hand side of the fuselage. I expect he was annoyed, because he was having a hot shower bath from the damaged radiator. Anyhow, I hope the water froze over him solid and gave him frostbite. After that I pulled up away from him and returned to my aerodrome, for I had very little petrol left, and on my way back I felt very disappointed at having missed the last Hun, for if my Vickers had not stopped at the crucial moment, I think I should have dispatched him with much celerity. When I landed, the Major said that our 'Archie' gunners had reported Huns falling out of the sky in pieces everywhere.[30] *Captain James McCudden, 56 Squadron*

Although McCudden was a conscientious flight commander and had a strong grasp of formation tactics, he did not have the widespread influence that Mannock achieved in 1918. His personal concentration was always on his solo patrols and hence in the crowded skies his influence was more localized.

Another kind of ace was Captain Gwilym Lewis. He had served in 1916 and returned with 40 Squadron in 1917. He claimed a number of victories himself, but he took far more interest in ensuring the survival of members of his flight rather than in increasing his personal score. He was well aware from his own experiences that not every scout pilot could hope to attain that deadly combination of flying skills, eyesight, shooting ability and tactical nous that made the likes of Mannock and McCudden such a deadly force. Lewis aimed to do his duty wherever possible, but his overall priority was making sure his men lived to fight another day.

> I was very keen on an efficient flight. That was my job. We became especially good with our formation flying. Perhaps we weren't a star turn but I liked everyone to have got a Hun. It wasn't so easy getting Huns as

all that. Fellows would fight quite hard and still not make the final hit. It was an extraordinary thing that a fellow coming out couldn't see half the things that were going on. Their eyes didn't register into the far distance. We had to see things – just a twinkle of the sun on a bit of metal – that's all we would need to make us conscious that there was something in the sky way in the distance. From that we might manoeuvre our position. But we would get into dogfights even and they hardly knew what was going on. They were shot down pretty freely. I didn't like this so any fellow coming out new to my flight as soon as he was ready to go over the lines flew next to me and outside him was an experienced man. So I never lost one of these boys who was new to the game. I kept my own eye on them and other people did too. As soon as they became better acquainted to what was going on then they were on their own then.[31] *Captain Gwilym Lewis, 40 Squadron*

Yet it was becoming increasingly apparent that the flight of about six to eight aircraft was becoming a thing of the past over the front. Increasingly squadron patrols, or even several squadrons operating together, were becoming the norm. In a sense, as in so much else, Richthofen had led the way with his flying circus Jagdgeschwader 1 composed of four Jasta. Early British attempts to secure dominating force by the use of multi-squadron formations had floundered when they merely served to frighten off any German opposition who generally either kept out of their way altogether or just sniped at any stragglers from the sidelines.

As the size of formations increased so the amount of routine overclaiming ballooned to excessive proportions. The problem was no longer the lone wolf ace claiming unwitnessed kills. Now it was the natural confusion in determining who had done what in the chaos of a dogfight. Look at it from the perspective of a flight of British aircraft flying well over the far side of the lines who dive on a German formation. Their experienced leader puts a long burst into his selected victim, then dives and is soon up to his neck in a dogfight; the next in his formation also puts a burst into the same aircraft and is caught up in the mêlée; behind him a more inexperienced pilot fires an erratic few rounds at the same target and sees it begin to tumble out of the sky. Finally, the fourth member of the flight bringing up the rear sees what is happening and although not personally involved is well aware that no-one can see what he is doing and decides he too can seize the opportunity to put in a claim to boost his all-important victory total. At the end of the dogfight when they report to their squadron all four duly put in their claims. Two are in essence 'legitimate': their shots must have caused damage or injury to their target, although neither can have any real idea what happened to their victim once they were dragged into the hurly-burly of a dogfight. The third claim is speculative in the extreme, but then he *did* see the German aircraft begin to fall; the fourth claim is utterly spurious. So what have we here: four victory claims, probably all granted by the authorities who naturally have little motivation for refusing claims. Yet in reality the German aircraft has merely spun down, taking violent evasive action until it was safely out of sight below the cloud level and then flown off home; damaged certainly, the pilot shaking in his boots perhaps, but all too ready, willing and able to fight again. As the action took place over German lines there could be no searching the ground for the mangled aircraft wrecks that were the ultimate confirmation for most German victory claims. So there it is: the British squadron has four more kills for its victory board; but they have shot no-one down. Ninety years later it is impossible for even the most conscientious of aerial historians to track down the identity of the four 'victims'; the reason is obvious – they don't, and never did, exist.

Lieutenant Thomas Traill recalled the atmosphere when the Bristol Fighters of 20 Squadron got back to their airfield to make their reports and file their claims after combat.

> Debriefing was a noisy free-for-all. After a fight the patrol, or most of it, would straggle in twos and threes with streamers of message bags flying from the rear guns of those claiming Huns. Each lot as they came in would beat up the hangars, and the intensity of this would indicate how individual crews were feeling and how the fight had gone. After taxiing in, the crews, still in flying kit, would gather round Major Johnstone and Packham. The crews who had not been on the show would gather round them, and the NCOs and air mechanics of the squadron would press in all round to hear as much as they could especially what had happened to the crews of their machines. Meanwhile the inner group made their verbal reports, mostly at

the same time to Johnstone and Packham. 'I fired a short burst and he turned over and went right down out of control' might mean what the speaker hoped it did, or it might mean that the Huns did a half roll and beat it for home – there was no way of telling – and many more aircraft went 'right down out of control' than ever hit the ground. One got to know who were the line-shooters who so often managed to 'see him crash' and who were the ones who tried only to report what they thought they had seen. It was usually the former who at the end of a fight were the furthest west and nearest home. Once after a show I had been leading, I broke in on one of those who was shooting a line to the CO that I knew to be untrue and I called him a, 'Bloody liar!' There was a silence for a moment as he turned and elbowed his way out of the crowd and then the gaggle went on as before.[32] *Lieutenant Thomas Traill, 20 Squadron*

Such direct challenges were rare; human nature meant that quarrels over claims were avoided and many squadrons had a cheerful 'You scratch my back, I'll scratch yours' attitude to the formal confirmation of kills.

Nevertheless it is emphatically not that they were all part of some dishonest conspiracy. After all, if the British pilots hung around to track the fall of their victims right down to the ground, then they too would be shot down in an environment where every ounce of concentration was required to survive. Worse still, in concentrating on confirming their own kills, they could easily be accused of leaving their comrades in the lurch. It seems that some pilots claimed only when they were certain and were occasionally wrong; many pilots claimed in good faith and were often wrong; others claimed in what can euphemistically be called an optimistic frame of mind; a few, a very few, were utterly fraudulent. *But all of them, one way or another, over-claimed*. It is only the actual proportion of over-claiming that is variable.

Whatever the skills they possessed or the qualities of the aircraft they flew, there was one factor that held back most of the scout pilots and even some of the aces. Unfortunately this was a somewhat basic fault: their lack of marksmanship and utter inability to hit anything they aimed at. There is no doubt that the overall standard of gunnery was appalling.

The most successful air fighter is the most aggressive; but at the same time, a cool head and a fine sense of judgement are essential. Angles are so fine, and speeds are so tremendous in the air, that a very accurate burst of fire must be put in to be of any use. I have seen pilots 'sitting on the tail' of enemy machines, and only a few feet off, fire away all their ammunition, and still the Hun tootles along unhurt. Then again, I have seen a careful pilot fire only about 10 shots – and down goes his opponent.[33]
Lieutenant Arthur Cobby, 4 Squadron, Australian Flying Corps

When gunnery tests cruelly exposed his inadequacies even against static or relatively slow-moving targets, the sensible pilot would attempt to use his other skills to counterbalance his inadequate gunnery skills.

The tests in the air were of two types and consisted of diving and firing on a floating target in a pond and firing at a canvas drogue towed by a BE2c. At my first attempt on the pond target I had 17 hits out of 200 possible and at a second attempt 15 hits out of 120 possible. On the towed target my one and only attempt produced 18 outers and 7 inners out of a possible 400. These were not very good results. Realising my low standards of marksmanship I resorted to surprising the enemy and only firing at point-blank range.[34] *Captain Leonard Rochford, 3 (Naval) Squadron, RNAS*

Major Sholto Douglas resolved to follow a similar line. If he couldn't hit his enemies then he would make damn sure that they couldn't hit him.

My one big failing was that although I was a good enough pilot I was not, for some unaccountable reason, a good shot, and good shooting was essential for any outstanding success in putting up a score. On the other hand, it would have taken a very smart Hun to get his sights on me.[35]
Major Sholto Douglas, 84 Squadron

And in the highly competitive world above the trenches of the Western Front there were always new aces, new supermen, ready to take on the world and create a formidable reputation for themselves. One of the most remarkable was Captain Anthony Beauchamp-Proctor who was soon made a flight commander with 84 Squadron. His manifold qualities were much appreciated by his commanding officer.

> He was a very good formation leader, and at long range his eyesight was extraordinarily keen. He seemed able to spot an enemy aircraft much further away than any of the rest of us. He also had great courage, and he had developed a particularly good sense of tactics; and after he had sighted the Huns he would proceed to stalk them with the greatest skill and patience, eventually taking them unaware and with the advantages all on our side. Although I still led the squadron at times, I was happier flying as Beauchamp-Proctor's deputy leader.[36] *Major Sholto Douglas, 84 Squadron*

Beauchamp-Proctor was a truly formidable combination of tactician and executioner in the Mannock mode. One typical incident was when his flight of SE5s sighted eleven Albatros.

> I manoeuvred for position and got well into the sun without being seen. Diving on the enemy aircraft formation I selected their leader and getting within 150 yards opened fire. After a burst of 1,000 rounds, the enemy aircraft fell over on its left wing and started to dive. I was compelled to zoom to prevent colliding with EA, but got onto EA's tail again and opened fire. The EA continued to dive and the dive got steeper until EA was in vertical nosedive with engine apparently full on. My Vickers jammed but I followed EA down to 3,000 feet and saw EA nosedive into the ground near Hengest.[37] *Captain Anthony Beauchamp-Proctor, 84 Squadron*

Meanwhile, as had been frequently practised, the men of his flight watched his back.

> My flight commander dove on the leader of the Hun formation. I dived immediately afterwards and got onto the tail of a 'V' Strutter flying on the left of the formation. The 'V' Strutter waited for Captain Proctor to fly over him and then stalled up underneath him. I immediately opened fire and got a good burst of about 100 rounds into him from very close range, The Hun machine then fell over into a vertical sideslip eventually developing into a nosedive.[38] *Lieutenant H. O. MacDonald, 84 Squadron*

The major aces on both sides exuded a massive power and confidence that made them seem like supermen even to strong and competent individuals such as Sholto Douglas. Men like Manfred von Richthofen, James McCudden and Edward Mannock were veterans and, in comparison with the short life span of the average scout pilot, they seemed to have been there for ever. They were eternal figures with apparently supernatural powers in combat that made them seem invulnerable to the young pilots joining their units. They had learned their trade, mastered the complexities of aerial combat and they were as ready as they ever would be for the next round in 1918.

Chapter 4
Impending Storm

The New Year – I wonder whether it will see the end of the war. Somehow I fancy it will be.[1] *Major Charlie Dixon, 29 Squadron*

ON 21 January 1918 the German offensive plans were finalized. Ludendorff had decided to strike at what he now considered to be his primary enemy – the British – in the sector between Arras and the river Serre south of the Somme. It was planned that the massively bolstered Seventeenth, Second and Eighteenth Armies would launch themselves on 21 March 1918 against the British Third and Fifth Armies under Operation Michael. There was of course no element of 'bite and hold' about the German plan; for 'bite and hold' above all needed time and hence was utterly irrelevant in the circumstances faced by Ludendorff. The plan was to break through the British lines and then, while the Eighteenth Army guarded their left flank from intervention by the French to the south, the main force was to drive vigorously to the north, rolling up the British line. Once utter confusion had been created the next phase of assaults was to be launched starting with Operation Georgette in Flanders. This would be the battle that would decide the war, for anything less than complete victory would inevitably doom the Germans to defeat.

They would use the new bombardment techniques developed by Oberst Georg Bruchmüller who had made his reputation at the Battle of Riga in September 1917. He had developed a highly efficient method of suppressing opposition to an attack. Preparation was vital, identifying key targets by means of aerial photographs and carefully calibrating the guns to minimize the need for prior registration. The barrage when it started would be short, but extremely concentrated, changing focus constantly between headquarters, artillery batteries and infantry defences, yet with the overriding aim of neutralizing any opposition, using a predominance of gas shells to prevent units from functioning rather than actually destroying them. This then culminated in a fast-moving creeping barrage as the infantry made their assault. Bruchmüller called the overall effect the *Feuerwalze* or, more poetically, the 'Fire Waltz'. It should be noted that his work was pioneering but only so far as the Germans were concerned. The British had already grasped the essence of Bruchmüller artillery tactics in planning their own offensives but now they were to experience more than a little of their own medicine.

The German Army had also thrown itself into a vigorous retraining programme to prepare the troops for the offensive. At the heart of its new infantry tactics was a concentration on infiltration led by the elite formations of 'storm troopers' who were specially trained to move forward fast, avoiding pockets of resistance but infiltrating as deep as possible to strike hard at the rear echelons. There were not many of the elite storm-trooper units but all the attack divisions underwent vigorous extra training, practising and enhancing their fighting skills in mock-up trench systems. Mobility and the necessity of pushing forward were emphasized at every stage. As an integral part of these plans the German Air Service was given a significantly increased role in ground-attack strafing missions to assist the infantry throughout the offensive. This was symbolized by renaming the Schutzstaffeln (defence section) as Schlachtstaffeln or battle section. They flew the Hannover CL.II two-seater armed with two forward-firing Spandau machine guns, a Parabellum machine gun for the observer and a number of fragmentation bombs. They were tough aircraft, built largely of plywood which gave them the ability to withstand considerable punishment. Their role was to go over the top with the infantry, alongside the first wave, flying low and attacking any pockets of resistance.

Yet this lay in the future. The prime concerns of the German Air Service in the two months leading up to the offensive were twofold. First, they must surprise the British, which meant that the enormous preparations for the attack must be concealed from the probing 'eyes in the sky'. Second, they must themselves secure the detailed reconnaissance not only of the British defensive system but also of deep behind the lines; after all if they did not smash through to the rear areas the offensive would have failed.

To conceal their own plans it was clear that they must intercept and shoot down not only the relatively slow and obsolescent photographic reconnaissance aircraft as epitomized by the RE8, but also wrest air superiority from the British scouts that day after day swarmed over the German lines. Yet their ability to achieve this was in considerable doubt. The technological superiority Germany had achieved with the advent of the Albatros Scout in the autumn of 1916 and which had blossomed into the successes of 'Bloody April' in 1917 had been effectively countered. The Allies were producing ever increasing numbers of the comparable, or even on some counts superior, SE5a, Sopwith Camel, Bristol Fighter and the French SPAD scout. The German aviation industry had begun to struggle in its efforts to find a worthy successor to the Albatros D.III. They needed a whole new generation of scouts capable of taking the fight to their enemies but they were limited by the standard 160hp engine which was all that was available. The most recent efforts, the Albatros D.V, Pfalz D.III, Pfalz D.IIIa and Fokker Triplane, were all designed primarily for a defensive role fighting behind the German lines and close to their own airfields. Their designers had therefore sought power and performance but in doing so had rather sacrificed endurance with a flying time of just 90 minutes. This compared rather badly with the 150 minutes achieved by the likes of the SE5a and Camel. All told, the German Air Service needed new aircraft and better, more powerful engines to drive them onwards and upwards. And it needed a lot of them.

> It could not be doubted that the mere accomplishment of the numerical schedule of the programme would never give us the equality in the air, to say nothing of superiority, when faced by the air forces of England, France and America, all working in unison. We had to surpass our foes in all matters pertaining to the technical side. Above all else we needed the design of a new pursuit plane.[2] *General Ernest Wilhelm von Hoeppner, German Air Service*

The aircraft designers of Germany engaged in a competition to determine the best design possible for a new single-seater scout. In the end it was the Fokker aircraft manufacturer that won: Reinhold Platz was the designer, assisted by the remarkable Anthony Fokker himself who contributed the final design touches using his own abilities as a pilot to finesse the basic design. After the competitive tests took place at Adlershof airfield in January 1918 large orders were placed for the Fokker D.VII, with even Fokker's rival Albatros being ordered to produce them under licence. The first production models were hampered by the same slightly outdated 160hp Mercedes engine that only generated a top speed of 116mph but whose high compression allowed it to retain speed at high altitudes. Yet the sturdy construction, streamlined fixtures and fittings and overall efficiency of the design made it a superb flying machine. It was very responsive to the controls, making average pilots look extremely good indeed. It particularly excelled at high altitudes where its controls still 'bit' and it could outmanoeuvre most of the contemporary Allied aircraft. However, in an echo of the British problems during 'Bloody April', the Fokker D.VII would not be delivered to the front until late April 1918 – long after the planned German offensive was scheduled to begin.

It was fortunate that the Germans had another string to their bow in concealing the time and place of their offensive. Recognizing that it was difficult to prevent aircraft from penetrating their hinterland, they made sure that whatever they might see could be easily misinterpreted or downright confusing. The age of the deception plan was born.

> The success of the German attack depended on whether we were fortunate enough to surprise the enemy. We learned a great deal from the mistakes of our foes, for they generally revealed their intentions to attack by increasing the number of their aerodromes and by an increase in aerial activity over the zone in question. Therefore, above all else, we had to avoid the appearance of numerous new aeroplane tents just prior to the attack. Another thing, in the construction of the permanent hangars which had been pushed vigorously during the winter, we did not dare to concentrate them along the front on which we intended to attack. They were divided up on practically an equal basis between all the armies.[3] *General Ernest Wilhelm von Hoeppner, German Air Service*

The German reconnaissance and artillery observation flights responsible for the preparations for the offensive were known as Flieger

Abteilung. Their pilots and observers were going to be exceptionally busy men over the next three months. One of the observers was Leutnant Fritz Kampfenkel. He knew what was to be done.

> Flieger Abteilung (A) 240 performed essentially three different missions: first, photographing enemy positions, including troop concentrations and approach roads; then, in support of our ground troops, reconnoitring the area where the positions of both sides dovetailed; and, seldomly, on bright moonlit nights directing our artillery against enemy guns or supply depots.[4]
> *Leutnant Fritz Kampfenkel, Flieger Abteilung (A) 240, Imperial German Air Force*

The German reconnaissance flights had begun the exhaustive process of photographing every inch of the ground that lay in front of the planned Somme offensive. They were replicating the tasks undertaken from the other side by the RFC during the great British offensives of 1916 and 1917. The German Air Service had never really needed this kind of excessively detailed picture of what lay before them in the past, as the ground over which the battle would rage was already in their hands. Their flights had primarily been to identify the signs of artillery and troop movements that would indicate the next point of frenzied assault. But now their own armies needed to know exactly what lay beyond the next ridge, invisible to observers on the ground. They needed to know the location of every Allied trench, machine-gun post, artillery battery and command post. And they needed to track troop movements to judge whether the Allies had determined the point of the oncoming assault.

> The air units were given the mission of taking a new set of pictures of all the enemy positions so that the High Command might have the data necessary for launching the attack. This was not limited to the front line positions but extended far into the enemy's defence zone. On the basis of these photographs all necessary maps were to be compiled by the Field Service Battalions. In addition to the maps with the usual data of all sorts, special maps were prepared giving distant targets for heavy artillery fire, and bombing raids (railway stations, bridges, crossings, headquarters, camps, depots etc.), another map showing the location of bad shell holes

in the area to be traversed, another giving the condition of roads behind the front, another with the enemy's telephone net so that we could use it after the front had been broken, and also a map showing the location of the hostile camps. In this way the enemy aerodromes could be assigned before the attack as objectives. Beside these maps a great many photographs were taken covering the area held by the enemy and giving details of the terrain and troops. This vast amount of work had to be done in the main by the units already with the armies; otherwise the increase in aerial activity would have made the enemy suspicious.[5] *General Ernest Wilhelm von Hoeppner, German Air Service*

Flying reconnaissance aircraft deep over the lines territory was always a dangerous business as Leutnant Fritz Kampfenkel and his pilot – always known colloquially in the German Air Service as 'Emil' – discovered when they were attacked by two British scouts.

Following warning shots from my 'Emil', I put my camera in a nook in my cockpit and made my light machine gun ready to use on its moveable track. At the sight of the first enemy fighter, whose speed was greater than ours – I saw the proverbial 'whites of their eyes' – and fired by the rules right at his engine. The second enemy fighter, right behind him, was a better shot, and from his stream of fire, I felt a shot pass along the right side of my chest. I gave many thanks to my very talented pilot, who, with bold and deft turns, made us a more difficult target for our opponent. So, with no further hits, we returned unimpeded to our airfield. There I was helped out of our 'crate', fortified with cognac and cigarettes and driven to the nearest field hospital. The wound was cleaned and sewed up.[6] *Leutnant Fritz Kampfenkel, Flieger Abteilung (A) 240, Imperial German Air Force*

IT was unquestionably the role of all British scouts to prevent the incursions of the German Rumpler and LVG reconnaissance aircraft. But in the January and February of 1918, there is no question that the greatest exponent of that art was still Captain James McCudden of 56 Squadron. His cautious tactics and stalking adroitness were simply irresistible, but his mechanical skills gained during his years as an engine fitter added a whole new dimension to the menace he posed to his adversaries. When new German models of the Rumpler and LVG reconnaissance two-seaters became virtually invulnerable to interception through their ability to fly far higher than the 19,000–20,000 feet that the SE5a could normally achieve, McCudden sought a technical solution. He acquired a set of non-standard high-compression pistons, which he successfully fitted to his engine to gain a huge increase in engine performance while trimming every spare pound of weight from his aircraft. His extra reserves of speed and height immediately began to take effect in a series of dispassionate victories. He became not only the top-scoring British ace but reached the fifty victory milestone on 16 February.

> I saw a Hun two-seater running away east. For he had apparently seen me before I had seen him, for I was not expecting Huns over, for the visibility was not too good. But I suppose he was out for some urgent information. I now opened the throttle of the high compression Hispano and I overtook the LVG just as though he was going backwards, for I should judge my speed to be 20 miles faster level than his. I quickly got into position and although the LVG tried hard, I presented him with a very excellent burst from both guns, and then he went down in a vertical nose dive, and then past vertical onto his back. The enemy gunner shot out of the machine for all the world like a stone out of a catapult and the unfortunate rascal seemed all arms and legs.[7] *Captain James McCudden, 56 Squadron*

McCudden could also now reach 21,000 feet. This however brought its own problems, for at that kind of altitude the extreme cold and, even worse, a lack of oxygen, had a considerable effect on even the hardiest of aviators such as McCudden. After one indecisive scrap at extreme altitude he found himself in real trouble as he descended.

> I felt very ill indeed. This was not due to the height or the rapidity of my descent, but was due to the intense cold that I experienced up high, so that when I got down to a lower altitude, I could breathe more oxygen, with the result that my heart beat more strongly and was trying to force my sluggish and cold blood around my veins too quickly. The reaction of this caused me a feeling of faintness and exhaustion that can only be appreciated by those who have experienced it. My word I did feel ill and when I

got on the ground: the blood returning to my veins, I cannot describe as anything but agony.[8] *Captain James McCudden, 56 Squadron*

Ace he may have been but McCudden was no doctor and few then understood the effects of extreme altitude. Oxygen deprivation or hypoxia had potentially severe effects and serious symptoms could start as low as 8,000 feet and it is salutary to remember that during the Second World War aircrew were routinely warned of the necessity of using oxygen masks at high altitudes. Many were put in a pressure chamber drained of oxygen and then filmed to illustrate the dire effects of hypoxia on their cognitive functions. The overall effect was that of 'stupidity' and all-embracing incompetence, with the key point being that they were rendered too 'stupid' to realize that anything was wrong. Effects varied with individuals but it is remarkable that McCudden was regularly flying well above 16,000 feet, at which height supplemental oxygen is now considered absolutely essential.

McCudden scored his last pair of victories on 26 February. In most ways the first of these was typical of his methods.

What a beautiful day it was, but I felt so bad, for my throat was very sore and the cold and height were affecting it. But there were a lot of the enemy to be fought, and so I stayed up and very soon saw a Rumpler a few hundred feet above me returning to his lines from above Arras. I followed him in the direction of Douai, and finally got to close range and fired a good burst from both my machine guns, and at once the two-seater burst into flames and then fell to pieces, the wreckage falling east of Oppy.[9] *Captain James McCudden, 56 Squadron*

The occupants of the Rumpler, Vizefeldwebel Otto Kresse and his observer Leutnant Rudolf Binting, were both killed, the latter tumbling out of the machine and landing within the British lines. But McCudden's second victory that day showed that he was beginning to stray from his own tactical precepts. In attacking a Hannover two-seater he took foolish and completely uncharacteristic risks. Hitherto he had always been frustrated in his attempts to shoot one down; this time he was determined to succeed whatever the risk.

I said to myself, 'I am going to shoot down that Hannover or be shot down in the attempt.' I secured my firing position, and placing my sight on the Hannover's fuselage, I fired both guns until the two-seater fell to pieces and the wreckage fell down slowly, a fluttering monument to my 57th victory and my last over the enemy for a time. As I looked at the machine I saw the enemy gunner fall away from the Hannover fuselage, and I had no feeling for him for I knew he was dead for I had fired 300 rounds of ammunition at the Hannover at very close range and I must have got 90% hits.[10] *Captain James McCudden, 56 Squadron*

Inside the fluttering monument to his accuracy were Unteroffizier Max Schwaier and Leutnant Walter Jäger. Both were killed. As usual McCudden's claims are easily verifiable.

Whatever McCudden's mental state, his physical condition was undoubtedly deteriorating under the strain of his continued high-altitude flying, exposed in an open cockpit. By now he was lecturing on his aerial tactics to neighbouring squadrons as well as his own. It was obvious to his superiors that after seven months with 56 Squadron at the front he needed a rest; even that he was perhaps more use at home instructing and raising the overall standard of British combat flying rather than setting an individual example. For such a habitually cool customer his over-emotional reaction after his dining-out by officers of the combined squadrons of III Brigade on 2 March showed that he really did need a break.

In bed that evening I thought over it all and I now more than ever regretted that I had to leave a life that was all; my everything to me, and I confess I cried.[11] *Captain James McCudden, 56 Squadron*

After a period of leave during which he was awarded the Victoria Cross and was generally lionized by London society, McCudden was posted as an instructor to the School of Aerial Fighting at Ayr. Here he began a relentless campaign to secure a new active service posting back to the Western Front. As far as he was concerned he had unfinished business.

Meanwhile the RFC was still carrying out its own reconnaissance missions, a never-ending task that was given special meaning by the need to locate where the Germans would strike. This was what the German generals and von Hoeppner were afraid of and what they were doing their best to conceal so the predator scouts of the German Air Service had their own deadly aces mirroring the efforts of Captain James McCudden. Both sides were playing for high stakes. While the RE8s probed over the lines photographing the most minute changes in the German front-line trenches, the multi-purpose two-seater Bristol Fighters were reaching further back to look for the telltale new ammunition dumps, the improvements to communication infrastructure, the new supply dumps, the new or reactivated airfields. The Bristol Fighter was powered by a 200hp engine, capable of up to 110mph, armed with a fixed Vickers machine gun and the observer's additional single or twin Lewis guns. It was a powerful machine, which generated a performance almost comparable with a single-seater, with the added advantage of an observer watching their collective tail.

> We were not so fast as the Fokker Biplanes who were our main opponents, but we held our height better in a dogfight, and, when a Fokker was turning inside you and almost, but not quite, getting his sights on you, he offered a good target to your observer. Over the lines the observer never sat down. His job was to see that he and his pilot were not surprised by enemy aircraft from behind and that gave him a hemisphere to search, and search, and keep on searching. On his search more than on anything else depended his own life and his pilot's. The pilot had plenty of searching to do too; there was no place for a stiff-necked type in a fighter squadron![12] *Lieutenant Thomas Traill, 20 Squadron*

Unfortunately the process of taking reconnaissance photographs took most of their attention, leaving little to spare for the vital business of self-defence and they were frequently caught unawares. As usual this was particularly the case with inexperienced pilots and observers. On one occasion Second Lieutenant Frank Ransley accompanied by his observer Second Lieutenant L. Lambe were coming back from a reconnaissance in their Bristol Fighter over the Cambrai and St Quentin sectors when he got the shock of his young life.

On the way back with the sun more or less behind us I heard a machine gun firing followed by an agonised yell. My observer was a fairly new boy and had not yet learned to look for hostile aircraft diving from the sun. I also had not been warned how difficult it was to spot aircraft diving from the sun. I turned my head to see how Lamb was. He was badly wounded and was obviously in great pain.[13] *Second Lieutenant Frank Ransley, 48 Squadron*

When he got the aircraft down his ground crew took over the machine and began to make good the damage. It was no small task, for the aircraft had been riddled.

I watched the mechanics stripping the canvas from the fuselage of my machine. They said the spars and longerons were riddled with bullet holes and were surprised the machine held together. So ended my first serious encounter with the enemy. Another lesson learned – to rely on one's own observation in future. I was very fortunate not to have received any of the shots fired.[14] *Second Lieutenant Frank Ransley, 48 Squadron*

When the photographs were safely back on the ground they were pored over by the experts. To the uninitiated the black and white photographs appeared of little value but after four years of war the new science of photo-interpretation was developing fast. One accomplished practitioner was Lieutenant Thomas Hughes who had been serving in the Ypres area since 1915. An irritable man, Hughes had little time for his superiors, but would tolerate them as long as they left him in peace to carry out his specialized tasks. Despite all the advances many were still sceptical of the value of aerial photographs and part of his duties lay in explaining to the uninitiated just what the RFC was accomplishing on their behalf. These sessions did not always go according to plan.

I started my course of 'Interpretation of Aeroplane Photographs' this morning. There were eight infantry officers – I rather think they were battalion intelligence officers – assembled round the table in the conference room at the Corps, where Sergeant Cowley, Second Aircraftsman Ripley and I arrived with the component parts of a magic lantern. After a bit of business getting the light to work, I got under way with my celebrated

lantern exhibition and was getting along quite nicely when the door behind the screen opened and the Corps Commander and the B.G.G.S. shuffled in, tripped over the electric light wire, put out the light and fused the arc lamp. The Corps Commander then fell over a chair and I felt it was time to pull up a blind, which I did. He then told me to carry on as if he wasn't there![15]
Lieutenant Thomas Hughes, 53 Squadron

The aircraft were not the only method of determining what was going on the other side of the wire. Observation balloons were used by both sides as a vital ingredient in the panoply of methods devoted to spotting and registering artillery batteries and generally monitoring everything going on over the lines. Yet this too was a risky business for the observers who would rise up to 3,000 feet above the ground, where they were left standing in a flimsy wicker basket, linked to the ground only by the restraining cable and a telephone line, lifted and held in position just by a temptingly flammable gas-filled balloon and with no capacity for any manoeuvre other than up or down – their situation seemed a definition of vulnerability. The diary of an intrepid kite balloon observation officer serving in the Ypres area provides a bewildering kaleidoscope of many faceted difficulties and threats that ranged from the laughable, via the genuinely dangerous, to the sublimely ridiculous over just a few days. Captain Walter Giffard insisted on serving at the front despite having only one leg as a result of a pre-war shooting accident.

Had a new batman, he is a dud, greatest difficulty in getting him to leave my leg, he wanted to take it out and polish it or something . . . Tried to get the balloon up, but the winch skidded off the road into a ditch and took an hour to get it out, by which time it was 'dud' . . . Went up for an hour with Smith and did some shoots, good visibility, but basket was jerking about too much for accurate observation . . . Went up with Whelan for a couple of hours, not good enough to shoot, but spotted some active hostile batteries, we could not find, however, the fellow who was shelling us once every five minutes for the last hour we were up. It is not pleasant being shelled in a balloon, especially when you see your next door neighbour shot down, give me a Hun aeroplane any day . . . There was a hell of a gale and we could see nothing and the gunner who came up with me having relieved himself of his lunch and breakfast, and I should think last night's dinner as well, I decided to come down . . . When at 4,000 feet a poor little mouse dropped right out of the rigging past the basket, but I could not catch him to put a parachute on to him and he disappeared into the clouds below . . . One of our aeroplanes returning home pretended he was a Hun and dived straight for us, awful funny joke, not appreciated at the time.[16] *Captain Walter Giffard, 13th Kite Balloon Section*

Lieutenant Arthur Behrend was one young gunner officer who accompanied another one-legged balloon officer, Lieutenant Colonel F. H. Cleaver commanding the Third Balloon Wing, on a balloon ascent.

One day my Colonel sent for 'Hoppy' Cleaver in order to complain about what we thought was the extraordinarily poor service we had been getting from his 'balloonatics' as we called them behind their backs. He came along to see the Colonel and said, 'I fully accept all you say, but you know it's not nearly as easy as you people on the ground think for our chaps to do their job, because you are always shooting at targets which are several miles behind the lines. I think it would help a great deal if you detailed one of your officers to come up with us and so we can show you exactly how difficult it is!!'[17] *Lieutenant Arthur Behrend, 279 Siege Battery, Royal Garrison Artillery*

The task fell to Behrend himself and next afternoon he turned up as arranged at one of Cleaver's Kite Balloon Sections. From ground level at least it seemed a perfectly pleasant day although there was a degree of low cloud and a fairly stiff wind. He soon found he was to go up with Colonel Cleaver himself.

The balloon was swaying in the wind above my head and the wicker basket was swaying too a few feet above my head. I saw that the thing was anchored to a winch on a fairly hefty lorry and I said to myself, 'The lorry may move but the balloon will never lift the lorry into the air!' The winch man put a parachute on my back and we got into the basket. There were no preliminaries at all, except he said to me, 'No smoking mind!' He said to the winch man, 'A 1,000 feet!' We started off almost immediately; you heard the hum of the winch as you went up. It was all very novel. In the

> basket all there was was an aneroid barometer for the height, a telephone to the ground and our parachutes. Up we went. Looking down you saw the winch and this wretched cable that connected you to the ground. It wasn't really a very pleasant feeling: because it was neither one thing nor the other, you were still attached to the ground and compared with being in an aeroplane there was an extraordinary feeling of insecurity about it. When we got up to our thousand feet and the winch stopped working, the whole motion of the thing changed and it was extremely unpleasant because the balloon started to sway about in the wind and the basket started to swing with it. I felt, 'Well good heavens, I'm sure I'm going to be sick!' and for the first time I felt very sorry for balloonatics. It didn't seem to worry Cleaver in the very least![18] *Lieutenant Arthur Behrend, 279 Siege Battery, Royal Garrison Artillery*

They began to range the guns onto a German battery and were soon engrossed in making the small corrections that would direct their shells bang on their target. Suddenly they became aware that they and the neighbouring balloons were no longer alone in the skies.

> The fourth balloon away from us was emitting great clouds of black smoke. It had been done by a German plane that had flown in quite quietly and pumped tracer ammunition into it. Out jumped the two chaps with their parachutes and I saw the parachutes open. The German plane came on to the next balloon, the third from us and it did exactly the same thing. I suppose the time would probably have been about 15–20 seconds. The feeling one had was one of great remoteness, it didn't seem to matter, it wasn't us it was people possibly a mile away. It was interesting rather than frightening at that stage. Well by this time every single anti-aircraft gun within range started shooting at it. Although the height of the AA fire was quite accurate, the shooting was very wild indeed and it didn't worry the German plane in the very least. It came on to the second balloon from us and shot that one down. The first balloon had completely burnt out and each balloon went through the phases: great clouds of black smoke then the flame then the balloon dropped exactly like a burning paper bag. I looked at Cleaver and he had put his parachute on the edge of the basket that was five feet high and clambered on top of the basket. Even that didn't convey much to me. I watched the German plane and it came on. Our winch

people were winding us down as fast as they possibly could, which wasn't very fast. The plane got to the next balloon, which was lower than it had been but not low enough. The two chaps jumped out and one wondered if their parachutes would open in time. I then realised that this really does mean me. I looked again at Cleaver and to my surprise discovered that Cleaver had got back into the basket beside me. I watched the plane and with a feeling of unreality saw the plane turn away from us and streak off across the lines for home. Cleaver said, 'Four balloons in one sortie isn't bad, I expect he ran out of "tracer!"'[19] *Lieutenant Arthur Behrend, 279 Siege Battery, Royal Garrison Artillery*

Later, while having a much needed drink in Kite Section officers' mess, Behrend asked Colonel Cleaver to explain something that was still puzzling him. Perhaps he should never have asked!

'Why did you jump back into the basket *before* the German plane turned off?' Cleaver said, 'Well you were my guest and I knew you had neither the sense nor the guts to jump and I was going to throw you out!'[20] *Lieutenant Arthur Behrend, 279 Siege Battery, Royal Garrison Artillery*

The German scout engaged in balloon-busting would have no doubt in his mind as to both the importance and inherent dangers of his mission. One of the most successful German balloon-busters, Oberleutnant Erich Löwenhardt of Jasta 10, explained how he ensured surprise on the balloon observers and their anti-aircraft defences.

I fly alone to the front, twilight is the most favourable time to attack. I go deeply into the front line, take note of the position and heights of the balloons and watch out for enemy planes. When the sun has set, on days of major battles, there are usually one or two balloons standing, probably doing evening reconnaissance and which will eventually guide the enemy's heavy artillery. I carefully keep these balloons in view, fly away from the front, and climb to a height of about 3,000–4,000 metres. Then I return to the front, and, when I think I can reach the balloon in a glide, kill the engine. Usually the English can then neither see or hear me any more. I have never been shot at before an attack. A short burst at very close range, not more than 50 metres, has always been sufficient to ignite a balloon.[21] *Oberleutnant Erich Löwenhardt, Jasta 10*

For the real balloonatics flying every day they could, the weather was one of the most implacable of all their enemies and there was a very real danger if they misjudged the wind conditions prevalent high up in or above the clouds.

Seemed to be a lot of wind so we stopped the winch at 1,500 feet and told them to take the tension. '1,000 kilos, Sir! And she's lifting the winch off the road, Sir!' 'Well tell the balloon crew to sit on the winch!' 1,000 kilos and anything over 800 is supposed to be risky. 'Hello, chart room, take the wind please?' '56 miles per hour, Sir!' 'Put me on to the Officer Commanding, will you?' Told the O.C. the circumstances, 'What about it?' 'For Lord's sake come down!' 'Hello, winch, haul down!' Five minutes later, 'Hello winch, have you started hauling down yet?' 'No, Sir! The engine won't start, there's too much strain!' 'Well put her into low gear and for Lord's sake haul down!' It took 25 minutes to get down from 1,500 feet – no more today thank you![22] *Captain Walter Giffard, 13th Kite Balloon Section, RFC*

However the wind would never be the greatest enemy of the 13th Kite Balloon Section; that honour belonged to an opposing German battery euphemistically known as 'Clockwork Charlie' due to its timed shell fuses.

Whelan went up and did some shoots at 12 o'clock. The Hun opened 'Clockwork Charlie' on him and had an aeroplane observing for him. The fifth shot cut the telephone cable and put 47 holes in the balloon, she came down quite gently and he did not have to parachute. Patched her up and had her aloft within half an hour. 'Clockwork Charlie' is getting too accurate; four out of the seven balloons in our neighbourhood were shot down today.[23] *Captain Walter Giffard, 13th Kite Balloon Section*

Time and time again 'Clockwork Charlie' filled the air with lethal shrapnel splattering all around Giffard's balloon. On many occasions his basket was hit and the balloon deflated so that he slowly sank to the ground. Unsurprisingly his nerves were stretched by the sheer tension of awaiting the 'next round'. Then it seemed retribution was nigh!

I went up. 'Clockwork Charlie' started again, but was shooting badly and I got his exact position behind Dadizeele, we immediately got a battery to fire on him, but before they were ready he put another one over and holed the bag pretty badly in about 30 places. I very nearly jumped for it, as I was at 4,500 feet and I thought she might start falling before they could haul her down, but she came down quite gently and I was glad I hadn't. She was ready again in an hour, but before going up I had taken the precaution to have 'something' ready for 'Clockwork Charlie'. A 12" howitzer battery and 6" battery were all laid on our friend behind Dadizeele and ready to fire as soon as I could see the target. In order to see him really well, I had to get to at least 4,000 feet as he was at least 9 miles away and behind a wood. Consequence was he put four over at me as I was going up, but they were poor shots and only made me doubly sure of his exact position. Then the fun began: both batteries shot toppingly and they soon ranged, then they started battery fire and at times they simply obliterated 'Clockwork Charlie's' position and also caused two explosions. What satisfaction, by Jove I did feel bucked then![24] *Captain Walter Giffard, 13th Kite Balloon Section*

At the outset Giffard had encountered some scepticism among the gunner officers as to the worth of corrections supplied by the kite balloon observers. But slowly officer by officer, battery by battery, they became convinced of their value as they realized the detail of what they could see from the higher perspective.

A battery I visited the other day did not believe in balloon observation. The Major said he didn't like shooting with them and for one thing they were too fond of giving 'OKs'. However I finally extracted a promise that they would give me a trial the first fine day, whilst I undertook not to give 'OK' without good reason. Well it came off today; it was on a couple of Hun guns in the remains of an isolated building. The battery shot toppingly and after a time I distinctly saw one shot demolish the building, so I sent 'OK'. The Major immediately asked why I said it was 'OK' and I told him; he said, I could not see the house going up in brick dust at that distance. A few minutes later there was another 'OK' and there was literally nothing left of the position. I did not give another 'OK' however and let them carry on. The next three or four shots I gave unobserved and after the fourth the Major asked what was happening, so I replied that there was no longer a target to observe on and he seemed more or less satisfied.[25] *Captain Walter Giffard, 13th Kite Balloon Section*

Giffard was clearly not a man to rest on his laurels and he ordered a photograph of the target sector which convincingly proved the point of his observations from the balloon and he duly forwarded it to the offending battery who were henceforth nowhere near as prejudiced against balloon observation as they had been.

Naturally the opposing German kite balloons performed an equally valuable function and they too were a much prized target for the British scouts. Their balloon defences were exceptionally strong, featuring anti-aircraft guns, machine guns and the dreaded 'flaming onions'. This last was the description given to the rising balls of light that the British thought were chained together in flight. In fact they were separate 37mm shells fired by a five-barrel revolving gun – it was the fast rate of fire and tracer rounds that created the illusion. Few officers would take the risk of attacking such a hotbed of trouble without distinct orders. When Captain Harold Balfour was once tempted to try his hand as a balloon-buster he almost instantly regretted his rashness.

The balloon was about 3,000 feet up and I was about 9,000 feet up. I dived down to about 6,000 feet when discretion overcame my momentary feeling of valour. I pulled away towards our lines, telling myself not to be foolish; not to run a very unnecessary risk; that I had no orders to shoot down the balloon and that a comfortable lunch awaited me at the aerodrome, so why not go to it without further ado? I flew towards the lines. The next mental process was one of remorse and shame at my hesitation in fulfilling my purpose due to honest funk. The shame was doubly strong as, owing to the splendid visibility, my altered plans must have been clear to every one of our kite balloon observers within 15 miles and also to our men in the trenches. So round I swung, and this time I went at the balloon properly. When I got near and opened fire, the observer jumped out in his parachute. Now the balloon itself is only rubber and silk filled with gas, comparatively

> valueless and easily replaceable, but the observer is a trained man who has sat in that balloon basket day after day, knows the layout of our trenches and has probably spotted most of our artillery positions. His knowledge is of value to the enemy and he is not easily replaceable. Therefore I followed him down as he swung helplessly below his parachute, and shot the best part of 100 rounds into him, or around him, which I do not know, as his body just continued to swing. Machine gun fire becoming unpleasantly close, so I sheered off.[26] *Captain Harold Balfour 43 Squadron*

Needless to say the watching observers in the British balloons were duly outraged at Balfour's ruthless action; from their perspective they could see that this was a really unfortunate precedent that the Germans might well follow up to their own personal and fatal disadvantage. For a while Captain Harold Balfour's name became absolute mud among the RFC Kite Balloon Sections.

DESPITE all the German efforts, even as early as late January the RFC had located sufficient signs of German preparations to convince Major General John Salmond commanding the RFC that the attack would be launched in the general area facing the British Third and Fifth Armies between Arras and the river Serre. This reconnaissance evidence was augmented by news from British intelligence sources that two of the most successful German generals had been moved into this sector. General Otto von Below, the recent victor at the Battle of Caporetto in Italy, had taken over the Seventeenth Army facing the Third Army commanded by General Sir Julian Byng, while General Oskar von Hutier had been appointed to command the German Eighteenth Army opposing Fifth Army commanded by General Sir Hubert Gough.

Gough was certainly convinced at an early stage that the blow was destined to fall in his Somme area. Gough was born in Ireland on 12 August 1870. After a fairly conventional regimental career his conduct of a mobile column during the Boer War had marked him out as a thrusting young officer and his career progressed apace. After staff appointments he had become entangled deep at the heart of the Curragh incident in March 1914, when he threatened to resign rather than suppress Unionist opposition to the proposed Irish Home Rule

Bill. The war saved him and indeed his career really took off as promotion followed promotion until he attained command of Fifth Army during the Somme offensive of 1916. Since then his reputation had been blemished by his performance in the Arras and Ypres offensives where he seemed to be unable to get a real grip on the complexities of modern warfare at the highest level.

Whatever Gough and Salmond might think, for Haig back at the General Headquarters the situation was nowhere near so clear-cut. His responsibilities extended to the whole of the British front. He had to sift the truth from the confusing mass of intelligence information pointing to offensive preparations all along his front, while at the same time contending with all the various German diversionary tactics. Of course the underlying concern that never left him was a fear that an attack in Flanders could expose the Channel ports. Even a minor advance in Flanders would threaten them with closure by artillery fire, while their outright capture by the Germans would be utterly catastrophic. Haig remained more determined than ever to keep the main concentration of his forces in the north.

THE challenge for the RFC now was to determine *exactly* where and if possible when the Germans would attack. Accordingly in March 1918 Salmond moved his Headquarters reserve, the newly reorganized IX Brigade, down to begin operations in the Somme area. The Ninth Wing (25, 27, 62, 73, 79 and 80 Squadrons) and the night squadrons of 54 Wing (58, 83, 101 and 102 Squadrons) duly began to add their efforts to that of Third and Fifth Brigades. In total there were 579 serviceable British aircraft (261 single-seater scouts) facing approximately 730 German aircraft (326 single-seater scouts) in the Third and Fifth Army sectors as the battle loomed. Reconnaissance patrols were being carried out from top to bottom of the British front, checking every scrap of intelligence and making sure that there had not been some awful blunder. For what if it was to be Flanders after all?

As part of this great effort, whenever the March squalls permitted, the Bristol Fighters of 48 Squadron were sent up on long-distance patrols. These high-altitude flights were physically challenging in the extreme.

We had to commence our flight before dawn. No flare paths. Having always flown in daylight it was at first terrifying roaring into stygian darkness hoping for the best until we were high enough to dimly see the horizon. Then on a particularly cold morning one felt frozen and, more often than not, actually getting frost-bitten noses. Considering pilots and observers were in open cockpits with no oxygen, it was a marvel we were able to do as well as we did for most of the time – both on patrol and reconnaissance we operated at 20,000 feet. I do not remember finding it difficult to breathe on the rare occasions one met enemy aircraft at that height. Any such encounter would not last long for both would lose height and break away. Diving down from 19,000 or 20,000 feet was extremely uncomfortable for we suffered from the different pressures as we hurtled down. Ears would sing and make clicking noises, but hearing would be generally restored when we reached a lower level.[27] *Second Lieutenant Frank Ransley, 48 Squadron*

One morning Frank Ransley was sent up with another new observer who had only arrived at the squadron that same day. Not everyone could face up to the combined physical and mental challenges of such patrols and it was soon apparent that his observer would be found wanting.

We had no sooner crossed the lines when we met an unusually heavy barrage of anti-aircraft fire which took me all my time to dodge. Black balls of dirty puffs were all round us. As soon as I had a chance I looked round to the back seat to see how my observer was taking things. He was on the floor in a faint. I immediately turned back to try and get a seasoned warrior in his place. I had only gone a short distance to the west when I received a tap on the shoulder from my pallid observer signalling for me to turn east again. Once more the anti-aircraft fire let us have it, I looked round and he had fainted again. This time I took him right back to the aerodrome. He was obviously not suited for aerial warfare and should have been given his baptism of fire more gently. But for our heavy casualty list he *would* undoubtedly have been eased in more gently. He left the squadron that same day not having unpacked his kit.[28]
Second Lieutenant Frank Ransley, 48 Squadron

There were many perils in flying so deep behind the German lines of which the most obvious, but equally easily forgotten, was the prevailing westerly winds. These were no problem whatsoever to anyone engaged in flying east over the German lines. It was only during the return journey that things could become awkward.

> I very soon realised we were making little progress westwards. I put the nose of the machine down a little at the same time losing precious height. We still seemed to be making little progress, so I pushed the nose down still more and at last we seemed to be moving slowly westward. It then dawned on me that we must be facing a strong gale. Visions of having to land on the German side passed through my mind for we must have been 30 or 40 miles on the German side. I had a horror of being a prisoner of war. I decided to go right down and hedge-hop home. Anti-aircraft guns were unlikely to get me so low down, and I hoped Richthofen and his boys were still abed. Down I went and picked up speed. After what seemed hours I crossed the lines; I heaved a sigh of relief. After I had landed I hurried to the squadron office to scan the weather reports which had not been available at 3.30am when we left. It read, 'Wind westerly at 15,000 feet 106mph. At 12,000 feet 85mph.' In the dark we must have been blown many miles over German territory. After we turned back our slow progress was understandable as the Bristol's top speed was 110mph.[29] *Second Lieutenant Frank Ransley, 48 Squadron*

As the evidence continued to mount that the Somme was indeed where the German offensive would be launched, the RFC began to move into its second raft of defensive duties as laid down in Trenchard's December 1917 memorandum. Its first priority was to cooperate in every way with the Royal Artillery. Thousands more photographs had to be taken of the German front lines to enable the identification and registration of potential targets to hamper their offensive preparations. The artillery observation aircraft, mainly RE8s, redoubled their efforts, hovering above the German lines and guiding shells right onto their destined targets. The RE8s were relatively slow, but on one occasion the prevailing wind conditions led to an almost surrealistic experience for a Second Lieutenant N. H. Anderson when his aircraft briefly became a fixed point in the firmament above the German lines.

On one occasion it was found possible to carry out a whole artillery patrol almost without moving. This was due to a strong south-west wind at about 5,000 feet which enabled one to head into it and throttle down to about 50mph in such a position, slightly to the west of the lines, that the whole of the allotted area for the patrol was in view in the area between the port bottom plane and the tail plane. Although the aircraft was stationary in this position for so long, not a round of anti-aircraft fire was sent up – in fact only one hostile battery of any kind in the whole area opened fire throughout the period – and it ceased after a few rapid salvos. This may have been pure coincidence, but one prefers to imagine that it was the moral effect of their being so easily and obviously watched. This effect may have been increased by their seeing the stationary aeroplane turn down wind towards the battery immediately it opened fire. In fact, as the sky was empty, one could not resist the temptation to go over, after sending down the usual 'zone call', and waste a few rounds of ammunition in the direction of the flashes, just for the moral effect. It took rather along time to get back, but altogether it was a very amusing patrol.[30] ***Second Lieutenant N. H. Anderson, RFC***

THE second priority, as prescribed by Trenchard, was to launch persistent bombing raids in an effort to disrupt the German preparations. In March the bomber squadrons found that their tactical role was growing in importance with every day that passed. Their duties were manifold. First of all they had to try to put the German Air Service out of action by bombing their airfields to perdition. If they could obliterate the German aircraft on the ground then they would of course be unable to fly the aerial reconnaissance missions, the artillery observation missions and ground strafing that the Germans would need when the offensive began. It was a great deal easier to destroy German scouts on the ground than when they were marauding in the air. Second, they were charged with the interdiction role. This was largely done by striking at railway junctions, stations, bridges and other key components of the communications infrastructure. Realistically, given the bomb loads and numbers of aircraft available to the RFC, it was always ambitious to think that they could 'seal off' the crucial battlefield. Nevertheless, the capacity to cause serious damage and interference was growing exponentially as the years passed and there is no doubt that, with a bit of good fortune, the bombers could slow down the reinforcement process. Third, bombers were required to cause damage to any other military targets considered worthwhile. Thus ammunition dumps, supply depots, High Command headquarters and billeting centres were all fair game for the tumbling bombs. Together this added up to a general harassing of the Germans, threatening them far behind the lines, ruining their sleep and cranking up the pressure.

The day bomber squadrons charged with the bulk of the work were equipped with the DH4 and DH9 bombers. The DH4 had arrived on the Western Front in the spring of 1917. It was a purpose-built day bomber able to carry a load of up to two 112-pound bombs and was powered by the Rolls-Royce 250hp Eagle engine to a speed of up to 120mph with a range of about 450 miles and the high ceiling altitude of 23,000 feet. Even a year later it was still a formidable aircraft and flying in formation their combination of forward-firing Vickers machine gun and twin Lewis guns for the observer was fearsome enough to keep the German scouts at bay. The main problem that had been identified was the distance between the pilot and observer cockpits. In contrast the DH9, intended as the replacement for 1918, was a dismal failure. Although the cockpits were closer together to facilitate communication between the crew, the original BHP 230hp engine was hopelessly underpowered, with the result that the DH9 struggled to lift its full bomb load to any reasonable altitude necessary for long-range bombing raids. Although the faults were realized early it was still too late to cancel the huge orders that had already been placed for the new aircraft. The bomber crews had no choice but to make the best of a bad job.

The weight of bombs the DH4 and DH9 could carry was quite startling in comparison to the pathetic efforts of 1914 aeroplanes. Yet they were still lacking in any genuine striking power and depended to a large extent on luck if they were to cause any real damage.

Above the undercarriage and under the wings were the bomb racks which could accommodate three 112pdrs or twelve 25pdrs. The bombs were released by means of a string which the observer pulled when the pilot told him. Then there was a bombsight which helped the pilot to drop his bombs somewhere in the neighbourhood of his objective.[31] *Lieutenant William Grossart*

There is no doubt that bomb aiming in 1918 remained a somewhat inexact science which few crews took seriously. As long as they were vaguely over the target they would let rip almost regardless. This was not precision bombing!

As far as bombing was concerned it was only the flight commander and his observer who had to use their judgement, with or without the help of the bomb sights which were strapped to the outside of the fuselage on the right hand side of the observer's cockpit. There were one or two factors in using the sights which could only be roughly estimated. There was therefore no guarantee of accuracy and as a result the majority of the squadron took a dim view of their use. The other observers, when they knew they were nearing the target, just had to keep their eye on the leader's plane and when they saw his signal – a white Very light fired by his observer – release their own bombs in a salvo.[32] *Lieutenant J. B. Heppel*

As the bombs fell they could watch their progress as they accelerated away, right down to the ground.

I was fascinated when watching bombs fall. They appeared to remain in the horizontal position and almost vertically below the moving aircraft, still retaining the horizontal velocity of the bomber, but rapidly receding from us, i.e. their observable motion was vertical. However, after about half a minute, probably when the bombs passed the halfway height they appeared to shoot forward and move at ever increasing speed parallel to the ground until the final burst.[33] *Lieutenant C. H. Latimer-Needham*

The German scouts were the main method of defence against the British day bombers. When they struck it could be absolutely terrifying. They surrounded the bombers, harassing them, trying to break up the formation so that they could be destroyed in detail. In turn the RFC sent first flights, then squadrons of their own scouts up to escort the bombers.

The ever increasing size of formations employed by both sides culminated in a huge dogfight on 18 March when a bombing raid by the DH4s of 5 (Naval) Squadron, RNAS, on the Busigny airfield and railway station was backed up by the Camels of 54 Squadron, the SE5s of 84 Squadron and the Bristol Fighters of 62 Squadron. Their collective aim was to clear the Germans right out of the sky. This huge unwieldy layered formation was intercepted by Richthofen and some thirty aircraft from Jagdgeschwader 1 and 20. His adjutant Leutnant Karl Bodenschatz watched his men taking off from their airfield at Avesnes-le-Sec.

> Then around 10.30 they came. At a great altitude, together as a unit these heavily concentrated squadrons wound their way to carry out their orders, come hell or high water: to fly over the German front and finally get a glimpse of what was causing the commotion back there; to ascertain the significance of the considerable nightly clamour they were hearing; to find out what was really going on. At an altitude of 5,000 metres, the most powerful squadrons of the English Army move towards the German front. The radio reports from the German air defence officers had arrived in Avesnes-le-Sec in good time. The commander took off with three Staffeln in a closed formation. It was a wonderful yet solemn sight.[34] *Adjutant Leutnant Karl Bodenschatz, Jagdgeschwader 1*

The men in the DH4s of 5 (Naval) Squadron saw them coming. To them it was by no means such a wonderful sight.

> Approaching Bohain the sky ahead seemed literally full of aircraft, three large formations of some twenty each to our north, and many smaller formations all about our height – but then too far to distinguish as friend or foe. Immediately after dropping our bombs and turning for home, every aircraft in the sky seemed to come together and there was a colossal mix-up.[35] *Flight Commander Charles Bartlett, 5 (Naval) Squadron, RNAS*

Tactics seem to have counted for little in the battle that ensued; it was just a confused mess from start to finish. This was the worst possible environment for the carefully nurtured aces of Jagdgeschwader 1, but needs must and Richthofen was determined to stop the incursion in its tracks. He plunged into action.

It was no longer possible to think of maintaining wing formations. Everyone pounced on the nearest opponent. The result was a pell-mell of individual dogfights. Frequently it was impossible to tell friend from foe. The air was crisscrossed by the white ribbons of tracer ammunition, in between one could see burning or disabled aircraft plunging to the ground.[36] *Rittmeister Manfred von Richthofen, Jagdgeschwader 1*

Both sides were equally confused; no-one could maintain their composure in such a maelstrom. Many felt it was the biggest dogfight that the war had seen so far. Aeroplanes seemed to be everywhere, filling the sky and with the brightly coloured triplanes of Richthofen's Flying Circus well to the fore.

We saw numbers of EA spinning down and on fire, our Camels following them right down; also a few of our own out of control. I had my front guns on to an Albatros at about 30 yards range for a few seconds as he cut across our bows, and got some 20–30 rounds into him, but he dived, coming up again under our tail. I slewed enough for Naylor to get a long burst into him and he went down pouring black smoke from his tail.[37] *Flight Commander Charles Bartlett, 5 (Naval) Squadron, RNAS*

Bartlett's claim was accepted and if the multiple British claims had any real justification then they would have had a field day. But in reality the élite scout pilots of Jagdgeschwader 1 rather went to town, carving their way through the ranks of their far less experienced opponents, shooting down eight for the loss of just four. The Camels of 54 Squadron suffered most, losing five of their men, and their Flight Commander Captain Francis Kitto was left utterly distraught.

I was talking over the telephone to Captain Kitto after we got back, and he said it was by far the biggest scrap he had ever been in. He seemed quite unnerved and kept repeating, 'Frightful affair, frightful affair.'[38] *Flight Commander Charles Bartlett, 5 (Naval) Squadron, RNAS*

The Germans had done well but the risks to the aces like Richthofen were equally apparent: in a chaotic struggle anything could happen. Chance was a far greater factor and collisions all too possible and anybody, no matter how good, could be brought down.

Over the last two days the Germans made their final covert preparations assisted by bad weather which blanketed them under a layer of cloud. The German diligence was typified by the efforts of Jagdgeschwader 1 as they constructed their advanced landing field.

> Night after night, the shovels fly, the trucks roll and industrious dark forms abound. When the first crack of dawn comes creeping over the spring landscape, every living thing disappears into the dugouts, into the shelters and underneath the tarpaulins. When one inquisitive Englishman, a couple of thousand metres up, actually approached and looked down, he could see only an unoccupied airfield and nothing else: no machines, no men, nothing.[39] *Adjutant Leutnant Karl Bodenschatz, Jagdgeschwader 1*

By the time the skies had cleared the British had still not worked out exactly when the offensive would be launched; they simply knew it would be very soon. Back at the General Headquarters it was only on 19 March that Haig finally accepted that the offensive would indeed be launched in the Third and Fifth Army area. Yet, true to form, Haig still would not weaken or imperil his line in Flanders – the cockpit of Europe. Haig remained confident that Gough could resist the impending blow with the troops at his disposal. And if he could not hold the line then after all there were no vulnerable strategic objectives in the Somme area. The Fifth Army could make a fighting retreat of up to 50 miles with impunity before the Amiens rail centres were threatened.

The Third Army sector of 28 miles from Gavrelle to Gouzecourt was held by 14 divisions and was facing 19 German divisions. The poor old Fifth Army in contrast would have to hold the 42 miles of front from just north of Gouzecourt to Barisis with only 12 infantry divisions and it was about to be attacked by 43 German divisions. The Third and Fifth Army combined artillery strength of 2,686 guns was dwarfed by the 6,608 guns and 3,534 heavy mortars amassed by the Germans.

As darkness fell on the night of 20 March the Germans began their final preparations. The gunners checked their complex firing programmes; the infantry took up their final positions; the pilots unveiled their aircraft. Everyone was ready; nothing, it seemed, had been forgotten.

> Only during the night preceding the day of the attack were the camouflaged tents to be removed from the planes. However, the crews had an opportunity to become familiar with the terrain in the attack area by flying the planes which were a normal part of the army.[40] *General Ernest Wilhelm von Hoeppner, German Air Service*

The men in the front lines on both sides were well aware of what they were about to receive and were nervous. It was a time of dreadful strain for the Germans confined in their forward jumping-off positions. Men getting ready to go over the top mused on their imminent fate, not unnaturally prone to mixed emotions and no little sentimentality.

> We were in high spirits because we hoped for our victory in this battle. At about three o'clock I went out of my dugout to look round. The night was silent, nothing was to be heard and there was a clear sky with stars shining and glittering and I thought, 'These are the same stars that my family at home are looking at.'[41] *Hartwig Pohlmann, 36th Division, Imperial German Army*

Even those German officers billeted well behind the line could feel the strain of what was to come. They knew how important the success of the offensive was, not just to their own continued survival, but to their whole country.

> The various officers of our group were quartered in a large house where we found a good piano. We all had our orders. Some had to leave the same night to join their outfits; others, like me, were kept in reserve. The piano was a great and unexpected attraction for the music lovers among us. One of the lieutenants had a fine baritone voice. His deputy was the director of the Kiel Philharmonic Orchestra and as we soon found out, a very fine musician. To top it all, this man, half an hour before, had met a former violinist of his orchestra outside our quarters. He was a non-combatant and worked in a field hospital nearby. Everyone was delighted to hear good music again. They had no notes, but until after midnight the baritone sang beautiful German *Lieders* and excerpts from Wagner's operas, accompanied perfectly on the piano by the orchestra leader who seemed able to play anything in all keys. The violinist performed a beautiful rendition of Bach's

Chaconne, a violin piece to be played as a solo. Once that evening I tried to play a little on his violin, but it sounded embarrassingly amateurish and I soon gave it up. During the pauses while all this lovely music was being played, we were quite aware that the enormous preparations for the next morning's attack were in full swing. We could hear the clatter of marching troops on the street outside and the constant, 'RRHUM! RRHUM!' of the heavy artillery. Our windows never stopped rattling.[42] *Leutnant Fritz Nagel, Nr 82 K-Flak*

At last the Germans were ready for *Der Tag*. But were the British?

Chapter 5

Götterdämmerung on the Somme

The Kaiserschlacht, or 'Kaiser's Battle', finally began at 04.45 on 21 March 1918 when the German barrage opened up with a deluge of shells from some 6,500 guns and howitzers. The barrage was the *pièce de résistance* of the German plans. Shells of all calibres crashed down onto the Forward and Battle Zones of the British defences, smashing down out of the morning mist on strongpoints, headquarters, identified lines of communications and of course the artillery batteries. The Bruckmüller system was employed to perfection and the gas shells forced the defenders to put on their gas masks, rendering them almost helpless: half deafened, almost blinded and with severely restricted breathing. At 09.40 the Germans launched some thirty-two first-wave divisions into a full-scale assault on the line held by the British Third and Fifth Armies between the river Scarpe and the Oise in the south.

The fog was roundly cursed by both sides. Visibility was so bad that the Germans could not judge how far their infantry had penetrated and so were unable at times to make the best use of their massed gun batteries. The fog also effectively stymied the morning plans made by the German Air Service. The Schlachtstaffeln ground support two-seaters should have been unleashed to strafe their way across the battlefield, adding to the confusion and general mayhem, while concentrating together as required to soften up specific strongpoints. Their scout pilots were also neutralized and unable to play their allotted role.

> As day breaks the fighter pilots are standing dressed and ready on the airfield, nonplussed, disappointed and furious, staring into a thick grey damp wall of fog. It is impossible to fly. 'One man's owl is another man's nightingale!' says the Rittmeister.[1] *Leutnant Karl Bodenschatz, Jagdgeschwader 1, German Air Service*

Bodenschatz had hit the nail on the head. As disruptive as the fog was for the Germans, the British were absolutely hamstrung by it. Not only were their artillery observers blinded but their lethal criss-cross fields of fire were effectively negated as the Germans' movements were cloaked by invisibility. At the same time the blanketing fog added to the sense of panic and dislocation promoted by the terrifying power of the German bombardment.

Led by the storm troopers the German troops surged over the British Forward Zone within a matter of minutes. Follow-up waves of troops surrounded and pinched out any strongpoints that were still resisting. Only a few redoubts held out past 11.00 and within a few hours the British had lost the best part of forty-seven battalions. On the Germans surged, crashing deep into the Battle Zone and overrunning whole gun batteries caught in the confusion and mist. Within a few hours it was obvious that a whirlwind of disaster had swept across the British Fifth Army.

For the men of the RFC the opening of the bombardment came as an unwelcome alarm call.

> I was suddenly awakened by the shattering noise of a colossal and extremely noisy bombardment, with tremendous reverberations of sound. It was the beginning of the most intense bombardment by artillery so far staged in the war. I leapt out of bed and hurriedly dressed, but as soon as I got outside I saw that the airfield was shrouded in thick fog.[2] *Major Sholto Douglas, 84 Squadron*

All along the threatened front the pilots roused themselves to find there was almost nothing they could do but wait for the thick ground mist to clear.

> At 4.30am we were all awakened by a continuous roar. We could hear the shells whistling overhead. It was, of course, impossible to sleep, so we stood outside our huts with our gas masks in readiness thanking God we were not in the trenches.[3] *Lieutenant Ewart Stock, 54 Squadron*

In the north the fog began to drift away by the late morning, but the intrepid efforts by crews of 59 Squadron to bring down 'Zone Call' concentrations of artillery fire on some of the spectacular targets revealed beneath them were all in vain. Desperately they repeated the calls and eventually resorted to the unusual 'LL' calls only to be used for really important targets. Still the reaction was minimal. This situation was duplicated in the Fifth Army sector. Here the Armstrong Whitworths of 8 Squadron commanded by Major Trafford Leigh-Mallory found great difficulty in getting any response from the guns. Leigh-Mallory sent out his wireless officer with as much spare gear as he could find but discovered that not a single battery he visited had even got their wireless mast up.

> As soon as the retreat had started all idea of cooperating with aeroplanes seemed to have been abandoned. Many batteries had simply thrown their wireless equipment away; others had retained the instruments only. The squadron wireless officer certainly did get many sets into action during the days of the retreat, but the trouble was that batteries remained such a short time in one position that the effect of his work did not last for many hours. Under these circumstances little use was made of the 'Zone Calls' which were sent down, the answering of which was probably the only hope the artillery had of effectively hindering the German advance.[4] *Major Trafford Leigh-Mallory, 8 Squadron*

Many of the telephone lines from the forward observation posts on the ground had been cut by the downpour of German shells and communications generally were completely haywire. It should not be forgotten that many of the batteries needed for an effective barrage in response to the 'Zone Calls' were already fully engaged in firing in support of local divisions or in some cases had simply been overrun by the fast advancing German storm troopers. The first duty of the RFC was to support the artillery, but the artillery was in no state to be supported.

As visibility improved the scouts began to fly more and more missions. By 11.30 Lieutenant Ewart Stock and Second Lieutenant N. M. Drysdale, both of 54 Squadron, were in the air and skimming above the trenches in their Sopwith Camels. They had been ordered to carry out a low-level reconnaissance near the St Quentin Canal. Lieutenant Stock had a distinctive perspective of the great battle; part of events, even in personal danger, but strangely detached. He was certainly close enough to grasp the tragedy and drama of the momentous events unfolding just beneath him.

> This was the first time I had witnessed a big bombardment from so low an altitude. As we neared the lines the ground seemed covered in a thin film of fog with bursts of flame coming from all directions. I could see bodies of our men lying on the ground firing all the time. We flew on at about 500 feet until the canal was reached when I looked down on to the road directly underneath me and saw large columns of grey forms moving west. There must have been several thousand on those roads and not a single shell bursting near them! We passed over the canal and still the roads were crowded with enemy troops and transport which would have afforded good targets, but our job was to get as much information as possible of the strength of the enemy in that area. It was not until we were east of the enemy observation balloons that we realised how far over the lines we had flown. When we saw all there was to see we turned to come home with our noses down and engines full on until we were out of the battle zone.[5]
> *Lieutenant Ewart Stock, 54 Squadron*

Other RFC personnel were even closer to events on the ground. There were signallers attached to the artillery batteries up and down the front for the purpose of maintaining wireless communications with the artillery observation RE8s. Sergeant C. R. Outen was attached to 215 Siege Battery of the Royal Garrison Artillery at their gun positions at Happencourt some 6 miles south-west of St Quentin. The wireless station was 300 yards in front of the guns and halfway up a small hillock with an attached machine-gun post just 10 yards in front of their dugout entrance.

> During the afternoon, hearing the sound of machine guns, I looked outside and saw one of our planes engaged in a scrap with a Hun. Both planes seemed to be making a bee-line for the dugout. I rushed to the machine gun pit and shouted to the gunner, 'Now's your chance, Gibbo!' One shot came from his gun and then the words, 'Blast the bloody thing has jammed!' It seemed that the Hun only cleared the aerial by a few feet, he got safely away and our fellow landed apparently unharmed about 600 yards away. I

then asked Bombardier Gibbons, 'Which one were you aiming at?' 'The one in front!' he replied. It was as well the gun failed – the one in front was ours![6] *Sergeant C. R. Outen, RFC attached to 215 Siege Battery, Royal Garrison Artillery*

By the early afternoon it was clear that the Germans had advanced deep into the Battle Zone along the front of Fifth Army. A few outposts were still holding out but were slowly being overwhelmed as the Germans swirled round them, isolating them from any support or reinforcements.

In one sense the RFC was never at the disadvantage of their comrades on the ground. It took days to move in reinforcements of infantry or artillery, but nowhere on the British section of the Western Front was further than a ninety-minute flight away from the Somme area. Squadrons could fly in within hours and others, while maintaining their own bases, could fly down to carry out sorties over the contested area before returning to their airfields. The overall air superiority of the Allies over the Germans on the entire Western Front was on the scale of something like three to one: on the Somme battlefront only 579 aircraft faced 730 German aircraft, but in the sector to the north there were some 489 aircraft facing just 172 German aircraft, while to the south approximately 2,600 French aircraft were being held by only 471 German aircraft. It was thus evident that the German air superiority over the Somme could only be short-lived.

By mid-afternoon the British scouts had begun to get the bit firmly between their collective teeth. They were ordered to engage in concentrated ground strafing to engage at will the multiplicity of targets that the German offensive placed before them. Previously, ground strafing had been relatively ineffective firing against troops concealed in trenches but now everything was right out in the open below them: the marching columns of infantry, the largely horsed transport, the precious artillery batteries. Given such enticing targets the airmen did not stint themselves.

After lunch I was ordered to lead a formation along the St Quentin-Estrees road and bomb and fire at the enemy infantry and transport. We had never undertaken this sort of 'job' before. We carried two 20lb bombs and about 800 rounds of ammunition. Our object was to get rid of our bombs at the earliest opportunity, as they were a handicap on a Camel owing to the weight. I led the formation along this road until we could see our infantry in action, then I dived down to 500 feet and looked for a good target. Enemy infantry were everywhere as usual, advancing in the open and in large columns on the road. I gave the sign to release the bombs when we were well over them. We were so low that their uniforms could easily be seen, especially their large helmets and long bayonets. I dived first and released both bombs at once; they must have hit the road squarely in the centre. I could hear the explosions and see the smoke. One by one the rest of the formation followed dropping each pair of bombs and scattering the enemy. I turned and led the formation west and dived on the Huns in the open. At one time I must have been at the level of their heads, they lay down on the ground when they saw us coming. We continued to dive and fire at them in turn until our ammunition was exhausted, when I led the 'flock' home.[7] *Lieutenant Ewart Stock, 54 Squadron*

They got back at 16.30 and Stock only had time to try to get his breath back while the ground crew rearmed his Camel, then he was off back up into the fray again.

We left the ground at about 5.30pm and flew towards the lines. It was a glorious evening and visibility was excellent. We saw the enemy still advancing and shells bursting everywhere. Once or twice I switched off my engine and heard the bombardment plainly. We encountered a Hun two-seater chasing an RE8. We were well above him so were able to get a good dive and a long burst in. Dugdale dived first and must have shot the observer because when I dived the rear gun of the enemy was not firing. He went east with his nose well down and when I looked a second time he was gone, whether he landed or not, we do not know.[8] *Lieutenant Ewart Stock, 54 Squadron*

The SE5s of 84 Squadron had originally been intended to take on the German scouts and thereby protect the artillery observation and contact patrols. But the pressure of events and the sheer desperation of what was happening on the ground meant that they too were thrown into low-level ground attacks to help the infantry and to slow the pace of the German advance. This posed their cerebral squadron commander, Major Sholto Douglas, with a whole new range of problems to consider.

> All our thought and training had gone into how to chase and destroy German fighters in the air, usually at fairly high altitudes. Now we were having to carry out very low-flying attacks with bombs and machine guns on the enemy troops on the ground.[9] *Major Sholto Douglas, 84 Squadron*

The low-flying British scouts also posed intractable problems for the German anti-aircraft units that had gone forward as far as they could with the intention of protecting the infantry from ground strafing. The K-Flaks were armed with an ordinary 77mm field gun mounted on an open truck in such a manner that it could be elevated high enough to fire at aircraft. However, the gunners found that the British scouts were flashing past them too low to be targeted by such a slow-moving gun.

> We rolled along but did not contribute much to the battle. RFC planes seemed to be everywhere and tried to stop the advance. Most of the time they were too low for us, diving down with machine guns going full blast, and never high enough to become safe targets. We could not fire on a plane operating over the heads of our own men. The chances of hitting such fast-moving targets were practically nil, while the danger of hitting our own soldiers and showering them with splinters was great. Ordinarily, good anti-aircraft fire forced the enemy to fly high, but this was a life or death struggle and these RFC fliers continued to dive in regardless of the risk. Only a direct hit could stop them.[10] *Leutnant Fritz Nagel, Nr 82 K-Flak*

When attacked by low-flying aircraft it was soon apparent that crossfire from machine guns was the best answer.

The aircraft of the German Air Service were themselves active once the fog had lifted. Leutnant Fritz Kampfenkel was acting as observer to his pilot Feldwebel Franz Jessen in a ground-support Schlachtstaffeln aircraft and their armour plating undoubtedly saved their lives when they ran into trouble.

During these close air support for the infantry flights over the forward trenches at no higher than 200 to 300 metres to reconnoitre where friend and foe were, our infantry laid out white panels as recognition signs. We had to look for them while dodging fire from the enemy trenches nearby. We used AEG and Albatros aircraft with steel armour plates that protected our cockpits. This time, I suddenly felt a heatwave as our engine had been hit and had caught fire. Thanks to the steel plate between the engine and my 'Emil', he was able to hold the control column comfortably in his hand and turn to a spot behind our own lines and set the aircraft down. The engine was completely burned up. Quickly, we climbed out of the burning wreck, which then came under heavy enemy fire. We found protection in our own trenches.[11] *Leutnant Fritz Kampfenkel, Flieger Abteilung (A) 240*

Another German pilot, Leutnant Gustav Lachman, accompanied by his observer, was ordered to destroy a bridge in front of the fast-moving German line. This was an extremely difficult task for a solo bombing mission even without the worry of being intercepted by the RFC.

It was a fairly hopeless order because we had to fly without any fighter protection. I was caught by five Spads – very good single-seaters! It was a very brisk encounter and I was really a dead duck because my machine was much less manoeuvrable and my observer was soon put out of action by a shot through his chest. I could never use my two machine guns because when I tried to turn the very manoeuvrable single-seaters flew rings round me. It was my first really sharp encounter in the air but I wasn't really scared. It was really this feeling of almost detachment. I believe that when one is near to death the second ego steps out and observes one – I had a feeling that I observed myself – and I was quite satisfied that I took the whole situation so calmly. I imagined that I had been wounded several times because I saw bullet holes appearing in my dashboard and I was surprised that it didn't hurt. Then I was wounded in the leg and it was like a sledgehammer blow. Then I did something that was totally against the book of rules. I went into a straight sharp nosedive. But it saved me because I dived into the layer of cloud which made visibility in the oblique direction. So with tremendous speed I approached the ground. My engineering instincts told me that if I pull up the machine too sharply then the wings would go so I pulled up very, very slowly and the machine recovered.

Then I was at very low altitude over the trenches. The apathy came now which is a characteristic of the shock after being wounded. My first instinct was to land – to be out of it. I had my packet and I wanted to be out of it. There I saw in front of me a mound completely covered with barbed wire – I was gliding straight towards it and I didn't care a damn – I wanted to be out. Then suddenly somebody knocked me on the head and yelled, Gas! So I opened the throttle again and I carried on. Then my calm decision returned and of course it struck me as ridiculous to crash into barbed wire and the right decision was of course to fly straight on until a town appeared on the horizon and to land on the field in order to get into a hospital as quickly as possible as we both were very severely wounded. That I did.[12] *Leutnant Gustav Lachman, Flieger Abteilung (A) 216*

The German Air Service could not fight defensively when their country was making its final attempt to wrest victory from the jaws of long-term defeat. The pilots and observers knew that beneath them thousands of their countrymen were risking and losing their lives in the supreme battle. But as they strove to turn the tide they naturally exposed themselves more than would usually be the case to their enemies. And the British had no qualms in pressing home any advantage they could get. There was no concept of a fair fight in this war.

I led a formation of 'B' and 'A' Flights on an offensive patrol, flying along the lines at 17,000 feet. Near Vaulx we encountered an Albatros two-seater. Poor chap, he had not a hope of escaping us and we fell on him like a pack of bloodthirsty foxhounds who had caught up with their prey. Nearly all of us took part in the attack and eventually the EA turned completely over and descended on its back in a flat spin until it hit the ground and was completely wrecked on our side of the lines.[13] *Captain Leonard Rochford, 3 (Naval) Squadron, RNAS*

Yet such victories were small fry compared with the success that had attended the German offensive. Indeed air casualties on both sides were not high as they devoted their attentions to the ground rather than on hunting each other out of the skies. The RFC and RNAS lost sixteen aircraft during 21 March, while the Germans appear to have lost only eight aircraft, some of them due to ground fire.

By nightfall it was evident that the Germans had made substantial gains that ranged from about 2,500 to 8,000 yards. In the north the assault by the Seventeenth Army had been held up by the stubborn resistance emanating from the stronger and better prepared Third Army. The British centre had also been able to hold on, although to a lesser extent. The serious breakthrough was in the Essigny-le-Grand sector, close to St Quentin. Here the German Eighteenth Army had crashed through the British Fifth Army Forward Zone and, more seriously, breached the Battle Zone, forcing a headlong retreat, back to the Crozat Canal. In all, the British had lost just over 500 vital guns and, perhaps worse still in the era of manpower shortages, suffered 38,500 casualties (of which a staggering 21,000 were prisoners of war). Yet the cost was high; attacking in even such advantageous circumstances was always a risky business and the Germans themselves suffered up to 40,000 casualties.

The German success was brought home to Captain Leonard Rochford when he, accompanied by his distinguished commanding officer Major Raymond Collishaw and a couple of ground crew, set off that evening to try to salvage what they could from the crashed Albatros.

> As we proceeded towards Bapaume, the noise of gunfire noticeably increased and shells passed over us and exploded on the west side of the road. A touch of humour was brought into the picture by Chief Petty Officer Finch who kept on exclaiming, 'That's one of ours!' and 'That's one of theirs!' As darkness fell the road became more and more congested with military vehicles of every description. We moved forwards at a snail's pace and sometimes not at all. The bombardment continued though fortunately none of the shells hit the traffic on the road as far as we could see. But the state of chaos was so great that 'Collie' decided that it was now quite impossible to reach the crashed Albatros and ordered our driver to return to Mont St Eloi.[14] *Captain Leonard Rochford, 3 (Naval) Squadron, RNAS*

The retreat had begun and it was soon apparent that many of the remaining gun batteries would have to move back swiftly if they were not also to be overrun by the fast-moving German infiltration troops probing behind the lines. It was perhaps unfortunate that in arranging the retreat of his gun battery one unknown artillery officer criminally omitted to inform his attached RFC signallers.

> Shortly after nightfall it became quieter and I got ready for an early kip. Round about half ten, my assistant, a battery signaller, asked if he could phone the Battery Command post and find out how we had fared. My retort was, 'Go to bed!' Later he repeated his request and realising that he would keep on until it was granted, I said, 'OK!' Imagine my surprise when he blurted out that about half the battery had left the position. In the turmoil the wireless had been forgotten. I was told to get out as quickly as possible with as much equipment as could be carried and make for the road some 500 or 600 yards away. Fortunately another signaller was with us and with his help we managed to get all the wireless gear and nearly all of our belongings to the roadside, where we found a number of the battery waiting for tractors, in order to pull out the remaining guns. The transport had not arrived by dawn and the Major ordered some of the gunners to make their way to the billets some distance to the rear. The offer to remain and load up the wireless gear was turned down – much to my relief – so I joined the men, but not without the wireless tuner. A meal, presumably breakfast, was interrupted by a shout, 'Jerry's coming!' and in the distance troops could be seen skirmishing so once again we made off.[15] *Sergeant C. R. Outen, RFC attached to 215 Siege Battery, Royal Garrison Artillery*

Next morning, on 22 March, the Germans prepared for the second day of their offensive by deploying a sinister array of *drachen* kite balloons, their observers looking down on the battlefield and communicating directly by telephone with the ground. The balloons had the tremendous advantage that unlike the ordinary artillery observation aircraft they could stay in the air all day as opposed to just a couple of hours.

> While it was still dark the balloons were sent up at a distance of about 5 kilometres from the enemy. When the fog lifted they could be seen following the advance of our infantry at a distance of 1–1½ kilometres lined up as in review and revealed to those of us far in the rear what fine progress was being made by our attack. When the visibility became excellent, nothing was concealed from these balloons and they gave the High Command

continuous information on the action. By means of balloon observation we were able to discover promptly, and give immediate warning, of the assembly of hostile reserves for a counterattack, and artillery which had just been unmasked could be brought under counter-battery fire.[16] *General Ernest Wilhelm von Hoeppner, German Air Service*

The misty morning once again hampered the aerial operations of both sides. Lieutenant Ewart Stock of 54 Squadron only got into the air for the first of another long series of low-level patrols at about 11.00. That afternoon he saw evidence that despite their successful advance the resistance of the British infantry was causing the Germans severe casualties in places.

In the afternoon when flying low and firing on the Huns in the open I saw what seemed to me to be a long wall of sandbags. I could not understand for a moment why I had not seen it before until diving at the enemy behind it I noticed that it was a wall of dead bodies heaped one upon the other! The enemy were on the east side of it so I was able to sweep this wall with machine gun fire until there must have been a hundred or so German soldiers to add to their human wall.[17] *Lieutenant Ewart Stock, 54 Squadron*

Everywhere he found inviting targets of opportunity. The diving scouts armed with their spitting machine guns and their 25-pound Cooper bombs took full advantage. All along the line they tore into the advancing German columns.

We promptly dived on them. There were enemy troops everywhere, and we went about shooting them up until we were all out of ammunition. Only an hour or two later the squadron went off again, and we immediately found a great many more targets than we could ever cope with, and again we waded into the attack until we were completely out of ammunition and bombs. The Germans were advancing literally in hordes, and since they were not taking any particular precautions against attack from the air we found that our low-flying against them was not as dangerous as we had anticipated. My pilots almost wept with joy as they fell upon these massive targets.[18] *Major Sholto Douglas, 84 Squadron*

The British pilots were learning the task of ground strafing almost from scratch. There was no manual for them to consult and by the second day each unit was making their own judgement as to the best way to proceed.

> Up to now we had been flying in a formation of five or six machines which we found was far too many for such a job as ground strafing as we were apt to hinder each other when diving. It was therefore decided that we should work in pairs.[19] *Lieutenant Ewart Stock, 54 Squadron*

Perversely, but for equally valid reasons, Major Sholto Douglas and his 84 Squadron came to exactly the opposite conclusion and resolved to attack in strict flight formation under the strict control of the flight leader.

> The method of attack that we evolved against these ground targets was first of all to fly over the enemy, always in formation, at a height of between 8,000 and 10,000 feet. At that height we presented to the enemy guns fast-moving targets that were difficult to hit, and we were too high for their machine guns to be effective. On the other hand, we could scan wide stretches of country in search of suitable ground targets. Having selected his target, the leader would dive at it, but not too steeply: more flying down to it from a distance with engine full on. When we were within range we opened up with our machine guns; and at about 200 feet away from the target we dropped our bombs. Immediately after our attacks we zoomed up as hard as we could go, usually turning at the same time. In the dive we would be doing between 150 and 180 miles per hour, and in the zoom that followed we rocketed up to about 1,000 feet.[20] *Major Sholto Douglas, 84 Squadron*

But the German aircraft had the same type of opportunities in harassing the retreating British columns. The German ground strafing brought the same scenes of confusion as disciplined infantry columns were suddenly thrown into wild confusion in the dash for cover, the roads blocked by strafed transport.

> Our attack squadrons found excellent targets in the British columns which were now streaming in jams that lasted for hours on the straight stretch of

the Romer road. Teams became badly mixed up; everyone sought shelter in the ditches to the right and left of the road, or rushed out in panic across the open fields.[21] *General Ernest Wilhelm von Hoeppner, German Air Service*

At a higher altitude there was more fighting between the scouts. In one clash some forty-five Fokker Triplanes and Albatros D.Vs of Jagdgeschwader 1 encountered twelve Camels from 70 Squadron and a flight of SE5s from 56 Squadron over Havrincourt Wood. The RFC claimed four aircraft in this dogfight alone but the German losses for the whole of the Third Army front were a maximum of six aircraft of which two were known to have been accounted for by British anti-aircraft fire. Elsewhere the SE5s of 2 Squadron, Australian Flying Corps, had been sent up with orders to prevent the Germans operating over the hard-pressed British lines at all costs. While patrolling over St Quentin they sighted five Rumpler two-seaters protected by a higher escort of five Albatros scouts. In the fight that followed Lieutenant Robert Mackenzie claimed a victory over an Albatros but then sighted the Rumplers sneaking away. Accompanied by Lieutenant Henry Forrest they dived to the attack.

The formation never wavered, each gunner crouching tensely behind his gun, waiting to open fire. Half a mile from the Rumplers we separated. Forrest's angle of dive steepened as he plunged to attack them from underneath, whilst I purposely overshot and did a spin turn to take them at the front and below at an angle. Soon the sky was full of lead. Those German pilots were a stout-hearted bunch keeping perfect formation, they offered no blind spots, as each plane was covered by the fire of the others. Forrest hung back, dipped, zoomed till I thought he would collide with the rear machine, fired and down went a Rumpler burning like a meteor. Just as I was all set to do a neat bit of execution, both guns jammed. Pounding at the breechblock of the Vickers, my momentary distraction was fully taken advantage of by the leader, who manoeuvred to give his gunner the best possible shot. He put in some fine shooting for his first burst sprayed my machine from nose to tail, shattering windscreen and instrument board and cutting the joystick clean in two within an inch of the bottom. The SE immediately went into a tight spin from which I could not come out. Seeking to press home his advantage, the two-seater followed me down, the pilot giving me all he had with the front guns. That pilot's shooting was every bit as good as his observer's and that I was not struck seemed like a miracle. Maybe it was. A good pair of goggles went by the board, followed by bits of a Sidcot suit. With only 3,000 feet of altitude and the lines immediately below, I prepared to give up the ghost. This is my finish I thought. A gun crackling in a different pitch proved to be none other than dear old Forrest, who, seeing my predicament, broke off his combat and came down to my assistance. Swerving to meet this new attack, the Rumpler offered him a perfect broadside and I was delighted to see the Rumpler go down minus his wings. How to get out of my own jam was now the all-important matter. Some frantic juggling with the controls and the stabiliser at last did the trick. The SE came out of the spin so violently as to almost throw me out of the cockpit, but the point was I was out, and that was all that mattered at the moment. Gingerly turning in the direction of our lines, not without some sleight of hand with the rudder, throttle and tailplane wheel, I very gradually lost height.[22] *Lieutenant Robert Mackenzie, 2 Squadron, Australian Flying Corps*

Mackenzie was indeed fortunate. He skimmed over the front lines at just 200 feet and managed a relatively controlled if far too fast forced landing. He was unhurt and was back with his squadron by nightfall.

By the end of 22 March it was evident that the situation had to a large extent stabilized on the Third Army front to the north of the Somme. It was a far different story on the Fifth Army front where the Germans were still pressing hard and the British line was falling back in considerable disarray. From this point the sheer pressure of numbers began to turn the tide of the close-fought battle in the air. As has been noted the Allies always had the edge when it came to overall numbers and soon the British and French squadrons were massing in the battle area. Aircraft from III Brigade began to intervene in the Fifth Army area as their own situation stabilized; aircraft flew in from as far afield as I Brigade which normally supported First Army far to the north. On arrival they may have been disrupted in their arrangements by the necessity of abandoning and changing airfields, but collectively they improvised well under pressure assisted by the sheer quantity of supplies and munitions available.

Next day increasing numbers of Allied aircraft threw themselves into the battle. They knew exactly what they had to do and they certainly knew what was at stake. They simply had to stop the German advance thrusting towards the town of Albert and threatening to open up a gap between Third Army and the beleaguered Fifth Army. To help their infantry, the RFC aircraft simply had to ignore the German scouts flying above them in large formations. To look up behind one's tail was to run the risk of a fatal collision with a passing church or tree.

> We were on a low flying patrol, intent on strafing the advancing German infantry, when we ran into a bunch of German fighters, Pfalzs, at an altitude that was too low for the use of any tactics that we had evolved. After a few moments of pretty hectic whirling around I managed to get on the tail of one of them and I gave him a couple of good bursts of fire, and he went down and crashed just the other side of the German lines. It was all over before I seemed to have even a chance to think.[23] *Major Sholto Douglas, 84 Squadron*

At this point in time, Second Lieutenant Frank Ransley of 48 Squadron returned from a brief leave and found himself, like so many others, thrown in at the deep end. All their previous wealth of experience of scout tactics in their magnificent Bristol Fighters at high altitude was as nothing. They may have once been the 'gilded elite' but their real status was now clear. The army was their parent body: the safekeeping of the army was their main concern, and their own survival was purely secondary in the overall scheme of things.

> We then began our 'Aerial Infantry' role. Our orders were to go as low as possible and concentrate on shooting up German troops or any other worthwhile ground targets. The '*Brisfit*', being a two-seater, was much larger than a scout machine and had a bigger wing spread and was not built for low flying. Many machines I flew were put out of action by fire from ground troops. Fortunately being on the trench line if one was not wounded one could nearly always glide over the lines and reach the aerodrome or put the machine down on a fairly level piece of land on the British side. At one time we had only three serviceable machines. The mechanics and riggers worked non-stop at this time to put us in the air again. Major Keith

> **Park inspired us all with his calm certainty that we should win through although he hated sending us out on these near suicide missions.**[24] ***Second Lieutenant Frank Ransley, 48 Squadron***

On the ground the squadrons were falling back from airfield to airfield under circumstances that were more than a little fraught. This was particularly the case for the ground crews who sometimes found themselves closer to the Germans than they would normally have expected or wished. Signaller Monty Pocock, a wireless operator of 53 Squadron, was caught up in the squadron move from Villeselve to Montdidier on 24 March.

> **A few 'volunteers', 'You, you and you!' were told to stay behind to set alight to the petrol and surplus stores, and being one of the 'yous' I certainly did not relish the job. We who were left behind to do the 'firing' were told to set alight as soon as we saw any signs of the Germans. What we saw being done on the aerodrome was the digging of a lot of holes, waist deep, and infantry officers chasing around looking for machine gunners, of course that wasn't our war. As soon as we saw the Germans, up goes the fire, much to the consternation of the infantry and we skiddadled hell bent. We found the Germans were already in most of the towns and villages, so we cut across country and were welcomed in quite a number of places with the sight of a barrel of champagne with the top open into which you dipped your tin hat and refreshed yourself.**[25] ***Monty Pocock, 53 Squadron***

On 24 March the great ace himself, Rittmeister Manfred von Richthofen, tore into action like a force of nature. It was almost a matter of routine for him by this stage of his career: take off, locate then shoot an aircraft down, write the brief combat report.

> **During a protracted single-seater combat between about ten SEs and twenty-five machines of my Jagdgeschwader, I attacked an Englishman at an altitude of 2,500 metres. Under my machine gun fire, both wings broke away from the aeroplane in the air. The pieces scattered in the vicinity of Combles.**[26] ***Rittmeister Manfred von Richthofen, Jagdgeschwader 1, German Air Service***

Whatever the risks, if the British pilots had the chance to intervene to protect the British troops on the ground then they had no choice but to spring into action. This was exemplified when Lieutenant Stock was on a low-level reconnaissance of the area between Ham and his former airfield, now abandoned. As he flew over he sighted British troops digging in west of the Somme who were being threatened by a body of German cavalry at Matigny.

> We dived down to about 200 feet over the Somme and flew with engines full out towards Matigny. The majority of the Hun cavalry were on a straight road running east from the village so I flew straight along the road and when we were above them we pulled the handle which released the bombs. Without any warning a bullet hit one of my landing wires cutting it in half, the one piece of it flew past my head just missing my goggles but I was able to turn in time to see the effects of our bombs. I have never seen such confusion among horses as I saw then. They were dashing all over the field knocking men down who were trying to catch them. Without a second thought I dived on what seemed to me to be a squad of about twenty horses running across the field. I got so low in my attempt to get level with them that my wheels hit the ground with such force that the machine leapt into the air before I could get a shot in. I managed to fire a long burst into them as soon as I turned round, but as I was pulling out of the dive I saw about four cavalry officers on the road and definitely saw one firing with a revolver at Crowdon who was about 200 yards from me diving at a target which I was unable to see. The officers were all mounted except one who was sitting on the side of the road. I saw all this in the space of about five seconds before I dived on them and fired about 100 rounds; two of them fell off their horses and one galloped off along the road. He was a tall man and was wearing the spiked Hun helmet. I hit either him or his horse before he got far down the road, for horse and man went crashing into a large hedge. I turned to get back when a machine gun opened fire on me and I could not seem to shake him off whatever I did.[27] *Lieutenant Ewart Stock, 54 Squadron*

Even against cavalry the low-flying scout was a reasonable target, especially for those cavalrymen with enough experience of game hunting to allow for deflection. When Stock landed he found just how lucky he had been, for the wings of his Sopwith Camel were riddled with holes, two flying wires had been shot through and there was a bullet through his rev counter. This kind of work was not sustainable by any individual not blessed with phenomenal luck and courage.

> We had very few pilots left of the old squadron by this time, about six were missing and at least five had been wounded – this meant more work for those that were left.[28] *Lieutenant Ewart Stock, 54 Squadron*

By this time the scale of the RFC intervention in the ground fighting can be charted in statistics. The 28,000 machine-gun bullets fired and 15½ tons of bombs dropped on 21 March had risen to 82,000 rounds and 36½ tons of bombs on 24 March. As Salmond proudly reported to his old boss Trenchard:

> We managed to concentrate one hundred machines on the threatened line. They had orders to fly low and take every risk; nothing was to count in carrying out their duties. I had news from the I Brigade that our machines were so thick over this point that there was every danger of collision in the air.[29] *Major General John Salmond, Headquarters, RFC*

To counter this aerial activity the Germans had their scouts, ground fire and of course their anti-aircraft guns. Leutnant Fritz Nagel and the crew of his mobile 77mm anti-aircraft gun found themselves moving forward, but from their perspective it hardly felt like a fast advance. As they approached Peronne they encountered a terrible bottleneck of troops probably caused by the bridge over the Somme river.

> We got into another incredible traffic jam. I had no idea what caused it, but our K-Flak was jammed in tight between horse-drawn field artillery. This time British planes came roaring in, four or five at a time, strafing without mercy. None of our fighters were in sight. We had to open up and fire as best we could right over the heads of men and horses only a few feet away. Nearby infantry let go with machine guns. To the left of us was the usual procession of the Red Cross vehicles. While we worried about the danger of these constant attacks from the air, I wondered how a wounded man

must have felt, completely helpless in these wagons while machine gun bullets spattered all around.[30] *Leutnant Fritz Nagel, Nr 82 K-Flak*

As the Germans advanced they overran the British supply depots, most of which had not been destroyed. Looting was widespread, for the German soldier had been on short rations for years and this was an opportunity not to be missed. Nagel sent his driver to investigate a dump and was delighted beyond measure when he returned a little later with a truck loaded to the gunwales!

They had loaded many cases of the most wonderful things to eat: condensed milk, tea, cocoa, corned beef, sugar, bacon, tinned butter, cookies, biscuits and countless cartons of English Woodbine cigarettes. They also brought an armful of raincoats made out of real rubber – something very scarce in Germany. Our mouths watered and we were most anxious for night to fall so we could stuff ourselves with these incredible goodies. It was a treasure beyond price. We were always hungry and completely sick of army slop. That evening some of the soldiers drank the first cup of real cocoa they had tasted in years.[31] *Leutnant Fritz Nagel, Nr 82 K-Flak*

Since the start of the German offensive the RFC night bomber squadrons had been directed to attack these long columns of German troops. Among the bombers was Second Lieutenant J. C. F. Hopkins of 83 Squadron who was flying an old FE2b.

The principal target for attack was the Bapaume–Albert road on which the Germans were advancing rapidly. The weather was very fine – bright moonlit nights. The road showed up almost white in the moonlight. You'd see an obvious column of troops marching, a long black blob along the road. Then you'd see vehicles, you could pick out individual vehicles from about 1,500 feet. We dropped as many bombs as we could. Most of the bombs were anti-personnel bombs. We had very little retaliation from the enemy because they were obviously holding their fire in order not to give away their concentration. Well that was all very nice; it was just jam for us! We just went out, dropped bombs, came back, loaded up, went out and dropped more bombs. We did a great deal of damage and stopped these columns

Major William Bishop VC, with pilots of 85 Squadron, RAF at St Omer, June 1918

Group photo of 22 Squadron, RAF

James McCudden VC

Major Edward Mannock VC

Major Sholto Douglas, MC, DFC, Commanding Officer of 84 Squadron, RAF, at Bertangles in the summer of 1918, standing in front of an SE5a

Above left Lieutenant Edward Lee, 98 Squadron, RAF

Above right Major William Bishop VC

Manfred von Richthofen (right) with his brother Lothar von Richthofen, standing in front of a Fokker Dr.I

Issuing Lewis guns

A mechanic handing ammunition to an observer in a Bristol fighter

Air mechanics prepare a Bristol fighter of 22 Squadron, RAF

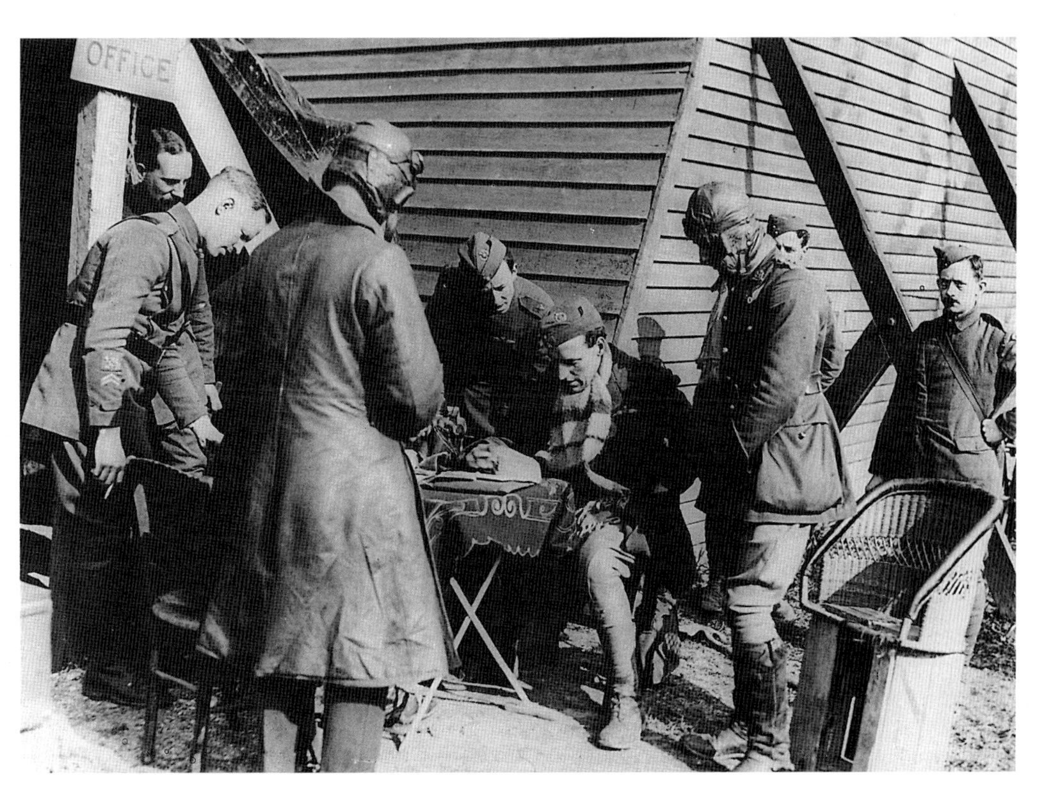

Pilots hand in reports to Major Stammers, 15 Squadron, RAF

An SE5a of 85 Squadron, RAF

A Sopwith Dolphin

A Sopwith Camel looping the loop

Post-war demonstration of air fighting using Bristol Fighters

Optimism ran wild in the RAF: 'Huns: 39 in 14 days'

from going along the road.[32] *Second Lieutenant J. C. F. Hopkins, 83 Squadron*

The Germans obviously moved as much as possible at night and Hopkins was also sent on reconnaissance patrols to try to determine the progress of the German advance and the likely direction of their next thrust.

Reconnaissance work was accomplished by flying at around 4,000 feet over a particular area and then dropping what were known as parachute flares. These were magnesium flares suspended on a parachute. They were rather like a bomb launched through a tube – as they went through an electrical contact fired the magnesium compound. It dropped a certain distance – say, 500 feet – and the parachute opened and at the same time the flare caught light. We would fly along, drop these flares in a line and then turn round and come back over the top of the flares to observe anything we could see. This was not a pleasant business because it was quite obvious to the Germans that having dropped the flares we were going to come back and they were waiting for us. At the height we flew we were within machine gun range and they had these things called 'flaming onions' which were great balls of fire on wires. These things were shot into the air and they looked like enormous roman candles – quite terrifying but as far as I know they never did any damage at all except put the wind up you.[33] *Second Lieutenant J. C. F. Hopkins, 83 Squadron*

Both sides were engaged in bombing tactical objectives as and where required by their armies. From the same squadron, Lieutenant G. W. Higgs and his observer were ordered to carry out a night raid on a German railhead to try to interfere with the smooth arrival of the German reinforcements who were gathering for the next phase of the offensive. They reached their target and after dropping their bombs without any real excitement they were flying back when they had a close encounter with one of their opposite numbers.

When we were about 40 miles from our home aerodrome at Auchelle, I encountered and all but collided with an enemy machine that had, in all probability, been engaged in a similar occupation to myself. So near were we before we sighted each other that my observer, who was perched in the nose of the nacelle, instinctively dropped down to avoid the impact. Telepathy has its adherents as well as its opponents, but since that night, I am a firm supporter of the pros in this matter, for as I violently urged my control lever in the direction necessary for descent, so did my *vis-à-vis* pull up his snout to virtually a vertical position. Neither the German pilot nor myself made any effort to engage in combat and the flames from his exhaust became less visible as second succeeded second. He probably thought, as I did, when sustained thought became possible, that one such escape from imminent death in one night was a sufficient temptation to providence. Anyhow we passed and parted.[34] *Lieutenant G. W. Higgs, 83 Squadron*

By 25 March the Germans were deep into the wilderness lands of the old Somme battlefields that had claimed the lives of so many on both sides in 1916. The man-made desert posed a serious threat to their communications. Many of the bridges across rivers and canals had been demolished. The RFC was also determined to add to their difficulties. The concentration on ground strafing was raised another peg in an order from Salmond to Headquarters of his tactical reserve Ninth Wing.

I wish you as soon as you can after receipt of this to send out your scout squadrons and those of No. 27, No. 25 and No. 62 Squadrons that are available on to the line Grévillers–Martinpuich–Maricourt. These squadrons will bomb and shoot up everything they can see on the enemy side of this line. Very low flying is essential. All risks to be taken. Urgent.[35] *Major-General John Salmond, Headquarters, RFC*

All unaware of the gradual gathering of the squadrons, Lieutenant Stock was once more up in the air carrying out ground-strafing missions accompanied by his partner Lieutenant Roy Crowden. He was horrified at the scale and speed of the German advance.

The situation apparently was very serious; the Hun was now in Peronne and Bapaume and was likely to be in Albert at any moment. It was a glorious morning when we set out for the lines. As far as I could see we were the only machines in the air around Albert when we reached it. We did not know how far along the Bapaume–Albert road the enemy had

reached so we were obliged to fly very low until we spotted grey forms and guns firing to the west. We discovered that the enemy were half way along the road at this time. A thin haze covered the ground and the clouds were only 2,000 feet high thus affording ideal opportunities for ground strafing. The area over which we flew was the old Somme battleground of 1916, one mass of trenches and shell holes, and a stump of a tree here and there. Albert was in ruins but the church still stood apparently untouched.[36]
Lieutenant Ewart Stock, 54 Squadron

But one thing was becoming increasingly apparent: when the massed squadrons of the RFC were coordinated they could make a real difference to events on the ground. They may have suffered high casualties but they killed hundreds and struck terror into the hearts of their German enemies.

We had a priceless evening. We suddenly had orders to send every available machine to bomb and machine gun a few thousand Huns who were massing to attack. The sky was simply filled with our machines and No 4 Squadron's were over first; and I was flying with the formation leader in the first machine of all – the first of all the Flying Corps to get over. We bombed and machine gunned him until he must have got vertical gust most horribly – 200 aeroplanes suddenly appearing and opening up on him just as he was massing to attack. My average amount of sleep in the last eight nights has been just four hours.[37] *Lieutenant John Baker, 4 Squadron*

It was worth the constant trickle of casualties that was constantly eroding the number of experienced pilots serving in the scout squadrons. Ground-strafing aircraft had no chance to check who might be approaching them from behind. If it was the likes of Manfred von Richthofen they were simply doomed. This was the morning that the 'Red Baron' claimed his sixty-eighth victim.

With five aeroplanes of Jasta 11, I attacked a couple of low flying English single-seaters north-east of Albert. I came up to within 50 metres behind one of the Englishmen and, with a few rounds, shot him down in flames. The burning airplane crashed between Contalmaison and Albert and continued to burn on the ground. The bombs which it was apparently carrying exploded a few minutes later.[38] *Rittmeister Manfred von Richthofen, Jagdgeschwader 1, German Air Service*

Threatened by the Jasta aces from above, the low-flying British scouts were also under constant ground fire. Fortunately, many infantrymen had no idea of deflection shooting, the necessity of firing ahead of the target to allow for the time in flight of the bullet. But at times the sheer number of soldiers shooting could create the effect of a hail of bullets all around them. Captain Leonard Rochford of 3 (Naval) Squadron, an acknowledged ace with at that point some fourteen accredited victories, had an extremely lucky escape while ground strafing on 25 March.

The sky was overcast with cloud base about 1,000 feet when I took off with my flight at 12.45. On reaching the appointed area we broke flight formation and proceeded to work independently. I flew eastwards at 500 feet searching the ground for enemy troops. I observed both German and British troops but everything was very confused and it was difficult to sort them out one from the other. I could hear the sound of rifles and machine guns firing and noticed bullet holes appearing in my top and bottom planes. Suddenly from out of the clouds a two-seater flew right across my bows and as he turned eastwards I got into a position close behind him. I was about to open fire when a bullet hit my main petrol tank. Thinking I was being attacked from behind, I turned quickly but could see no EA, so the bullet must have been fired from the ground. Petrol fumes entered the cockpit, the engine spluttered and stopped, and I thought my machine was about to catch fire. I cannot deny that I was frightened as I descended with the intention of landing near our troops. But I soon recovered my self-control and switched on to my auxiliary fuel tank. The engine started and I eased the machine out of its dive only 50 feet above the ground and headed westwards.[39] *Captain Leonard Rochford, 3 (Naval) Squadron, RNAS*

After refuelling twice he flew back to Mont St Eloi where he was just in time to stop the despatch rider from setting off with a report that he was 'missing in action' with all the grief to his family that would have entailed. It was no wonder that the scout pilots for the most part hated ground strafing.

> These low-level missions were thoroughly disliked by most of us as one became a mere target to be shot at all the time and it was a matter of sheer luck whether one got hit or not. Nor was it always easy to identify German from British troops, and while this was being done one became even more vulnerable. My method was to take the flight to a height from which likely targets could be seen clearly, then to dive down on them firing off all ammunition as quickly as possible and, having made a mental note of the positions of all enemy troops and transport, return home.[40] *Captain Leonard Rochford, 3 (Naval) Squadron, RNAS*

General von Hoeppner was an astute man and he could not but be aware that he was beginning to lose control of the vital air space above the ground offensive.

> The counter-attack of the enemy became stronger. The condition of our aviators in the combat area was constantly becoming more difficult and our infantry began to complain about hostile bombing attacks. Our foes had already acquired a numerical superiority in the air. It was especially disadvantageous to us that we had to undertake to advance our aerodromes into the area where the ground had been torn up fearfully by shell fire during the previous Battle of the Somme. We encountered great difficulties in this respect and our air units huddled together on the few suitable spots that could be found. Our foes knew all about these locations and through bombing raids delivered by both day and at night, they sought to wear down the combat effectiveness of our air forces.[41] *General Ernest Wilhelm von Hoeppner, German Air Service*

The reason was simple. The British had by this stage concentrated twenty-seven squadrons onto ground-strafing duties, while a further six squadrons were engaged in normal offensive patrolling trying to sweep the German aircraft from the sky. On 25 March they fired some 92,000 machine-gun rounds at ground targets. Next day it would rise to 228,000. To achieve this they had left most of the rest of the front denuded, but the Germans were equally preoccupied with the Somme and could take no advantage. The German Air Service had other problems as well. It too had been suffering a high rate of casualties in the bitter fighting. Both sides were concentrating on events on the ground but contacts were frequent and when the scale of air fighting increased so inevitably did the number of casualties and damaged aircraft. As the Germans moved forward from one airfield to the next they began to have trouble replenishing aircraft, fuel and munitions. To add to the problems the hitherto smooth liaison with the infantry and artillery began to break down due to the complexity of the situation.

Yet Manfred von Richthofen and the men of Jagdgeschwader 1 were getting into their stride. For the old master it must have seemed almost like old times – he was now 25 years old but had lived a lifetime in the dangerous skies of the Western Front. On 26 March he shot down his sixty-ninth and seventieth victims.

> With five gentlemen of Jasta 11 at a low altitude, I encountered, with Leutnant Udet, a Sopwith single-seater at the front. At first my opponent tried to escape me by skilful flying. From an aeroplane's length I shot him down in flames. The plane disintegrated into pieces during the crash. The fuselage fell into the small forest of Contalmaison. A quarter of an hour after downing the first aeroplane, in precisely the same place, I encountered an RE two-seater, at an altitude of about 700 metres. I went into a dive behind him and shot him down in flames with about 100 rounds from close range. At first the Englishman defended himself with the observer's machine gun. The aeroplane burned in the air until impact. Half an hour later the aeroplane was still burning on the ground.[42]
>
> *Rittmeister Manfred von Richthofen, Jagdgeschwader 1, German Air Service*

For the RFC pilots the strain was beginning to tell on the likes of Lieutenant Stock and his comrades in 54 Squadron who had been flying mission after mission for five seemingly endless days. They were men at the end of their tether: they would soon have to be rested or one way or another they would be put out of action.

> Lieutenant Crowden and myself had reached such a condition that a meal had lost all of its former pleasure and we merely ate because we had to, a cup of tea and a piece of bread was all I took for a breakfast. The strain of ground strafing was beginning to tell on us; the only thing I ever looked

forward to on returning from a 'job' was a cigarette.[43] *Lieutenant Ewart Stock, 54 Squadron*

Everything they did seemed to have become a macabre, almost unreal routine. Their tired minds clung to this, as well they might.

We strapped our helmets on, wound scarves around our necks and fixing goggles on walked to the hangars. The faithful flight sergeant always awaited us with everything in readiness. The only thing he ever said was, 'Good morning, Sir!' as we arrived and, 'Good luck, Sir!' as we prepared to take off.[44] *Lieutenant Ewart Stock, 54 Squadron*

Off they went, knowing full well what lay ahead of them. Even that take-off to possible catastrophe had become routine.

Crowden followed me in the usual position, slightly behind and on my right, when we took off; we had flown thus for so many times now that we were able to keep together in the thick of machine gun fire from the ground.[45] *Lieutenant Ewart Stock, 54 Squadron*

By this time it was becoming apparent that for many of the scout pilots repeated ground-strafing missions were deeply unpopular. Major B. E. Smithies commanding 64 Squadron had given some thought as to why his men were reluctant.

Low flying in strongly protected areas is unpopular with scout pilots. This is only to a small extent due to the risk of machine gun fire from the ground; it is partially attributable to the inability to defend oneself from attack from enemy aircraft above. The real objection arises from the personal factor. If a pilot can shoot down several enemy aircraft observed to crash, he gets personal credit and possibly a decoration. If he does equally or more valuable work for a month by shooting up transport vehicles, troops or aeroplane sheds, his feats tend to become included in the general results of the flight or squadron with which he is working. The squadron may get a chance word of congratulation on its performance; the individual has no confirmed and positive result to show. This 'individualism' is not talked about; it may

> be petty, unmilitary and regrettable, but it exists.[46] *Major B. E. Smithies, 64 Squadron*

On the night of 26 March, 54 Squadron were given at least a little recognition from 'above' in appreciation of the work they were doing and an indication of just how important it was considered by higher authorities.

> General 'C' congratulated us on our work during the last few days and by means of a pocket flashlight and map explained to us the seriousness of the situation on our front. We were to do all we could to harass the enemy on the Bray–Corbie road the next morning. The General said, 'Good night!' and drove off in his car – probably to some other squadron.[47] *Lieutenant Ewart Stock, 54 Squadron*

That same night the French Chief of General Staff General Ferdinand Foch was appointed as Commander-in-Chief of the combined French and British Armies on the Western Front. The origins of the appointment lay in Haig's attempts to get agreement for a combined Anglo-French response. His intention was that Third Army should fall back pivoting on its left flank; meanwhile all available British reinforcements would gather in the Amiens area ready for a counter-attack. But Haig needed the French Commander-in-Chief General Henri-Philippe Pétain to cooperate by also concentrating a French Army in the area. Yet Pétain had been less than forthcoming. He was prepared to cooperate in assembling the troops under General Marie Fayolle but expressly reserved the right for them to fall back covering Paris if all did not go well. Haig was not unnaturally appalled: such a retreat would open up a gap between the British and French and defeat in detail would become a real possibility. As a result immediate measures were taken. The British Minister of War, Lord Milner, and General Sir Henry Wilson, the Chief of Imperial General Staff, came out to France where a conference was organized at Doullens between them and the senior French politicians and generals. What was agreed would have been sacrilege to Haig at any other time: the preservation of Amiens was agreed as the priority but the strategic direction of military operations was to be handed to Foch. For the rest of the war he would coordinate the action of all the Allied armies on the Western Front.

For the men in the field this was all a million miles away. On 27 March Lieutenant Stock and 54 Squadron were once again flung back into action as they carried out an offensive patrol commanded by the 'C' Flight Commander, Captain Francis Kitto. This patrol marked a return to their more conventional scout role, once more searching the skies assiduously for their enemies.

> We were directly above the river flying eastwards with loaded guns and eyes for ever on the alert. As the Somme reached Peronne it makes a sharp turn to the south towards Ham; it was here that we first spotted a formation of Hun scouts. They were under us and flying south above the river. As far as I could see they were Pfalz and seemed to be in a formation of eight machines. Our leader went down directly in a dive and the rest of us followed him. I turned as we dived, it being my job to watch the rear of the formation, and was surprised to find yet another formation of Huns of the same type making for us.[48] *Lieutenant Ewart Stock, 54 Squadron*

This was a tricky situation, for the second body of Pfalzs were still above them and it was obvious that Captain Kitto, their patrol leader, was unaware of the threat lurking behind them.

> The only thing to be done was to fire a burst over the leader's machine to attract his attention. We were diving by now at about 170mph and every moment saw the rear formation of Huns nearer. So I fired accordingly and turned to avoid the foremost Hun who no doubt was about to fire. I met the Hun nose to nose at a distance of about 200 yards. As I approached him I could see him looking first to one side and then the other in hesitation as to which side to pass me. I waited until I was almost upon him, a matter of a few seconds, and zoomed up over his top plane and turned sharply round to keep my leader in sight. Needless to say the Hun turned too in order to keep me off his tail. Then we turned round and round, each trying to make a sharper turn than his adversary to gain the most advantageous position. But the Hun did the wrong thing, a movement which in aerial fighting is oft-times fatal. He changed, or attempted to change, from left-hand circuits to right, that giving me my opportunity and I let him have it.

I was quite close to him, since my machine which was fitted with a rotary engine, was able to make a sharper turn than him and I had been able to catch him up as we were circling. He did not need much, about thirty or forty rounds and he went down in a steep nose-dive and burst into flames a few hundred feet below me. A glorious sight at the time, since one does not realise that a human being like myself is within; for after all as far as war is concerned it is merely a 'mechanical bird'. I looked around after watching the Hun dropping in flaming pieces earthwards, to find that I was completely alone except for a solitary Camel.[49] *Lieutenant Ewart Stock, 54 Squadron*

In the Third Army sector the Germans had managed to enter the town of Albert on the night of 26 March. After this symbolic capture, with its 'Hanging Virgin' still suspended, there was some intensive fighting in the mangled ruins. This certainly came as a surprise to Fritz Nagel and his anti-aircraft gun crew, who were assigned to move forward and help protect the newly captured Albert. They found the battle was still raging in the suburbs and indeed used their 77mm gun to help destroy an Australian machine-gun post.

I saw explosions in front of us while we drove along one of the side-streets, and I wondered where they came from. I did not believe at all that they were aimed at us. Then the man behind me touched my shoulder, drawing my attention to an explosion behind us. The dust was still settling. Looking up, several Bristol double-deckers carrying two men and two machine guns could be seen milling around over our heads, looking enormously big as they flew no more than 100 feet above us. I still was not certain whether they were after us or some other target.[50] *Leutnant Fritz Nagel, Nr 82 K-Flak*

As the bombs fell around them it became obvious that one way or another they were a target and they stopped and dropped into action.

After blowing, 'man the gun!' on my whistle, the crew jumped on the truck under orders to set shrapnel at point-blank range, maximum elevation, straight up, load and wait for my signal for rapid fire. I was glad to have such a fine crew. They understood perfectly. When I saw the wings of the

Bristols coming over the rooftops to my left, we blasted away so fast I thought the whole gun might topple over. Within seconds I saw one plane hit, coming down squarely as if it would fall on top of us.[51] *Leutnant Fritz Nagel, Nr 82 K-Flak*

Over the next few days the mobile anti-aircraft batteries such as that manned by Fritz Nagel would indeed provide an unpleasant surprise for the unwary British aircraft accustomed to flying over Albert with impunity.

Went further north towards Albert. 'Archie' evidently watched our unsuspecting approach and carefully waited for us. Had not thought of an 'Archie' battery being up so quickly. Had nearly got over Albert when he put up a fearful burst at us. The first one did all the damage. It was as near a direct hit as possible. Blew about a dozen large holes in the tail and fuselage, shot the main spar of the lower plane through and sprinkled the whole machine liberally with small holes. The observer's luck was dead in as a chunk went right through his seat while he was standing up and missed him by a fraction. The machine went right out of control with the explosion and I thought the tail had gone. However I soon got control again, found she was alright and proceeded to go home very carefully. The machine was so badly damaged that it was written off.[52] *Second Lieutenant William Butler, 8 Squadron*

Meanwhile, on 27 March, Richthofen was on patrol above Albert with the pilots of Jasta 11, including a newcomer to their ranks, Leutnant Ernst Udet, who had just shot down an RE8. They then sighted a group of low-flying Sopwith Camels.

Richthofen set the nose of his red Fokker towards the ground and dived, with the rest of us following close on his tail. The Sopwiths scattered like chicks from a hawk, but one of them was too late – the one at the end of the Rittmeister's sights. It happened so quickly that one could hardly call it an aerial fight. For a moment I thought that the Rittmeister would ram him, so short was the space that separated them. I estimated it at 30 feet at the most. Suddenly the nose of the Sopwith tilted downwards, and a cloud of white smoke shot from the exhaust. The ill-fated machine crashed in a field close to the road, and burst into flames.[53] *Leutnant Ernst Udet, Jasta 11, Jagdgeschwader 1*

Then something new. The aces of Jasta 11 risked everything in ground strafing a column of British guns and marching troops on the road below them. And they were led by the greatest of them all.

Richthofen continued to dive until he was close above the Roman road. Tearing along at a height of about 30 feet above the ground, he peppered the marching troops with his two guns. We followed close behind him and copied his example. The troops below us seemed to have been lamed with horror, and apart from the few men who took cover in the ditch at the roadside, hardly anyone returned our fire. On reaching the end of the road, the Rittmeister turned and again fired at the column. We could now observe the effect of our first assault: bolting horses and stranded guns blocked the road, bringing the column to a complete standstill. This time our fire was returned. Infantrymen stood, with rifles pressed against their cheeks, and fired as we passed over them. Machine guns posted in the roadside ditches fired viciously at us as we flew overhead. Yet, despite the fact that his wings were riddled with bullets, the Rittrneister still continued to fly just as low as before. We followed in close formation behind him, firing burst after burst from our Spandaus. The whole flight was like a united body, obeying a single will. And that was how it should have been.[54] *Leutnant Ernst Udet, Jasta 11, Jagdgeschwader 1*

But on the ground the German advance on Third Army north of the Somme was definitely beginning to grind to a halt. It was at this point that Ludendorff changed his tactical direction.

The Seventeenth Army was already exhausted; it had lost too heavily on the 21st and 22nd, apparently because it had fought in too dense formation. The Second Army was fresher, but was already complaining of the old shell holes. It could get no further than Albert. Its left wing had been more delayed by having to cross the Somme than by the enemy. The Eighteenth Army was still full of fight and confidence. Soon the enemy formed a new front north of the Somme, which was sure to be difficult to overcome. In the direction of Amiens the enemy's resistance seemed weaker. The original idea of the battle had to be modified, and the main weight of the attack vigorously directed at that point.[55] *General Erich Ludendorff, General Headquarters, Imperial German Army*

He still hoped to break right through to attain the Holy Grail of open warfare. The left wing of his Second Army was reinforced and it and the Eighteenth Army began to drive on towards the perceived point of Allied weakness at Amiens. But as we have seen, the British and French Armies were slowly beginning to work as a team under the direction of Foch.

Meanwhile the RFC had also now completed its reorganization and on the single day of 27 March they managed to fire a lacerating 313,000 machine-gun rounds while also dropping 50 tons of bombs on the advancing German Army. General Herman von Kuhl, the Chief of Staff at the Crown Prince Rupprecht Army Group Headquarters, claimed that, 'The very disagreeable enemy air activity . . . had caused about one half of all casualties suffered.'[56] Although this seems an exaggeration it certainly showed that the effect on morale of the ground strafing was matching and exacerbating the actual damage caused.

By this time both the RFC and the German Air Service were approaching exhaustion, given the frenetic nature of the fighting. Captain Gwilym Lewis had returned from leave to find his beloved 40 Squadron had fallen to pieces.

Tilney had broken up diving on a Hun. Tipton got a bullet through the abdomen and died a few days later, like the hero he was. I never expect again to see a fellow lying halfway between life and death, knowing it, and yet showing such wonderful pluck. And a fellow called Foster has never been seen or heard of since. While I was on leave Wade was killed, and Herbert wounded. Since then Smith and I had a crash just alongside one another, and his machine burst into flames, and by a miracle he got off with a slightly burnt face. I arrived back to find myself in command of the squadron, my flight, and also Napier's, which was a sort of training show for half a dozen new pilots. From that Sunday to this I seem to have lived in the air.[57] *Captain Gwilym Lewis, 40 Squadron*

Their aircraft had reached the limits of mechanical endurance, at which point they duly began to fail with catastrophic effects. Casualties had thinned the ranks, and the pilots were at the end of their tethers, physically and mentally exhausted. Lieutenant Stock certainly had other priorities on his mind when he awoke on the morning of 28 March. He was utterly delighted to find that the weather was 'dud' and their first patrol was cancelled.

> Rain at last! I turned in my bed at 7.30am to find our batman standing at the side of my bed balancing two large cups of tea on a battered piece of boarding from a petrol box which served as a tray. 'Dud, Sir!' he whispered as he handed me a cup.[58] *Lieutenant Ewart Stock, 54 Squadron*

His relief was to be short-lived indeed. There was to be a second rude awakening for Stock as he and the rest of 54 Squadron were ordered to fly whatever the weather conditions by their Wing Headquarters. It might be a useless sacrifice but the battle was in the balance and anything that the RFC could achieve might make all the difference.

> To send us up in the driving rain and low clouds was before unheard of. We were compelled to fly very low owing to the clouds which were only at 500 feet. Several times I looked over the side of my machine in order to pick up familiar landmarks to find that the rain cut my face and blinded me for a few seconds. The first warning I had of being near the line was a big thud directly underneath me 'bumping' my machine several feet. We were over a battery of 60pdrs apparently firing towards the river as hard as they could go. We were flying at about 100 feet so were able to see what was going on a distance of a mile or so around us. The rain still poured down with the clouds about 200 feet so we did not expect to see any Hun machines about that morning. The Hun was attacking across the river at Mericourt and Cerisy apparently trying to outflank our troops on the Amiens road about 4 miles south. Everywhere was a mass of smoke and flame of 60pdrs and heavies of all kinds all firing on Mericourt and Cerisy. We reached these villages on the river in a few seconds and were welcomed with a bombardment of machine guns, flaming onions and field guns. I have never experienced such a volume of din above the sound of my engine before. My outer struts were all splintered before I had reached the river. I lost sight

of Crowden almost immediately in the rain and mist. I throttled my engine down and still turning about as much as possible – to fly straight would be fatal – came down to about 100 feet. I at once noticed what all the din was about; the large stone bridge over the river at Cerisy was covered in a mass of Huns edging their way across while our guns pounded them for all they were worth. The side of the road on the south of the river was lined with our men firing hard on the north bank. The Bosche had already managed to cross the bridge but not in very great numbers. They had lined the bank and were apparently bringing machine guns into action. It was obvious to us that the Hun was making a determined attempt to cross the river and so outflank Villers Bretonneux, the last village before Amiens.[59] *Lieutenant Ewart Stock, 54 Squadron*

As they dived again and again into action the Sopwiths suffered the inevitable results of attacking such a hornets' nest. What their efforts achieved in the context of the wider battle it is difficult to say, but they had certainly given everything they could in the common cause.

On looking back I think that this day, 28 March, was perhaps worse than all the others during the push. We lost more in our squadron than any other single day. Our machines by the evening were in an awful state, bullet holes everywhere. We came back from the firing lines several times utterly 'done' and caring naught for anything or anyone to find the CO awaiting us or perhaps about to take off in his own to go and trench strafe. Some poor fellows came back with half an arm or leg and others not at all. Crowden looked upon these gruesome sights with perfect calm, in fact it was partly through his cheerfulness that we managed to carry on together, when nearly everyone else was either wounded or missing.[60] *Lieutenant Ewart Stock, 54 Squadron*

In essence 54 Squadron was finished, at least for the time being, but they had done their job magnificently, just one of many squadrons brought to the brink of extinction in trying to stem the German advance.

The Allied line had finally coalesced beneath them on a line that stretched from just behind Albert through to Villers-Bretonneux. The critical moment had come and gone. In a hugely symbolic gesture, Gough and his staff were immediately removed from the command of Fifth Army, which temporarily ceased to exist. The military authorities judged Gough harshly for his conduct of operations in March 1918; historians have been more understanding. From the night of 27 March Fifth Army's place was taken by Fourth Army which was removed from reserve and reconstituted under General Sir Henry Rawlinson to take over the area south of the river Somme.

On 28 March the Germans had launched a further attack under Operation Mars when nine of their divisions attacked four divisions of General Byng's Third Army positions north of the Scarpe river. They used the same tactics but this time they found the British infantry and artillery were well dug in and ready for them. There was no fog to blind the machine gunners and artillery observers, and the result was a disaster for the Germans. They made next to no progress and suffered severe casualties. This defeat has been largely forgotten as it does not fit in with the popular image of the unstoppable German '*über* tactics'. Operation Mars was stillborn and the attention switched once again to the dying embers of Operation Michael. For the next few days the Germans hammered on trying to capture Villers-Bretonneux. The fighting was hard, often desperate, but the line held just firm enough. From the air Lieutenant G. M. Knocker could see just how thinned out the khaki line had become.

> I was sent out to locate our front line. The ground between the St. Quentin road and the Somme presented a remarkable spectacle. The British front line consisted of a line of men holding a hedge; then it ran across an open field upon which lay a single line of troops in extended order; then it consisted of some troops lining a sunken road from which another road forked east to the Bois de Vaire. The enemy was lining the road separated from our troops by 100 yards of open grass field. Behind our lines were parties furiously digging rifle pits, stretcher-bearers, riderless horses galloping about and 1,000 yards or less in the rear, field gun batteries in the open firing with open sights. Anti-aircraft guns mounted on lorries were also being used as field guns. Our shrapnel was bursting over the Bois de Vaire while to the south Villers-Bretonneux was burning fiercely. The clouds

were at 1,000 feet but there must have been fully thirty of our aircraft flying in the narrow strip between the road and the Somme.[61] ***Lieutenant G. M. Knocker, 65 Squadron***

On 5 April the exhausted Germans admitted they had failed to break through. Their entire offensive had been a failure judged on its own terms. They had sought to rip open the British line and roll it up to the north. They had failed to maintain this aim and were distracted into a thrust towards Amiens in an effort to maximize ground gained and in an effort to separate the British from their French allies. But the ground won had no real tactical value; certainly there were no strategic goals to be gained. In the end they had created a huge, ungainly salient some 40 useless miles deep and consisting of a statistically impressive 1,200 square miles. Most of it was a desolate wasteland they themselves had left without a second thought when they fell back to the Hindenburg Line in March 1917. The British had retreated in disarray under the phenomenal pressure, teetering on the edge of dissolution, but in the end they had maintained their links with the armies on either side. The Germans had inflicted 255,000 casualties on the Allies, who had also lost over 400 aircraft, 1,300 guns, 200 tanks and 2,000 or so machine guns. Yet the Allied war machine was in unsurpassable flow in 1918. Over the next month the overall number of aircraft and pilots deployed would actually increase to pre-offensive levels, there were nearly 2,000 replacement guns on their way, tank production had reached 100 a month and machine guns were pouring out at a rate of 2,500 a week. The Germans had lost some 239,000 men themselves; but more importantly for both sides the Allied front was still unbroken and the war went on.

There is no doubt that both the RFC and the German Air Service had been through a trial that had pushed them to the limits. But in the end the Germans had simply been outnumbered and slowly the British had gained the air superiority that allowed them to make a real difference to the battle that really mattered below them. They may not have caused the level of ground casualties attributed to them but the Germans *thought* they had and that was what counted. Yet another piece of the 'all-arms battle' jigsaw had fallen into place. Ground strafing had thoroughly come of age, and it was evident that a well-aimed burst of machine-gun fire coupled with a scattering of 25-pound Cooper bombs could kill and maim more than any ace could manage in a whole year. The nature of air warfare had changed for good.

Chapter 6

The Battle for Flanders

That day, 5 April, brought a natural end to the great Operation Michael offensive – the Kaiserschlacht. Yet the Allies were still under an enormous strain, for although the German threat had been held at bay for the moment it had not yet been dissipated. The strategic situation had not greatly changed and although the Germans were fast running out of time they had plenty left up their sleeve in the short term. One of the advantages of the planning process that had preceded 21 March was that full-scale plans and preparations had been drawn up for alternative offensives up and down the front which could still be triggered into action with minimal delay. The German losses had been heavy, but the loss of troops had not yet become crippling; their morale held firm. The Americans had not arrived and the British and French were short of men. In the air they had held the ring and performed valiantly but the front-line pilots were suffering ever increasing strain as the toll of the fighting showed not only in the lengthening casualty list but also in the shattered nerves and exhaustion of those who remained. The squadrons at the front line of the battle were stretched to their very limits.

Yet it was at the height of the battle that the RFC and RNAS had to suffer a root and branch reorganization that turned them upside down and inside out, adding a whole new layer of stress through sheer irritation. The origins of these changes lay right back in June 1917 when the German Gotha bombers had bombed London,* the very heart of the British Empire, in broad daylight, and a series of events had been set in chain that would rock the flying services to their very foundations. As a result of the general hue and cry a public enquiry

* See Chapter 12: Bombers over Germany.

had been established to consider not only the question of the air defence of Britain, but also the organization of the air services and the general direction of air operations. The enquiry was headed by the South African soldier-politician Lieutenant General Jan Christian Smuts. After a hasty deliberation they presented their findings to the War Cabinet in August 1917. These were somewhat drastic in their nature and based on a 'visionary' view of the powers of aerial bombing that looked far to the future – well beyond the reality of the situation in 1917 or 1918. Smuts considered that aircraft would soon be the prime means of waging war, eclipsing the forces of land and sea. He wished to create a new force, The Independent Air Force, to carry out strategic bombing of the German industrial heartlands. He believed that it had to be independent to ensure that its operations were not sublimated to the routine operations demanded by the army. He also believed that it could be equipped using the 'Surplus Aircraft Fleet' that was faithfully promised by civilian ministers responsible for aircraft production. At the same time he proposed that the existing air services – the Royal Flying Corps and the Royal Naval Air Service – should be amalgamated to create one air force bound together with one command system, a single supply system and under the overall control of an air board and staff.

This was a controversial plan that somehow seemed to leapfrog all the many obstacles placed in front of it in 1917. The very idea of joining together two disparate services, with different cultures, uniforms, ranks and operational practices, was startling indeed. It certainly caused Major General Sir Hugh Trenchard, then commanding the RFC on the Western Front, a great deal of anguish.

> **I thought that if anything were done at that time to weaken the Western Front, the war would be lost and there would be no air service, united or divided. I wanted to unify it, but later on at a more suitable opportunity.**[1]
> ***Major General Hugh Trenchard, Headquarters, RFC***

He was firmly backed up by his ultimate commander, Field Marshal Sir Douglas Haig, who had a keen appreciation of the vital role of the RFC and had appreciated his sound working relationship with Trenchard.

Trenchard is much perturbed as to the result of this new departure just at a time when the Flying Corps was beginning to feel that it had become an important part of the army. The best solution would be to have one Minister of Defence with the three offices under him, viz: Admiralty, War Office, Air.[2]

Field Marshal Sir Douglas Haig, Headquarters, BEF

Here were two peas in a pod; both hard practical men utterly committed to fighting and winning the war against their prime enemy – the Germans on the Western Front. Trenchard's idea of a future union was simple: that the Royal Naval Air Service should be swallowed whole and become part of the Royal Flying Corps. Neither he nor Haig believed in the easy 'paper' promises of a 'fleet' of surplus aircraft which underpinned the creation of the Independent Air Force. The RFC still had not reached the levels of squadrons, aircraft and men agreed back in 1916.

Somehow their objections failed to make headway. Preoccupied as they were with the grinding battles on the Western Front in late 1917, their gritty arguments did not carry sufficient weight with a War Cabinet in London that had already made up its collective mind. The proposals were duly approved and set under way with Smuts himself placed in charge of the interim Air Organization Committee. Parliamentary approval for the Air Force Bill encapsulating his schemes was duly received on 29 November 1917. As a result the Air Council was created in January 1918; the question then was who would take up the post of Chief of the Air Staff? Trenchard wanted to stay in France, Haig wanted him to stay, but who else was there for such a prestigious post? The other main candidate was Major General Sir David Henderson who had been the first commander of the RFC in the field back in 1914–15. But within the vastly expanded RFC, Henderson seemed a figure from the past and furthermore was tainted by his close links with Smuts and advocacy of strategic bombing. Despite it all, Trenchard was duly knighted, appointed as Chief of the Air Staff and, as we have seen, was replaced by Major General Sir John Salmond as commander on the Western Front. The new force was given the name of the Royal Air Force (RAF) and, awe-inspiringly to the modern mind, the date chosen for its creation, with a complete lack of self-awareness, was to be 1 April 1918 – 'All Fools' Day itself.

The threat posed by the German offensives was irrelevant to the process of imposing a complete reorganization of the British air services against the wishes of almost everyone actively involved on the Western Front. Just at the very moment when their every sinew should have been strained in effort against the German advance on Amiens the RFC and RNAS squadrons were required to scrap their hard-won independence and meld together seamlessly, ignoring all their previous differences. It was a ludicrous distraction. At a trivial level all the former RNAS squadrons had 200 added to their number: thus for instance 3 (Naval) Squadron, RNAS, became 203 Squadron, RAF. If this was all it would not have mattered greatly but there was a far greater level of disruption that was certainly not appreciated in the various officers' messes up and down the Western Front.

> All that happened was a complete hotchpotch. They were trying to join together two disparate forces. The Navy tradition was very firmly embedded and the Army had a regimental tradition. The ex-RNAS rating would take off his hat to receive his pay; the Army man would keep his on. Where the ex-RNAS man would double across the parade ground the ex-RFC man would march across it. There were all sorts of incongruities of this nature. Of course there was no uniform to distinguish them as a complete corporate force. We still wore RNAS uniforms – they still wore the old maternity jacket. The biggest possible pot mess that I ever came across, absolutely terrible. In the officers' mess ex-naval squadrons still sat down to toast 'The King' whereas the Army people got up – where you got a combination in one mess it was absolutely ludicrous – 'Fred Karno's Army' – nothing else! Whoever thought that Jan Smuts was the fount of all knowledge in recommending this beats me![3] *Pilot Officer Thomas Thomson, 217 Squadron*

There is considerable justification for Thomson's skepticism, for although the two services had been united in name, the powerful 'Senior Service' RNAS tradition would linger long. Indeed it would later be formally rekindled when the incompatibility of role and function was generally recognized with the formation of the Fleet Air Arm in the post-war years.

To some it was a disgrace that while the men at the front were desperately fighting their corner as best they could against the Germans, back at home the ripples caused by the formation of the RAF continued to rebound around the goldfish bowl that was the newly created Air Council. The Prime Minister David Lloyd George had appointed a newspaper proprietor, Lord Rothermere, to be Air Minister and to the surprise of almost no-one he immediately fell out with his gruff Chief of Staff. Trenchard was supremely loyal to Douglas Haig and was appalled both by the simplistic air policies and the rampant political intrigues against his old chief that he found polluting the air back in London. Both he and Rothermere were natural autocrats, accustomed to their own way and furious when thwarted. It could not go on and on 19 March, two days before Ludendorff struck on the Somme, Trenchard had resigned in a fit of pique. Persuaded to resume his duties during the crisis he eventually was to stand down on 13 April. Rothermere's triumph would be stillborn; he could not withstand the repercussions of Trenchard's departure and would himself resign on 25 April. This was a disastrous blow to the reputation of the Air Council both at home and at the front.

> I wonder what damned political intrigue is behind Trenchard's resignation. It's bound to make an enormous impression out here. 'Boom', as he is nicknamed, has been the life and soul of the RFC since its inception. We all know him to be, doubtless, a hard taskmaster, but a 'man' strong and resolute. With his whole heart wrapped up in the Air Service. To the majority it is nothing less than a tragedy. He and he alone is responsible for our magnificent morale and in the Air Service that is the main factor leading to success.[4] *Major Charlie Dixon, 29 Squadron*

In the end the situation calmed down as two far more pragmatic men took the vacant roles. The industrialist technocrat Sir William Weir became the Air Minister while Major-General Sir Frederick Sykes became Chief of Air Staff.

As to the newly constituted RAF, their initial role on the Western Front was to be defined by no less a person than Marshal Ferdinand Foch himself, acting in his capacity as Supreme Commander. He was required to ensure that the French Air Service and the new RAF cooperated fully, driven forward with a common purpose. The continuing urgency of the situation as they awaited the next great German offensive was evident in the way he clearly set out their priorities. They could not waste a scintilla of effort on non-essential targets.

> At the present time, the first duty of fighting aeroplanes is to assist the troops on the ground, by incessant attacks, with bombs and machine guns, on columns, concentrations or bivouacs. Air fighting is not to be sought except so far as is necessary for the fulfilment to this duty.[5] *Marshal Ferdinand Foch, Allied Forces*

This firmly placed the aces in their place. The 'real' work in the crisis of the war was the mass machine gunning and bombing of German troops wherever they might be found. The stiletto work of the aces with their clever stalking and pinpoint accuracy to down German aircraft was simply irrelevant in contrast to the cruder but vital mass slaughter that the generals now required from their pilots.

The bombers were also firmly directed as to their primary function. It had been apparent for a while that spraying bombs at a multiplicity of targets achieved very little in terms of long-term damage. With the size of bombs then available an awful lot of aircraft needed to concentrate on very few objectives if any real long-term damage was to be achieved by anything other than a lucky hit.

> The *essential* condition of success is the concentration of *every resource* of the British and French bombing formations on such few of the *most important* of the enemy's railway junctions as it may be possible to put out of action with certainty, and keep out of action. Effort should not be dispersed against a large number of targets.[6] *Marshal Foch, Supreme Commander, Allied Forces*

WHILE the British continued to deal with the fallout of their ill-timed reorganization of their air forces into the RAF, the Germans were ready to launch their next offensive. After the failure of Operations Michael and Mars to win the war the German High Command looked elsewhere for a decisive success. General Erich Ludendorff duly selected the Lys valley and the frontline sector between Armentières and La Bassée as the next arena of battle to be codenamed Operation

Georgette (as a slight diminutive of the previously planned Operation George) and this, in essence, was the assault in Flanders that Field Marshal Sir Douglas Haig had always feared. The Channel ports of Dunkirk and Calais lay just a few miles behind the front line and these were the conduits through which everything flowed. All the BEF infrastructure of communications, bases, depots, training areas and hospitals was centred on these ports and it was emphatically *not* just a matter of switching to different French ports. Their loss would undoubtedly have thrown the entire BEF into complete chaos to such an extent that it was questionable whether it would be able to continue the war. Nearer to hand for the Germans was the vital rail junction of Hazebrouck. Ludendorff planned to instigate an attack by his Sixth Army, striking hard at the junction between the British Second and First Armies. Ludendorff was well aware that, despite Haig's attempts to maintain the number and strength of the divisions holding the line in Flanders, nonetheless the strain imposed in resisting the juggernaut that was Operation Michael had been such that of the fifty-eight divisions available on the Western Front no fewer than forty-six had already been through the mill in 1918. Under the pressure the line had been weakened in the north and the Lys valley was particularly weakly held, with a long section of line under the somewhat shaky tenure of a Portuguese division. The date selected for Operation Georgette was 9 April 1918.

The German reconnaissance aircraft were soon active above the Flanders fields taking photographs and logging the exact nature and layout of the defensive positions: the trenches, the fortified strongpoints, the machine-gun posts, the headquarters, the all-important artillery batteries. As ever these photographs would be the raw 'tools' of the staff officers of the German Sixth Army.

During preparations for our infantry's assault we were ordered to make a reconnaissance of the area. Once at the scene, we saw a horrible and alarming sight. All around the meadows outside the city were shell holes filled to the brim with water. Of Ypres itself, however, there was nothing to be seen; the smoke of the shell hits and the fires in the city covered the whole region with a thick fog-like cloak, which every shell hit that we saw tore apart with a circular burst of air that then immediately closed around itself again. As we flew through the continually thundering rounds of our artillery, for the first time I asked myself, as well I might: if we were hit how could we survive after a crash in this morass of shell holes?[7] *Leutnant Fritz Kampfenkel, Flieger Abteilung (A) 240, Imperial German Air Force*

The British were aware that something was brewing, but once again it was difficult to determine exactly where and when the axe would fall. The Germans were helped in their preparations by the unseasonable dryness of the weather and as they began the final countdown it was apparent that some of the blanket secrecy and cautious build-up that marked the previous assaults were being sacrificed for speed. Captain Robert Archer, a very experienced, if somewhat pompous, artillery observation officer with 42 Squadron, noticed that there was an unusual degree of German activity behind the lines as he carried out an evening counter-battery mission on 7 April.

I became aware that something was on. The first sign I saw was railway activity at Don station. It was a longish way behind the lines, out of range of even our longest range guns, or I would have opened onto it. But during the three-and-a-bit hours of our flight in daylight, I had made a list of twenty-four train timings at Don station. This includes arrivals and departures. Angus independently observed much the same. A second sign I saw was the outcome of some fire which I called for. When ranging a battery on some close flashes I got a round into a hedge some distance behind my flashes, which lit a fire obviously due to burning propellant. Now when propellant burns it makes the cartridge cases, if there were any, instantly hot and the heat of the metal colours the flames with the appropriate spectrum colours. Now I have often hit enemy ammunition but this was the only occasion when I saw no such colours, and I concluded that the piece whose ammunition we had hit was a breech-loader and not a quick firer. I did not know what their smallest BLs were, but I did know that the 21 centimetre (8.2 inch) howitzer was a QF. Now I had found a BL battery pushed up too close to be of use in the present position of the line. He must be lying silent in order to support the later stages of an advance. That at least was my reading of the signs.[8] *Captain Robert Archer, 42 Squadron*

By 8 April, thanks to the weight of reports like this, the British High Command was fully aware of what was coming; the question was whether it could withstand the onslaught with the forces at its disposal.

The Germans were using the same tactical framework that had been so successful in the first assault on 21 March and, of course, which had so signally failed at Arras. The Sixth Army had seventeen divisions available to go over the top on the Lys and it was planned to launch a coordinated follow-up assault from their Fourth Army a day later around Ypres. The British had just four divisions with two more in reserve in the Lys sector.

The Germans were lucky with the weather once again. When Operation Georgette began the battlefield was blanketed in dense fog, with even worse visibility conditions than had prevailed on the Somme. The barrage commenced at 04.15 and the first blow fell at 08.45 on 9 April on the XI Corps of First Army. The inexperienced Portuguese division holding the line in the north of the Aubers sector broke and fled as the field-grey masses emerged from the swirling mists not 50 yards away. As the front began to fold the Germans broke through, facing nothing but the already badly battered 50th and 51st Divisions. Before anyone knew what was happening they were across the Lys river and had reached Estaires, an advance of just under 4 miles all along the 10-mile front.

In the first instance there was little the RAF could do as the weather conditions were completely unsuitable for flying and most of the squadrons found themselves grounded. The mists endured deep into the day and although by then patchy or localized in effect, they still thwarted many squadrons' courageous attempts to get into action.

> In the afternoon we had a great alarm. News came through that the Bosche had broken through and taken Armentières and all machines were got out, four bombs on each. Every pilot had to stand by his machine ready for instant flight. It was arranged that 'B' Flight should leave the ground first and fly down to Armentières sector and drop bombs on the Huns and fire from about 500 feet all our ammunition on advancing troops. Everyone had fearful wind up. After half-an-hour's suspense I went up on a weather test. I found clouds at 500 feet and couldn't see the ground and could only see

the ground immediately underneath. As a result nobody went up.[9] *Second Lieutenant Henry Blundell, 21 Squadron*

Once again, as on the Somme, the speed of the advance meant that within just a few hours the British gun batteries were forced to pull back or be overrun. Captain Archer found that in his sector the visibility was better, but by then it was too late.

I did my own first flight after lunch, which was an error of judgement. Many of the batteries were on the move by then, and that reduced my effect. I alone in the squadron had experience of handling several batteries at once, therefore I should have gone up when there were plenty to handle. When I did fly, I took Angus. Visibility was again very bad, and I had to sit down on the enemy side lower and longer than I had ever done before. I saw a lot and did a fair amount of shooting. For the first time in the war I heard the noise of ground musketry loudly throughout the flight over the noise of the engine, and a good deal of it appears to have been aimed at the machine, as when I landed I found a great deal of damage by rifle and machine gun fire. It was quite unfit to fly.[10] *Captain Robert Archer, 42 Squadron*

As the Germans broke through, several of the RAF airfields close to the front line came under imminent threat in a situation severely complicated by the local weather fluctuations. Most were swiftly evacuated but all eighteen Sopwith Camels of 208 Squadron based at the La Gorgue airfield found themselves trapped in near farcical circumstances.

About 4.00am on the morning of the 9th we were aroused by the sound of very heavy gun fire which increased in intensity towards dawn. There was considerable hostile shelling of Merville and La Gorgue and the surrounding districts. A large number of French civilians were passing west through our camp, followed by considerable quantities of Portuguese troops in open disorder without either rifles or equipment and apparently unofficered. By about 7 o'clock the shelling became very intense, but owing to the fog it was practically impossible to ascertain definitely where the shells were falling. I gave orders to have the machines removed from the hangars and spread out over the aerodrome in case of a concentrated shelling of the hangars.[11] *Major Chris Draper, 208 Squadron*

Meanwhile the officers and men packed up their belongings in case the evacuation of La Gorgue became essential. Already German shells were falling around them, but the Headquarters of XV Corps could only inform them that the Germans had attacked and they discovered from a despatch rider that the Germans were already in Laventie.

The General commanding XV Corps asked me if I could carry out a reconnaissance, but I had to definitely refuse, it being quite impossible to see across the aerodrome through the fog. The General did not wish me to leave La Gorgue but said if it was to save the machines from shell fire we could fly them away. I replied it was quite impossible to fly at all.[12] *Major Chris Draper, 208 Squadron*

The telephone line to the Headquarters of XV Corps then broke down and Draper was left to his own devices. The underlying situation as he saw it was that aircraft were relatively plentiful but pilots took months of hard graft to train. Although his men were willing to risk taking off into the murk, Draper finally took the plunge.

After careful deliberations with my flight commanders I decided that I was not justified in risking personnel by flying away in the fog, though the majority volunteered to try. We then collected the machines in one bunch in the middle of the aerodrome, the idea being for everyone to clear out and leave one officer with a cycle and sidecar to standby until the last moment with orders to destroy the machines if necessary.[13] *Major Chris Draper, 208 Squadron*

As the Germans grew ever closer and the fog kept its clammy grip on the airfield, Draper was forced to make an extremely difficult decision.

The fog was as thick as ever and it was quite impossible to fly. I fully realised the seriousness of the situation but, being unable to communicate with any reliable authority, I had to act on my own. If there had been British troops in the area I should have left the machines for them to destroy, but

I felt it extremely improbable that a panic-stricken crowd of Portuguese troops retiring in open disorder would carry this out, even if they had received orders to do so. The machines were burnt and everyone cleared out by 11.30.[14] *Major Chris Draper, 208 Squadron*

Whatever the rights and wrongs of Draper's decision it should be noted that when the squadron got to Serny airfield they were re-equipped with Camels within forty-eight hours. (Although it should also be noted that the irrepressible and boisterously unrepentant Draper then had the cheek to complain that they were the inferior models with the 130hp Clerget engines.)

On 10 April the German attacks widened as planned when the Fourth Army fell upon the British Second Army entrusted with defending the 'Sacrificial Ground' of the Messines Ridge and Ypres Salient. As one might expect the weather was foggy and low cloud cover prevailed all day. The fighting was desperate all along the front with no quarter given or asked. Among those on ground strafing that morning was Lieutenant Jack Weingarth of 4 Squadron, Australian Flying Corps. It was a brutal business, not for the faint-hearted.

When about 10 miles over the lines we dropped our bombs upon a wood full of Huns from about 200 feet. Then we saw some transports nearby, about twelve horse-wagons; we tore into these, firing our machine guns all the time we were diving on them. It nearly made me sick, killing the horses, but it had to be done. We did not have it all our own way, for there were a lot of Germans about with machine guns and rifles. Just after we cut up the transport one of my mates was hit; he glided down and hit a hedge along a road that he was trying to clear, turned over and crashed. I followed him down, but could see that I could not help him, so I turned back to find the leader, who was then firing into another line of transport, and was pulling up out of the dive when he was shot. He turned over on his back and dived straight into the ground from about 150 feet. You can imagine my feelings: two killed and myself well into German territory, absolutely lost in the thick mist and smoke, which made me keep low. If I kept low they would get me sooner or later, machine guns were chattering all around, besides firing shrapnel at me. I thought I'd never get into the mist; it seemed like two hours but it only took seconds. At last I got into the mist, which was only

500 feet from the ground, and tried to steer by compass, but it was spinning round and round and I could not go straight, Of course, they kept firing at me all the way home, mostly at random. In the mist they can see sometimes, but one cannot see the ground at all; in fact one has to rely on one's instruments to steer. I kept climbing until I got a hazy glimpse of the sun; I got this on my back and kept it there until I thought I was over our side. I nosed down to have a look at the ground, but found that I had drifted over the lines again, and promptly got black 'Archie' at me. I steered west again, and eventually tacked onto some other machines going the right way home. The Bosche threw everything at us except the grand piano; it was worth it though, as we did a lot of damage. I was just about done up when I got home; on an empty stomach too![15] *Lieutenant Jack Weingarth, 4 Squadron, Australian Flying Corps*

Although the Germans once again broke through on 10 April, their advances were not excessive. But the situation remained utterly chaotic and when the much needed French reinforcements began to arrive in the battlefield area their appearance caused considerable additional confusion.

We had a hectic day trying to stem the German advance. Some of the reinforcements were French and they forgot to warn us. I was mystified to see troops whose uniforms I thought were grey, confronting the enemy in the front line. I felt sure that the Portuguese would not do that so presumed that they must be Germans and facing westwards. But I was suspicious and went very low at I estimate 30 feet above the front line and with my goggles off I tumbled to it. It was extreme luck that I had not shot them up.[16] *Captain Robert Archer, 42 Squadron*

Archer had his own firmly held eccentric theories on aerial tactics. His most often expressed belief was that the RE8 was fully capable of taking on and beating any German scouts.

I had my first fight in an RE8. My passenger was Harvey, a Second Lieutenant in the Dorsetshire Regiment. At the time when he drew my attention to the enemy, we were about 3,000 feet and just about over the front line. It was quite an unjustified fight as I had plenty of time to escape without fighting, but I felt annoyed at being disturbed in an interesting battle and attacked, making a serious attempt to get one with my front gun while Harvey took the other on and protected my tail. My attempt to fight the RE8 like an SE5 was not victorious, but at least it was successful, as after an astonishingly short time the enemy abandoned the attempt, and made off. I made a gesture of pursuit, but it was only a gesture as they were at least half as fast again as me. It completely confirmed my view that the RE8 properly fought was equal to two enemy scouts, provided of course that the fight took place within a reasonable distance of friendly territory.[17] *Captain Robert Archer, 42 Squadron*

Emboldened by this relative success he resolved to miss no opportunity to try out more of his unique theories. One cannot help but speculate as to the reactions of his observer had he known what was being planned for him.

It seemed to me that there was a technical surprise that I could bring off. If I could go down in a straight dive with a heavy sideslip, his sights would be put out of action by reason of the fact that my real and apparent direction of flight were different. My passenger's gun however was on a wind vane which would allow for my real direction. There was a hope further that the enemy could mistake me for a beginner and take dangerous liberties with me. The plan had a curious characteristic. I meant to rely on the accuracy of my enemy's aim to make him miss me, therefore the better shot he was the safer I should feel.[18] *Captain Robert Archer, 42 Squadron*

He did not have to wait too long to try his spectacularly risky plan, which relied entirely on meeting a German pilot too inexperienced to have encountered a side-slipping target before. He was flying with Second Lieutenant Green acting as his observer when they were caught a little too far over the German lines by no fewer than five German scouts and with a nasty head-wind to cope with to boot. He had wanted to try his new scheme but this was a little too rigorous a trial for even Archer's optimistic nature.

When they were about 300 yards away I played the innocent and dived straight. As I hoped and expected two stayed up to piquet against

> possible helpers for me, and only three came down on to the attack. When they were still too far away to open fire I put on maximum sideslip and ruddered against it producing a sideslip of at least 70 or 80 feet per second. The rudder disguised my manoeuvre and to my great delight firing one burst, two of the three broke off the fight, leaving the one to administer the *coup de grâce*. Green got going and I watched with interest expecting every second to see my enemy fall. Then his gun stopped. He tried to remedy it but could not.[19] ***Captain Robert Archer, 42 Squadron***

By the end of the action Archer was sure that only luck had saved that German scout; others might ponder his and Green's own good fortune in escaping alive.

On 11 April the Germans had reached the towns of Merville and Nieppe. It was at this point that Captain Archer's considerable expertise in artillery observations, his ability to range the shells from more than one battery exactly onto their intended targets, was called into play.

> Corps Headquarters got an idea that a tank attack was coming between the canal and the Fôret du Nieppe and they ordered that the two bridges that admitted tanks into the sector must be destroyed. They allotted unlimited ammunition to it, 9.2" to one bridge and 8" to the other. I thought them easy targets. I started on the 9.2". The third round was a hit. It cleared the metalling off the road and left the two main girders. I dropped a message, saying that I thought the bridge easily repairable, 'Were Corps satisfied or would they carry on?' Corps were not satisfied. I was therefore left with two girders about 30 feet long and 1 foot wide each to hit, the most hopeless target I have ever tackled. It took a further 429 rounds to break a girder![20] ***Captain Robert Archer, 42 Squadron***

Next day the situation had indeed reached crisis point. Although the British retreat was far more controlled and indeed limited than the debacle suffered by Fifth Army on the Somme, the proximity of the Channel ports meant that there was no more room for error. It was at this point that Haig issued his inspiring 'Backs to the Wall' order to his embattled troops.

> Every position must be held to the last man: there must be no retirement. With our backs to the wall and believing in the justice of our cause each one of us must fight to the end.[21] *Field Marshal Sir Douglas Haig, General Headquarters, BEF*

That such a phlegmatic leader, able to withstand the shock of battle with no outward sign of emotion, should issue such an appeal speaks volumes as to the stress the whole British Army was labouring under. Yet the situation was by no means hopeless. As long as the British flanks could hold firm, then the Germans were essentially driving deeper and deeper into another huge unwieldy salient. But the British line was by no means complete and the German success in infiltrating through the gaps meant further British retreats were required in the desperate effort to maintain the integrity of the porous khaki line. British reinforcements were on their way; would they be in time?

It was the RAF's good fortune that the foggy weather temporarily cleared away for the duration of 12 April and the German movements were consequently laid bare to the British reconnaissance and artillery observation aircraft. As the artillery batteries settled down into new positions and generally sorted themselves out, they were able to open up with a series of increasingly devastating barrages which further slowed the German advance. The scouts flung themselves into ground strafing to considerable effect, concentrating their efforts on stopping the German advance on Hazebrouck and hitting targets in the Merville sector. Among them was Captain Arthur Cobby of 4 Squadron, Australian Flying Corps.

> The short distance we had to fly enabled our sorties to be made much more rapidly than in the previous 'do' and the number of trips we could make in a day naturally increased our hitting power. Again, the order of the day was to get out and back again as quickly as possible and it was ding-dong from before dawn until after dark. Again it was point-blank warfare. It was a case of every time you saw a head you hit it, and there were plenty of heads. Bombs and bullets would create havoc among formations and before they could reform, another relay of machines would arrive and smash them again.[22] *Lieutenant Arthur Cobby, 4 Squadron, Australian Flying Corps*

This was the 'day of days' with more hours flown, more bombs dropped and more photographs taken on the Western Front than on any previous day since the war began. Well over 100,000 machine-gun rounds were fired in ground strafing. Inevitably the German scouts were also active, flying abroad in large formations and diving to prey on the low-flying British aircraft. Once again the tension was ratcheting up.

That day, 12 April, marked the return to the fray of Captain Edward Mannock as a flight commander with 74 Squadron who were to operate for the next couple of months in the Flanders area. Although he had wanted to get back to the front, driven by a sense of duty, there is no doubt that he was still suffering from the nervous debilitation that had built up during his previous tour which had only ended in January 1918. He should have stayed at home to impart his tactical methods to a new generation of scout pilots. Yet it was difficult for the authorities to take the long-term view when the whole of the newly constituted RAF was stretched to the utmost. In these circumstances if a skilled ace wanted to be thrown back into action then they were unlikely to try overly hard to stop him. His immediate value to the newer pilots was soon in evidence as the squadron threw itself into action. One young pilot, Lieutenant Ira Jones, only managed to escape a brisk encounter with Fokker Triplanes by following to the letter the detailed instructions previously imparted to them all by Mannock on how to escape just such a peril. Once he had managed to break away he experienced feelings of dreadful despair and overwhelming inadequacy on the flight back home.

> The feeling of safety produced an amazing reaction of fear, the intensity of which was terrific. Suddenly I experienced a physical and moral depression which produced cowardice. I suddenly felt I was totally unsuited to air fighting and that I would never be persuaded to fly over the lines again. For quite five minutes I shivered and shook.[23] *Lieutenant Ira Jones, 74 Squadron*

Here Mannock showed his greatest strength as a patrol leader. He could help nervous young pilots in such situations, where a colder type of man, exemplified perhaps by James McCudden, probably could not. He took young Jones to one side and revealed that he himself had often experienced exactly the same terrors earlier in his career. He then followed this up by giving positive motivational advice as to how to overcome such fears, all of which went a long way to allay Jones's fears and helped him to face up to the challenges of the next dawn patrol. Jones would hero-worship Edward Mannock for the rest of his life. Yet Mannock still harboured his own inner doubts, even though he had himself claimed two more victories that day.

> **In the thick of it. Things are a bit funny at the moment and I am not at all content. Maybe it's OK. Much work, much fighting and much 'wind up' at times, but OK at present.**[24] ***Captain Edward Mannock, 74 Squadron***

But there was good reason to be afraid. A few days later one of his protégés, Lieutenant Sydney Begbie, met his fate in terrible circumstances at the centre of a wild dogfight over Armentières. There was no romance or glamour in the manner of his death.

> **I spotted a machine commencing to smoke – then, burst into flames. Quick as thought, I wondered if it was a comrade. It was. I recognised by the marking that it was poor old Begbie. A sudden feeling of sickness overcame me, and I felt I was about to vomit. A shiver of horror passed through me.**[25] ***Lieutenant Ira Jones, 74 Squadron***

Many pilots serving with squadrons who had by then been in the thick of it for nearly a month began to find the unremitting strain was too much to bear. They had passed almost immediately from all their hard work in the Somme area to this new crisis in Flanders. Those who survived had learned a lot; but they were not the only ones to gain experience: the Germans were also learning to deal with low-flying scouts.

> **Since the Huns attacked down south they have learnt a thing or two. They saw this machine gunning was quite good sport for two or more players, and now they have nests of those beastly machine guns waiting for us, and they simply wipe years off one's life in a flash!**[26] ***Captain Gwilym Lewis, 40 Squadron***

When the small tight-knit group of men that made up a squadron suffered a steady trickle and occasional flow of casualties in just a few weeks, it was bound to have a considerable effect on their morale.

> Our work in the past weeks had consisted mainly of bombing and shooting-up ground targets from low altitude, much of the time in heavy rifle and machine gun fire, and it was then that I experienced some mental and physical ill-effects besides noticing them in my fellow pilots. These special missions – sometimes four or more in a day – imposed a much greater strain on one than did the offensive patrols. At the same time we lost more pilots, some shortly after joining us, others being old friends who had served in the squadron for a year or more. The element of doubt as to the outcome of the German advance was also a cause of tension not to mention the unsettling, tedious and frequent moves to new aerodromes. The cumulative effects of such strain depended upon the individual temperament, of course, but invariably those who best survived these pressures were those who, by nature, were calm and disinclined to panic reaction. All pilots were very tired after each day of intensive and dangerous low-flying strafing. However, it was the self-controlled and unruffled ones who managed to get a good night's sleep. And that made all the difference.[27] *Captain Leonard Rochford, 203 Squadron*

There is no doubt that in many squadrons the young pilots and observers used alcohol as a relaxant, although this aspect of their lives has often been exaggerated. A few drinks helped them let off steam, to forget temporarily the dangers that faced them on a daily basis.

> With regard to alcohol I say unhesitatingly that it played a big part. It would have been impossible to have had the hundreds of successful dinners and wonderful evenings we had without it, but no one who reads this need think life was one 'orgy' or that we were carried to bed every night, because alcohol was damned hard to get, and what we did manage to obtain had to be 'nursed' for special occasions. However, I don't think we were at any time actually 'dry' though occasionally our guests had some queer mixture for cocktails.[28] *Major Christopher Draper, 208 Squadron*

Sometimes, however, the drinking did get a little out of hand. Judging the exact point of personal inebriation as an evening progressed and, more importantly, the likely severity of the hangover are things that come only with hard-won experience. No active service pilot was likely to live long if he overdid it and was left trembling and shaking when he had to take off on a dawn mission.

> It was after midnight when I was deposited in my bed. Goble gave us a lecture on inebriety – the only time I ever deserved it. The worst of it was I was flying on an early morning bomb raid and at 6am we left the ground and I felt like nothing on earth. I could hardly tell which leg of the 'V' was which. I learned a lesson I can tell you, for if we had met any Huns I wouldn't have known what to do with them![29] *Lieutenant William Grossart, 205 Squadron*

A big guest night in the mess could be a fairly lively affair and many officers had developed amusing eccentricities or special turns that never failed to entertain no matter how many times they were repeated.

> No one ever knew why Jordan, when in post-prandial mood, imagined he was captain of a ship and insisted in walking the quarterdeck. So harmless a pastime could cause no offence if the room was clear, but it seldom was, and woe betide those who got in his path, for he simply walked straight through them. On these occasions he wore his hat at the 'Beatty' angle, a set expression on his fine ascetic face and his hands behind his back.[30] *Captain Robert Compston, 208 Squadron*

Some of the guest nights on special occasions were splendid affairs that had more than a whiff of the amateur dramatics about them. These would only take place when there was nothing too distracting occurring at the front. They offered the chance to celebrate in style.

> Then I proposed a bullfight. Turnbull was the matador, Rusby was the bull and the others took part as picadores, horses, bandilleros etc.. I was the beauteous lady who sits in a box and is Queen of the Festival. We all dressed up. Rusby put on a woolly fur coat and snowboots on his hands and feet, Turnbull wrapped our beautiful curtain round his middle and draped

a tablecloth over his shoulder. Of course he carried a red cloak and a sword (stick). All the others had various coloured cloths draped round them and Hamilton looked perfectly priceless in a piece of old sacking and a flying glove stuck on his head as a hat. He really is the ugliest man I have seen. First of all we had the parade to appropriate music played by Poole. That ended with a flourish and from my box – the top of the piano – I flung the key into the arena, the parade continued and the door of the bull's den was opened. Out rushed the bull and I nearly fell off the piano with laughter. The matador played with him first of all in the approved style and then the picadors on horseback plunged in. As it looked like becoming a most awful schmozzle I called off the gee-gees and sent in the bandilleros. Then came the kill. The pianist rose to frenzied efforts, I beat the drum, Payne blew the clarinet and everyone was dancing wildly round the room. Suddenly the door opened and in walked the General. The sight that met his eyes must have been perfectly priceless. There was a hideous silence, which Turnbull and the bull didn't pay any attention to because Turnbull chose that particular moment to kill the bull. I leaped from the piano and confronted the General. He was highly amused and insisted on us finishing the show, which we did.[31] *Major Charlie Dixon, 29 Squadron*

Some of the mess games were a little overly boisterous but the release of tension in such circumstances was seen as a healthy expression of good morale, rather than the altogether more threatening sullen silence or secretive drinking of men with real problems.

Practically the whole squadron went to dine with Sutton's squadron. They gave us coffee cocktails before dinner and plenty to drink during and after dinner. The result was a most hectic evening. We danced and generally ragged about. They had a comic game of their own called, 'Going over the Top'. Two big sofas were put across the room, the piano played, the attacking party prepared and at a given signal the barrage opened. The barrage was produced by beating with sticks on drums, pieces of tin, bits of iron, etc. and a fiendish din resulted. At zero hour the barrage ceased and the first wave went over the top. A fierce fight ensued but we captured Sutton and brought him back our side all right. We then had to defend. Sutton's crowd rushed the barrier O.K. and collared Hay and self. The most awful scrimmage resulted. Hay and I finally went through the door, but accompanied by half of one of the sofas. Oh we had a great time. My yellow cardigan hasn't been the same since.[32] *Major Charlie Dixon, 29 Squadron*

Practical jokes and 'jolly japes' of all kinds were prevalent. It extended to all ranks and newly joined pilots at 74 Squadron had to undergo a strange rite of passage at the hands of their commanding officer and flight commander.

Mannock was always full of pranks; his favourite one was to enter a comrade's hut in the early hours of the morning after returning from a 'night out'. He would enter, usually accompanied by Caldwell, who would be carrying a jug of water. Once inside Mannock would pretend that he had wined and dined too well and would make gurgling noises as if he was going to be sick. As each 'retching' noise was made, Caldwell would splash an appropriate amount of water on the wooden floor. The poor lad asleep would suddenly wake up and jump out of bed to the accompaniment of roars of laughter as his legs would be splashed with the remaining water.[33] *Lieutenant Ira Jones, 74 Squadron*

This wheeze was inflicted on a particularly pompous neighbouring squadron commander to the general satisfaction of *almost* everybody.

ON 14 April one of the hardest pressed units, 40 Squadron, was asked to conduct an urgent reconnaissance to find out exactly what was going on. After the formation of the RAF, Major Roderic Dallas, who symbolized the nautical essence of the RNAS, had been given command of 40 Squadron where he was duly nicknamed 'the Admiral' by his stolidly 'RFC' pilots. Dallas was born on 30 July 1891 in Queensland, Australia. He enlisted in the Australian Army in 1913 and at the onset of war he had joined the RNAS after being rejected by the RFC in 1915. After qualifying as a pilot and being commissioned, Dallas was initially posted to 1 Naval Wing based at Dunkirk where he patrolled over the North Sea and soon began to score victories. When 1 (Naval) Squadron was formed and equipped with Sopwith Triplanes, Dallas found his true vocation fighting alongside the RFC above the battlefields of Flanders in 1917. By the end of that year he had claimed a total of twenty-two victories. Now that the pressure was on he realized that in such a disordered situation his previous experience of the area would be invaluable in determining the limits of the German advance.

> I took them out because I knew the country better. We became split up in the mist and low clouds, and I found myself over enemy country with German troops shooting at me from below with rifle and machine gun fire. I saw a long row of German motor wagons going along bringing up supplies, so I fired into the leading one and set him on fire. He crashed into the ditch at the side. Just then a bullet went through my leg above the knee and ripped my breeches and out through the machine. This did not worry me a great deal so I flew on and later I saw a German officer and a lot of men marching below, then I saw our shells blow up a German gun and horse team. I was just getting my bearings when they got on to me again with machine guns and, by God, they riddled the machine but only hit me once. This time a bullet hit an iron bar and then splashed into my ankle and heel making three wounds. This made my foot stiff and filled my boot with blood and then I thought perhaps I had better go home.[34] *Major Roderic Dallas, 40 Squadron*

On landing he was surrounded by some of his pilots who did not at first realize that he had been wounded. Playing the wounded Australian hero perfectly, Dallas recounted his adventures to his rapt audience.

> While he was entertaining us with various descriptions in an amusing way somebody said, 'What did that, Sir – a bullet?' and pointed to a little strip torn from his leather coat. 'Yes,' said Dallas, 'they shot me!' And he lifted his coat to one side and the inside of his left thigh was all blood and raw meat and torn breeches. A bullet had come through the floor, hit a Lewis gun drum, spread itself and torn his thigh. 'Good God!' we said. 'You must get that dressed!' 'Yes,' said Dallas in his quiet way. 'Yes, I must get that dressed!' And he began hobbling away towards the sick bay. Then, after going some distance he half turned back and said, 'There's one in my heel too!'[35] *Second Lieutenant Cecil Usher, 40 Squadron*

At such a desperate time Dallas was determined to continue his tour at the front and, as his wounds looked far worse than they were, once he had been cleaned up he continued to lead 40 Squadron into action.

Although the town of Bailleul had been captured on 15 April, the advance culminated in the prolonged battle for the dizzy heights of Kemmel Hill, a tactically significant high point in the generally featureless Flanders plain. By now the British and French reserves had arrived and were beginning to make their presence felt. German attacks were becoming prohibitively expensive and casualties ballooned as the advantages of surprise diminished. As their communication lines extended there were difficulties in securing the all-important artillery support and as they pushed forward they were increasingly vulnerable to hard-hitting counter-attacks.

The RAF continued to do whatever it could to disrupt German preparations for the next stage in the assault. Whenever they could the day bombers flew into action, spraying their bombs liberally where they would do the most damage possible.

> Alquines was fog bound and our 18 machines were ready loaded with two 112lb bombs waiting for the fog to clear sufficiently. Our orders were to attack Bailleul which the Germans had captured two days before, and where they were now reported to be massing fresh troops for a further push forward. When we took off at last we flew in at 500 feet, just under the clouds, and were so low we could hear our bombs explode and feel their concussion. This raid was so effective that the enemy attack was wrecked before it could start and they never did succeed in pushing on any further in this sector.[36] *Sergeant H. W. Williams, 206 Squadron*

Of course the reconnaissance and artillery observation aircraft were up on their never-ending tasks. They too were suffering from the sheer pace of the war in the air, which was unremitting except when 'dud' weather intervened. Although the scout aircraft were their most obvious natural predator there was another set of implacable foes that never seemed to rest – the German anti-aircraft batteries lying below them. Many pilots and observers had developed a contemptuous attitude to their percussive efforts and the puffs of black smoke that sometimes surrounded them. Like a lightning strike it was obviously a catastrophe if you were hit; but it was a rare sight to see an aircraft being hit and of course in their heart of hearts they believed that it would never happen to them. Who after all was ever hit by lightning? Yet the German anti-aircraft guns *did* hit their targets on occasion. Lieutenant Percy Hampton and his observer Lieutenant L. C. Lane of 62 Squadron were patrolling in their Bristol Fighter flying south from Ypres towards Armentières when Hampton received empirical proof with a stunning bolt from the blue.

> I dived from 15,000 feet to about 12,000 to attack some enemy aircraft. I was almost within range when an 'Archie' shell burst under me, hitting my front petrol tank and wounding my observer in the thigh. The petrol then caught fire and I unfastened my belt and got almost out to jump from the flames, but got back again and put the machine into a violent side-slip. I couldn't breathe and my leather coat, boots and gloves started to burn and then my own ammunition, about eleven hundred rounds, started to explode. Five enemy machines followed me shooting all the time. They hit my 'bus' alright but didn't hit me, they hit my instrument board in front of me. I became unconscious several thousand feet from the ground, but my observer prevented a very bad crash. When we hit the ground my 'bus' went on to its nose and I was thrown out, also my observer. Then the rear tank caught fire and there was nothing left of the 'bus'. We were taken to Lille after being dressed at a field dressing station and I woke up in hospital. Both my feet were a bit burned, also my right hand and arm. My nose was knocked almost flat between my eyes and a little to one side. I had a very narrow escape with my right eye; I have a nasty cut between the eyeball and eyebrow. My neck was almost broken: I could not move my head for several days.[37] *Lieutenant Percy Hampton, 62 Squadron*

Percy Hampton landed, literally, on his nose, which was why it ended up flattened back against his face. The burns were painful, but not that serious. Although he was a prisoner of war, he had made the right decision as it was unlikely he would have escaped so lightly if he had jumped from around 15,000 feet. They had been both very unlucky and very lucky. Shot down, wounded and prisoners of war; but alive and out of the war.

Men who survived unscathed knew that they were lucky but they had the insight to guess that their good fortune was in finite supply.

Luck, for no apparent reason, seemed to play a big part in the fortunes of air crews. For instance, a newcomer known to me, very briefly, had hardly unpacked his kit before being wanted on a show. During that flight, it was thought that he met a high trajectory shell and large parts of his aeroplane were never found. Others, like myself, bore what is popularly known as a 'charmed life'. It cannot have been on the principle that 'only the good die young'.[38] *Captain Alan Curtis, 103 Squadron*

One common response to their predicament was to use humour to deflect or conceal the reality of their stressed mental state. This was common in the mess and even in their letters home to their families.

I have things which fait it *très difficile* for me to *penser ce coir.* To start with I did *trois heures et un demi* in the air yesterday and *j'ai* done *un autre* blinking three hours today; and you can't imagine how *fatigué* your eyes get in this snowy weather. Secondly, we are all sitting round the fire and somebody is playing the gramophone so *je* have to stop and collect *mes pensées* every minute. However thank you awfully for your letter, it was a *magnifique* effort – you can take that in French or English! Do you know I have not had any mail for three days? I am *très* fed up about it as *vous pouvez imaginer.* However *ne vous dérangez pas. Nillum doubtum!* (Trans: indubitably.) I shall have some tomorrow. I had quite an exciting time yesterday. I took, or rather went up with, a new pilot to do a shoot. He had not really met 'Archie' before and when the Hun started firing at us he just went happily on. Then he got one just underneath us, which nearly turned us topsy-turvy, and blew holes in the wings and tail, and shoved bits in the engine and wireless set. Gracious! He waggled about 'some' after that. I could not get him to fly straight even when it was the bangs of our own guns firing. Bother! I have stopped the French stunt: however '*Ça ne fait rien*' – my brains really are wonky tonight.[39] *Lieutenant John Baker, 4 Squadron*

There was also the bleak nature of the task that lay before them every day. They were killers and the men they killed did not die easily. The sheer horror of a flaming Fokker was something that did not fade quickly from the sensitive mind. But many simply treated it as an impersonal task, erecting a wall between them and their more human response to an awful death.

> I did not feel anything personal about the man I was trying to kill, and who was trying to kill me, even when my tracers seemed to be going in between his shoulders. The German pilot and his aeroplane seemed one impersonal thing to be destroyed before it destroyed you. Once or twice I felt, 'This chap is good!' but I did not continue to think of the enemy pilot as a man. Our feelings were too stretched to include the enemy in love or hate. A Bristol Fighter going down in flames with its crew made me feel sick, I knew the men in her. But not a Fokker doing the same thing – that was just the end of a satisfactory affair.[40] *Lieutenant Thomas Traill, 20 Squadron*

This constant tidal flow of lost acquaintances and friends could sometimes be sharply brought home by the most trivial of things. For Lieutenant William Grossart it was a meaningless game of bridge in the mess that brought home to him what a fine line he was treading.

> After dinner we had a foursome of bridge in the anteroom: Scott, Mellor, Theron and myself. All were new pilots, Scott being the most experienced. Once only did that foursome sit together: Scott died next day, Mellor three months later, Theron four months later. The fortunes of war were kind to me.[41] *Lieutenant William Grossart, 205 Squadron*

It was not that their courage was found wanting; it was just that no-one could endure such things for ever. Each time they went into action they had to screw up their nerves.

> It was in the minute or so before the fight that I knew the feeling of fear. During the time when the enemy aeroplanes developed from being small black specks in the distance into something that one could recognise, and then came closer and closer, and I knew that in a moment or so I would be in the middle of them. Then one knew, in one's fear, the temptation to cut and run. Once I was in the middle of a fight, and I had to fly with all the skill that I could summon up, I knew a certain amount of a sense of elation, almost of inspiration; and as I twisted and turned and dived and zoomed and fired and was shot at, I sometimes found myself shouting absurd battle

> cries and even singing at the top of my voice.[42] *Major Sholto Douglas, 84 Squadron*

The trouble was that every time it got harder to dissipate the accumulating fears. Every battle survived just seemed to postpone the moment when it would be them suffering defeat in the air.

> We would be in our machines waiting to take off, revving engines in short bursts to prevent plugs from oiling. Perhaps No.3's motor was proving difficult to start or the No.5 crew was not quite ready. It was then that I began to wonder, more and more, if the impending raid was likely to be as 'hot' as the last sortie, butterflies that would disperse, however, as soon as the engine was opened up to full throttle. I was jaded and had lost that 100% feeling; this does not mean that there was any likelihood of 'letting the side down'. Experience prevented me from doing anything silly and, subconsciously, I was still living on the principle that, 'It can't happen to me', but the zest was missing; rather it was a case of 'Let's get it over and tonight we'll have a binge in St Omer!' Moreover the small voice that had previously seemed to suggest that it could not happen to me now appeared to add, all too often, 'It jolly well can you know! What makes you so sure that you are going to be one of the lucky ones?'[43] *Captain Alan Curtis, 103 Squadron*

One other young man who understood the effect of nerves was Captain Harold Balfour. As a terrified young pilot he had been found wanting during the early aerial battles over the Somme in 1916. Gritting his teeth, he had come out again in 1917 for a second tour of duty. He held himself reasonably together, despite the awful danger of flying obsolescent Sopwith 1½ Stutters with 43 Squadron around Arras at the worst of times during 'Bloody April', until his nerve gave way again after a bad accident and he returned to be an instructor at the School of Special Flying in Gosport. But whatever he was, Balfour was no coward; back he came in 1918 for another tour of duty, this time flying Sopwith Camels with 43 Squadron. His accumulated experience began to tell and he claimed seven victories to make nine in total before, inevitably perhaps, he once again began to suffer from his nerves.

> For some weeks I had felt the same old troubles coming back; unable to sleep at night, a general desire to shirk battle and a complete inability to eat a decent meal. One day in the mess I half fainted. The Wing doctor happened to be lunching with us that day and insisted in examining me. He told me that my heart, which had a murmur as a result of diphtheria, was enlarged and in a bad state, and that I should have to go to hospital. I suppose that mental debility can bring about a physical reaction. This was so in my case, for with nerves near to breaking strain, I will admit that in the doctor's verdict, I found nothing unpleasant, as perhaps I should have done had I been a tougher warrior, without any feelings, imagination or temperament.[44] *Captain Harold Balfour, 43 Squadron*

It is perhaps worth noting that after his three arduous tours on the Western Front, Balfour was still only 20 years old.

One of the duties of the commanding officer was to monitor the mental and physical condition of his men. There was no point in driving a man to destruction when a period of home service could restore him to well-being.

> Two high patrols a day rendered officers inefficient at the end of five summer months, and necessitated their being withdrawn for a period of rest. In the autumn, winter and early spring, when flying was at lower altitudes, pilots could stand up to longer periods, eight or nine months. Continuous flying at over 16,000 feet, without oxygen, renders fifty per cent of officers unfit for flying till after a long rest on ground duties. Unless carefully checked the highly strung 'enthusiast' wears himself out by extra voluntary patrols just when he has become most valuable to his squadron.[45] *Major Keith Park, 48 Squadron*

It was the job of men like Major Park to point out the obvious to any of their pilots who had done too much.

THE battle on the ground was hard-fought but the Germans were eventually held up on the slopes of Kemmel on 17 April, which they would take only on 25 April. That loss left the troops manning the Ypres Salient exposed to a real risk of encirclement and General Herbert Plummer took the morally courageous decision to evacuate almost all the ground they had won in the Third Battle of Ypres, pulling back in haste to a far more coherent defensive line along the Pilckem Ridge and thereby flattening out the salient. The German attacks continued unabated for a few more days, but their losses increased as the Allied front solidified to such an extent that it was obvious to Ludendorff that his fondest hopes of a breakthrough to capture the Channel ports were doomed to disappointment. Operation Georgette had finally run out of momentum and was suspended on 29 April.

Overall the British Army had suffered around 250,000 casualties and the French a further 92,000 losses since 21 March 1918. But the Germans had themselves suffered around 320,000 casualties and the Allied line still held firm. The Germans had not shifted the juggernaut course of the war. Soon the Americans would be on the Western Front in real strength: time was running out for the German Army.

These had indeed been fraught times for the RAF. The statistics are stunning in their simplicity: on 21 March the total number of aircraft serving on the Western Front was 1,232; yet in between 21 March and 29 April 1918 they had lost 1,032 aircraft from all causes. Of these 195 were missing in action, 141 deliberately destroyed during the retreat, and 696 written off through serious damage. Of course the metaphorical conveyor belt from across the English Channel had more than replaced these with new aircraft and men, but the seriousness of the fighting can be judged by the sheer scale of loss replacement that was necessary. The RAF had passed through the fire and emerged on the other side, battered, frayed at the edges but still ready, willing and able to take the fight to the Germans whether in the air or on the ground.

One man typified that continuing aggressive spirit of the RAF, even during the natural lull in air operations as the Flanders front calmed down. Major Roderic Dallas considered the temporary disappearance of the German aircraft from the skies as a personal affront and duly found the perfect way to express his frustration at the lack of opposition. On 2 May 1918 he crossed the lines alone in his SE5a, proceeded low down over La Brayelle airfield and strafed the aerodrome before dropping a parcel onto the centre of the landing strip. In it were an ironic gift and brief note intended for the Imperial German Air Service.

If you won't come up here and fight, herewith one pair of boots for work on the ground, pilot's for the use of![46] ***Major Roderic Dallas, 40 Squadron***

As a group of Germans gathered round the package, Dallas added real injury to insult by dropping a couple of bombs and opening fire with his machine guns. This exploit was rumoured to have been unique in that it subsequently moved to laughter those twin graveyards of humour, Trenchard and Haig. But the Germans were not really hiding. They were gathering their strength for the next major confrontation. Soon the British would have all the action they could wish for.

Chapter 7

The Death of Richthofen

For nearly a month the focus of attention in the air war had been centred on Flanders but the ambivalent German attitude to Operation Georgette can be judged by their failure to deploy Richthofen and his élite Jagdgeschwader 1 in the fray. The embers of Operation Michael still glowed brightly under the surface and both sides were more than mindful that the Germans might at any moment resume their drive on Amiens. Neither the RAF, nor the German Air Service, could afford to neglect the Somme front for a moment. That April Richthofen seemed to be in his usual irresistible form. His efforts peaked on 20 April 1918, as he claimed his seventy-ninth and eightieth victories. They occurred when a twelve-strong patrol of Sopwith Camels from 3 Squadron led by Captain Douglas Bell was intercepted by a group of five or six Fokker Triplanes led by Richthofen. Bell already seems to have lost half his patrol in the heavy cloud and the sides were about equal, although as usual both seem to have exaggerated the number of their enemies in subsequent reports. Within a few moments Richthofen had got on the tail of the commanding officer of 3 Squadron who had accompanied the patrol. His quick accurate burst sealed the fate of Major Richard Raymond-Barker as his petrol tank exploded and the Camel tumbled to earth a mass of burning wreckage. Richthofen immediately switched his attention to Second Lieutenant David Lewis who had got on the tail of a blue Fokker. It was to prove no contest.

> I then saw a bright blue machine slightly below me, and impetuously dived on him. I think I should have stayed above him, and so been more or less on an equality in height with the Triplanes, whose lift was greater than the Camels. I saw my tracer bullets enter his machine but do not think I did him any damage, for I had to turn round to save myself from bullets which I could see were ripping the fabric off my machine. I saw at once that my

attacker was Richthofen himself, who had probably been waiting for some indiscreet pilot to get well below him. Then started a merry waltz; round and round, up and down to the staccato of the machine guns of the other fighters. Only once did I get my sights on his machine, but in a trice the positions were reversed, and I felt he was so much my master that he would get me sooner or later. Try as I would I simply could not shake him off my tail, and all the time the bullets from his hungry Spandau plastered my machine. His first burst shattered the compass in front of my face, the liquid there from fogging my goggles, of which, however, I was relieved when a bullet severed the elastic from the frame, and they went over the side. My position was not improved, however, for my eyes filled with water caused by the rush of wind. Flying and landing wires struck by the bullets folded up before my eyes, and struts splintered before that withering fire. I do not think Richthofen was more than 50 feet from me all this time, for I could plainly see his begoggled and helmeted face, and his machine guns. Next I heard the sound of flames and the stream of bullets ceased. I turned round to find that my machine was on fire. My petrol tank was alight.[1]
Second Lieutenant David Lewis, 3 Squadron

It was all so much less dramatic and far simpler from the point of view of the destroyer close behind him in his red Fokker Triplane.

I attacked a second Camel of the same enemy squadron. The adversary dived, caught his machine and repeated this manoeuvre several times. I approached him as near as possible when fighting and fired 50 bullets until the machine began to burn.[2] *Rittmeister Manfred von Richthofen, Jagdgeschwader 1*

Lewis was faced with an awful outlook from the cockpit of his Camel. His aircraft was severely damaged and on fire; he had no parachute; he was thousands of feet up in the heavens.

I put my machine into a vertical nosedive and raced earthwards in an endeavour to drive the flames upwards and away from me, but every now and then the flames overtook the speed of the machine and were blown back into my face. When about 500 feet from the ground the flames seemed to have subsided, so I pulled the control back to gain a horizontal position

> and was horrified to find the machine would not answer the elevators. I held the stick back instinctively, I suppose, and then noticed that the aircraft was slowly attaining the desired position, and I thought I should be able to land on an even keel. This was not to be, however. I hit the ground at terrific speed, but was hurled from the machine unhurt except for minor burns and bruises. Major Barker's machine was burning fiercely not far from me, so I went over to see if I could pull his body out, but was hopelessly beaten back by the flames. A German officer assured me that they would decently bury his remains.[3] *Second Lieutenant David Lewis, 3 Squadron*

But how had Lewis survived? How had his crippled Camel responded to his desperate tugging on his joystick? The answer was simple: he had been very lucky indeed.

> I later saw that not a stitch of fabric was left between my seat and the tail, but noticed that a few strips of the material left on my elevators had saved me. The back of my Sidcot was in charred strips and my helmet crumpled when I took it off. I also had one bullet through my trouser leg and one through my sleeve.[4] *Second Lieutenant David Lewis, 3 Squadron*

Above him the Red Baron was delighted by his latest successes and celebrated reaching 'Eighty not out' in an almost imperial fashion, flying above the upturned heads of his enrapt countrymen as he flew back to base.

> Richthofen went down very low so that everyone could recognise his red machine and waved to the infantrymen and the columns of men. Everyone knew who was in the machine and all of them had seen the burning Englishmen shortly before. Enthusiastically they all waved and flung their caps into the air.[5] *Leutnant Hans Joachim Wolff, Jasta 11*

Richthofen seemed to be back at the peak of his powers. Perhaps he should have listened to the siren call of a training or publicity role. But he was determined to fight on. Perhaps he could reach a hundred; then perhaps he might take another rest.

The next day was 21 April. What happened has generated countless articles, books and even television programmes – all devoted to tracking down who exactly shot Manfred von Richthofen. The issue can never be resolved but the protagonists battle on, refighting endlessly a skirmish that took just a couple of minutes all of ninety years ago. The reason is simple. Richthofen was an enormously potent symbol of German nationalism. He was seen as their 'knight of the air' flying out to do battle with the best the Allies could throw at him and his 'band of brothers'. Whatever happened he emerged victorious, proof of the supremacy of German manhood. Until 21 April 1918: then suddenly it was all over. How could their champion have been defeated? Who could have done it? Surely he could not have been defeated in a fair fight?

The incident started in conventional fashion. Three flights of Sopwith Camels from 209 Squadron were carrying out an offensive patrol over the Somme area. After shooting down a German two-seater in flames they were regaining height when they were attacked by a formation led by Richthofen.

> We saw a large formation coming at us with a considerable height advantage. There was no element of surprise and the attack of Richthofen's circus found our three flights using the marvellous manoeuvrability of the Sopwith Camel to turn sharply into the enemy's initial dive. There was no doubt about the determination with which Richthofen and his 'circus' pressed their attack. In a matter of moments there was a complete mêlée. At first we managed to maintain our flight formations, but as the mix-up intensified, it became a matter of individual action in violent manoeuvre and in short bursts at very fleeting targets. For myself, I recorded at the time one or two passing and ineffective shots at Richthofen's red Triplane and a sustained encounter with another German aircraft, tastefully and impressively painted in a combination of light blue and sea green. I could claim no positive success; and, as so often happened, the sky which at one time had seemed over-full of milling aeroplanes, suddenly became empty. The engagement had started at 12,000 feet and we finished up right down on the ground.[6] *Lieutenant Robert Foster, 209 Squadron*

Lieutenant Wilfred May was an inexperienced pilot and he had been firmly ordered to try to stay out of such dogfights, but he was soon sucked into the fray. To him it was all a formless blur of action in which he was a next to useless makeweight.

> The enemy aircraft were coming at me from all sides, I seemed to be missing some of them by inches, there seemed to be so many of them the best thing I thought to do was to go into a tight vertical turn, hold my guns open and spray as many as I could. The fight was at very close quarters; there seemed to be dozens of machines around me. Through lack of experience I held my guns open too long, one jammed and then the other. I could not clear them, so I spun out of the mess and headed west into the sun for home. After I levelled off I looked around but nobody was following me. I was patting myself on the back, feeling pretty good getting out of that scrape. This wasn't to last long, and the first thing I knew I was being fired on from the rear. I could not fight back fortunately, so all I could do was to try to dodge my attacker. I noticed it was a red Triplane, but if I had realised it was Richthofen I would have probably passed out on the spot. We came over the German lines, troops fired at us as we went over; this was also the case coming over the British lines. I got on the Somme River and started up the valley at a very low altitude.[7] *Lieutenant Wilfred May, 209 Squadron*

Leutnant Hans Joachim Wolff saw the ill-assorted pair leave the general dogfight.

> While Oberleutnant Karjus and I fought against two or three Camels, suddenly I saw the red machine near me, as he fired at a Camel that first went into a spin, then slipped away in a steep dive toward the west. We had a rather strong east wind and Herr Rittmeister had not taken that into account. As I now had clear air around me, I got closer to a Camel and shot it down. As the Camel went down, I looked over at Herr Rittmeister and saw that he was at extremely low altitude over the Somme near Corbie, right behind an Englishman. I shook my head instinctively and wondered why Herr Rittmeister was following an opponent so far on the other side.[8] *Leutnant Hans Joachim Wolff, Jasta 11*

As May desperately tried to get back and to shake off the red triplane his predicament was seen by May's friend and fellow countryman,

Captain Roy Brown, a practised veteran with nine victories to his credit.

> At 10:35am I observed two Albatros burst into flames and crash. Dived on large formation of fifteen to twenty Albatros scouts DVs and Fokker Triplanes, two of which got on my tail and I came out. Went back again and dived on pure red Triplane which was firing on Lieutenant May. I got a long burst into him and he went down vertical and was observed to crash by Lieutenant Mellersh and Lieutenant May.[9] *Captain Roy Brown, 209 Squadron*

For Brown that was where the action ended. He had no idea at the time it was Richthofen as he flew away to join up with Mellersh and May before returning to their airfield. However it is generally accepted that, whatever Brown *thought* had happened, Richthofen carried on pursuing May for some time after Brown had fired on him and flown off.

> I kept on dodging and spinning, I imagine from about 12,000 feet until I ran out of sky and had to hedge-hop over the ground. Richthofen was firing at me continually, the only thing that saved me was my poor flying. I didn't know what I was doing myself and I do not suppose that Richthofen could figure out what I was going to do.[10] *Lieutenant Wilfred May, 209 Squadron*

The next major protagonist in this puzzling affair was a Sergeant Cedric Popkin of the 24th Australian Machine Gun Company on the ground. He opened fire from a position to the left-hand side of Richthofen's flight path.

> I opened fire immediately the British plane left my gun sights and followed the Fritz around. He would be perhaps 100 to 120 yards in front of me when I opened fire and about 200 to 400 feet in the air. He would be below the top of the ridge which is about 500 to 600 feet high.[11] *Sergeant Cedric Popkin, 24th Machine Gun Company, Australian Expeditionary Force*

One interested observer on the ground watched the two aircraft flying up the Somme valley. Lieutenant D. L. Fraser was the intelligence officer for the 11th Infantry Brigade.

I was in the wood and saw two aeroplanes approaching flying westward directly upwards the wood, at a height of about 400 feet above level of River Somme over which they were flying. I had noticed that the leading machine had British markings just as it reached the wood and immediately afterwards heard a strong burst of machine gun fire coming from direction of south east corner of the wood.[12] *Lieutenant D. L. Fraser, Headquarters, 11th Infantry Brigade*

This would presumably be Popkin's burst and indeed Fraser seems to indicate that this burst of fire from the Vickers took effect.

Immediately afterwards the red painted enemy machine appeared overhead flying very low and unsteadily and probably not more than 200 feet from the ground. I lost sight of the British machine and my attention was concentrated on the enemy plane which was flying as if not under complete control, being wobbly and irregular in flight.[13] *Lieutenant D. L. Fraser, Headquarters, 11th Australian Infantry Brigade*

This evidence will prove significant, but not quite as Fraser undoubtedly intended it. Meanwhile Lieutenant May had no real idea what was happening some 20 yards or so behind him. Skimming along, dodging trees and ridges in the ground, he had no time to watch what the red Fokker Triplane was doing. His only aim was to get away.

Richthofen was very close on my tail. I went around a curve in the river just near Corbie, Richthofen beat me to it and came over the hill. At that point I was a sitting duck. I was too low down between the banks to make a turn away from him. I felt that he had me cold, and I was in such a state of mind at this time that I had to restrain myself from pushing my stick forward into the river as I knew that I had had it.[14] *Lieutenant Wilfred May, 209 Squadron*

As Richthofen climbed over the ridge it is at this point that a third serious claimant appears in the story, as the two aircraft flew directly towards the two Lewis machine-gun posts of 53rd Battery on the high ground of Morlancourt Ridge above the Somme river.

The Triplane flew steadily on, still firing short bursts at the Camel; it was now barely 20 yards behind and 10 feet above May. Very close indeed. I was at the ready with my finger on the trigger, waiting the clearance. It came. I can still remember seeing Richthofen clearly. His helmet covered most of his head and face and he was hunched in the cockpit aiming over his guns at the lead plane. It seemed that with every burst he leaned forward in the cockpit as though concentrating very intently on his fire. Certainly he was not aware of his dangerous position or of the close range of our guns. At 200 yards, with my peep sight directly on Richthofen's body I began firing with steady bursts. His plane was bearing frontal and just a little to the right of me and after 20 rounds I knew that the bullets were striking the right side and front of the machine, for I clearly saw fragments flying. Still Richthofen came on firing at Lieutenant May with both guns blazing. Then just before my last shots finished at a range of 40 yards Richthofen's guns stopped abruptly. The thought flashed through my mind – I've hit him! – and immediately I noticed a sharp change in engine sound as the red triplane passed over our gun position at less than 50 feet and still a little to my right. It slackened speed considerably and the propeller slowed down although the machine still appeared to be under control. Then it veered a bit to the right and then back to the left and lost height gradually coming down near an abandoned brick kiln 400 yards away on the Bray–Corbie road. I looked to my gun. It was empty. I had fired a full pannier.[15]
Gunner Robert Buie, 53rd Battery, 14th Australian Field Artillery Brigade

Buie had discerned a great deal from the blur of the red Triplane passing about 150 feet overhead at more than 100mph. As Richthofen turned sharply back, reversing his course and heading back to the German lines, Popkin had the chance of a second burst although this was at a longer range.

I opened fire the second time at the peak of his turn. I don't think that I was firing so long the second time as the first. I would be firing about half to three-quarters a minute each time.[16] *Sergeant Cedric Popkin, 24th Machine Gun Company, Australian Expeditionary Force*

The red triplane crashed into the ground where another member of 209 Squadron desperately evading the German scouts saw it crash and assumed that Brown shot him down although it is also clear he had not seen what really happened.

> I was forced to spin dive to the ground and return to our lines at about 50 feet. Whilst so returning a bright red Triplane crashed quite close to me and in looking up I saw Captain Brown's machine.[17] *Lieutenant F. J. W. Mellersh, 209 Squadron*

So there we have it. Richthofen was shot down by Brown from behind, by Popkin from below and on the left, by Buie and Evans from straight ahead and slightly below, or by Popkin's second burst from below on the right as Richthofen turned back to the east. Or of course any British or Australian soldier in the Somme sector could have hit him with a casual rifle shot out of the blue.

Richthofen was dead, most believe, before his Fokker triplane hit the ground. There was no autopsy, although a selection of medical officers examined the body at various times, drawn, one suspects, by morbidity rather than any academic rigour. Their slightly confusing and contradictory reports show that just one bullet had hit Richthofen, entering the body from slightly behind the right armpit, passing through the body and emerging from the chest by the left nipple. He had some minor facial abrasions and a possible fractured jaw caused by the crash. The body was *not* opened up and the track of the bullet was merely hazarded at by inserting a wire to probe for its passage. This is not particularly scientific, certainly open to question and thus leaves some impressive theoretical constructs wobbling about on very insecure foundations. The habit of trusting accounts that contain demonstrable falsehoods has also fatally stirred the pot of evidence until almost everything appears possible. Thus one witness who is often given credence for other parts of his story, Lieutenant G. M. Travers, explicitly says he saw the body and somehow confuses the relatively minor impact damage to Richthofen's face with 'A machine gun bullet had passed from the left side of his face and near bottom of jaw and came out just behind the right eye.'[18] Then there are the equally puzzling claims of Gunner Robert Buie who unequivocally states after seeing the body that:

Richthofen was struck in the left breast, abdomen and right knee. I examined these wounds as his body lay on the stretcher. The wounds were all frontal. Their entrances were small and clean and the exit points were slightly larger and irregular in the back.[19] ***Gunner Robert Buie, 53rd Battery, 14th Australian Field Artillery Brigade***

No chance of confusion here then. Simply put, either *all* the doctors were mistaken or Buie was embroidering the truth to try to show that the bullets came from the front – the only way he could claim the 'kill'.

Common sense, backed up by studies of the angle at which the bullet presumably hit Richthofen using a mock-up of the cockpit, seems to indicate that the bullet must have hit him from his right-hand side, and both slightly behind and below.[20] The question is often seen almost in medical terms. Could Richthofen have lived another sixty seconds as he travelled the 1,500 yards from the point where Captain Roy Brown last attacked him to the point at which he pulled up and crashed? Some say he could; some say he couldn't; but in truth it is impossible to know. Without a proper autopsy there is insufficient evidence for modern doctors, no matter how expert, to give anything other than a guess as to how long he could have survived the wound. It is therefore significant that the sober account of Lieutenant D. L. Fraser seems to indicate that Richthofen was flying unsteadily *before* he turned back to the east. Why indeed did Richthofen keep missing May's helpless Camel during this phase? But then again experts have also surmised from examination of his surviving Spandau machine guns that Richthofen had a nasty combination of jams which hampered his shooting; deeply ironic in view of Richthofen's strongly held belief that all such were entirely the responsibility of the pilot. Lieutenant Fraser's account was originally intended to boost the claims of Popkin, but it actually confuses the issue, for Popkin could only have hit the *left-hand* side of Richthofen at this time. If only Popkin could have hit Richthofen in his *right* side during this phase of the fight then all might have been reasonably clear. So Popkin's claim is only really feasible if he hit Richthofen *after* he had turned back to the east and after the time when he had already, according to Fraser, begun to fly erratically. The Australian Lewis gunners, Buie and Evans, could not have wounded Richthofen in the back from their position on the hill in front of him.

Their claim seems to lack credibility, but perhaps they hit him *after* he had turned back, although this is explicitly against the thrust of Buie's 'head-on' statement.

So who fired the fatal bullet? Although many distinguished analysts feel it *must* have been Sergeant Popkin after Richthofen had turned back and therefore presented his right-hand side to him, it would require a remarkable deflection shot to hit at long range a small scout moving at over 100mph at low-level right across his line of sight and with an unwieldy Vickers gun. Contrast this to the relatively easy 'straight' shot briefly available to Captain Roy Brown, an acknowledged ace. But to believe Brown was the killer is to believe that Richthofen survived his fatal wound for a whole minute. In the absence of any real evidence to the contrary, I have always sentimentally preferred to believe that it was indeed Brown and that Richthofen spent his last dying minute, as he would surely have wished, trying to get his eighty-first 'kill'. No-one will ever know and one cannot be dogmatic at this distance in time. What is certain is that Richthofen had committed a catalogue of errors that fatally contradicted his own *dicta*. If he had flown like that in 1916 he would certainly never have survived to become an ace; in 1918 it was suicidal to pursue a scout extremely low down over the British lines, with faulty machine guns, under heavy fire from the ground and under attack from an unseen scout on his tail who was an ace in his own right.

For both sides it was almost impossible to grasp what had happened: Richthofen *was* dead. The curious and the morbid gathered around his Fokker triplane where it came to rest in a mangel field close to the road leading from Corbie to Bray. In the rush for souvenirs they stripped away much of the evidence that could have settled the vexed claims once and for all.

> **When the remains of the Fokker Triplane and Richthofen's body were brought in there was immense curiosity about them. The only suitable place in which to keep the body of Richthofen was a canvas hangar belonging to my squadron that happened to be empty. He was laid out in the hangar on a small raised platform, and many of us went to see him as he rested there more or less in state. It was a curious experience, after all we had heard about him, to see him lying there.**[21] ***Major Sholto Douglas, 84 Squadron***

The Germans were utterly distraught at the loss of their hero. The first to realize that something was wrong was the rest of his formation. But the process was slow. In a dogfight they had plenty to attend to and aircraft could be difficult to spot in the wide open skies. Yet Richthofen's red Fokker Triplane was certainly distinctive.

> I looked around for Herr Rittmeister, saw no one else except Oberleutnant Karjus, who was close to me. Then I became a bit uneasy, as I certainly should have seen Herr Rittmeister. We circled the area for a time and were attacked by an Englishman, who followed us to about 900 metres over Corbie – but of Herr Rittmeister there was no trace. With a sense of foreboding I came home.[22] *Leutnant Hans Joachim Wolff, Jasta 11*

Another pilot contributed some more ominous news.

> I had a numb inner feeling that something had happened to Richthofen. As I flew back, east of Corbie, I had seen a small machine on the ground on the other side of the lines that had not been there previously. The machine appeared to be red.[23] *Leutnant Richard Wenzl, Jasta 11*

When they attempted to return to the spot they were thwarted by a superior force of British scouts. Meantime, desperate efforts were made by adjutant Leutnant Karl Bodenschatz to find out what had happened to his commanding officer.

> In frantic haste, over and over again, the same sentences are uttered, 'Jasta 11 has returned from a combat mission. The Rittmeister is missing. The men of Jasta 11 report that the Rittmeister went down. Has a red triplane made an emergency landing in your sector? Have you observed a red triplane landing on this side or on the other side of the lines?' And in the headquarters of the artillery and infantry, all the phone clerks raise their voices and ask, 'Red Triplane?' ... 'Red Triplane?' ... 'Red Triplane?' The couriers and messengers stumble hurriedly through the communication trenches, passing it on with shouts and notes, 'Red Triplane?' ... 'Red Triplane?' ... 'Red Triplane?' In the foremost trenches, all the telescopes,

trench periscopes and field glasses – all the eyes of the infantry – scour the terrain. 'Red Triplane?' . . . 'Red Triplane?' . . . 'Red Triplane?' God help us, every minute counts. If he has made an emergency landing somewhere he must be helped immediately.[24] *Adjutant Leutnant Karl Bodenschatz, Jagdgeschwader 1*

But there would be no reprieve. First an artillery observation post reported the red triplane making a smooth landing behind the British lines. For a while the Germans clung to the belief that Richthofen had landed under control and was merely a prisoner of war. When the news came that he was dead they were devastated anew. A huge memorial service was organized in Berlin. A nation mourned its fallen hero.

His brother, Lothar von Richthofen, was helpless in hospital when he first heard the news. As soon as he could bear it he wrote home to his grieving parents. Germany had lost a hero but they had lost a son aged just 25 years old. His twenty-sixth birthday would have been on 2 May 1918.

I could find no words for this pain. Since I had to learn the news from the newspapers, a frightful apathy has come over me. Outwardly, I am quite prepared for it, and I am glad that father was also. But I know I will miss Manfred at every step for the rest of my life. We have lost much with him, but we can be proud of him.[25] *Leutnant Lothar von Richthofen, Aaper Wald Clinic, Düsseldorf*

He was determined to return to action as soon as possible. The RAF had certainly not seen the last of the Richthofen family.

The RAF has long prided itself on the chivalry with which it dealt with the corpse of their most successful enemy. A commemorative plaque was made up and a decent funeral organized on 22 April when he was interred at Bertangles. Yet in reality the men of the RAF were deeply ambivalent about Richthofen and his death. Many sought to decry his achievements and that tradition lingered long after the war was over. They considered there was little about Richthofen that was worthy of their respect.

After all he was a typical Hun – he always led his circus and had about ten machines protecting him, and only attacked when he was pretty sure of success. If by any chance his bullets missed his opponent he would go straight on down in his dive and not come up again to the attack as we would. A fellow like that is bound to have a long life. His favourite people used to be stragglers in a formation who are always easy prey. However he appears to have bitten off more than he can chew this time at any rate.[26]
Lieutenant Pat Walmsley, 55 Squadron

The underlying message was clear: Richthofen was a fake, his achievements grossly exaggerated. But whatever they might think, Manfred von Richthofen was the 'real thing'. His claims have been verified time and time again by investigators: the aircraft he shot down and their occupants have almost without exception been traced and at the end of the exercise his reputation stands untrammelled – as does his final total of eighty victories. Perhaps the best response to his death for a young RAF pilot was simple relief.

I read a book called *The Red Air Fighter* by von Richthofen. It strikes me that it is a good thing he is dead![27] *Captain John Middleton, 40 Squadron*

Chapter 8

Fading Hopes

Throughout May the Allies were well aware that the Germans had not yet finished their series of offensives. The consensus was that the next blow would be struck in the Somme area as a follow-up to Operation Michael. As a result reconnaissance flights and photographic interpretation officers once more found themselves poring over the Somme hinterlands looking for evidence as to the German intentions. It was true that Ludendorff was indeed planning their next major offensive, but once again he was able to wrong-foot his opposite numbers in the Allied High Command. This time it was Operation Blücher, to be carried out by the German Seventh Army and intended to hit the French Sixth Army positions in the Chemin des Dames area. It was sheer bad luck that five British divisions caught up in the previous offensives were smack in the firing line. In May they had been exchanged with French divisions and had taken over the 'quiet' Rheims sector of the front line where it was intended they would bed down their new reinforcement drafts, reorganize and generally recuperate after their earth-shattering experiences. As they settled into the unspoilt country, they were unaware that the woodlands on the other side of the river Ailette concealed a multitude of Germans with malicious intent, including over 3,700 guns. The Germans prepared in their normal secretive manner and although the first inklings of something brewing were detected in the last couple of days it was by then far too late.

> On the evening of 26th May, the Commanding Officer and I dined with the French Squadron which was also on Fismes aerodrome, and here we heard that two prisoners captured that morning had given details of an overwhelming attack to be made the very next morning. The bombardment, they said, was to commence at 1 o'clock and the attack at 4.30am. We

strolled back to our quarters about midnight, discussing this unbelievable news. It was one of those nights when it never gets dark, a perfect clear night with a thick mist lying in the valley below us, covering the quiet little town of Fismes. Not a sound broke the stillness. Could it be true? It seemed impossible. We went to bed full of wakeful thoughts. We certainly did not sleep long![1] *Lieutenant W. E. Theak, 52 Squadron*

The German bombardment duly opened up at 01.00 on 27 May 1918. The barrage was incredible and the earth-shattering power of the guns was described in almost Wagnerian terms.

The whole earth and everything on it – ground and trees, houses and huts, man and beast – seem to tremble and shake incessantly, and the air layers seem to whirl. High in the air and deep within the earth, millions of sounds pound and thunder, howl and roar; noises that soon collapse within their ears into a single unbroken deep and powerful organ note of immeasurable strength. The organ of the German artillery is playing the overture.[2] *Adjutant Karl Bodenschatz, Jagdgeschwader 1, German Air Service*

At 03.40 the German infantry surged forward along a 27-mile front. Once again the bombardment had done its work, the line was weakly held and the units that held it were crushed. From above, the army cooperation aircraft of 52 Squadron charted the collapse of the British and French front lines and tried to bring down fire from the artillery. But the batteries were not able to respond, their communications were shot to pieces and they were for the most part retreating or overrun where they stood. Soon 52 Squadron themselves were forced to withdraw, bouncing back from airfield to airfield. What followed was a definition of chaos.

With the first light of day we saw to our dismay that the sky was full of German aircraft. Our first two patrols left at 05.00 hours, and were never seen again. Shortly after that hour the whole French squadron also left and that was the last we saw of them; but they had disappeared in the direction of Paris! The events of that day are difficult to describe. The Commanding Officer having detailed patrols to report the situation every two hours, left for Corps Headquarters and we didn't see him again until the next day. The poor RE8s were helpless in such a situation. Everywhere they were driven to the ground by flights of hostile scouts. One of our pilots was driven on to the aerodrome by three Pfalz scouts, who continued to shoot at him after he had landed. We had no British scouts in that sector, and the French fighters, who were responsible for our protection, were nowhere to be seen. At 10 o'clock a German two-seater was sitting over the aerodrome ranging a battery onto the hangars, offices and quarters. By midday German batteries appeared on a ridge a few miles across the valley and commenced shelling the aerodrome with direct observations. Our patrols carried on all through the morning and early afternoon, and brought back a wealth of information as to the strength of the German columns and the positions their troops had reached. This information was obtained largely by flying at a few hundred feet above our own forward troops, thus getting the protection of their small-arms anti-aircraft fire, in range of which the German scouts would not follow us.[3] *Lieutenant W. E. Theak, 52 Squadron*

At last orders came from their errant Commanding Officer, sent via his driver, instructing them to move back. It was not before time and their lorries were vigorously shelled as they departed. The information gathered by the patrols may have been of value but it was purely theoretical as for the time being there was no-one to staunch the German flow.

On the ground the British 8th and 50th Divisions who had taken the full brunt of the attack had ceased to exist as coherent formations and the Germans had advanced some 12 miles by nightfall. The bedraggled 52 Squadron were seeking temporary shelter at a French aerodrome. The airfield was packed solid with aircraft and it was a target the German bombers found irresistible.

As soon as dusk fell, so arrived the German night bombers who commenced an attack on the aerodrome which was continued without intermission all through the night. With my observer I walked away to a little hill half a mile from the aerodrome, and there at the edge of a copse, we sat all night watching. One of the early bombers with a well directed salvo of bombs hit one of the French hangars. In a flash the ten or twelve machines inside were all blazing furiously, and this made a guiding beacon for the relays of aircraft that attacked that night. The attack was most determined. Bombs were dropped from about 1,000 feet, and every machine, even the twin-engined Gothas, flew down to about 200 feet and directed a heavy machine gun fire on the camp, every corner of which was brightly lighted by the rising flames of the burning hangar.[4] *Lieutenant W. E. Theak, 52 Squadron*

Yet despite all this, next morning Theak found that the aerodrome was still functioning. The anticipated scene of desolation by no means met his expectations; a salutary lesson, perhaps, when analysing the regular claims of devastation made by bomber pilots of all nationalities.

It is surprising how little material damage is done even by intensive bombing such as this, except by the rare lucky shot. Conditions could not have been more favourable for the attackers. They met with no opposition, weather conditions were perfect, they had a short flight of only 25–30 miles from their base and no difficulty in identifying their target. And yet the next morning we found very little damage done. In our squadron we had no casualties and slight repairable damage to one machine only. The French were less fortunate, but apart from the burnt out hangar and its contents, I think they had only two machines seriously damaged, and three or four casualties to personnel.[5] *Lieutenant W. E. Theak, 52 Squadron*

To be effective air raids had to be relentless, occurring night after night, allowing no repairs and gradually destroying all the hangars and machines, killing the pilots, observers and mechanics. A one-off raid had little real impact.

The Germans continued to advance, brushing aside the faltering opposition until they reached the river Marne on 30 May. Yet as in 1914 this marked the high-water mark as nearly thirty French reserve divisions were moved up, first to fill any the gaps along the Marne, then to create a defensible front line and finally to throw back any further attacks. Alongside them were a couple of American divisions slowly 'feeling' their way into the war. As the offensive wound down on 6 June another door to German victory had been slammed shut.

By this time the German Air Service was beginning to be afflicted with a problem that would dog them for the rest of the war: a serious fuel shortage. This was not something that could be laughed away and it meant that harsh choices had to be made as to their operational priorities.

> **Stringent measures were caused by the shortage of gasoline. At the beginning of June the monthly consumption had been set at 7,000 tons. At the same time the staff ordered us to avoid all flights that were not urgent and to make a great limitation of photographic reconnaissance. Furthermore the production of aeroplanes was not maintained at the desired level. The difficulties in getting fuel were delaying our use of raw materials and unrest was growing among the workers. Difficulties were on the increase everywhere, but there was no let up in the requirements of our air units at the front.**[6] ***General Ernest Wilhelm von Hoeppner, German Air Service***

Ludendorff had problems of his own. His strategy had resolved itself into a series of bludgeoning attacks on the Allied lines designed to wear out the Anglo-French reserves prior to launching a final war-winning thrust for victory in the Somme or Flanders areas in mid-July. Following the fighting in the Chemin des Dames area, the French were sure that the next attack would also be in their area, with all the indications they could discern pointing to an assault in the Montdidier to Noyon front directed towards the river Matz. But the British still had their eyes nervously fixed on their Achilles heel at Ypres as they rightly feared the possibility of a renewed attack in Flanders.

It was over Flanders that Major Roderic Dallas would fly his last mission. 'The Admiral' was perhaps too aggressive for his own good. He had enjoyed great success on solo patrols which he continued to fly on a regular basis in the crowded skies of 1918. He took off at 10.10 on 1 June 1918 on yet another lone mission aiming to prey on German high-level reconnaissance aircraft. He was unaware that his promotion to lieutenant colonel in command of a wing was 'in the post' that very day. He was to cease flying duties immediately. . . .

There is some confusion over what happened late that Saturday morning, but it seems that Dallas was unlucky enough to encounter three Fokker triplanes over Liévin. In the fight that ensued he was shot down and killed with the victory being assigned to Leutnant Johannes Werner of Jasta 14. Dallas's final accredited total of victories was thirty-nine. He had been an inspirational leader to the men of 40 Squadron who could hardly believe he was dead. Rumours of all kinds of knavish German tricks were conjured up to try to explain what to them was simply unexplainable.

> The world is upside down. I don't know how to start. In the first place Dallas has been killed; I can't think why, but he has been. Too good for this world, I suppose. We simply couldn't believe our ears when we first got the news, but all the same it was true. It wasn't a matter of admiring the 'old fool'; we simply adored him. He must have had a most wonderful influence because the squadron has had awfully bad luck, and a very large element of new pilots. Yet the spirit has been wonderful. There never was such a happy bunch of lads. I feel I have lost a very good friend as well as a commanding officer. Since I returned from leave we got to know each other awfully well, and had all sorts of discussions on the squadron and pilots in it. He had got everyone summed up properly, and knew everything worth knowing about the lads. He seldom, if ever, said, or seemed to think anything but nice things about everybody. The worst of the whole thing was that he had almost fixed up to take charge of all testing in England, and we all saw possibilities of a sort of reunion in England under him. He would have been largely responsible for the selection of new machines. However, that is no more, and we no longer have our 'Admiral'.[7] *Captain Gwilym Lewis, 40 Squadron*

The squadron would survive. A new commanding officer arrived in Major Arthur Keen, himself an ace with twelve claimed victories. He lasted six weeks before he was severely burnt in a flying accident. So the baton of command passed on again. It was a dangerous business.

Flanders was not the target for the next German thrust. The French had been right: with Operation Gneisenau the Germans *were* intending to strike towards the Matz. They duly launched eleven divisions into the attack at 03.20 on 9 June. They were faced with an almost equal number of French divisions and although the Germans made progress in the centre they had not penetrated through the well-drilled French system of defence in depth. It was now that the benefits of a coordinated command were self-evident. Foch had asked that the RAF earmark five scout and three day bomber squadrons to be rushed to reinforce the French front if required. Arrangements had been made and they had been duly moved to the afflicted sector as the situation became clear. On 10 June Lieutenant Glasspoole was sent out in his Sopwith Camel on a ground-strafing mission.

> The enemy troops had good cover; they showed their disapproval of the strafe in the usual manner, and I lived through that. At length, after parting with, I should think, 500 rounds, I turned my back upon war for that day and set off home. I took a last look back at the German side and to my surprise saw flash after flash from clumps of trees which a minute ago I'd been stunting over. I was staggered that guns could be fired, reloaded and fired again so quickly. 'And they're dropping shells on the French' I said to myself with an empty feeling in my tummy. It was so, shells were now bursting in the French lines. Poor Poilus! Hell! I'd give 'em a burst. I pulled the 'bus' round and shoved her nose down for the spot. 'Crackerty-crackerty-crack!' said the two Vickers. Not a flash was seen during this performance.[8]
>
> *Lieutenant G. H. Glasspoole, 80 Squadron*

It was apparent to Glasspoole that the well-camouflaged German batteries in the woods were ceasing fire whenever he was in their vicinity. As he only had about 100 rounds left there seemed to be little he could do. He then came up with an ingenious plan, heavily reliant on sheer bluff.

> I thought that if I flew away at high speed and came back slowly they might think it not worth the candle to fire on such an intermittent basis. Forthwith, I beetled off, nose down at 160mph. They did not fire; 10 seconds later I turned and throttled down to 90mph, gently zig-zagging towards them. On my repeat performance, however, I had no sooner started rushing away when a gun in the left clump fired. I flew straight at that spot and at 50 feet sprayed it with a dozen. A third time I rushed away; towards the end of my beat of half a mile or so, a gun in the right-hand clump fired. I tore back at that spot, full out, delivering a longer burst this time, right at things. 'This would learn 'em!' I hoped. Well it did do, apparently, for that was the last gun of this 'pet' collection to fire for the remainder of my stay. I flew to and fro after that, feeling a joyful thrill at the success of the wheeze. Guns on the flanks up and down the line were flashing every now

> and then, but my little lot were behaving like lambkins.[9] *Lieutenant G. H. Glasspoole, 80 Squadron*

He kept up this performance for some twenty-five minutes before the warnings from his petrol gauge brought an end to his harassing.

Next day the French counter-attacks went in and not only stemmed the German tide but managed to regain some of the ground lost. The Germans did not want to get involved in a grinding attritional battle *per se* and they soon abandoned the fight. The question was once again where would they strike next? It had been discovered that German reserves consisting of twenty-five divisions had been concentrated facing the British in Flanders. This was of obvious concern to Haig, but Foch was still convinced that this was a distraction from the real assault about to be launched on the French Army. Throughout June there remained considerable confusion as to where exactly the Germans might be intending to strike. Salmond had by this time realized that the Germans had in place the transport infrastructure and supply arrangements so that they were in essence ready to attack anywhere along the line and that it was the move forward of the assault troops that offered the best chance of determining the moment of attack.

> In order to prevent surprise, such as apparently occurred on the last attack on the Aisne, it is a vital necessity that his approach march be discovered. The time during which this approach march takes place is, without doubt, during the night, and the very early hours of the morning during any period up to five nights of the day selected for attack. Responsibility that the British Army is not surprised is on the Royal Air Force.[10] *Major General Sir John Salmond, Headquarters, RAF*

Twice-nightly and dawn reconnaissance missions were therefore ordered to look for even the smallest signs of unusual troop movements. Meanwhile the French Air Service monitored day and night the traffic of German troops on the entire rail network. The British and French bombers would then try to maximize the interference in that traffic by concentrating on just a few targets to achieve not only a substantial weight of bombs hitting the targets but also a frequency of raids and consequent disruption of repair work. The RAF would concentrate on just four target junctions and associated railway mainlines designed to hinder any possible German troop concentration in Flanders and northern France: Valenciennes, Tournai, Fives (south of Lille) and Courtrai.

In the lull in the ground fighting that followed the failure of Operation Gneisenau the aerial war continued at a vigorous level. During this time new heroes had stepped forward to replace Manfred von Richthofen. Of these one stood out for his sheer courage in the face of constant adversity, while at the same time continuing to hand out copious punishment and death to his enemies. Hauptmann Rudolf Berthold was born on 24 March 1891 and had joined the army in 1910, learning to fly as early as 1913. He had fought throughout the war in the air, but his injuries were legion and would have stopped a lesser man in his tracks long before 1918. He had been wounded on several occasions and had broken most bones ranging from his skull via his pelvis to his thigh. His defining moment proved to be in combat on 10 October 1917, when he was badly wounded in the right upper arm. The bones were splintered and he lost any effective use of the limb. At this point he had claimed some twenty-eight victories and it seemed his career as an ace was over. But Berthold had an intense inner drive, and although he had already been awarded the *Pour le Mérite* he was determined to return to the fray. In March 1918 he was appointed to command Jagdgeschwader 2. He taught himself to fly left-handed, in itself no mean feat, and although his wounds had by no means healed he began to fly operational missions. His efforts accelerated after the loss of Richthofen on 21 April. It was medically ill-advised but it is fair to say that Rudolf Berthold was not as other men. He had a fanatical belief in the cause of his country and above all he was a leader of men.

> **Richthofen is killed, daily the comrades fall, the English are numerically superior. I must show the young ones that duty stands above everything else.**[11] ***Hauptmann Rudolf Berthold, Jagdgeschwader 2***

He began to drive his Jasta commanders even harder, insisting on an ethic of constant hard work and the necessity of disciplined tight formations in combat. Those he felt let him down he dismissed. He himself began to score regular victories, but they came at a terrible personal cost.

> It is raining today. Thank God, because otherwise it would have been impossible for me to fly with the others. My arm has got worse. It is rather swollen and infected underneath the still open wound. I believe the bone splinters are forcibly pushing themselves out because the swollen area is very hard. The pain is incredible. During my air battle yesterday, in which I shot down in flames two English single-seaters, I screamed out loud from the pain.[12] *Hauptmann Rudolf Berthold, Jagdgeschwader 2*

A man like Berthold does not naturally show his feelings and certainly would expect no sympathy, but his sufferings even as he killed have a resonance.

> I shot down in flames my thirty-seventh. My arm is still no good. Since the lower wound has broken open again, the pain has diminished somewhat and the swelling has reduced. Last week was horrible, I screamed from the pain, at times I went into a fit. It appears to have been only a bone splinter. From outside you could directly follow the path which it wandered. In the end it got stuck in the old scarred wound and the fun really started for me. After a few days, as the scar popped open and the pus sprayed out in a high arc, a bit of relief at least came. I know that I feel every – even the slightest pain – double and triply because since being wounded I have not had time to bring my body up to its old capability for resistance. But I must hang in there, no matter what it costs. After the war we can slowly bring my old bones back into order again.[13] *Hauptmann Rudolf Berthold, Jagdgeschwader 2*

Another man stepping into the breach to replace Richthofen was Leutnant Ernst Udet, who had returned to the front and been placed in command of Jasta 4 after a spell of sick leave with a serious ear infection. Udet was a brilliant combination of tactician, pilot and marksman; his score grew rapidly. He was helped by the arrival of the delayed Fokker D.VII. The superb manoeuvrability and general all-round qualities of this aircraft were a superb platform for a man of Udet's abilities. Yet even the best can make mistakes and on 29 June Udet's career nearly ended when he committed the basic fault of underestimating his enemy. His life was only to be saved by a relatively new innovation recently issued to German scout pilots – the parachute.

> I attacked a plane which was flying at an altitude of 800 metres over an area under artillery fire from the French. On my first attacks the Breguet turned towards me and flew past below me. I then noticed that its observer was no longer standing to his gun, and therefore assumed I had already hit the observer. Contrary to my usual habit, I attacked the enemy plane from the side. Suddenly, however, I noticed the French observer re-appearing from the fuselage and at the same moment was hit by several rounds, one low down in the machine gun, another in the petrol tank. At the same time my elevator and aileron cables must have been shot through for my Fokker D.VII was plummeting down out of control. I tried everything I could, partly using the throttle and partly the rudder, to bring the plane under control again, but in vain. At an altitude of about 500 metres the plane went into a vertical nose-dive and could not be pulled out. It was high time to get out. I unfastened myself and stood up in the seat. Next moment I was blown backwards by the immense pressure of the air. At the same time I felt a violent tug and noticed that I had caught my parachute harness on the front edge of the rudder. With a final supreme effort I broke off the tip and in a rush was free of the plane, tumbling head-over-heels several times behind it. I thought at first that the parachute had failed me when I suddenly felt a gentle deceleration; shortly afterwards I hit the ground. It was a fairly violent landing and I sprained my left leg.[14] *Leutnant Ernst Udet, Jasta 4*

Udet found himself in the middle of the heavy French barrage but just managed to regain the German lines – against all the odds he had survived and would be back in the air to resume his depredations next day. The parachute had saved his life and left him free to continue his lethal career.

The parachute question has acquired a spurious significance that really reflects our own preconceptions rather than the situation as it was actually perceived in 1918. The Germans had only started selectively issuing parachutes in the spring of 1918 and only about forty of their scout pilots seem to have used them – and not all of them survived the experience. The British were a little behind in the sense that although parachutes had been used from balloons on many occasions they were not employed in a British service aircraft until Captain Clive Collett made the first jump in January 1917. Two things held them back from general issue. The first was a practical matter: the cockpits of their aircraft were tight-fitting at best and there was simply no room for the bulky parachute as it was then configured. More development work needed to be done to make their use feasible, especially for the single-seater scouts. Second, the authorities had decided that the availability of parachutes might tempt a pilot to abandon his aircraft and parachute to safety before it was strictly necessary instead of continuing the fight. This was an unfortunate and tactless position, but they did not stick to it for very long. Parachutes were eventually sanctioned for use but the end of the war intervened before they could be issued in any numbers. So a *faux* controversy was born.

Most deaths were unaffected by the question of parachutes which were only usable in very limited circumstances. But every day that high summer there was a trickle of casualties up and down the line. Some of these deaths were like meteorites blazing across the heavens; others almost pitiably anonymous, men dying quietly amid the screaming engines and spluttering machine guns. One such casualty occurred on 2 July 1918.

> Engaged eight Pfalz scouts – I got one in flames who was on a Bristol's tail and did not see me coming. Jones thought he got one too. Then, when the formation was a bit scattered, ten Fokker Biplanes came out of the sun, astern and suddenly the sky was full of tracer. A Bristol wrapped in flames spun slowly ahead of us while two Fokkers danced a jig around it. Jones leaned over my shoulder for a moment and then everything happened at once. Jones tapped me on the top of the head, our 'extreme emergency' signal and I kicked full left rudder, stick hard forward to the left and ducked. There was a very brief stuttering burst from a Fokker's twin guns, I felt a blow on my left elbow as if I had been hit by a hammer, the aileron controls went out of action, one of the landing wires flew free and thrashed the fabric of the bottom plane, and a bullet went through my windscreen 6 inches in front of where my nose had been a moment before. Then, as suddenly as it had happened, it was over. I expect another Bristol made a pass at the Fokker who had me cold, only able without ailerons to fly

straight and fairly level. Having found the aeroplane would fly and pointed her for the lines, I looked round to see Jones sitting quietly on his little seat, his head resting on the butt of his gun. When I put my hand on his shoulder I knew he was dead. I discovered that my arm which I had thought shot through had only been bruised by a round from one of Jones' ammunition drums that had been hit; or perhaps by a bullet that had spent itself penetrating Jones' gun mounting. I decided to land at Marie Capelle, the first field I came to, though I felt sure nothing could be done for him. One of the undercarriage struts had been shot through and collapsed when we touched down, but we crunched to a stop without turning over and I shouted to some men for an ambulance. A stretcher party came quickly and Jones was lifted from his cockpit, but there was nothing to be done: he had died instantly.[15] *Lieutenant Thomas Traill, 20 Squadron*

Lieutenant Jones had been Traill's observer and rear gunner for more than a month. They had fought together as an integrated team in the air, but on the ground they were almost as strangers.

Jones was an almost fearless man whose aim was to shoot down German aircraft. I never knew his Christian name, or where he came from, or whether he had a family; but as far as we did know each other, we knew and trusted each other completely. Except for a fortnight when he was on leave, we flew together till his death. He was not a gregarious man: I was the nearest thing to a friend he had in the squadron, but we never talked of anything but our work, of flying, fighting and tactics – and how to do it better. He had a hot, potentially violent temper and no one pulled his leg much in the mess. I was very happy to have him behind me and I think he was glad to fly with me.[16] *Lieutenant Thomas Traill, 20 Squadron*

It appears from the records that his name was Lieutenant Percy Jones and he came from Mold in North Wales. He died at the age of 29 on 2 July 1918 and is buried in the Longuenesse Cemetery in France. Jones was just one of many who never came home. And what of his pilot, Lieutenant Thomas Traill? He seems to have reflected rather more on the implications of his narrow escape from a Blighty wound than on his amazing escape from death.

I was disappointed: to go home wounded would have been an honourable way out of immediate danger and a temporary relief from the conflict between, on the one hand fear, mostly of burning, and on the other end whatever it is that holds a man in the line – a fear of being recognised as one who will leave his comrades to carry the can; the knowledge that you will have to live with yourself afterwards, knowing that it is the only right and honourable thing to do, and that the men around you whom you most respect feel the same.[17] *Lieutenant Thomas Traill, 20 Squadron*

BY early July the Germans had completed preparations for their offensive in the Champagne area. In a sense both Foch and Haig had been right in their conjectures as to German intentions. The Germans meant to attack the French Army first on 15 July, but then planned to generate their final killer blow in Flanders, which was provisionally timed for five days later. The French aviators knew by this time what they were looking for and soon the reports and photographs made it obvious that an assault would be launched in the Rheims sector of Champagne in a matter of days. Once again Foch requested and received assistance from the British who duly despatched several divisions and a selection of scout and bomber RAF squadrons south. They also began a series of operations north of the Somme designed to pin down German reserves. These included the Battle of Hamel on 4 July, a small but significant tactical operation conducted by Lieutenant General Sir John Monash and his Australian Corps, part of Fourth Army commanded by General Sir Henry Rawlinson and charged with holding the Somme front. All in all this was a notable collective Allied effort, for Haig still harboured entirely justifiable fears that Flanders could be the next German target.

The Germans attacked across the river Marne towards Rheims following the usual crunching bombardment at 04.00 on 15 July 1918. The French were ready for them and although some progress was made the Germans once again failed to break through the French careful system of defence in any depth. As the French, British and American reserves marched to the sound of the guns it was soon obvious that for all their planning and sacrifice the Germans were not going to break through to recreate the siege of Paris in 1870. This, the Second Battle of the Marne, had much the same result and a lot of the import of the First Battle of the Marne which had saved Paris from capture in 1914. The German offensives of 1918 were effectively at an end. Another significance of this battle was that the counter-attack that followed on 18 July was the first real test of the Americans both on the ground and in the air.

The Americans had conceived splendidly grandiose plans to create an air armada which had comically lurched in size during the summer of 1918: first 260 squadrons, then up to 358, and finally back to 202 squadrons. All these programmes were piously intended for fulfilment by mid-1919. As we have seen, this latent American threat had troubled the Germans for the last eighteen months but in reality the only American threat on the Western Front had come from the initial trickle of pilots like Lieutenant Edgar Taylor who served directly with RAF squadrons, or the volunteers flying with the French Escadrille Lafayette. However by the time the French and Americans launched their attack on 18 July, there were all-American squadrons available to fly into action above the US troops as they pushed forward on the ground. As he flew over the battlefield of Château-Thierry, Lieutenant O'Neill of the 147 Aero Squadron could see the turning of the tide as the German offensive collapsed in disarray.

> We were on dawn patrol out over the lines, just about sunrise, when the zero hour hit. The sight below us, over the entire sector, which was probably 80–90 miles long, it couldn't have been any less than ten thousand pieces of artillery, firing in rapid fire, as fast as they could go. The flashes of the artillery guns were almost constant, and over the German lines you could see dust rising, smoke rising and fires in all directions. It was the most formidable attack that I have ever seen in my life, and, of course, it did the cockles of my heart good to see that at last the Germans were getting a bit of their own.[18] *Lieutenant Ralph O'Neill, 147 Aero Squadron, 2nd Pursuit Group*

The inexperienced American pilots became veterans very quickly in the skies above Château-Thierry. But as so many had learned before them there was a terrible randomness about aerial warfare. On 24 July Lieutenant Wilbert White of 147 Aero Squadron was leading a formation of fifteen Spad XIIIs when he suffered engine trouble and soon lost his men in the prevailing heavy clouds. As his engine perversely then seemed to pick up, he climbed high to burst through the cloud ceiling where he suddenly found himself presented with two German scouts barely 200 feet away and completely at his mercy.

> If I had been ten seconds earlier, I would have been 'meat' for them and the positions would have been reversed. As it was I was sitting right in the sun and it was a wonderful chance. I gave one look around for some more, and seeing none, started after this pair. I literally sneaked up on the trailing Hun and was somewhat closer than 50 yards when I opened fire. I saw the pilot look around, throw one hand to his head and fall forward. His machine 'zoomed', turned on its side and started to spin down. The first man by this time had probably heard my guns and started to dive, so I started after him. He went into the clouds and I followed shooting at him whenever I could see him. When we got through the clouds, I closed on him and gave him all I could until he went into a straight nose-dive and I circled around until I saw him crash into the ground head-on. Now this may all seem terribly cold blooded and callous, but in this war it is either a case of get or be gotten, and I choose the former if ever there is a choice in the matter.[19] *Lieutenant Wilbert White, 147 Aero Squadron, 2nd Pursuit Group*

THE war was changing: new weapons, new counter-measures and now a whole new American adversary both in the field and in the skies. The defeat on the Marne was so comprehensive that by the end of July the final German master-stroke intended for Flanders had been first postponed and then abandoned. Ludendorff's window of opportunity before the American Army arrived in strength on the Western Front was now emphatically slammed shut. As these first American divisions surged forward into action, hammering against the increasingly exhausted Germans, they were just the strong advance guard of a vast army of some 3 million men who would gradually be deployed in action on the Western Front in 1918 and 1919. But even so, credit should be given to the equally worn-out British and French Armies who together had done the bulk of the work in holding the line before the Americans reached the front. It had bulged this way and that, but it had never given way, and the two armies not only maintained physical touch, but had been united under a common cause by the leadership of Foch.

Chapter 9

Falling Aces

Retrospectively it is strange to think how little heed was paid to the aces on either side by the men with real power. A recently published compilation of the correspondence and diary of Douglas Haig reveals no anguished pondering on the threat posed by Manfred von Richthofen, or indeed of any exultant celebrations following his death in action on 21 April 1918. In the titanic battles involving millions of men and dominated by weapons capable of inflicting hundreds of casualties in one burst of fire any one individual, no matter how influential, was not of any real importance. Haig was interested in the performance of the RAF as a whole, in accordance with the operational priorities laid down first by his General Headquarters and now by Marshal Ferdinand Foch. The Red Baron was a cult figure to the Germans, whose deeds had been used as an inspirational propaganda weapon both at home and abroad; but many aerial historians have long been guilty of grossly exaggerating the impact of individual aces on the course of the war. Who can discern any 'real' effect of the death of even Richthofen, indubitably the greatest of them all, in the midst of the massed air battles of April 1918? Did the morale of the German Air Service collapse? Did the Jasta scouts stay at home in mourning? On the contrary it was evident that they would fight on regardless under new leaders and with fresh new aces emerging constantly from the ranks.

Mannock's reaction to Richthofen's death had been unambiguous. When a member of 74 Squadron proposed a toast to the memory of their fallen enemy he refused point blank and allegedly expressed the wish: 'I hope he roasted the whole way down!'[1] By this time Mannock seems to have thoroughly detested the Germans, probably through a combination of his fervently held socialist opinions reacting to the threat posed by imperialist Germany and then all briskly stirred by his naïve patriotism. Yet one also may suspect that his hatred grew because the Germans directly or indirectly put him through hell as he wrestled day and night with his own jangled nerves. Others have also conjectured that he exaggerated his hatred and determination to secure kills and to encourage the young pilots 'onward and upwards'.

Mannock now began his most productive period, shunning the easy unwitnessed victories of solo patrols and concentrating entirely on the collective success of his squadron flights using his own personal marksmanship as the razor-sharp cutting edge – much, in fact, on the Richthofen pattern. His only real departure from that norm was his habit of sharing victories with young pilots. He clearly believed that once pilots had broken their 'duck' and got their first victory under their belt, then they would be liberated from personal doubts to emerge as competent combatants in their own right.

Seventy-Four Squadron was exceptionally fortunate in that they had another accomplished formation leader in their ranks, their Commanding Officer, the New Zealander Major Keith Caldwell. Unfortunately, although Caldwell was a superb pilot, he was severely handicapped in action by his inability to hit a target.

> No pilot in France goes closer to a Hun before firing than the CO, but he only gets one down here and there, in spite of the fact that his tracer bullets appear to be going through his opponent's body! Mannock on the other hand takes an angle shot and – Hun goes down in flames![2] *Lieutenant Ira Jones, 74 Squadron*

Caldwell persevered gamely enough, though, to finish the war with twenty-five allotted victories. With better shooting many of his contemporaries believed he could have doubled this score. Nevertheless, with leaders like Mannock and Caldwell, 74 Squadron rapidly began to gain a fine reputation. During May, Mannock had shot down a veritable stream of scouts, many of which can be verified to an above-average extent from the German records. He was awarded the DSO on 24 May, to be immediately followed by a Bar just two weeks later. But by this stage Mannock was beginning to fall prey to the curse of so many successful aces. He began to measure his success against the numerical achievements of his peers, in particular his friend James McCudden, then still languishing on Home Service. 'If I've any luck I may beat old Mac. Then I shall try and oust old Richthofen.'[3] Such references become increasingly common in his correspondence and just a little later he promises to beat McCudden's score or 'die in the attempt'. These were worrying signs of the beginning of a fixation.

On 9 July Mannock's friend and rival, the illustrious James McCudden, travelled back to the Western Front to resume his career of destroying German aircraft. His relentless campaign to secure an active service posting had finally been successful. He had already rejected a well-intentioned compromise when he was offered command of 91 Squadron which were however nowhere near ready to go to France. McCudden had also been considered for the command of 85 Squadron after they had lost their charismatic leader Major William Bishop. Bishop's brief second tour of duty in France had culminated in a series of unbelievable solo exploits over a frenetic few days before he was withdrawn to help pave the way for the formation of the Canadian Air Force. Yet 85 Squadron desperately needed to be sorted out, being a conglomeration of undisciplined and underachieving 'free spirits' who thought themselves an élite, but who had so far achieved very little. Understandably, they did not fancy the idea of McCudden, a noted disciplinarian, taking over command. At the time much was made of his working-class origins, for as the son of a non-commissioned officer in the pre-war regular army, he was beyond the pale for a certain kind of officer. There were also unpleasant rumours that he maximized his own kills by denying anyone else in his flight any opportunities. These can be dismissed as the usual jealous mess tittle-tattle: all the great aces dominated the formations they flew with as they were the best shots and had the best chance of a clean kill. Shamefully rejected by 85 Squadron, McCudden was finally promoted to major and sent out to command the more malleable 60 Squadron which was based at the Boffles airfield in France.

McCudden had only just completed his memoirs, *Five Years in the RFC*, which was and remains by far the best account of life in the RFC in the Great War. In his closing paragraphs he suggested that if the war continued much longer, 'One or two perhaps of the Allied aviators will have exceeded a total of one hundred enemy aeroplanes shot down'.[4] There is no doubt that McCudden had himself in mind as the prime candidate to be first of the centurions. He was a naturally confident, forthright young man: he believed in his own abilities, proved time after time in action, he would be flying the trusty SE5 and his new squadron had an excellent reputation. But he would take no chances; in his own words there would be no 'dashing stunts'[5] for him.

McCudden took off in a brand-new SE5a from Hounslow airfield and seems to have flown to the RAF Headquarters at Hesdin *en route*. On resuming his journey at about 17.30 he found himself in hazy weather over the airfield of Auxi-le-Château, a mere 5 miles short of his destination. Aware of the recent fluctuations in the front line McCudden decided to land to get directions rather than risk some awful embarrassing blunder on his first day back. The landing field was the home of both 8 and 52 Squadrons flying two-seaters and had the reputation of being quite tricky for the faster scouts as it was slightly sloping, narrow and had woods on two sides. McCudden made a neat landing, and after asking for directions, immediately took off again.

> The aircraft took off into the wind and at about 100 feet did a vertical turn and flew back across the aerodrome by the side of the wood. The engine appeared to be running badly. The pilot rolled the machine which failed to straighten out, at approximately 200 feet. It crashed nose down into the wood.[6] *Lieutenant L. M. Fenelon, 52 Squadron*

Ground crew and off-duty pilots ran to the scene of the crash where they found the SE5a scrunched into the trees on the south-east edge of the airfield. There was little hope, but at least the wreck had not caught fire – yet. They found James McCudden had been thrown out and was lying beside one of the wings. As they removed his flying helmet Corporal W. H. Burdett, who had served as an aircraft rigger alongside McCudden way back in 1915, recognized him immediately. The unconscious McCudden was carried by stretcher and taken to the casualty clearing station where he was discovered he had a badly fractured skull. He never regained consciousness and died at 20.00 the same day. The greatest, most deadly British ace of the war was dead, his career stalled at fifty-seven victories, most of which are irrefutable. He was just 23 years old.

It seemed incomprehensible and rumours soon sped round the RAF to explain what seemed unexplainable: that McCudden was drunk; he had been stunting on take off; that he had crashed trying to turn back to the airfield, when his engine had failed – the classic beginner's mistake. Later, the rumour mill was boosted by the strange failure of the RAF authorities to issue any official report on the cause of the crash. Yet some investigations had been undertaken, for Captain Hubert Charles, a senior accident investigator, was sent ot the scene of the crash. On examining the engine he found that the air intake of the carburettor was identical to the type fitted the early SE5 he had encountered in June 1917 when acting as the engineering officer of 56 Squadron. It had been found that near vertical turns and violent manoeuvres flooded the carburettor, causing loss of power, and the intakes had been modified to allow adequate petrol drainage. Lieutenant Fenelon had seen McCudden employ a vertical turn on take off, so if the SE5a had an unmodified carburettor McCudden would have been in immediate trouble. As the angle of the bank increased McCudden would have needed exta power, but when he opened the throttle the engine would promptly choke and lose power – his SE5a lost flying speed, turned over onto its back and crashed. In the last moments, with no chance to recover, he switched off the engine to reduce the risk of fire, undid his safety belt and took his chance in the inevitable crash. Perversely, this last precaution may have been his downfall.

James McCudden's death had a considerable effect on his comrades in the RAF. Edward Mannock in particular took it badly; he had been in part taught to fly by McCudden and they had a lot in common. They were both of 'lowly' origins, both had scaled the heights thanks to their own abilities and carefully applied intelligence and they both had an unwillingness to take unnecessary chances. But by June 1918 Mannock was a man coming to the end of his tether. He had always used humour to disguise his own jangling nerves, in essence laughing away his fears, but in the course of this he developed a macabre mania for describing the consequences of being shot down in flames.

> Whenever he sends one down in flames he comes dancing into the mess, whooping and hallooing, 'Flamerinoees, boys! Sizzle, sizzle, wonk!' Then at great length, he tries to describe the feelings of the poor old Hun by going into the minutest details. Having finished in a frenzy of fiendish glee, he

> will turn to one of us and say, laughing, 'That's what will happen to you on your next patrol, my lad!'[7] *Lieutenant Ira Jones, 74 Squadron*

His nerves were clearly shattered and his letters reveal a chaotic jumble of thoughts tumbling out onto the paper.

> Things are getting a bit intense just lately and I don't quite know how long my nerves will last out. I am rather old now, as airmen go, for air fighting. Still, one hopes for the best. These times are so horrible that occasionally I feel that life is not worth hanging on to myself, but 'hope springs eternal in the human breast'.[8] *Captain Edward Mannock, 74 Squadron*

He was evidently suffering from combat fatigue and he should have been sent home. On his last leave in June he had been more than usually moody, convinced he would be killed, and his pre-war friend Jim Eyles reported physical reactions that illustrated the insupportable nervous strain he was under.

> He started to tremble violently. This grew into a convulsive straining. He cried uncontrollably, muttering something that I could not make out. His face, when he lifted it, was a terrible sight. Saliva and tears were running down his face; he couldn't stop it. His collar and shirt front were soaked through. He smiled weakly at me when he saw me watching and tried to make light of it; he would not talk about it at all.[9] *Jim Eyles*

Yet patriotic duty or the driving ambition to be the highest scoring ace beckoned him still, and on his return from leave he was promoted to major and posted to take over the command of 85 Squadron. It seems that his rumbustious character was considered more acceptable in their mess than the more reserved McCudden. Also, as the popular press had not yet caught up with Mannock's exploits, his new élitist comrades were unaware that he was the son of a corporal. Once installed as their squadron leader, Mannock concentrated on developing the efficiency of his pilots in flying and fighting in tightly controlled formations, and he took a full and active part as a patrol leader himself. The squadron responded exceptionally well to his inspirational leadership and soon began to function effectively as a collective unit.

By mid-July Mannock had won the hearts and minds of his new charges in 85 Squadron. Whenever they flew in flights at varying altitudes he was always willing to take the lower and hence more dangerous station.

> He would always be the low man, not high man, that's where I always admired Mannock. He was always low, and I knew it because I was with him. When a bunch of Huns came along he would goad them into attacking him while the rest of the boys were off in the distance, waiting. It worked magnificently. Mannock was such a hell of a fighter and such a good shot that he could afford to get himself into the worst position and still shoot his way out. He was a highly imaginative pilot, and the best shot that I ever saw in my life.[10] *Second Lieutenant Larry Callahan, 85 Squadron*

This growing willingness to take on all risks and his confidence that he could shoot or manoeuvre his way out of any trouble, so different from his former caution, all increasingly coexisted with premonitions of his own death. In particular on a couple of occasions he followed tumbling German aircraft right down to the ground to ensure their destruction. This entirely contradicted his own 'always above' watchwords, but he was no longer entirely rational. This did not, however, stop him from continuing to chastise others for committing exactly the same offence! On meeting his former 'pupil' Captain George McElroy on 21 July at a party with old comrades from 40 Squadron, Mannock sternly lectured his friend, now a formidable ace in his own right, on his reported habit of flying low to make certain of kills.

> I remember him telling McElroy, 'Don't throw yourself away, don't go down on the deck – don't do that, you'll get shot down from the ground.'[11] *Lieutenant Gwilym Lewis, 40 Squadron*

McElroy took it in good part and reciprocated warmly, though he may well have been suffering a little from strain because he had just had an extraordinary escape that very same day when the engine of his SE5 caught fire and he had been forced to throw himself out of the cockpit as he made a desperate forced landing. In any case he ignored Mannock's warnings. He would only last another ten days before, as Mannock predicted, he was shot down and killed by anti-aircraft fire while flying low over the lines after achieving his forty-seventh victory on 31 July.

But what of Mannock himself? On his arrival at 85 Squadron Mannock had continued his policy of 'blooding' promising new pilots; spoon-feeding them their first kills by himself removing every possible obstacle to their success.

> He was determined to win. He hated the Huns and he wanted to kill all of them. He wasn't interested in just killing them himself. He wanted a lot of them killed, and he trained us how to do it. That was why, on several occasions, Mannock made way for a new pilot to come in and finish off an enemy aircraft that he had already winged. It was to give the new boy confidence.[12] *Second Lieutenant Larry Callahan, 85 Squadron*

This habit of Mannock's was certainly unusual, though not entirely unique among the very best flight leaders, but it should not be exaggerated. He seems to have done this about five or six times and certainly usually claimed a share in the kill himself. It was while carrying out such a munificent mission that Mannock's luck finally ran out. On 26 July 1918 Mannock took a young New Zealand pilot, Lieutenant Douglas Inglis, up on a dawn patrol to try and break his 'duck'. At about 05.30, Mannock sighted a two-seater LVG piloted by Vizefeldwebel Josef Hein with his observer Leutnant Ludwig Schöpf. Inglis had been ordered to stick close to Mannock's tail.

> A quick turn and a dive, and there was Mick shooting up a Hun two-seater. He must have got the observer, as when he pulled up and I came in underneath him I didn't see the Hun shooting. I flushed the Hun's petrol tank and just missed ramming his tail as it came up when the Hun's nose dropped. Falling in behind Mick again we did a couple of circles round the burning wreck and then made for home.[13] *Lieutenant Douglas Inglis, 85 Squadron*

From the ground Private Edward Naulls of the 2nd Essex Regiment, who were occupying the front line in the sector between Robecq and Bois de Pacaut, saw the two aircraft flying low down.

> I watch fascinated as tracer bullets from a German machine gun post enter Mannock's engine just behind the cowling; there is a swift tongue of flame followed by belching black smoke and Mannock's machine falls away helplessly to hit the ground not far from his victim.[14] *Private Edward Naulls, 2nd Battalion, Essex Regiment*

It all happened so quickly, right in front of the disbelieving eyes of Douglas Inglis.

> I saw Mick start to kick his rudder and realised we were fairly low, then I saw a flame come out of the side of his machine; it grew bigger and bigger. Mick was no longer kicking his rudder, his nose dropped slightly and he went into a slow right-hand turn round, about twice, and hit the ground in a burst of flame. I circled at about 20 feet but could not see him, and as things were getting pretty hot, made for home.[15] *Lieutenant Douglas Inglis, 85 Squadron*

Inglis himself had his petrol tank holed and only just gained the British front line before making a forced landing by the trenches at St Floris, although by this time he had been liberally sprayed with petrol and hardly knew what he was doing.

> The pilot was badly shaken and covered in petrol. He was rather incoherent, shouting, 'They've shot him down!' A young lieutenant came along and took him into a dugout. The pilot was quite distraught and nearly in tears.[16] *Sergeant John, 24th Battalion, Welch Regiment*

Back at the airfield the realization of Mannock's death only sank in gradually. Every report that came in from the front line was more definite as to his fate and it was soon apparent that their charismatic leader was indeed dead. In such circumstances it was traditional in the RAF to try to hold a defiant party and that night the men of 85 Squadron stiffened their resolve and tried their best. But their hearts were not really in it, even when his old comrades from 74 Squadron turned up to help.

> It was a difficult business. The thought of Mick's charred body not many miles away haunted us and dampened our spirits. There was more drinking

than usual on these occasions; the Decca worked overtime; we tried to sing, but it was painfully obvious that it was forced.[17] ***Lieutenant Ira Jones, 74 Squadron***

Mannock's reputation as the finest patrol leader of the war within the RAF was secure, but few civilians had ever heard of him and he was only belatedly awarded a posthumous Victoria Cross in July 1919 – a year after his death. Yet stranger things were to happen. There was widespread scepticism within the RAF, as opposed to the Royal Canadian Air Force, over the seventy-two victories claimed by Major William Bishop. It is now generally believed that these doubts were the motivation for posthumously raising Mannock's claimed score of around sixty-one victories right up to a frankly dubious seventy-three, 'coincidentally' just one more than Bishop had claimed. It was Mannock's occasional practice of giving or sharing his kills with his wingmen that provided a cover for this artificial post-war increase. And there he would remain, lauded in the history books as the highest scoring British ace of the Great War. One can only imagine that had Edward Mannock ever known he would have laughed.

THE aces were tumbling from the sky by mid-1918. Yet the strange thing is that nothing really changed. The hard work of exploring the capabilities of the aircraft had been done long ago; the development of aerial tactics had been completed; the wise words of the importance of preparation and caution had all been spoken. Men may have mourned Manfred von Richthofen, Edward Mannock and James McCudden, but what were they mourning? How many really knew them? Part of the sadness felt on their deaths was surely a projection of individual pilot's own fears: if men like these, with all their manifest skills, knowledge and experience, could be killed then what chance did they themselves have? Even more germane: had the war in the air been altered in any way after their deaths? In essence the answer is not at all. The numbers of scout pilots flying over the front, well organized by numerous competent tactical leaders, was such that any individual ace's work was almost redundant.

Chapter 10

A Black Day

After the failure of the series of the Kaiserschlacht offensives, the German High Command could see the writing was on the wall. It consequently placed the whole Western Front onto a defensive basis. They knew what had to be done; indeed it was in one sense merely a return to the status quo of awaiting the next Allied onslaught as they had throughout 1916 and 1917. However, by now the German Army and the state from which it was drawn had reached the end of their hangman's rope. There was no longer a question of who would win the war; the only question was whether the Allies would attain the victory in 1918 or 1919.

It was the French who got the ball rolling with a series of counter-attacks after the German thrust on the Marne in early July. It soon became apparent to the Allies that there was a whole new situation on the Western Front. Once again they could plan for the offensive. Field Marshal Sir Douglas Haig ordered his subordinate army commanders to prepare options for attacks.

The most promising plan to emerge was put forward under the auspices of General Sir Henry Rawlinson commanding the British Fourth Army. The active front-line patrolling of the Australian Corps had revealed that the Germans were not behaving in their normal fashion. In particular it was evident that they were not employing their usual diligence to prepare the layered defences in depth that they would need if they were to beat back a determined assault. The battle-worn German divisions holding the line had sunk into an unhealthy state of stupor. When ordered to take up a defensive stance, they simply lacked the energy to ensure the necessary work was done. Rawlinson realized that he had the chance to make a real difference to the war situation. Here also was the chance to try a new kind of operation.

The initial Fourth Army concept was starkly limited in scope, seeking only to regain some of the ground won by the German spring offensive in the Somme area and to push the Germans back to the old British defensive line between Méricourt and Hangest. But Rawlinson was determined to use the new all-arms tactics deployed at Cambrai in November 1917 and recently improved and road-tested with spectacular success by Lieutenant General Sir John Monash commanding the Australians in the explorative Battle of Hamel on 4 July. The emphasis was now firmly on the suppression of German resistance until it was too late to have an impact, rather than the lengthy process of outright destruction formerly considered essential before an assault could be undertaken.

In the all-arms battle there was a clear stress on using the emerging panoply of machines and engines of war, rather than the flesh and blood of the poor benighted infantry to break down the German defences. The massed heavy guns would first suppress the German artillery batteries with veritable deluges of high explosive and gas shells. Then the field artillery would fire the all-important, but tortuously complicated, creeping barrages that edged forward clearing the way for the infantry assault. Armoured warfare had finally come of age with the deployment of the heavy Mark V tanks which would take out strongpoints; while if the German line broke, the fast-moving medium Whippet tanks were to range ahead and keep the Germans off-balance, preventing them from reorganizing their defences. Meanwhile, above them, in the third element, the bomber squadrons would strive to seal off the battlefield by disrupting German rail and road communications, while swarms of scouts engaged in ground strafing would strike hard at any targets of opportunity. It was a multi-faceted attack, pummelling the hapless Germans, but most of all it was flexible, able to switch focus between weapons as the situation demanded. It was a variegated weapons system that had been forged by painful experimentation over the last three years of war.

The new tactics were expressly designed to be relatively economical with the lives of the infantry. They had to be. The British Army was depleted not just by four years of war and the enduring effects of the massive casualties inflicted upon them during the German offensives, but also by the Prime Minister Lloyd George's continued reluctance to deploy manpower reserves on the Western Front. At heart he sought to control Haig and prevent him launching further costly offensives. Perversely this caution was then exacerbated by Lloyd George's addiction to the extravagant side shows across the Middle East so beloved of amateur tacticians.

By 1918 there was also a qualitative difference in the infantry available for deployment on the Western Front. There is no doubt that the morale of the British soldiery was in a peculiar state. They were depressed and downtrodden, worn down by the myriad horrors of war. There were more and more cases of 'shell hole dropping', of outright malingering, even of downright cowardice in the face of the enemy. When things were going wrong there is no doubt that the British 'Tommy' was no longer the indomitable warrior of 1916, but they *were* willing to keep going as long as they felt they had a chance of survival and success. And the new tactics gave them that chance.

The British Army did not favour overtly élite units in the fashion of the German storm-trooper divisions. It preferred to try to raise the overall standard of *all* its formations and the latest tactical methods were widely disseminated across the BEF through a series of instructional pamphlets. These clearly encapsulated best practice as known at the time so that others could follow their lead. Ideas of lines of men advancing with only their rifles and bodies to add weight to the attack had long been outmoded. Now there was a concentration on firepower at all levels. There may have been fewer of them but collectively they packed far more of a punch. The battalions were under strength in mere numbers of infantrymen, but they now deployed thirty Lewis light machine guns, they had rifle grenades, they were backed up by lethal concentrations of Vickers heavy machine guns firing indirect barrages that rained bullets down on their enemies, by mortars belching out high-explosive, gas or smoke bombs and of course the massed panoply of the Royal Artillery – indubitably the greatest weapons system of the Great War.

As the reports came in from Fourth Army, Haig also became convinced that the German Army was vulnerable to attack. Although he had thought the same in both 1916 and 1917, that did not lessen his inner certainty. With the Germans weakening he saw the possibility of widening the scope of the putative Fourth Army offensive. Foch, as the overall Allied commander, readily agreed and at his instigation it was decided that the French First Army commanded by General Marie Debeney would be placed under Haig's command for the planned attack. The Allies were working as a team. Of course their differences had not vanished, there were still grievances and petty jealousies, but overall they were being sublimated for the common good. The end result was that the old outer Allied defence line in front of Amiens was now regarded as just the first stage. Haig directed Rawlinson to be prepared to push on towards Chaulnes while Debeney made for Roye, with the liberation of Ham a further 15 miles back their final objective. While Haig chivvied his subordinates with ever grander ambitions, Foch was doing exactly the same to Haig, checking that the exploitation of any success should be as forceful as possible.

Yet all the long painful years of trench warfare and the failure of countless breakthrough attempts had not unnaturally dulled the ambitions of Rawlinson and his hardworking staff officers. In a sense he had been the first to appreciate the worth of the 'bite and hold' tactics way back in March 1915 at Neuve Chapelle. There was no doubt that whatever lip-service he paid to the idea of breaking through to the green fields beyond, he felt the initial planned advance of 8 miles was quite enough to be going on with. The force deployed by Fourth Army was considerable: the III Corps were on the left between the Ancre and the Somme rivers, next to them was the much vaunted Australian Corps between the Somme and the Villers–Chaulnes railway line, then the Canadian Corps attacking between the railway and the Roye–Amiens road. In all, three British, two Australian and three Canadian divisions would make the initial assault supported by 1,386 field guns, 684 heavy guns, 342 tanks and 72 of the Whippet tanks. In reserve, ready to follow up, were three more divisions and, of course, the Cavalry Corps, reinforced with yet more Whippets, stood ready for any exploitation. To the right of Fourth Army, the French First Army would attack between the dividing line of the Roye–Amiens road and the Avre river. They had a superiority of manpower of three to two over the Germans which was not excessive given the bloody noses and worse suffered with a far greater numerical superiority in previous offensives such as that on 1 July 1916 in the self-same Somme area. But this time it was a battle using the latest tactics, not just blood and guts taking on the power of unsuppressed German artillery and machine guns. And thanks to the reconnaissance efforts of the RAF they knew exactly where the German guns were – 504 of the 530 guns facing Fourth Army had been pinpointed.

Now it was the Germans' turn to wonder and worry over where the attack would be launched. Ludendorff and Hindenburg knew full well that only an effective concentration of their military reserves at the decisive spot could hope to thwart the Allies. The problem was finding this spot. This placed a special responsibility on the shoulders of the German Air Service commanded by General Ernest Wilhelm von Hoeppner.

> Since each Army front might now become a critical point in the action with surprising quickness, it was no longer possible to go through with the usual preliminary step of a methodical concentration of aviation, as had been the custom in the previous offensive and defensive actions. Measures had to be taken to provide for a simultaneous withdrawal all along the front and all available air units, especially the pursuit and attack squadrons, had to be held concentrated so that they could be despatched to the threatened points. This rapid concentration was to be carried out not only in the individual Armies, but also in the entire Group of Armies where all air strength must help out in case of an attack.[1] *General Ernest Wilhelm von Hoeppner, German Air Service*

But von Hoeppner well knew that he and his men had a particular responsibility in that it was, of course, the task of his reconnaissance aircraft to discover exactly where and even when the Allies intended the blow to fall.

> To determine in ample time the enemy's carefully concealed preparations for an attack, was a vital question for our Western Armies during these very serious days. This task was far more difficult, for the enemy had available at this time all the material needed in an attack which he had been years in accumulating, piled up along the entire front from the coast to Switzerland. Beside this, he had learned how to follow German methods and he was now able to conceal completely the preparations for an attack.[2] *General Ernest Wilhelm von Hoeppner, German Air Service*

Indeed Rawlinson was making a fixation out of secrecy. At every level of command there were precautions to prevent the leaking of information to the Germans. The batteries, tanks and battalions moved in to the area as late as possible, just a week before the planned start date on 8 August 1918. In the past the preparatory bombardment would have already started, but the guns remained safely concealed out of sight and would rely on the latest map registration techniques to be ready to fire the moment the attack began. The RAF and French Air Force had also to conceal their concentration of squadrons into the Somme area from the Germans. This was done with a sham concentration of squadrons and increased air activity in the Ypres area in an attempt to channel German attention to the well-worn battlefields of Flanders.

Over the Somme it was crucial that there should be no abnormal air activity before the air assault was launched in synchronization with the men on the ground. This was difficult to achieve as they still had to fly the usual photographic and artillery observation missions that were obviously more important than ever, but which had to be undertaken without attracting too much attention; similarly the RAF had the additional responsibility of thwarting German attempts at high-level aerial reconnaissance without making it obvious that they 'had something to hide'. This called for a neat sense of balance. In the end they were blessed by the poor weather conditions prevalent in early August that severely restricted flying by either side. When the clouds cleared and the sun sheepishly emerged on the afternoon of 7 August it was already too late for the effective photographic reconnaissance and intelligence interpretation that the Germans would need to realize what exactly lay before them. The British scouts managed to fend off the German scouts without overreacting.

By August 1918 the RAF operated in strength everywhere along the front and could achieve the photographic reconnaissance and artillery observation missions that might be needed without the need for major reinforcements. Only in the last few days would the various squadrons begin to move forward onto airfields close to the front; many still remained where they were and would strike hard from their normal bases well outside the Amiens area. The total concentration of air power amassed in support of the attack was some 110 army cooperation aircraft, 376 scouts, 147 day bombers, 92 night bombers and 75 scout/reconnaissance aircraft – a statistically satisfying 800 aeroplanes, each with their place in the order of battle. In addition the French Air Force had concentrated no fewer than 1,104 aircraft in similar proportions, adding up to a total of 1,904 Allied aircraft. The Germans faced them with just 171 army cooperation aircraft, 140 fighters, 36 bombers and 18 ground-strafing fighters – a total of only 365 aircraft. They could move in reinforcements from elsewhere, indeed many of their squadrons were still languishing in the Champagne area, the site of their last failed offensive, but would they arrive in time?

The RAF squadrons were carefully briefed to let them know exactly what they were meant to be doing and how it would fit in with the general scheme of things. One such briefing took place in the officers' mess of 205 Squadron on the very eve of the attack.

> Major Adams, Brigade Intelligence Officer, arrived at the squadron on the eve of battle, the 7th August. He dined with us and after dinner described the operations of the Fourth Army for the morrow. The line had been stationary since my arrival in France in April. Tomorrow it was to move and he described the layout of the operations. Adams' address inspires quiet confidence. Our job was to bomb and shoot up aerodromes, dumps, roads and railways from dawn to dusk. On much of our good work depended the fate of the infantry.[3] *Lieutenant William Grossart, 205 Squadron*

Only a few of the pilots and observers in the hushed room had formerly served in the infantry and from bitter personal experience knew exactly what it meant for the 'poor bloody infantry' to go over the top next morning. One who had was William Grossart himself. As he listened to the dry details of the briefing his experiences on the Somme in 1916 resurfaced in his mind.

> Adams threw a little of that eve of battle atmosphere into the hushed mess though possibly none but myself appreciated it. Stirring times ahead, zero hour, attack at dawn. Soon the lads who won the war would be on their way to the communications trenches with their interminable 'hole on the right' or 'wire overhead'. The screech and crump of the 5.9 as it found its way near and often into the packed avenue. A few men less for the first

wave, but on they go. Well could I see them – all in battle order waiting for the magic of zero hour.[4] *Lieutenant William Grossart, 205 Squadron*

That night, despite poor weather conditions, the Handley Pages of 207 Squadron were already flying over the Somme area so that the deep-throated roar of their engines would cover the noise of the tanks as they rumbled slowly forward to take up their allotted jumping-off positions. When dawn broke, the day bomber squadrons, aided and abetted by escorting scouts, were to attack all identified German airfields along the front in an attempt to strangle any aerial response at birth. When the infantry and tanks went over the top the corps aircraft would engage in the usual contact patrols and liaise with the artillery to bring down extra fire support wherever it was required. Scout squadrons stood ready to deal with any German aerial activity that managed to get itself off the ground. Throughout the day squadrons of all types would be engaging ground targets of opportunity to harass the Germans and deflect them from the organization of an effective defence to the advancing tanks and infantry. Later, by day and night, bombers would strike home on the crucial railway stations. Raids on the junctions at Peronne and Chaulnes were intended to cut off or at the very least disrupt the flow of German reinforcements that would be hastening pell-mell to the threatened front.

As dawn broke on 8 August the men of the RAF dragged themselves out of their beds. Some had had an understandably troubled sleep, knowing the trials that would face them that day; others had slept like the proverbial babes.

At 3.30am the adjutant awoke me. Soon the camp was astir. Usually we lay until the exasperated CO almost pulled some of us out for the very early shows. I was soon in the mess in my flying kit drinking my coffee and watching the lads come in in ones and twos, some arm in arm, others giving each other a hearty, more than hearty, 'Good morning!' slap on the back. An air of subdued excitement prevailed. The rumble of distant gunfire broke the silence only to be submerged by the sound of our engines starting up on the aerodrome. Busy mechanics with torches were warming up the engines which this day would never cool. It was still pitch dark at 4am when I found my way to the 'drome, ghostly figures moved about each intent upon his own allotted task.[5] *Lieutenant William Grossart, 205 Squadron*

All was set for the opening of the crunching barrage at 04.20. This was the moment when the British Army began to repay the Germans for all it had suffered during the last few months. The new offensive tactics blending the use of massed artillery power, infantry, tanks and aircraft worked almost perfectly. The German divisions facing it melted away like snow in summer sunshine with significant numbers surrendering *en masse*. The sheer power of the Allied barrages was inspiring for the aviators above them. Among them were Lieutenant William Grossart and Lieutenant J. B. Leach in their DH4 which Grossart had quaintly named Emma.

We were flying in flights. Dickson led 'C' and I brought up the rear. Low clouds hung about and Dickson was soon leading us up between two banks. It was weird, mystic, wonderful. High grey walls towered above us on each side, stars in the sky above were not yet obscured by the coming dawn. We wound our way between the banks of cloudland to the Somme which we followed for a while, its course marked by a grey winding ribbon on a dark featureless landscape. All the hollows below were filled by grey mist. At Amiens we cut off to the southeast for Chaulnes and the hellfire vision of the French barrage met our gaze. The landscape was a mass of flame, the stabs of fire from guns and shells only lighting up a haze of smoke. It was an inspiring sight and many were the shells that swept unseen past our planes. The greatest day of the war in the air had begun.[6] *Lieutenant William Grossart, 205 Squadron*

In the event most of these very early morning missions achieved little, for the battlefield was swathed in low mist and cloudy conditions that posed the usual mixed blessings for the attacking forces. While they cloaked the advance of the infantry and tanks from the threat of German machine guns and artillery, at the same time they made it hard for the RAF to accomplish its planned roles. Contact patrols and air cooperation were difficult, ground attack almost impossible, bombing hopelessly inaccurate and German airfields invisible.

One innovation was the assignment of 8 Squadron as the air cooperation squadron specifically assigned to the Tank Corps. Each of the constituent tank brigades was assigned its own flight to work closely with it and Major Trafford Leigh-Mallory found his twenty-four Armstrong Whitworths duly spread out right across the Third, First and Fourth Army fronts. His pilots and observers had already spent a considerable time liaising, exercising and even socializing with the tanks officers they would be working with. By this time they had grasped both the strengths and weaknesses of tanks, which meant their reports from the skies were realistic in their assessment of what was and could be achieved.

> All tank brigades had message dropping stations. Information was frequently dropped on these dropping stations, and at tank rallying points, giving the latest information concerning the progress of our own tanks and infantry, and the dispositions of the enemy. These reports also gave tank brigade commanders a clear idea as to how many tanks had been knocked out, and consequently assisted them to decide what proportion of the reserve would be required for the next phase of the operation. Wherever there was a chance of assisting the tanks by direct action with bombs and machine gun fire, this was done.[7] *Major Trafford Leigh-Mallory, 8 Squadron*

The fog played havoc with the carefully laid plans but one of the Armstrong Whitworths, crewed by Lieutenants Freddie West and William Haslam, braved the mists on a low-level tank cooperation flight. Tank cooperation was still in its absolute infancy and although they tried hard they had considerable difficulties.

> All our means of communications were flags and the trouble was that these flags were yellow and green, white and so on. When these were stored inside the tanks they became disfigured and it was very difficult from the air to tell the colour. We had to come down very low to receive the information the tanks wanted to give us.[8] *Lieutenant Freddie West, 8 Squadron*

As they skimmed low across the tanks they were vulnerable to the barrages of both sides crashing down all around them.

I remember seeing the shells of our barrage, which were very much at the height at which we were flying and you could see them every now and then – they didn't worry me. We went on looking for tanks and reporting where they were. When we turned west to go back there was a lot of fog ahead of us. Amiens Cathedral spire gave us a good line for Villaincourt airfield which was not far away and we started to come down in the fog. The next thing we saw was Villaincourt church much too close but West dodged that and we came up again for breath. This I suppose made the squadron aware that we were nearby and wanted to land and they fired Very lights which broke above the cloud and showed us where the aerodrome was. So we came down again. West must have picked a very good line because looking straight down was what I was sure was the aerodrome, but I couldn't see ahead at all. We came down lower and lower and the next thing was we saw a hangar straight ahead of us! West saved us from a bad crash by swinging the aeroplane strongly so that we hit one side and corner of the hangar with one wing, folding it back on the fuselage and then we heeled over on that side and slid down the corner of the hangar. We were out of the aeroplane well before it had properly settled; fire was the one thing at the back of our minds.[9] *Lieutenant William Haslam, 8 Squadron*

They had survived relatively unscathed although West had badly cut his lip and Haslam had knocked his knee about. In the circumstances they could genuinely consider themselves fortunate.

When the dust had died down, the tanks, although effective in crushing the wire and taking out pockets of resistance, had suffered dreadful casualties. Time and time again they were ambushed by German anti-tank guns and the inevitable mechanical breakdowns meant that of the 415 tanks that went into action only 145 were ready to resume action next morning. It was obvious that the next task the RAF had to address was the identification and then neutralization of anti-tank batteries with fast scouts attacking with bombs and machine-gun fire to cover the lumbering tanks' slow-motion approach. In 1918 tanks were not the super-weapon that they would become in future years. They had finally attained a high value as part of the all-arms equation, but once again it was evident that the artillery was the super-weapon of the Great War. But only as part of a greater whole. If the learning curve endured by the British soldier had been about anything it was the necessity of applying the right mix of weapons to any given situation.

As the aircraft flew over the German lines, whether they were seen or merely sensed from below, the massed anti-aircraft guns still managed to blaze out at them in fine style.

> Without deviating right or left Dickson led us straight for Chaulnes through an inferno of bursting 'Archie' showing up with terrifying effect in the still darkening sky around us. Once or twice we shivered as 'Emma' heaved from a nearby shell; once or twice I blinked at the bursting shell in front and felt the smell of TNT as we passed through its smoke.[10] *Lieutenant William Grossart, 205 Squadron*

Grossart's first mission was brief but he did not spend long on the ground before he and his observer were back up again and looking to target Bouvincourt airfield. Their aim was to prevent the German aircraft from intervening in the battle. This time they lost contact with the rest of the flight in the heavy cloud cover.

> We sped on alone to the German aerodrome. But we were destined never to get there for the cloud in the bottom of whose haze we were flying came to an end and we ran below three Pfalz scouts sitting about 1,000 feet above us. They immediately dived. My first concern was to get rid of the bombs. I pulled over an encampment of huts, signalled Leach to drop and sent out two hundredweights of steel and ammonol towards what now appeared to be a field hospital. We had no time to delay. The Pfalz were now diving under us and as they zoomed up I threw 'Emma' round in a vertical bank. Leach sent one to eternity with his guns; his Pfalz burst into flames south of the long road near Proyart. The other two sheared off. I thought we had escaped lightly and it wasn't until we reached the hangars that our flight sergeant spotted the little propeller of one petrol pump was not working. A bullet from the Pfalz had penetrated the casing and bent the spindle. We were sorry about the hospital afterwards, but squared our consciences by remembering the German attacks on Etaples hospital and the nurses who were killed there.[11] *Lieutenant William Grossart, 205 Squadron*

Once the mists had cleared at about 09.00, the British scouts flew across the length and breadth of the battlefield firing at targets of opportunity. As the Germans fell back in disarray the machine guns and 25-pound bombs added to their crippling sense of dislocation and overwhelming panic.

The German front was crumbling under the hammer blows of Fourth Army. By noon it was obvious that the German front-line divisions had been shattered by the sheer ferocity of the assault. As they fell back it was evident that they must either be massively reinforced, or retreat across the Somme river before they could achieve relative safety. Cutting the bridges across the Somme would hinder the frantic German efforts to get reinforcing divisions into the battle while, even more significantly, if they could be destroyed then all the Germans to the west of them – some 70,000 soldiers with all their equipment – would be trapped and left no escape route. There were in all eleven road and rail bridges within the area and Major General John Salmond cancelled his existing orders and launched a series of hell-for-leather bombing attacks with the avowed intention of destroying these crucial bridges. These bridges would become the scene of great heroism for both sides over the next few days: Bray, Cappy, Eclusier, Feuillères, Peronne, Brie, St Christ, Falvy, Bethencourt, Voyennes and Offey – the fate of these few bridges would decide the fate of thousands of lives on the ground.

One of the first raids was launched by 107 Squadron, whose DH9s attacked the bridge at Brie carrying the main Amiens to St Quentin road. As such it was a target of obvious importance and the Germans had duly amassed impressive anti-aircraft defences around it.

> We set off at 1.30pm and crossed at 4,000 feet only. We immediately ran into a terrific barrage of anti-aircraft shells. We reached the bridge at 2.15 and went low and dropped our bombs amongst thousands of retreating Germans camped around the bridgehead awaiting their turn to cross. We then went down to about 100 feet and machine gunned the troops. I have never before seen such a charnel house of dead and dying. We must have killed hundreds. Having done our job we made formation for the return flight, midst a perfect inferno of antiaircraft fire. One machine containing Gaukrodger and Doncaster was hit and went down in flames. Both were

killed. On landing I found ten shrapnel holes in my wings.[12] *Second Lieutenant George Coles, 107 Squadron*

Once again ordinary men were killing and wounding far more than any ace could hope to achieve in a whole career of air fighting.

By the afternoon the German Air Service was beginning to regain its collective composure and fought back hard in the finest traditions of that remarkable group of men.

After the fog had lifted, dense squadrons of hostile aviators shattered the resistance of the support troops, and the air force with the Second Army was too weak to prevent it. Only in the course of the afternoon was it possible for our combined pursuit strength of the Seventeenth and Eighteenth Armies to defeat our enemy in the air.[13] *General Ernest Wilhelm von Hoeppner, German Air Service*

The idea that the RAF and French Air Service were defeated is perhaps fanciful, but the level of German opposition certainly began to escalate as the long day wore on. Among the reinforcing German units was the 'Flying Circus' itself. Manfred von Richthofen's old command, Jagdgeschwader 1, was by this time under the command of his brother Oberleutnant Lothar von Richthofen in the temporary absence of their designated leader, Hauptmann Hermann Göring, who had certainly chosen the wrong or right time (depending on perspective) to go on leave. In the late afternoon they moved into the Ennemain airfield about 5 miles from Peronne, ideally placed for the task at hand. Their normally cautious battle tactics were now of little relevance in this battle to the death. These German aces could not stand back to conserve their forces for another day; *this was the day.* For the next few days they simply had to throw caution to the winds, and, like the heroes they were, that is exactly what they did.

Lothar von Richthofen raced into action; he was never as cool and calculating as his late brother. But he was a hero in his own right. He claimed three victims that day, as did Erich Löwenhardt and Ernst Udet, superlative aces all, whose achievements have never been seriously challenged. In his final kill of the day Richthofen got behind the SE5 piloted by Second Lieutenant James Hall of 60 Squadron.

At tree level we raced on towards the front. At an altitude of about 10 metres, I race after the Englishman. I can only fire a few rounds at a time since I am so busy with other things. Below I see various kinds of troops watching this wild chase in amazement. Now I've hit him. He's proceeding to land – or is it just a ruse? I was dying to give him just another couple of rounds. He apparently means to land at this insane speed. At least, he rushes towards the ground as if he means to land and then goes into the ground. Splinters fly in all directions. I have to put my machine into a steep climb to avoid being hit by the fragments flying round. By the skin of my teeth, I manage to clear the nearest tree.[14] *Oberleutnant Lothar von Richthofen, Jagdgeschwader 1*

After a day of triumph Richthofen then committed the blunder of landing too fast on his return to the airfield and wrote off his Fokker D.VII.

The increasing pace of the air battle was noticeable from the perspective of Lieutenant Grossart who was on his third mission strafing and bombing the roads when he saw the scouts swirling around in combat above them.

We passed high above us a magnificent dogfight of some thirty fighting aeroplanes. One of ours broke up in mid air and a pair of wings with the red, white and blue of the Allies fluttered down to earth past us while the main part shot down like a stone.[15] *Lieutenant William Grossart, 205 Squadron*

Heavy casualties were inevitable in such a vicious battle. The German aces were masters of their trade and they found victims easy to come by as the British pilots concentrated on the task in hand rather than the exigencies of aerial combat. This was a dangerous business. At 17.00 Lieutenant Ronald Sykes took off for another mission behind the fragmenting German front.

Low observation patrol in pairs. Flying behind Captain Kinkead. Saw Lieutenant Stone killed behind the lines by a Fokker which dived out of low cloud. Stoney was due for leave that day. Flew low over his Camel burning after crashing on a road on which he had been about to dive. Chased Fokker

D.VII away east. Lieutenant J. M. Mackay was shooting at German infantry when they hit his Camel and he came down 300 yards behind the enemy lines. Making a dash for freedom, he met one of our tanks and got inside. Finding it to be going further into action he opened the doors at the side and hopped out again and, under sporadic rifle fire made off westwards, and eventually rejoined the squadron at Bertangles.[16] *Lieutenant Ronald Sykes, 201 Squadron*

In all there were 205 bombing missions and some 12 tons of bombs were dropped on the main Somme bridges on 8 August. It was a day of concentrated effort; not just by the individual pilots and observers, but also by their ground crews who worked round the clock to put the aircraft into the air, time after time during this, the longest day.

All day long we kept it up. Flight succeeded flight as each arrived and left. Everyone was working hard and the hardest of all were our mess orderlies. Never from morning till night were the tables cleared; the orderly routine of early coffee, breakfast, lunch and dinner gave way to a running buffet. Never during the day did many have off their flying suits. Leach and I were an exception, being held up for two hours for a new bit of petrol pump, one of which got a bullet though it when I was attacked by three Pfalz scouts upon our second raid. As soon as a flight landed, mechanics swarmed over the machines filling with petrol, oil and water, bombs and ammunition, looking over shock absorbers, bracing wire and control wires. The day was one of enthusiasm, interest and excitement, such as I never knew in France. These were enhanced greatly about mid-day when reports came in of the success of the Australians and Canadians. The surprise attack had succeeded beyond the most sanguine hopes.[17] *Lieutenant William Grossart, 205 Squadron*

When the fighting resumed on 9 August, the British were still, rightly or wrongly, fixated on destroying the Somme bridges. It seemed an obvious objective, for thousands of German soldiers would be trapped within the Somme bottleneck if the bridges could be destroyed; the question was whether it could be achieved before the German reinforcements arrived.

On the 9th, 10th and 11th the big battle raged to the same tune as on the 8th. From daylight to dark the engines tore their murderous loads to the heavens, the passes of the Somme, Peronne and St Christ Bridges being the objectives to cut the lines of communication.[18] *Lieutenant William Grossart, 205 Squadron*

Grossart found there was a strange dichotomy between the biting tension of their aerial tasks and the relative comfort in which they lived on the ground. Just a few minutes after they had been engaged in a potentially life-or-death struggle over the bridges they would find themselves far behind the lines.

Finally we got home to our aerodrome and were strolling over to our tents in the sylvan peace. Flying is a dirty business and a good scrub was indicated. Our orderly had provided warm water and had our portable canvas wash buckets in position outside our tent all ready for us. We had just time to have a good wash and brush-up and get over to the mess for dinner. Everything at our table with its snow-white covering seemed so permanent. Even the solid construction of the mess, timber though it was, its walls decorated with pictures, the curtains giving access to the ante-room, all suggested peace, not war. And the mellow evening air coming through the open windows gave a never to be forgotten charm to the setting. What a glorious contrast to the war on land! Here we were little more than an hour after being in 'action' sitting down before a five-course dinner in the comfort and security of our mess – 30 miles from it all. The noisy, happy chatter gave me an impression of make-believe. It didn't just seem like war somehow. But it was, for we were front line soldiers. In effect we had the privileges, comforts and amenities of the 'base wallah', without his conscience; for we knew the thrill and satisfaction which only the front line soldier knows.[19] *Lieutenant William Grossart, 205 Squadron*

When the bombers were once again in the air the Germans knew where they were going and the battle ratcheted up in intensity until it seemed that no-one could survive for long.

The bombing of Peronne was the biggest project. Anti-aircraft guns galore and enemy squadrons were prepared to defend it. We were attacked before

> we reached it, shelled to hell while we went through the barrage only to meet the enemy fighters sitting waiting when we emerged from the 'Archie' range. Worst of all were the 'flaming onions' sent up in strings. They were said to be balls of burning phosphorous held together by wire and ascended in curtain to a height of nearly a mile.[20] *Lieutenant William Grossart, 205 Squadron*

After days like these the 205 Squadron mess in the evening resounded with tales that ranged from the fantastic to the ludicrous: of the streams of bullets from red-painted Fokker D.VIIs that passed between Clark's legs without affecting his marital prospects; of how Danger was shot down with only a flying suit covering his pyjamas and how he spent three days wandering behind the French lines before he finally got back to the squadron; of how a bomb by a sheer blind fluke hit and wrecked a Pfalz Scout flying far, far below, before continuing on its 'innocent' way to detonate on the ground as planned; and, best of all for the purposes of mess 'banter', how Crossthwaite shot up his own DH9 tail in the chaotic excitement of combat. Pilots and observers proudly counted up the physical signs of battle bespattered across their machines that denoted their every close shave. But at the same time they knew they were living on borrowed time and most could not help thinking of the friends that they had lost.

> Perhaps the most impressive sights I saw were the burned out wrecks on the ground. Scarcely 100 yards square it seemed but contained a wreck and many a time I wondered which of these often rusty collections of steel contained the remains of my old friend Scott.[21] *Lieutenant William Grossart, 205 Squadron*

The bridges were worryingly close to the German airfields, and on 9 August the men of 107 Squadron faced utter disaster when they twice encountered Lothar von Richthofen at the head of a combined force from Jastas 11 and 27. He personally claimed two victories to bring his total to thirty-seven, but 107 Squadron lost nine aircraft in all. No unit could withstand this rate of casualties for long.

> The few of us who were left sat down and at mess that night cried like children as we looked around at the vacant chairs. In two days we lost

fourteen men out of a complement of twenty-seven. As I write the names of my late comrades, it is hard to believe that they are dead. With me, they set out in possession of life and glorious health – within an hour or so they were charred and mangled remains. *This* is War!![22] *Second Lieutenant George Coles, 107 Squadron*

His pilot developed the harrowing symptoms of nervous exhaustion as a direct result of his awful experiences and shortly afterwards had to be invalided back home, a broken man. And was it worthwhile? The raids on the bridges had still not succeeded.

THE tank cooperation aircraft of 8 Squadron had also been in the thick of the action. Lieutenant Freddie West and his observer Lieutenant William Haslam had already crash-landed on 8 August, been shot down by ground fire while tracking the progress of the tanks on 9 August and on 10 August they were once again flying over the front. They had been sent to track the progress of tanks in the Rosières sector.

Very soon after we got on the line, I saw a formation of what I surmised were Fokker D.VIIs. Throughout our flight this formation of seven were in what I would call a threatening vicinity; never more than five miles away and at heights from round about 5,000 to 10,000 feet. But there were a lot of big cumulus clouds about and West seemed to contrive to keep us the right side of a cloud and we continued our work with the tanks reporting where they were.[23] *Lieutenant William Haslam, 8 Squadron*

While they were doing this, West saw what he considered to be significant numbers of German forces marshalling for a counter-attack in the area around Roye some 8,000 yards behind the German front line. They immediately headed off to reconnoitre further and at the same time expend their bombs and ammunition on a worthy target. Just as they were about to return they found themselves in the deepest of trouble.

The formation of seven appeared from somewhere, pretty close to us and turning towards us. I realised we were in for a scrap. Their leader straight away went down below us and attacked from under our tail. I could see

> him just round our tail but almost immediately he opened fire – before I expected and before I thought he was within the sort of range that my fire would be effective. His first burst hit us, I think straight away and I was hit though not badly, in the left leg, just neatly between the two bones, a flesh wound, though only just! I remember the flicker of tracers coming through the cockpit. West had been hit; the initial shock must have knocked him out.[24] *Lieutenant William Haslam, 8 Squadron*

Whatever his observer might say, West was convinced that he had not fainted, but whatever the truth of it there is no doubt that he had suffered a terrible wound as bullets had all but severed his left leg.

> Everything around me was confused and hazy. The terrific pain was the only thing that seemed to keep me from going off entirely. The machine was diving. I felt too weak to control it. I could not bring it up. It was too strong for me. Something told me I was crashing, and that I must not do so. I had to get back. With all the strength I could muster I heaved again on the joystick and the machine slowly levelled out. I could not turn round but from the desperate spatter of Haslam's guns we were still in danger. Blood was gushing in fountains from a big hole in my left leg. Waves of sense intermingled with drowsy numbness in my brain.[25] *Lieutenant Freddie West, 8 Squadron*

Haslam was indeed firing at the marauding Fokkers and had just changed the drums on his twin Lewis gun when he got a brief opportunity to take some vengeance.

> The leader appeared just up level to us and to the side of the tail. I shot at him and saw a shoot of what must have been water; presumably I had hit his radiator. I altered my aim a little to get him and he certainly went down and stopped firing at us. The other fighters didn't attack us any more. I turned round to see what had happened to West and his head was right over on one side – he was very pale. Whether he was dead, or had fainted: I think he was out at that moment.[26] *Lieutenant William Haslam, 8 Squadron*

In extremis Haslam looked for the emergency controls to allow him to control the aircraft, but as he did so West seems to have revived.

> One does a lot by instinct and I knew from my army training if you did a tourniquet you could stop a certain amount of bleeding. I twisted my pants as tight as I could and made some sort of tourniquet which reduced a little bit the amount of blood coming out of my wound. The pain kept me going.[27]
> *Lieutenant Freddie West, 8 Squadron*

A few tattered scraps of sinew or bone was all that attached the bloody remnants of his lower leg. Unfortunately, though, it was caught up in the rudder bar and as his right leg had also been wounded he was unable to control the aircraft.

> I must free the rudder bar for better manoeuvre or I might come to grief. My left leg was in the way. It was useless. I lugged and heaved at it, pulling it clear of the controls.[28] *Lieutenant Freddie West, 8 Squadron*

With a supreme effort West managed to stay conscious enough to make it back across the front lines to make a forced landing.

> I kept on recollecting the enemy troop location behind the woods. Everything was dreamlike, hazy and unreal. I saw the ground coming close and saw an open field to starboard. I managed to manoeuvre into a landing glide and came in. I managed to keep the machine level and we bumped, but torturing pains shot through me.[29] *Lieutenant Freddie West, 8 Squadron*

Once the aircraft had rumbled to a stop, William Haslam got out of his rear cockpit and rushed round to help his ailing pilot.

> My own wound wasn't worrying me in the least, I got out and went to see what was up with West and to try and help him out. By the time I got up to him I realised that he was very badly hurt, I think by the sight of his face. I started to try and get him out of the machine because I knew something had to be done but very fortunately some field ambulance men came up.[30]
> *Lieutenant William Haslam, 8 Squadron*

West was put through agonies as they struggled to get him out of the cockpit.

> 'Hang on, Freddie! Hang on! There's help coming.' A sunburnt Canadian came panting up, looked into my cockpit and shouted to the others. 'The pilot's badly hit. Come on, boys! Get him out!' One huge fellow tried to lift me, while another grasped my buttocks. The pain of their tugging was excruciating. I felt sick and began to vomit, retching saliva. They made a large triangular gash in the cockpit beside me. Then they began to lift me out.[31] *Lieutenant Freddie West, 8 Squadron*

Falling in and out of consciousness, in his own mind West was still determined to stay conscious and pass on the latest details of significant German troop movements behind their front lines.

> They eventually got me out of the machine and put me on a stretcher, but I was able to tell the Canadian captain who came up to my machine, I stressed the importance of passing on the information of the location of the German troops. Later on when I was taken to a small chapel, the recording officer of the squadron came over to visit me and I was able to tell him the location that I was anxious to give him in detail. I was on a stretcher along a corridor and a doctor came up to me and said, 'This man must be operated on immediately!' Then the doctor saying to me, 'Try to count!' I remember counting and then I lost consciousness.[32] *Lieutenant Freddie West, 8 Squadron*

Despite William Haslam's nonchalance on getting out of the Armstrong Whitworth, his own wounds were serious and the two of them found themselves laid out in a church being used as a field dressing station.

> We were on stretchers, side by side and I think it was then that West managed to get somebody to make a report to. The last I remember is a padre bringing round cocoa.[33] *Lieutenant William Haslam, 8 Squadron*

Freddie West was operated on and awoke to find that his left leg had been amputated from above the knee. He would be awarded a Victoria Cross for his courage.

From 10 August, although the RAF attacks on the bridges continued, the balance of daytime bombing attacks was widened to attack the Peronne and Equancourt railway stations. This too was something the Germans could not allow and the aerial battle continued unabated. The Germans were scoring kill after kill, but in this kind of battle they were bound to suffer their own casualties and it was not always the inexperienced pilots who died – the Germans suffered a series of particularly painful losses among their established aces.

Of these the greatest loss was probably Oberleutnant Erich Löwenhardt. He was born on 7 April 1897 and had served as an infantry officer on the Eastern Front during the first year of the war before transferring to the German Air Force in October 1915. He began his career as a scout pilot with Jasta 10 in March 1917 and proved to have all the right talents for the task. He scored regularly but not spectacularly until he was promoted to command Jasta 10 in April 1918. His rate of success blossomed and he proved a master of the Fokker D.VII. His friendly rivalry with Ernst Udet led both pilots to attain the very heights of success and he had claimed sixteen victims in July 1918. As he led his men over the Somme battlefield he had already shot down a total of fifty-three victims, he was the highest scoring German ace left alive and to his men he must have seemed all but invulnerable. But once caught up in a dogfight then everyone, no matter how talented and deadly, was in danger.

Löwenhardt had badly sprained his ankle the previous day, yet he refused to think of going on leave as the battle reached its frenetic climax. When he took off on 10 August he was accompanied by Lothar von Richthofen and elements of Jastas 10 and 11. The two aces had formed a fighting partnership that both seem to have valued highly.

> Flying with Löwenhardt was wonderful, almost like flying with Manfred, at least the first to compare with it. In just a short time, we had become well attuned to each other, and we could communicate splendidly with each other in the air. I was blessed, after Manfred, to have again found someone on whom I could depend. Löwenhardt expressed the same thing about me.[34] *Oberleutnant Lothar von Richthofen, Jagdgeschwader 1*

Löwenhardt was leading when they sighted, and moved to cut off, a British formation trying to get back to their lines. Suddenly there was an unwelcome distraction that caused confusion.

Then a lone Englishman got through a couple of 100 metres below us. Löwenhardt no doubt wanted to take him quick – the rest of the Englishmen could wait. He quickly put his machine on its nose and attacked the lone single-seater. The whole horde of novice pilots went diving down after Löwenhardt, as if they all meant to shoot down that one Englishman. I was the only one who stayed overhead, swearing loudly. To attack the enemy squadrons alone would have been madness. So I followed them down in a slow glide and watched the action below. The scene was as follows – Löwenhardt in his bright yellow machine was right behind the Englishman. I saw right away that everyone else was superfluous. But four or five of them didn't realise this but were flying right behind Löwenhardt, apparently to take part in the fight. Then, all of a sudden, I see the Englishman dive straight down, a trail of smoke behind him.[35] *Oberleutnant Lothar von Richthofen, Jagdgeschwader 1*

Among the young beginners following Löwenhardt was Leutnant Alfred Wenz of Jasta 11. Doubtless confused by the sheer drama of the moment, in his frenzy of excitement he lost sight of Löwenhardt and made a disastrous assumption that he had broken off the action. He sought to take over the chase, filled with a determination to shoot down his first victim.

With a short dive I got behind the 'Tommy' who was maybe about 200 metres below me. I got him in my sights and my series of machine gun bursts rained into his visibly cowering body from close range. Sticking tight to him in my machine, during my last rounds I was no more than 15 metres away from him; for in diving on him I had reached a very high speed. Suddenly, just above me to the right, and close enough to touch, I see Oberleutnant Löwenhardt's yellow machine and in the next instant, the wheels of his machine's undercarriage, probably the left wheel, strike my upper right wing.[36] *Leutnant Alfred Wenz, Jasta 11*

The two pilots had both been firing at the hapless British pilot; both diving from different angles of attack, both concentrating on their target to the exclusion of all else and neither able to see the other – until it was too late.

Somewhat stunned for just a few seconds I saw Löwenhardt's yellow machine shooting away over me in a jerky manner. A piece of fabric, almost the size of a tablecloth, tore away from my upper right wing. Instantly, my machine went over on its nose and went down. All of the controls failed. Several quick movements of the control stick produced no effect on my crate. Spinning for a few seconds, it then plunged straight down at a rate of speed considerably higher than the maximum for in my poorly contained excitement I forgot to throttle back the engine. During the plunge, looking straight down to the far-distant ground, I was sitting on my parachute pack, fastened in by leg and shoulder straps which were supposed to prevent my being thrown out during loops and spins and so on. What to do? I certainly had no feeling of fear; I was young – 20 years old – my nerves were intact. At the moment, despite the altitude of more than 4,000 metres, I fancied myself still quite safe sitting there, I simply couldn't believe that it could all be over for me so quickly. Unstable at that terrific rate of speed, my machine raced on towards the ground.[37] *Leutnant Alfred Wenz, Jasta 11*

He was heading straight for the wilderness of shell holes that marked the old Somme battlefield. Wenz dithered for a few vital seconds as he made the life-or-death decision as to whether to cling to the falling aircraft, or throw himself out into the blue, trusting to his parachute.

At first I made up my mind not to jump. Maybe the impact would result in nothing more than some broken arms and legs, but this was, of course, sheer nonsense. Anything that landed down there was pulp. So – out of the crate! I pulled on the wire pin, which would release the belts connected at my chest, but it stuck too tightly, I tore at it once more, it released, and in the next second I was pulled out of the machine with a jerk, I was without any support. Below me, the plane, now left to its own devices, plunged on towards the ground. Suddenly I felt a strong jerk upwards. It felt to me as if someone above me wished to tear the flight suit from my body. The parachute had opened. I floated and swung slowly down towards the ground.[38] *Leutnant Alfred Wenz, Jasta 11*

However, he was not yet out of trouble. He had no practical experience of parachuting, of the many risks involved and the techniques he needed if he was to survive unscathed.

Due to the powerful jerk at the opening of the parachute, however, both the main harness around my body, which consisted of strong hemp cords about 10 centimetres wide, as well as one leg strap, had broken. The straps slid up to my armpits. With one hand, I reached up to where they were connected to the parachute. I did that quite automatically because I had no real understanding that the straps breaking could have been my undoing. I was quite calm and waved happily to my comrades who were flying around watching me. I knew I was saved.[39] *Leutnant Alfred Wenz, Jasta 11*

Wenz floated down in apparent safety to face a somewhat fraught landing in the front line area amid a British artillery barrage.

Erich Löwenhardt had also taken to his parachute. But they were not then the reliable means of succour that they later became; Löwenhardt's parachute failed to open properly and he plunged like a stone to smash into the ground close to Chaulnes. The then current top-scoring German ace had perished, a fact that Leutnant Wenz only found out when he made it back to his airfield.

I was looking forward to a jubilant reception at the airfield, but I saw only sorrowful faces. Lothar von Richthofen told me that Löwenhardt was down, too, but he was dead! I cannot describe the emotional blow I took. I suffered over him a long time and he returned in countless dreams. It was simply incomprehensible to me. I could not believe it. Only one single comfort helped me through the next few days: the assurance of my Staffel leader, Baron Lothar von Richthofen, that I was not to blame. 'Such things often just happen,' he said to me. 'It has already happened to others as well.'[40]
Leutnant Alfred Wenz, Jasta 11

From the accounts given it may well be judged that Wenz was in fact largely to blame for the accident. But Lothar von Richthofen rightly realized there was no point in pillorying an inexperienced young pilot for an accident in the frantic chaos of a dogfight. And it had indeed happened before. Hauptmann Oswald Boelcke, the father figure of Jasta 2, had been killed in a very similar collision with his best friend Leutnant Erwin Böhme back in October 1916. Recriminations could serve no possible purpose. As a unit they had to move on.

Unfortunately there was another severe blow to German morale that same day when the Jagdgeschwader 2 lost *their* leader. Hauptman Rudolf Berthold had continued his active-service flying despite suffering the tortures of the damned with his smashed right arm. Berthold simply refused to give up flying, determined to lead his Jagdgeschwader from the front – in sharp contrast to the slightly more negligent attitude taken by Herman Göring commanding Jagdgeschwader 1. By this time Berthold was heavily dependent on morphine to mask the pain of his injuries, but he had shot down two more victims on 9 August to reach the considerable haul of forty-two victories. On 10 August he tore into a formation of DH4s and shot one down, but in bringing down a second victim he actually ran into the DH4 and thereby rendered his Fokker D.VII uncontrollable. It plunged down to smash into a house in the village of Ablaincourt. He was lucky to survive but his unhealed arm was again badly broken and he was once more despatched off to hospital. This amazing man then managed to leave the hospital unofficially and turned up once again at Jagdgeschwader 2 announcing that he was utterly determined to carry on regardless. It was his contention that with his experience he could be of value in the frenetic fighting and after all he had scored sixteen of his forty-four victories with only one functioning arm – what had changed? However the condition of his arm worsened and the Kaiser himself intervened to give him a direct order to return to hospital until he was fully recovered. The Allies had finally seen the last of this most implacable of foes; Hauptman Rudolf Berthold had flown his last mission.

The steady trickle of such losses suffered among the ranks of the Jasta may not have been particularly significant in comparison with the thousands of lives being lost or ruined in the ground fighting. But the Jasta were very small élite groups, the aces were incredibly highly skilled practitioners of their arts and their numbers were being eroded on a daily basis. Finally, on 13 August, Jagdgeschwader 1 was condensed to form just one Jasta. Things would only get worse when Lothar von Richthofen himself took to the skies that day, absolutely determined to break a superstition that was slowly beginning to take hold of him. The previous day he had got two more victories, to reach an accredited total of forty victims.

Upon awakening that morning I immediately realised, 'Today is the thirteenth – your unlucky day – the day on which you've been wounded twice already.' One mustn't be superstitious. I now intended to fly just to dispel my last misgivings about it being the thirteenth. On a different day, perhaps I wouldn't even have taken off, for I had three different urgent car trips to take care of. But no – today this spell of the thirteenth had to be broken.[41]
Oberleutnant Lothar von Richthofen, Jagdgeschwader 1

Perhaps he should have taken the day off after all, but like his brother, he had a strong sense of duty driving him on. No mere superstition would keep him grounded during such an important battle. Hence he was soon aloft leading what remained of his pilots in a joint operation with Jagdgeschwader 3.

I attack a two-seater, see the observer crumple under my fire. The aeroplane has to fall within the next few seconds. The pilot appears to be wounded already. I look around for my Staffel, there are six 'Lords' pursuing me, instead. I have no choice but to quickly let my victim go, in order to now escape myself. This works quite well, for they all leave me alone. Just one man is following me, at a distance of several hundred metres. I let him pursue me for the time being, in order to separate him from the others and then deal with him alone. The fellow fires at me from 600 metres. I calmly fly on, for you certainly can't hit anything at that range. Suddenly there is a terrible pain in my right leg. I'd taken my usual bullet. The only hit on the entire machine. At first I was in such pain that I was incapable of operating the controls. My right leg had fallen from the rudder. I couldn't move it so I held it tight with both hands. After having plunged several thousand metres, the ground was coming alarmingly close. I checked the altimeter – only 500 metres. And so it was time to get my machine under control again. I didn't trust the parachute, but I no longer had the strength to bale out, anyway. For a moment it seemed I was losing both strength and consciousness. So I took my right leg in both hands and placed it on the rudder bar. I could now right my machine and fly straight ahead. I landed where I happened to be. Found a spot in the shelled terrain of the Somme battlefield where landing was possible. I was so weak from loss of blood that I couldn't have kept myself in the air one minute longer.[42] *Oberleutnant Lothar von Richthofen, Jagdgeschwader 1*

It is difficult to be sure but it is believed that Lothar von Richthofen had been shot down by either Lieutenant Field Kindley or Lieutenant George Sebold of 148th Pursuit Squadron, United States Air Force, who had bounced Richthofen's formation after emerging from a large cloud. The American pilots claimed three kills and one possible, although it seems that only one other Fokker was forced to land. Once again Richthofen was badly wounded and this time he was out of the war for good – his 'curse' of thirteen had indeed struck again!

THE Battle of Amiens had all but petered out on the ground, despite the vicious aerial exchanges that would continue as 'aftershocks'. The Germans had managed to bring up sufficient reserves to stabilize their front line on the western side of the Somme. The RAF had tried its best to bomb the bridges and undoubtedly caused many casualties to the Germans funnelling themselves through the bottlenecks, but the bridges themselves survived all but intact. This concentration on the bridges was a change in policy, which had its origins in the confusion in the RAF over the 'continuing' battle. The significant expansion of the overall Fourth Army objectives, introduced at Haig's behest, had not been properly registered by either Brigadier Lionel Charlton commanding, V Brigade, RAF, who was locally responsible, or indeed by Salmond himself. They still thought of the attacks as essentially limited, lasting little more than a day or so. The intended interdiction role of sealing the battlefield off from German reserves by attacking their rail centres and airfields had therefore been partially dropped for the glittering prizes promised if they could destroy the Somme bridges and cut off the Germans in the loop of the Somme. In the event the arrival of those reserves meant that the German positions were stabilized.

Throughout the whole battle some 700 aircraft undertook raids on the bridges, managing to drop in the process some 57 tons of bombs. Yet most of the bombs missed their targets to fall innocuously into the river. Even if they hit the bridge it was an unfortunate fact that their bombs, mostly weighing 112 pounds, were simply not powerful enough to destroy well-constructed bridges; any damage caused was usually so superficial that it could be repaired in a matter of hours. *Aficionados* of bombing claimed that 'if only' every resource had been devoted to the bombing to the exclusion of all else then the bridges could have been destroyed; in particular the Independent Air Force should have been diverted from its raids on Germany to this task. They were in all probability wrong but there was no doubt that the bombers' time would come. Individual aces could not stem the tide; it took large, well-drilled formations of scouts to fend off the massed bombers and even then it was becoming apparent that the bombers would always get through if they had the sheer determination to press home the attack regardless of losses. The losses had been high for the RAF, but the German Army Air Service had been roughly handled and they did not have the personnel or aircraft at hand to replace their losses.

Overall, although the Allies had achieved a notable advance of some 12 miles in the Battle of Amiens, success in the Great War was not measured by ground gained but by the damage inflicted on the enemy. Yet here too there had been a tremendous success as there were a minimum of 48,000 German casualties (of whom nearly 22,000 certainly were prisoners of war) and 400 guns had been captured. Allied losses were also high at 22,000 British and 24,000 French casualties, but their reserves were deeper now that the Americans were finally making their presence felt. Ludendorff famously described 8 August as a black day for the German Army. He was right.

> The losses of the Second Army had been very heavy. Heavy demands had also been made upon its reserves to fill up the gaps. Our reserves dwindled. The losses of the enemy, on the other hand, had been extraordinarily small. The balance of numbers had moved heavily against us; it was bound to become increasingly unfavourable as more American troops came in. There was no hope of materially improving our position by a counter-attack. Our only course, therefore, was to hold on. We had to resign ourselves now to the prospect of a continuation of the enemy's offensive. Their success had been too easily gained. Their wireless was jubilant, and announced – and with truth – that the morale of the German Army was no longer what it had been.[43] *General Erich Ludendorff, General Headquarters, Imperial German Army*

After this debacle Ludendorff realized that Germany had no feasible option left other than to sue for peace as soon as possible.

The British and French had at last demonstrated a mastery of the grammar and syntax of 'attack' in modern war. They had shown that they could progress against whatever defensive measures the Germans cared to put up against them. And in one particular matter there was a vital new flexibility. When the German resistance stiffened and the Allied attacks began to flounder in the past a long-drawn-out battle of attrition might have been anticipated in an effort to wear down the German reserves. But Rawlinson had detected that the German reinforcements had arrived. After a period of confusion with Haig and Foch over the wisdom of a renewed mass assault on 15 August, the baton of attack was passed to Third Army, next in line to the north. The Allied generals were collectively hammering out the new framework for the all-arms battle and this battle would mark the point where they finally realized the necessity of continuously switching the focus of the attacks to try to keep the Germans constantly off-balance. There would be no pause for consolidation: 8 August was just the start of the advance to victory, the last hundred days that would bring the war to an end.

Chapter 11

Ordinary Boys

As the aces one by one tumbled from the skies it was increasingly clear that the future of aerial fighting lay with the thousands of anonymous young men who fought, died or survived without fanfare or general acclaim. Who remembers them now? From a thousand stories just two at random: Lieutenant Edgar Taylor, the young livewire American, the coyote hunter, born in the wilds of Camas Meadows in Idaho on 9 January 1897, who we have briefly seen in training and gauchely marvelling at the louche vistas of London. The other that of Lieutenant Jack Wilkinson born a year later in Kirkby Overblow, Yorkshire, on 10 January 1898, a man generally more cautious in his overall outlook and of whom we saw a great deal in his training, first as an observer and then as a pilot.

Edgar Taylor got out to the front first, joining 79 Squadron on the Flanders front on 22 April 1918. He was still confident that his flying skills and his mastery of acrobatics would serve him well in combat. He was also delighted with his new aircraft – the Sopwith Dolphin. This aircraft was a big change in the usual Sopwith design philosophy as consummated with the Camel. It abandoned their rotary engines for the powerful inline 200hp Hispano-Suiza engine as used in the SE5a, which gave a good top speed of just over 120mph and maintained a reasonably responsive performance right up to 21,000 feet. It had a substantial armament with two fixed forward-firing Vickers machine guns and an added Lewis gun on the top wing. The strangest feature to the naked eye was the back-staggered wings, with the result that the pilot sat with his head poking through the gap in the centre section of the upper wing. The all-round unrestricted view upwards and backwards was a definite bonus, but some pilots were nervous of being decapitated if the Dolphin crashed and tipped up over its nose – a not uncommon occurrence. Certainly Lieutenant Jack Wilkinson – as a

Sopwith Camel pilot – did not fancy what he saw of them when he got to the front.

> We had a look at these Dolphins and decided, in spite of their higher ceiling and superiority in speed, that we still preferred our Camels. The pilot of a Dolphin sat with his head above the top plane where he had an excellent view above the horizon but, as against this, his wings covered large areas where he was blind. Moreover, in the event of a rough landing and the whole outfit turning over on its back, the wretched pilot had to shrink as best he could into his cockpit – or be squashed into it – and then open a comic little door in the side of the fuselage, most likely jammed, and get out that way; or wait until kind friends came to release him. 'No,' we thought as we got into our Camels and looked with gratitude at the substantial centre-section protecting our heads, 'You can keep your perishing Dolphins!'[1]
> *Lieutenant Jack Wilkinson, 46 Squadron, RAF*

Although Lieutenant Edgar Taylor was sure he could cope with active service flying his commanding officer was perhaps not so sanguine and there was a three-week period of test flights, formation flying and gunnery practice before he was allowed into action. Even training flights could be dangerous to a relatively inexperienced pilot.

> I was up for a joy ride and I thought I would dive at a target on the ground. I was at 2,000 feet so I came down vertical until within 30 feet of the ground then I pulled her out. The funny thing was the engine stopped on me. There I was going straight for some trees at 130mph. I took goggles off ready for a crash. However I got over the trees and landed down a will in a ploughed field. I landed perfectly.[2] *Lieutenant Edgar Taylor, 79 Squadron*

His attitude to his survival prospects was unblinkered and he could clearly see the risks of what he was doing.

> The fate of a pilot is a foregone conclusion. Some of the most brilliant fliers who have come to the front and shot a score of Huns down went home for a rest only to 'do it' in a training camp. Of course nothing can be perfect in this world so why worry. You cannot afford to waste time thinking of tomorrow when today is so important. I am afraid we are in for a long and

deadly war. We must all buckle to, and do our bit until we take 'the longest flight of all'.[3] *Lieutenant Edgar Taylor, 79 Squadron*

Nevertheless, he showed an unusual capacity for foolish risk-taking – even when he was on the ground. In a scene of almost cartoon surrealism he caused utter consternation among his tent mates after a DH4 crash-landed on their airfield on 15 May loaded with bombs that fortunately did not explode.

I went to the machine and picked up a live bomb. When I got to my tent a gang were chatting, but you should have seen them scatter. There was a stampede! I then sat down to take it to pieces, and a bunch hid in their dugouts until I had finished. I got some cute souvenirs from it.[4] *Lieutenant Edgar Taylor, 79 Squadron*

He was obviously keen to get started on something really dangerous, and it was perhaps no coincidence that on that very day he was included in his first offensive patrol. Taylor was confident in himself, his comrades and his aircraft that he had duly named 'Idaho'. His first real dogfight could easily have been his last.

I was flying with the commander of the squadron. We chased a Hun but he got away so we started for our own lines being almost out of gasoline. Looking above me I saw a bunch of machines twisting and turning about. It only took me an instant to spot there was Huns in the mêlée. I went straight in because our fellows were outnumbered and in need of assistance. I opened on one Hun but one of my guns jammed. I attacked another at close range and put about 300 shots in and around him. He went down in a spin, but I was unable to watch him to see if he crashed because I heard bullets going past my head and I was obliged to turn quick to get clear. I then saw one flying straight toward me so I attacked him. We were both flying head on and I could see his bullets going over my head about 6" too high. They were using a bullet that leaves a trail of smoke behind. We passed so close together that as I looked down I could see his face and the colour of his helmet. I was getting in a tight place because my petrol was all gone and my engine kept stopping. And I hated to leave while our fellows were so badly pressed. We were a long way over Hunland so as I

saw the last of our machines start for home I came with them. I landed safely behind our lines. My leader was shot down but he was OK and managed to land behind our lines. When my machine was examined it was found to be riddled with bullets. It was a great experience; well worth the risk. But as long as I live I will remember it: the plunging, diving, firing etc., all above 15,000 feet is a sensation never to be forgotten.[5] *Lieutenant Edgar Taylor, 79 Squadron*

One wonders what his squadron leader thought of being dragged into such a dogfight at the end of a patrol when nearly out of petrol. Yet they had both survived unscathed.

Over the next couple of weeks it slowly became apparent that for all Taylor's natural ebullience there was something wrong. Despite all his hunting experience back in Idaho, all his talk of coyotes, he was simply a rotten shot.

I then went up to 20,000 feet and I ran into a Hun two-seater. He started to run but I was above him and he couldn't get away so easy. He sure did some dodging around. I followed him putting lead into him. I chased him for a long way over Hunland and he finally went down in a spin. Whether I got him or not I couldn't tell because my ammunition was all gone and I was so far over I couldn't stop to watch him.[6] *Lieutenant Edgar Taylor, 79 Squadron*

This is in marked contrast to the clinical marksmanship of James McCudden. Whether Taylor grasped exactly what he was doing wrong is open to debate. He had been in an almost ideal position, but had been unable to clinch the kill. The various forms of inexperience were usually obvious to everyone except the individual concerned, as Taylor himself gleefully recorded having watched the trials and tribulations of a fellow pilot committing another basic error.

One of our fellows was very amusing. He had a Hun Albatros on his tail and thought it was one of ours. The Hun was slinging lead all through his machine and the poor cuss just kept on tipping his wings so he could see his markings. At last I thought it time to get him out of it, so I went after Fritz. He beat it pretty fast. When I got to the aerodrome the chap was showing our commanding officer the bullet holes and telling him it was one of our machines. We sure had to laugh. He was riddled with bullets; a wonder he was not hit.[7] *Lieutenant Edgar Taylor, 79 Squadron*

As a new pilot he was heavily dependent on the tactical skills of his flight commander if he were to survive in skies filled with predators who knew their angles, whether it be simple direct flying or deflection shooting. On one evening patrol Taylor was with a patrol of four Dolphins that had wandered too far over the German lines. Too late they sighted a bunch of German scouts who had climbed to take station between them and home.

A fight was unavoidable even though there were about twenty or thirty to four, so we lambasted them as we dove through them. This scattered them, but they were all round us like a bunch of hawks. One started for me but I was a little quicker and I riddled his machine before he got into me. He dove away. I then heard bullets go whizzing upwards. One was under me. I dove at him and he beat it fast. In the meantime others were all around us firing. It sure gives you a sensation when you can see the bullets come. Our leader was getting it pretty hard but we managed to knock the Huns off if they closed in too near. Finally we got to the line. Our leader was wounded but the rest got out safely which was very lucky considering the circumstances.[8] *Lieutenant Edgar Taylor, 79 Squadron*

Taylor was typical of many new pilots. He flew his patrols conscientiously, he tried his level best in combat but he simply could not open his 'account'. Soon he realized that his innocent pride and faith in his aerobatic ability had been sorely misplaced.

A dogfight as we call a general air mix up is much like a fight on the ground amongst a bunch of men. The man who gets his gun going first and shoots straightest is the one who will win. It is worth far more to be a good shot than a clever pilot. All our famous fighters in the air are crack shots. Some are really poor flyers. It is the experience that counts. If you survive your first few fights you have a good chance to get out OK. To be in a general mêlée with our own dark coloured machines and the Huns' brilliantly coloured machines is an experience. You get fascinated with the long red line of fire coming from your own gun, at the same time you are ready to do some lightning stunt the instant you see the flaming bullets of Fritz coming past you.[9] *Lieutenant Edgar Taylor, 79 Squadron*

His overall confidence had not been damaged by his teething troubles. He was still determined to make the grade as a scout pilot.

I have not got any Huns yet. They are a bunch of cowards in the air. I will drop onto one yet when he isn't ready then I'll pot him just like shooting a coyote before he has chance to run. I like flying here very much. It is just like being on a big game hunt. You have your guns all ready and if you don't look out he will see you first! Flying comes second nature to me. I very seldom spin or loop now as the novelty has worn off long ago.[10] *Lieutenant Edgar Taylor, 79 Squadron*

If the German pilots were cowards then they were brave ones! Taylor himself had already been a distant witness of a scene of German heroism that would have a considerable resonance for his own future.

It was a crystal clear evening and everything was as quiet as if no war was going on for miles. We had finished our last show for the day and were busy getting our machines ready for the next day when our 'Archie' commenced firing furiously. We all commenced looking for the Hun whose machine guns were commencing to rattle. We soon spotted him at about 4,000 feet above us. He had come over after one of our observation balloons. It was a very plucky thing for him to do. It is very rare that we get to see such a nice show on our side of the line. Our 'Archies' just plastered shrapnel all around him at such a rate that the sky was covered with fleecy white puffs of smoke. For a few minutes he seemed bewildered and uncertain what to do. He had missed the balloon and the observer was slowly coming down in his parachute. He turned towards his own lines but a gang of our Sopwith Camels who were far above saw the white 'Archie' (the Hun use black) and of course knew there was a Hun. Down they came like a great flock of giant hawks, their machine guns rattling spitefully. The poor Hun did all kinds of tricks, but our boys stuck to him like leeches while the chaps on the ground went wild with delight. We were so pleased with the Hun's

> bravery that we almost wished he would escape. However we soon saw that he was done for. His machine came down tumbling like a leaf and crashed. We found he had been shot and killed before he hit the ground. He must have been one of their best men.[11] *Lieutenant Edgar Taylor, 79 Squadron*

By the end of June 1918, Taylor was an experienced scout pilot. He may not have shot anyone down but he had grasped the basic tactics and perhaps more importantly now had developed the 'air vision' that allowed him to see what was happening around him. He was hence far less likely to be ambushed and shot down. Through it all he had retained his essential youthfulness and *joie de vivre*, seen here in his envy of the multicoloured hues of his adversaries.

> We saw a gang of Fokker Biplanes chasing one of our men so we went to the chap's assistance and he got safely away. The Huns were above us but we couldn't tempt the cowardly cusses down to fight. Their noses were painted red, also their tails, while their wings were green and yellow striped. I wish they would allow us to fix our machines up like the Huns do. We are all obliged to be painted the same colour. All Huns are painted up like Indians.[12] *Lieutenant Edgar Taylor, 79 Squadron*

Emboldened with the confidence and invulnerability of youth, Edgar Taylor was immune to inner doubts, or at least chose not to reveal even a hint of such in his letters home to his family. To him it all seemed like a glorious game.

> Sometimes, when flying over the fields gets tiresome, I slip up to the clouds and dart in and out amongst them. They are far prettier than mountains. Often you go through one and out at the other side. You cannot tell whether you are upside down or not if in a cloud. But it is great sport just the same. My leader tried to give me the slip one day. We sure had a merry chase. No Huns were up so we had only to watch him. Over clouds and under them, through and around he went, but we had him beat. Every time he looked around we would be following him like a pack of hounds. When it was time to come home we all commenced to stunt.[13] *Lieutenant Edgar Taylor, 79 Squadron*

The wreckage of a German aircraft

The badly burned bodies of Manfred von Richthofen's 74th victory near Mericourt

Fokker Dr.I Triplanes

Fokker D.VIIs

Manfred von Richthofen's face in death

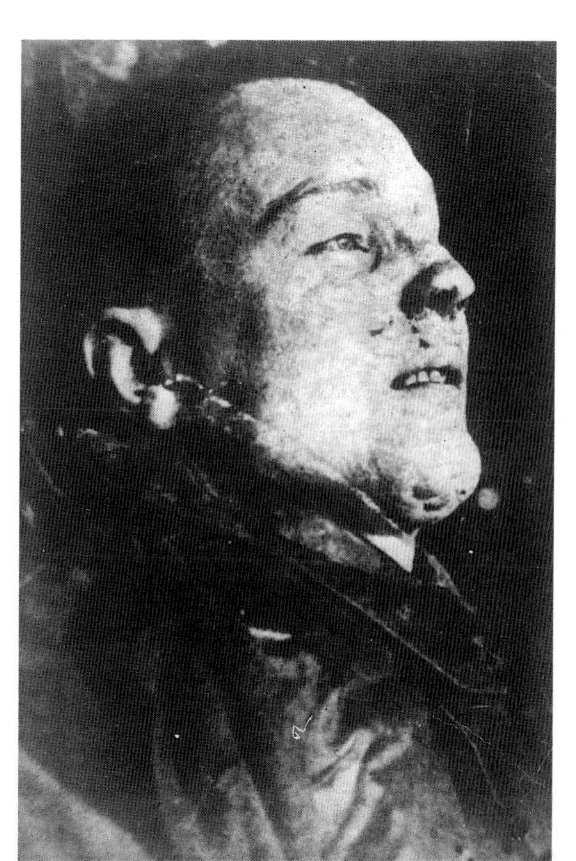

Richthofen's crashed Fokker Triplane Dr.I

A kite balloon in flames

OPPOSITE PAGE
Above The basket of a kite balloon
Below A kite balloon ascending

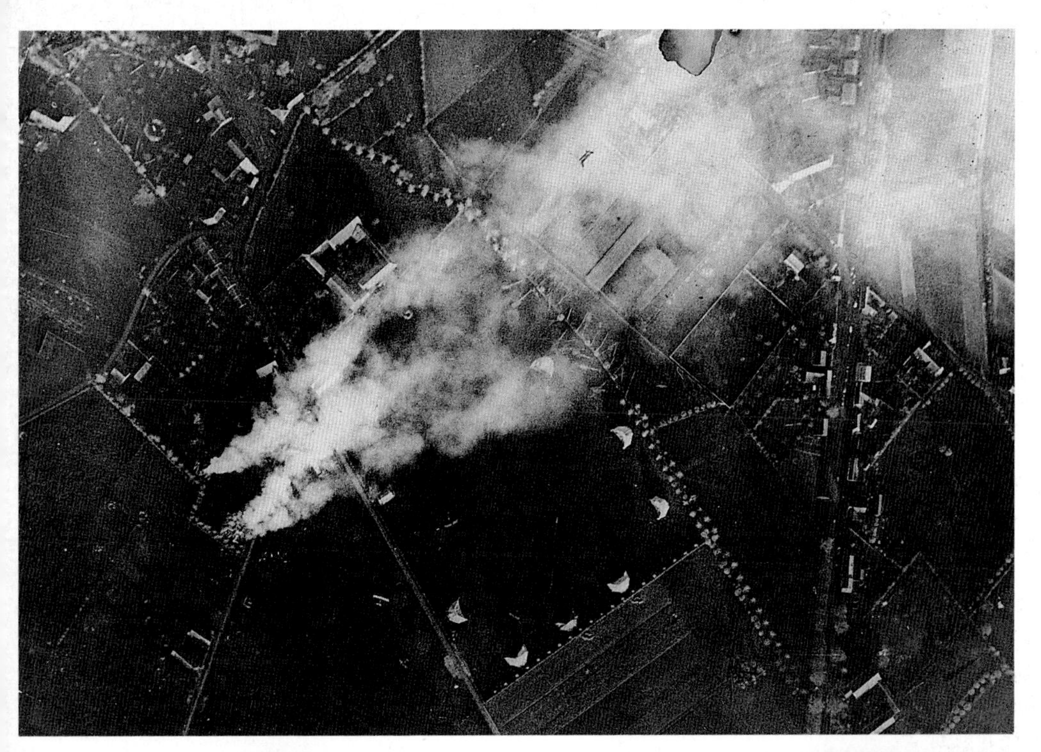

Top Aerial view of Marcq aerodrome under attack; *Above* A glimpse of the future: the remains of a German factory after a British bombing raid

OPPOSITE PAGE *Above* A train being attacked; *Below* Ground crew inspect a bomb before loading to a DH4 bomber.

Railways were a major target for the Allied bombers

German defeat symbolised by a heap of dismantled fuselages after the war

What could be better than the life they led as 'Lords of the Air'? It was dangerous but there was a natural exhilaration in flying in the open cockpits of their fast Sopwith Dolphin scouts with the wind blowing away their inhibitions.

> I was up this morning and though it may sound funny I sang every minute! I felt just topping and spoiling for a fight. Of course I wouldn't dare let anyone in the squadron know I sing while up. They would laugh! But though drowned out by the roar of my engine I have that same feeling of freedom I used to have when on old Prince riding out on the hills in good old Idaho.[14]
> *Lieutenant Edgar Taylor, 79 Squadron*

There was a new direction in the offing for Taylor at the start of August. If his poor marksmanship meant he was unable to hit German scouts, then what about a bigger target? What about the kite balloons that loomed high above the trenches?

> There was a layer of clouds all over so I sneaked through them until about ten miles over, then dropped out suddenly amongst their kite balloons. I laughed to see those observers jump over in their parachutes. Every one of them jumped. But imagine my chagrin when I found my guns had frozen and I was unable to shoot any of them down. The Huns awoke to the fact I was there and they accordingly proceeded to entertain me. Dozens of machine guns and 'Archie' batteries for miles around slung 'hate' at me. Gee, but I had some queer sensations. The air was literally black with high explosive shells bursting. I thought I was a goner several times. I started home opening up to 130mph and in less time than it takes to tell it I was safe on our side. There was a long trail of black smoke across the sky where I had flown a few seconds before. My plane was shot up, but no vital parts were damaged.[15]
> *Lieutenant Edgar Taylor, 79 Squadron, RAF*

Taylor was at a crossroads in his career as a scout pilot: would he avoid the temptations of the huge 'gasbags' flaunting themselves before him, offering death and all too perishable glory, or would he return to the routine of normal patrols? Only time would tell . . .

*

OUR second 'ordinary boy' was Lieutenant Jack Wilkinson. After the completion of his training he was posted out with a draft of new pilots to fly Sopwith Camels with 4 Squadron, Australian Flying Corps. On arrival he soon found that he had to ditch all his previous preconceptions as to what constituted acceptable language in the 'polite' society of the officers' mess.

> To English ears that were sensitive their language was often crude in the extreme. The word 'bastard' was continually on their lips, but they thought no more of it than we should of 'blighter'. 'Had a good scrap this morning?' Waddy would say as he climbed out of his Camel, loosening the chinstrap of his helmet. 'Get a Hun?' 'You bet!' was the reply. 'Fried the bastard!' meaning that he had seen the Hun go down in flames. Or there would be a group listening to Taplin, who specialised in stalking enemy two-seaters. 'And how did it finish, Tap?' 'Well,' he drawled, 'I went into the cloud again, and when I came out the bastard was just above me. So I pulled up the bus and blew the observer's bum through the back of his neck!' Yes they were tough, but they had hearts of pure gold.[16] *Lieutenant Jack Wilkinson, 4 Squadron, Australian Air Corps*

Fortunately, Wilkinson's previous experience with the London Rifle Brigade combined with a natural tolerance meant that he was able to fit in with the rough humour. It perhaps helped that there were other Englishmen present to dilute the overall Australian atmosphere.

> I was soon made to feel at home by the Aussies, and occupied a canvas hut with Youdale, a genuine 'Digger' and McRae. There were probably half a dozen non-Australian pilots in the squadron under the arrangement that they were to stay there until sufficient Australian-born pilots came along to maintain it at full strength, when we 'outcasts' or 'lepers', as they called us in fun, would be drafted elsewhere. Major McClaughry was in command. For the first three days I flew round about the aerodrome, sometimes firing at the ground target; sometimes following another pilot further afield to get accustomed to the landmarks of the countryside.[17] *Lieutenant Jack Wilkinson, 4 Squadron, Australian Flying Corps*

Wilkinson was a thoughtful man who understood the theory of what was required in formation flying. But the nitty-gritty of practice was not something that came naturally to him with the touch-sensitive controls of the Sopwith Camel.

> Sitting in a Camel, a pilot's head was almost beneath the trailing edge of the top plane's centre section. It followed that his vision was considerably obscured by the upper and lower planes, and, to counteract this, it was customary for the leader to throw his machine into vertical banks every few minutes so that he could see above and below him and thus avoid being caught napping. Even such a supposedly simple job as flying in formation became, under these conditions, a task needing full concentration. There were continual variations of throttle, joystick and rudder position in order to keep pace with the leader. When he made a turn the pilots on the inside of the turn dived and came up on the opposite side of their leader, while those on the outside of the turn flew straight across the leader's tail and took station on the other side. A 'V' type formation was always used, the leader being at the apex of the 'V' and the remainder in station on either side like wild geese on flight. In the intervals of keeping close formation it was our business to keep screwing our necks round in all directions – looking out for Hun machines. In air fighting he who gives first knock and better still manoeuvres into a good position for giving it is at an immense advantage. We were not concerned with attack from below; it was the sky above and behind that needed close watching.[18] *Lieutenant Jack Wilkinson, 4 Squadron, Australian Flying Corps*

As a conventionally reared and somewhat reserved young man Wilkinson found the crudeness of some of his Australian comrades a little shocking, but at the same time he was not too stiff to enjoy their natural indiscipline and humour.

> We tried to accustom ourselves to the experience of having a sponge down in our canvas baths in full view of the villagers of both sexes when they were out for a stroll on a Sunday. The orchard where our tent was pitched was, either by accident or design, beside the path they so often frequented. A polite, '*Bonjour!*' on both sides, a jest on our part, which seemed to fall on stony ground and our visitors passed on, most probably adding open-air

bathing to their already long list of our insane customs. One pilot, more conventional than the rest, always insisted on wearing his slouch hat with its 'Rising Sun' badge to compensate for the scantiness of his birthday uniform, and gave an impeccable salute to all and sundry![19] *Lieutenant Jack Wilkinson, 4 Squadron, Australian Flying Corps*

Once his acclimatization period was over, on one of his first trips across the lines he made acquaintance with the German anti-aircraft batteries.

At once 'Archie' greeted us with big, black bursts of smoke and the dog-like, 'Whoof! Whoof! Whoof!' as he tried to get our range. Sometimes a turn would put him off, sometimes a slow side-slip, but, so long as we were on the German side of the lines, their batteries gave us little rest. In addition to trying to damage us, which they very seldom did, the black 'Archie' smoke was a useful pointer to enemy aircraft, giving them our position if they had not seen us already.[20] *Lieutenant Jack Wilkinson, 4 Squadron, Australian Flying Corps*

Slightly more terrifying was an early exposure to the joys of ground strafing the advancing German troops during the crucial stages of the Battle of Lys. Every scout pilot was needed whether ace or callow beginner. Wilkinson had an amazingly lucky escape during his first ground-strafing mission.

I saw a white Very light fall away from McClaughry's machine in front. Well, I thought, this is where we see what shooting up trenches is like. Down we went in a steep dive, still in formation, until I could clearly see the shell pocked ground in front of Merville. As we came lower 'Archie' sent up innumerable shells but they exploded in a long line above. We were moving too quickly for him. At about 1,000 feet the formation broke up and indulged in individual firing into the Hun trenches. Now and then a heap of earth would rise lazily from the ground as a shell burst, but, now that we were too low for the anti-aircraft guns to fire at us, we became running targets for their machine guns on the ground which were clacking away full bore. I had had two quick dives with my guns hammering and was climbing for another dive when there was a sudden 'CRACK!' and the joystick was jerked clean from my hand. The Camel lurched and reared up its nose until

I grabbed the stick as it jiggled between my knees and put the machine on an even keel. Had something broken? I flew to our side of the line in a few seconds of gentle zig-zags. The controls seemed all right, and I wondered whether to go back and join in the trench-strafing. But it seemed to have lost a lot of its attraction now – McClaughry's signal was becoming worth its weight in gold and I sloped off to the aerodrome still puzzling what could have knocked the stick out of my hand. Once back on the ground again it did not take my rigger long to find out. He and the fitter had barely started to check over my machine when he called, 'This'll be what caused the schemozzle, I'll bet!' and pointed to a bullet hole in the lower plane. I told him I didn't see how a hole like that could have given the joystick such a clout and he gave me a pitying glance, 'You know what's inside this here wing, I suppose?' he said patiently. 'Yes; wooden framework and so on!' 'And so on is right – your aileron control wire runs in here.' He removed a strip of fabric that the bullet had pierced. 'I thought so,' he remarked with satisfaction and showed me the control wire which instead of being nice and round was holding together by three strands. 'Just as well you came home when you did!'[21] *Lieutenant Jack Wilkinson, 4 Squadron, Australian Flying Corps*

Wilkinson found that his early experiences in aerial combat were also less than satisfactory. Although the theory was simple, the practice once again proved extraordinarily difficult. There was just so much to remember and any small detail forgotten, any trivial mistake could render a pilot redundant in action – as when Wilkinson was in a mass formation of seventeen Camels operating over the Nieppe Forest.

As we were about to cross the line I noticed a puff of 'Archie' smoke appear level with us on our right. The fact that it was white and not black was sufficient to show that our gunners were trying to tell us that there was a Hun machine about, and while I was staring around trying to see it my leader turned on his side and dived like a hawk swooping. I followed, and there, hundreds of feet below us I could just make out the outline of an aeroplane making for Hunland. Its black crosses were only just visible and it was so low that it appeared to be crawling along the ground. In the excitement of the dive I had forgotten to keep my engine full on with the result that most of the other Camels in the flights behind me overtook me and began firing at the escaping Hun. By this time so many Camels were in front of me that I could not get off a single shot at the easy target for fear of hitting one of our own machines! In less than 10 seconds a feather of smoke was streaming from the German machine, it made one sweeping lunge upwards and then fell in a slow spin to the ground, the smoke increased in volume as it dived earthward and crashed on our side of the line.[22] *Lieutenant Jack Wilkinson, 4 Squadron, Australian Flying Corps*

There were just so many different mistakes for the young pilot to make. Towards the end of June, Wilkinson was sent off on a high-flying patrol, looking to intercept German photographic aircraft at around 20,000 feet. He had been advised to wear three or four of everything, but basking on the ground in the hot June sunshine this seemed totally superfluous. He thus took off dressed only in his normal flying gear.

The pointer of my altimeter touched the 15,000 foot mark. In spite of the intensity of the sun's rays the air was becoming much colder and I wished I had taken him at his word – and some of his clothes – and put on three or four of everything. Higher and higher we soared, but the rate of climb was slowing down considerably. At 17,000 feet I was continually beating my hands in turn on my knees to try to help the circulation for the immensity of my field of vision was poor consolation for the piercing cold I was experiencing. And truly the vista was tremendous! Away to the north-east the Belgian coastline could be seen, while to the west, much clearer was the coast of France and, in the dim distance, the white cliffs of Dover. I felt like a wasp suspended above an enormous bowl from which I could never completely escape, for, of course, the horizon rose level with me whatever my altitude. I had seen no planes of any nationality so far, but as we topped 19,000 feet I caught a glimpse of some specks near the sun. Were they ours, or theirs – or was I seeing things? Here they came, a neat formation of three, and as they passed over me my half-frozen brain registered relief when I identified them as Spads. I was in no condition to take on a scrap just then for, in addition to my struggle against the cold, my engine was quickly becoming weaker and weaker owing to the rarefied atmosphere. I became pettish and angry with myself like a child. Why had I come on this mad patrol? How the devil was I supposed to take on photographically inclined Huns with my Camel barely answering to the controls and nearly at stalling point? If there were Spads that could cruise so easily over my head, what could I do if all the confounded machines in the German Flying Corps decided to sit above me taking photographs. Oh hell! I felt thoroughly miserable, lazy and careless.[23] *Lieutenant Jack Wilkinson, 4 Squadron, Australian Flying Corps*

Wilkinson was no physical 'freak' as James McCudden had been, capable of overcoming the debilitating effects of oxygen starvation and cold on body and mind. After a terrible struggle he had clambered up through the thin air to 20,000 feet but encountered nothing. When it was time to return he found that the worst was still to come as he began his long descent. Soon he was really suffering.

My limbs developed an agonising 'hot-ache' as we descended to warmer temperatures. I could have cried with pain. I decided that I was coming down too fast for comfort – my ears had begun to pop with the different pressure, and I alternately swallowed or pinched my nostrils and tried to blow my nose. I steadied her into an easier glide. While this reduced the intensity of the aching the descent naturally took longer, and I was glad indeed to see our aerodrome slide under my wings. I landed to see mechanics going about their work without tunics; their shirts wide open at the neck.[24] *Lieutenant Jack Wilkinson, 4 Squadron, Australian Flying Corps*

Despite his problems, Wilkinson had managed to survive his first few weeks at the front. Indeed his career as a scout pilot stood neatly balanced. Would he go on to conquer his various teething troubles and emerge as the 'real thing' or would he flounder along unsuccessfully?

Youdale was at the same stage of novitiate as myself. Neither of us had yet brought down a Hun machine. Somehow the fact that a Hun had not brought *us* down did not arise! In order that this state of affairs might be remedied McClaughry called us aside one evening after mess and suggested that we might like to try for a balloon that was wound down each night near Estaires. We jumped at the idea – first one and then another of our pals had been chalking up a Hun to his credit. We arranged to go over very early in the morning before the balloon rose at the end of its cable. That evening we went across to the hangars, saw that every third round in our machine gun belts was an incendiary cartridge, and gave instructions to be called at 4.30am. It was quite dark when, next morning, we staggered, bleary eyed and sleepy, into the mess kitchen to gulp down hot cocoa and munch a few biscuits. We spun a coin for who was to have first crack at the balloon. Youdale won and said that he'd go first. I was to wait above our lines and watch the fun, and if he missed the balloon it would be my turn. We took off a few minutes before five and made straight for the lines, it being too dark to keep together. What a wonderful sight the sunrise was that morning! At 5,000 feet I had the feeling that over in the east someone was turning up the wick of a stupendous lamp. The ground was a very dark grey – almost black – while over La Bassée way little pinpoints of light flickered and blinked where a bombardment was in progress. Someone was getting it in the neck! But above the horizon first one patch of cloud and then another was turned to dull, and then bright gold until all the eastern sky was suffused in waves of light. Roosting above Nieppe Forest I looked down over to Estaires trying to catch a glimpse of Youdale. For some minutes I thought it would be impossible to see him in that growing glare of light, and then there was a flash as the sun caught his wings and he banked over and dived at the balloon. At the self-same moment the Bosche gunners spotted him and his progress was marked by burst after burst of black smoke. As he got lower he disappeared against the blackness of the ground, but I could still tell where he was by the strings of green fireballs – flaming onions we called them – that rose to meet him from the ground in graceful curves, and I guessed that what with these and machine guns on the ground he was having a lively time. I was still peering towards where I imagined the balloon lay when I saw him streaking for our lines, and in a very short time he was alongside and signalling that he had missed the balloon. He came closer and I could see that he was laughing, though it seemed that there was precious little to laugh about now that he had stirred up the wasps' nest I was about to tackle! Putting down the nose of my machine I made off for Estaires, and, as soon as I judged I was above the balloon, I shut off my engine and screwed over into a dive. Just for a second or two I thought that the German 'Archie' must have gone back to bed, but I was soon disillusioned. 'Wang! Wang! Wang!' came their shells. They seemed to have got the range to a nicety and I was soon surrounded by their belches of black smoke. I opened up the engines and, just when the flaming onions started to soar in my direction, I saw the balloon – a grey smudge on the ground. Even when I got down to 1,000 feet it still seemed miles away, and by this time machine gun bullets were clack-clacking their way in my direction. At length I thought I must be in range and opened up on it with both guns. My tracer bullets seemed to be going straight into the beastly thing, but there was no sign of it catching fire. Zooming up at the end of the dive, I made up my mind to have just one more go and this time got it plumb in the middle of my ring-sight. Surely I couldn't miss it now? With both guns hammering away I came down once more. The balloon loomed nearer and nearer, and as I shot over the top of it I was sure I could see a wisp of smoke coming out of its fat back. I swung round to take another look, only too glad not to be flying straight amid that clatter of gunner, but it was only my imagination. The balloon was apparently undamaged. By now things were uncomfortably hot. The excitement of the attack was over, and it seemed a long, long way back to our lines with the feeling that at any second a stream of bullets from the ground would come crashing into me or my petrol tank. 'Gosh,' I thought, 'fancy sitting with your back against 20 gallons of petrol with all this going on!' And I sat more upright – as if that would help! I circled over our own trenches and went down to have a look at our own lines. Here and there a white face showed as a sentry stared up, wondering, I knew, how long before he would be relieved and he could 'get down to it', if his missus was managing all right at home, and what the devil this flying bloke above him thought he was up to buzzing round and round and round.[25] *Lieutenant Jack Wilkinson, 4 Squadron, Australian Flying Corps*

To add insult to near injury, on landing Wilkinson found that Youdale had returned for another attempt and actually succeeded in shooting down the blasted balloon! Wilkinson had failed, but he had tried; he had not stinted in his efforts to shoot down the balloon. His courage had been tested and he had not been found wanting. But he still had not scored that elusive first victory.

So there we have it: two ordinary boys: one from Yorkshire, the other from faraway Idaho. Though they had not scored a kill, both had learned the basics of their grim trade, yet it is fair to say that neither had exactly prospered. At this point in their careers how they would have loved a generous-spirited patrol leader, such as the late lamented Major Edward Mannock, to ease their way by sharing a kill with them, thereby to assuage their doubts and give them the confidence to push on to greater things. But they were on their own. How would they cope in the months to come on the Western Front as the air fighting escalated to a hitherto unknown frenzy? Who would live and who would die?

On 4 August Lieutenant Edgar Taylor of 79 Squadron managed to score his first victory although it would be unconfirmed through lack of witnesses. Yet Taylor himself was confident that he had succeeded and that for the moment was enough for him.

> I looked down and saw a Hun dash over the line and attack one of our slow artillery machines. I knew that unless I got down quick it was all up with the artillery observation 'bus'. In my haste to get down I was unable to signal to my pals who flew on never missing me. As soon as the Hun saw me he beat it back not showing any desire for a fair scrap. I was so raging that I made up my mind that I would get him if I got it myself after. I riddled him and he went down, but I could see that he was only trying to get down to his own trenches, where the machine guns would get after me. As I suspected, at 300 feet he straightened out but I was ready for him and shot him to pieces. That settled his 'Watch on the Rhine'! I had gone a very long way over in my excitement and when I looked up four Huns were above me. They were in an ideal position to shoot but they only followed me at a respectful distance until I got safely back. The fun of it was that I was out of ammunition. The Huns didn't know what an easy mark they had missed.[26] *Lieutenant Edgar Taylor, 79 Squadron*

He was on his way at last; success born of grim determination to secure the kill. Not so ordinary any more – Edgar Taylor had finally broken his duck even if it was unoffical.

Meanwhile Lieutenant Jack Wilkinson of 4 Squadron Australian Flying Corps had still not scored a victory although he had participated in a mass dogfight early that August, an experience that seems to have exhilarated and shaken him in equal measure. The whole squadron had been ordered up after they received reports that the sky was 'black with Huns'. It is noticeable that he was not the first to sight the German scouts. His air vision was still not really up to scratch.

The leader waggled his wings, 'Enemy in sight!' I looked round. A few black specks seemed to be floating round the sun, or was it biliousness? Before I could discover what they were, we were off in a long steady dive. It took a few seconds to make out what we were diving at, it was a curving dive too, and I was still puzzling what we were really doing when I spotted the Huns, six Fokker biplanes flying due north. I was flying in the lower of our two formations and found it difficult to hold my fire until I was well within the range of 200 yards which was the maximum at which we were supposed to engage enemy aircraft. Then one of the Camels behind shot past, waggling his wings at my leader and pointing up and behind. What – *more* Huns? Good heavens – we *were* in for a lively time! It now became a race as to whether we could reach the Fokkers below us before the four Huns above, Fokker Triplanes, could reach us. It was hard to say who won. The Huns underneath must have spotted us as they swung up and round in a climbing turn to try and meet us at the same height; we swung round and down to get a crack at them while we had the advantage of height, and the merry-go-round was completed by the 'Tripehounds' snapping at our tails. The next part of the scrap was almost too instantaneous to bear recording. The air was full of machines flying around each other at every possible and impossible angle. I had been told to 'stunt and go on stunting' when I found myself in a dogfight, and this seemed to be the time to put precept into practice. It was a case of each man for himself while it lasted, and I put my machine into a tight turn, climbing to get behind a 'Tripehound' flying in the opposite direction. Before I could get him in my ring-sight there was a 'clack-clack-clack-clack-clack!' and the white streaks of tracer bullets appeared between my wings on either side. Hun on my tail! Over with the stick and rudder, and, as my assailant zoomed to dive again, I got off a short burst at a Hun diving in front of me, only to take my thumbs off the triggers in time to avoid hitting one of our Camels that was hard on the tail of the Hun. And so it went on – a short burst from the guns, and a wriggle to dodge a Hun on my tail – round and round, up and down, until the sky and the earth seemed to reel round each other in sympathy. At the end of perhaps a minute, during which time I had seen one enemy machine fall smoking and another in evident difficulties, the air cleared as suddenly as the fight had begun. I looked about me, and was scarcely able to believe my eyes – not a machine was in sight! No: I was wrong! Over towards Bois Grenier there were two of our chaps, and I darted off after them as hard as

I could go. I was feeling lonely after so much company! It takes a long time to catch up with an aeroplane flying in the same direction as I found out only too well that morning. Where the other three Camels had got to I did not know; I was too intent on catching up with these two to bother about the others. But the more I looked at the two Camels ahead, the more mystified I became. Somehow they didn't look like Camels! And then, quite quickly, the problem was solved, for they turned to the right and there, on their white tail-fins, were neat black crosses. In my excitement I had been following a couple of Fokkers! They made no attempt to attack. To be truthful I gave them no opportunity, I half-rolled away and tore back for our lines as fast as my engine would rev! Later, like a fool, I told the others what had happened and, in the ragging that ensued, I was openly accused of 'desertion'! Needless to say, the accusation was all in fun and would probably have never been made if they had known how frightened I was at the moment when I realised my mistake! The net result of our dogfight was three Hun machines crashed and two out of control, and none of our machines missing.[27] *Lieutenant Jack Wilkinson, 4 Squadron, Australian Flying Corps*

But Wilkinson had again failed to score – although not for the want of trying. A few days later, on 9 August, his confidence was not enhanced when an Australian pilot arrived to take his place in 4 Australian Squadron and he was posted to 46 Squadron where again he was flying Sopwith Camels. He would have to make himself at home in a new mess with a whole new set of comrades. At this point his career was finely balanced.

Both Wilkinson and Taylor had to become acquainted with the rigours of the dawn patrol; which meant just that. This was in itself a severe test of young men who had to get up in the middle of the night to take off as the sun glinted over the horizon at the height of summer. There was only one hope of remission – rain!

'The following pilots will be ready for an offensive patrol at 4.30am.' Of course those of us who were included in the list gave a groan and decided to get to bed at once, to be sure of getting enough sleep. Leaving orders with our batman to call us at 3.30am in order to have a little breakfast before going up. As we trooped off to our hut we all looked at the sky in hope of seeing some indication of a storm. If only it would rain *then* we could sleep. I was soon fast asleep in my bed.[28] *Lieutenant Edgar Taylor, 79 Squadron*

Young men being as they were, some of their favourite mornings were marked by bad weather that meant that the dawn patrol was cancelled, perhaps even meaning that the whole day's flying programme would have to be abandoned. The sound of rain or high winds was the very best mood music a pilot could hope for as he drowsily emerged from his slumbers.

The next thing I remembered was when I woke up and it was broad daylight. Holy smoke! I wondered if I had fallen asleep after the batman had woken me. I looked at my watch and saw it was 7am but – oh – I suddenly heard a pleasant sound. The rain which must have stopped for a few minutes commenced again. How good it sounded! It was music to me. I just ducked under the bed clothes and got ready to sleep until noon. My Irish terrier, who acts as squadron mascot, came in and laid down at my feet. In a few minutes I was asleep again. I dreamed I was in a fight, how it finished I don't know because I woke up again, looked at my watch and it was 10.30. The dog came up and chewed my ear so I decided to get up. As I put on my breeches I yelled for my batman to bring me some hot water. By the time I had shaved and washed I began to feel refreshed and all the lingering sleep had left my eyes. I then headed for the mess where one or two others were having breakfast, 11.15! I soon sent the orderly after two scrambled eggs and some bacon finishing off with marmalade and toast. Also I had some kind of liquid coffee, but it wasn't a bit like the stuff we call coffee in the USA.[29] *Lieutenant Edgar Taylor, 79 Squadron*

Such intervals were but deferments and each day of continued survival only seemed to bring their eventual deaths closer. They had watched so many young men come and go over their months at the front. The problem of mess life was that it was almost by definition transitory; a meeting of passing strangers who may be well disposed to each other but have little chance of developing a long-standing or meaningful relationship.

You may have breakfast with a chap and be discussing general topics with him; by night he is gone – God knows where – but you don't worry. He goes out with the past, you can only afford to think and plan for the present.[30]
Lieutenant Edgar Taylor, 79 Squadron

By mid-August, Taylor had become bored with routine patrols. He craved excitement and quicker results for his warlike efforts. And, after all, the balloons did look easy to hit, if only he could get past the anti-aircraft defences. The temptation was too much for him to resist and he began a career as a 'balloon-buster'.

I got off the ground this morning at 7am and headed straight for the lines. I was the one detailed to attack the balloons therefore I was carrying incendiary ammunition which you are allowed to use for balloons only. Also I was carrying a written statement from my CO saying that I was out to attack balloons only. This is just a precaution in case you are captured with incendiary ammunition in your machine. I saw several balloons up so I crossed the line and went for them. It was rather a ticklish job because you are obliged to go down to 1,000 feet after them and besides you are about 10 miles over. They are about 50 feet in diameter and 100 feet long, made of silk. The 'Archies' opened up at once making my journey too interesting to be enjoyable. They also started to pull the balloon down. I dropped a bomb just to square matters with the machine gunners on the ground, then attacked the balloon. The air was full of black 'Archie' and dozens of machine guns were blazing away. I kept diving at the balloon and shooting then I would climb away and dive again. It seemed impossible to down it. However at last it burst into flames and went down. I was sure glad. It is great sport *but* it is very often too good to last. However we must all do our best and let our personal safety take care of itself.[31] *Lieutenant Edgar Taylor, 79 Squadron*

Like several other scout pilots before him, Edgar Taylor soon became rather obsessed with the concept of shooting down German balloons. Something about their very existence in the skies seemed a personal affront to such men and they began positively to relish the chance to dash them from the skies, whatever the very obvious risks. Just a few days later he was at it again.

I got up at 4am and went out alone. I saw two balloons put up so I went after them, but they were so far over that they were on the ground before I arrived. The 'Archie' and machine guns were something terrible – I was sure scared. There were literally thousands of 'Archie' shells bursting. They all seemed to concentrate on me. As I passed over some Hun infantry I dropped my bombs. That evened things up a bit, making 'Archie' madder than ever. The Huns seemed to think that they had me scared out, because as soon as I reached our line they put two kite balloons up. I waited until they were up a few hundred feet then I dashed back. I put a stream of incendiary bullets into one and down it went in flames. I just yelled with delight. The machine guns were so busy that I had to clear away at once. There were bullets all through my machine. I started after the second balloon, which was about 3 miles away. How those Huns struggled to get it down before I got there. My engine was hit so it kept stopping. This delayed me so long that the balloon was only 500 feet up when I got there. They immediately put a barrage up between me and the balloon. I could see their flaming bullets going through my machine. It was not a pleasant job. I could see where bullets had gone through my main spars. I dived through the barrage and fired incendiary bullets into the balloon at close range. The observer jumped out in his parachute. The 'sausage' burst into flames so I was once more moved to let out a yell of delight, also hoping that the observer would break his neck landing. Mad – say those Huns must have been wild! They threw more hate at me than ever. I'll bet the shells they used cost the Kaiser ten times as much as my machine cost the RAF. I crossed No Man's Land at 1,000 feet and thanks to the Huns' rotten marksmanship I got through safely. Two Huns before breakfast – isn't that luck?[32] *Lieutenant Edgar Taylor, 79 Squadron*

Such behaviour may or may not have been compulsive, but it was certainly life-threatening to its practitioners. Luckily Taylor could console himself with the thought that he had not got long before he was due to go on leave.

Well, my much-postponed leave is to come through at last. I have definitely decided to go on the 28th August and am expecting to have a good time. Irene and I have patched things up again, so all's well that ends well![33] *Lieutenant Edgar Taylor, 79 Squadron*

Unfortunately, on 24 August, just the day after writing that letter, Taylor tried his luck once too often and this time paid a grim price. Major Anthony Arnold, his commanding officer, wrote home to pass on the bad news to his family.

> He left the ground to go over and bring down a hostile kite balloon. He was seen to fire at one, which was at a height of about 1,500 feet, which smoked but did not catch fire. He then went on to the second, which was much lower – about 500 feet – which he brought down in flames, but shortly after this he was himself brought down by anti-aircraft fire. His machine was seen to land apparently under control, so that it is probable that he is a prisoner.[34] *Major Anthony Arnold, 79 Squadron*

His family received another letter from one of Taylor's friends, Lieutenant M. Munden; it too offered some hope that their son had survived. Perhaps it helped the family to have a transitional period of optimism before having to accept the loss.

> As I have been a room mate of Edgar's for the past two months, I thought I should write to tell you how sorry we are to learn that he is missing, and to offer you our sincerest sympathy. However we feel very certain from reports that he is quite safe, and we know he is the kind of chap that soon escapes. We had a mutual agreement in case either of us was taken prisoner by which we could send for supplies, and I will communicate with you at once as soon as I receive some word from Edgar. Your son has been doing wonderful work and we learn that he has been recommended for the Distinguished Flying Cross. It is agreed that no one deserves it more than he, and we are all looking forward to the time that we can congratulate him personally. The whole squadron misses him tremendously for he was greatly liked and admired by us all, and we are all anxiously awaiting further news of him. I trust you will have had good news by the time you receive this letter.[35] *Lieutenant M. Munden, 79 Squadron*

The 'ordinary boy' from Idaho had flown over a hundred offensive patrols, claimed one German aircraft confirmed, three unconfirmed and four of the balloons that would be his nemesis. He had succeeded in his ambition of becoming an ace but had been killed taking it all just one step too far.

SADLY, by September 1918, despite all his best efforts over the front, Lieutenant Jack Wilkinson found that he was being ground down by the unrelenting pressure of aerial fighting. He tried his best to cope, but could not. Without the release of a confirmed kill the stress and nervous tension increased. Like so many other young pilots he became afflicted with chronic fatigue, which made him suffer more both in the air and on the ground. Wilkinson was caught in a classic vicious circle. Soon his self-confidence, so utterly vital for a scout pilot, began to drain away.

> For some days I had been feeling low. All day long I wanted to sleep, and sleep, and sleep. Even when on patrol it needed a big effort to make myself take an interest in what was going on. The war seemed never-ending, and all the fun went out of flying. There appeared to be no chance of my ever becoming a first-class scout pilot with a string of enemy machines to my credit, and when I began to shiver and ache all over it was with a sigh of thankfulness I climbed into an ambulance and was deposited at No. 41 Stationary Hospital some miles further back. I wrote home that I was sorry to lose the squadron, ten days absence meant that I should be struck off the strength automatically – but in reality I was tired of the strain of flying under war conditions; tired of the incessant squirming round in my seat looking for Huns; sick of the coughing bark of 'Archie' shells and the taste of burnt castor oil. I was weary of waiting to be shot down, for I knew it could only be a question of time before that happened. Either that or my nerves would crack up completely. In many ways it was galling to find that I could not stand the racket as long as the other pilots. But there it was – I was squeezed dry.[36] *Lieutenant Jack Wilkinson, 46 Squadron*

His response to the pressures of conflict is entirely understandable. For the ordinary man there was only so much of this awful business that they could stand before their physical or mental health began to leach away. It was a common response and in a sense Wilkinson was lucky. Many young pilots not blessed with phenomenal eyesight, preternatural reflexes, natural marksmanship and amazing flying abilities were simply shot down in their first couple of flights. Wilkinson had lasted several months, he had played his part and although ultimately found wanting, he surely warrants nothing but admiration and sympathy.

TWO ordinary boys: different characters, different fates, but both in their different ways typical of so many young men trying to face up to the terrible pressures of aerial fighting on the Western Front in the high summer of 1918.

Chapter 12

Bombers over Germany

The raids launched on strategic targets in Germany by first the 41st Wing, RFC / RAF and then the Independent Air Force were intrinsically much the same as the shorter-range tactical bombing raids; it was their target that was significant. These raids were designed to affect directly the Germans' ability to carry on the war by either severing the main rail routes to the Western Front, or by massively disrupting the production of munitions. There were three ways of doing this: by striking at the armaments factories themselves, by attacking the production of the raw materials of munitions, or by cutting the rail communications that allowed the distribution of weapons or materials. This meant striking deep into Germany and hitting targets within the major conurbations. It was a new way of waging war.

One of the manifest evils launched on the world by the Great War was the widespread aerial bombing of civilian targets. This was not really a surprise as the rules of war are in essence a movable feast that reflect the prevailing sense of what society will and will not accept in the pursuit of victory, rather than any deeply held overriding moral code. Yet the bombing of women and children in their homes – whether accidentally or with malice aforethought – surely marked a significant step in the brutalization of mankind. This is not to say that civilians had not borne the brunt of untrammelled military aggression before; indeed helpless civilians had never been safe from their marauding enemies as was shown time and again in the gory scenes that followed the capture of defended towns. Yet some attempt to hold the barbarians at bay had been made at the first Hague International Conference of 1899 when it was henceforth clearly prohibited to drop projectiles or bombs of any kind from flying machines. This had been revised in the subsequent conference in 1907 to outlaw only the bombing of 'undefended localities' in accordance with the then current naval and military practice. Such tinkering showed that the Great Powers were as ever unwilling to lose any prospect of effective offensive action against their enemies.

The spectre of iron devastation tumbling down from the sky onto helpless cities was raised in that very next year by H. G. Wells with the publication of his seminal fictional work, *The War in the Air*, in which Wells positively revelled in the concept of a fleet of German airships bombing the population of New York. The novel was a huge success, really firing up the popular imagination. As the naval race accelerated after the launch of HMS *Dreadnought* in 1906 there were many who pointed to the Zeppelins as the equivalent aerial behemoths and wondered why the British seemed to have no effective counter-measures.

When the war began in 1914 there was no doubt that Germany had every intention of using its air power to attack the homeland of the British Empire. Yet it could be held that the first 'strategic' bombing raids were carried out by the British when the Royal Naval Air Service launched pre-emptive raids on the Zeppelin sheds at Düsseldorf and Cologne in September and October 1914. Such British raids were infrequent and mostly ineffective, but they pointed the way to the future. The Germans began their assault on Britain with a series of aeroplane and seaplane raids on the Kent coast, finally penetrating as far as the outskirts of London on Christmas Day 1914. However the German Zeppelin campaign did not begin in earnest until January 1915. What followed over the next two years was inevitable. Bombs may have been legitimately directed at 'war targets' and defended localities, but nasty 'accidents' were bound to happen. Slowly but surely the acceptable boundaries shifted, freeing the bombers to drop their bombs to gain maximum physical and moral effect. It was just as certain that the British would invest resources in counter-measures to the Zeppelin threat. By the late summer of 1916 they had a developed a combination of anti-aircraft guns and aircraft that left the much vaunted Zeppelins exposed as little more than bags of highly inflammable gases that could not defend themselves in the hostile skies over Britain. They would return in high-flying raids in some desperation later in the war and would ultimately drop 5,806 bombs that killed 557 and injured 1,358.

The next escalation in the bombing war came with the German aircraft raids, first by day, and then by night in the summer of 1917. The twin-engined Gotha was a signpost to a grim future for Londoners. The counter-measures designed for Zeppelins initially proved inadequate in the face of the relatively high-performance Gothas and as the bombs sprayed randomly the casualties began to escalate. Whatever the legitimate military or economic targets the Germans may have aimed at they rarely seemed to hit them. Most of the bombs fell unerringly on civilians. Worst of all was during on the morning of 13 June when a bomb crashed through the ceiling of the Upper North Street School in Poplar, exploded in the infants' class and killed eighteen children.

The British were once again stung into action and squadrons of modern scouts were wrenched back from the grip of Trenchard and Haig, who desperately needed them on the Western Front, to guard the capital of the Empire. With the benefit of hindsight it is apparent that one of the important lessons of aerial warfare was that bombing campaigns were incredibly effective at diverting massive resources to the home front for a relatively minimal outlay in bombers. The Germans were soon forced to suspend the daylight raids, but the Gothas, followed by the even bigger and better Giants, merely switched to night raids for the remainder of the war. Once again, after a pause, the scouts followed them into the night skies, making the German raids increasingly hazardous and consequently less frequent. Nevertheless the aircraft raids were responsible for 857 deaths and 2,508 wounded.

The military solution to the raids had been relatively easy, if costly in diverting aerial resources from the real war. But the political outcry that ensued was to have far-reaching consequences. One result, as we have seen, was the formation of the Royal Air Force. A second, more germane effect was the escalation of attempts to bomb Germany and ultimately the formation of the Independent Air Force. Back in the summer of 1916 the No. 3 Naval Wing based at Luxeuil had begun, in conjunction with the French, a series of bombing raids directed at the German steel works in the Saar valley. This had provoked, or forced, the Germans to establish a gradually improving system of aerial defence incorporating searchlights, anti-aircraft guns, machine guns, balloon barrages and, of course, flights of scouts.

The scope of the raids widened and crucially included a genuine reprisal raid when, in the aftermath of the submarine sinking of the hospital ship *Asturias* on 20 March 1917, bombs were dropped indiscriminately as an act of revenge over the helpless civilians of Freiburg by British and French bombers on 14 April. However, in the spring of 1917 the operations were suspended when the No. 3 Naval Wing was broken up and despatched to assist the main battle against the German Air Service that had reached a crucial phase in the campaign over Arras. The lull did not last for long as the popular outcry and widespread hysterical reaction across much of the political spectrum in Britain prompted demands for reprisals for the Gotha raids of 1917. Haig was ordered to respond and the buck was duly passed down the chain of command to Trenchard who in October 1917 formed the 41st Wing based at the Ochey airfield in the Nancy area under the command of Lieutenant Colonel Cyril Newall. Their mission was summed up by Haig as, 'Long range attacks on German commercial towns as reprisals for enemy air raids on Allied towns.'[1] Or to put it another way:

> I sincerely hope that before the middle of this year we shall have spread terror and dismay among the noble Rhine towns. If only we could lay everything in ruins.[2] *Captain Lennox Beater, 55 Squadron*

There were plenty of tempting targets within range of Newall's bombers: iron and steel works, coalfields, engine manufacturers, chemical factories and of course the railway lines that were responsible for moving the raw materials and finished products of so much industry. The French staff considered the rail targets of prime importance as they sought to cut off Germany from the crucial raw iron ore supplies that originated in Lorraine and Luxembourg. This viewpoint may have had intellectual rigour, but it was not what the British public wanted – they wanted a real gesture of vengeance and craved the vicarious satisfaction of bombs falling on German towns. And a gesture was all that they were going to get – for just three squadrons made up the bomber force: all that was available for daytime raids was 55 Squadron flying the DH4 with their two or three 112-pound bombs or their equivalent; while at night there was 100 Squadron flying the clearly obsolescent FE2b which could carry a similar bomb load. The Admiralty contributed 16 Naval Squadron RNAS who were flying the far superior heavy Handley Pages that could carry a relatively impressive twelve 112-pound bombs. The first raids were made by day and night on the Burbach Works at Saarbrucken in October. Bad weather restricted the bombing opportunities over the next two months but a strong raid by ten DH4s bringing unseasonable cheer to Mannheim on Christmas Day marked a declaration of intent for 1918.

These raids continued throughout the year. Thus it was that on the morning of 16 March 1918 Lieutenant A. S. Keep found himself *en route* for the town of Zweibrucken in the Rhineland on the border of the Palatinate Forest, over 100 miles behind the German lines. As they took off for such raids there is a strange sense of generational slip to the scene that would be seen on airfields all across East Anglia just twenty-five years later.

> The start of a raid is an impressive sight: the twelve machines, six in each formation set out in battle flying order on the aerodrome; the propellers revolving easily with the engines throttled right back; the streamers of the leader and deputy leader fluttering from the struts; heavy ominous-looking bombs slung under the wings; machine guns pointing upwards; pilots and observers tense and waiting for the signal to start. Last but not least Roger the squadron dog running excitedly round. The low note of the engines becomes a full throttle roar and the leader machine followed by the rest of the formations move forward and rapidly gaining speed leave the earth behind.[3] *Lieutenant A. S. Keep, 55 Squadron*

As they passed over the battered front lines the first resistance came from the anti-aircraft batteries.

> Below we could see the shell pocked earth and the wiggling lines of trenches, here and there the smoke of a bursting shell. For the time being one seemed curiously detached and aloof from all this but this feeling was quickly dissipated once the line was reached and showed that the people below were by no means unmindful of your existence. What had previously been clear air now became filled with puffs of black and white smoke preceded by a little flash of flame. We were in the 'Archie' barrage. The

> sensation was weird. The little round black puffs of smoke apparently appearing from nowhere with nothing to herald them as unless they are very near you can't hear the noise of the bursting shell above the roar of the engine. It is only when you see jagged rents appearing in the planes that their full significance is properly realised.[4] *Lieutenant A. S. Keep, 55 Squadron*

Once they had got past the anti-aircraft bursts near the front lines they were heading direct for the Vosges Mountains, while beyond that lay the mighty Rhine and the Fatherland. All seemed to be going well. Yet they were moving into the area defended by the German home defence squadrons.

> With a cold thrill I saw a red light soar into the air from the leader's machine. Red always means danger and a red light fired from the leader's machine meant enemy aircraft approaching; close in and prepare to fight. Away on our left were some little rapidly growing black specks which speedily resolved themselves into hostile aircraft bearing down on us and a few seconds later spurts of flame appeared from the leading machine. I heard the never forgotten crackle of the machine guns and saw the streaks of blue smoke from the tracer bullets as they sped on their way. Before I realised it I was mixed up in an aerial fight with a Hun who was coming up behind. My own observer was blazing away with his Lewis gun and other observers were doing the same. To put it mildly I was frightened.[5] *Lieutenant A. S. Keep, 55 Squadron*

The brief combat was indecisive as the Germans failed to press home the attack in the face of the well-maintained formation adopted by the 55 Squadron pilots.

> We sped on and shortly reached Zweibrucken our objective. The leader fired a white light warning us to prepare to drop our bombs. Shortly after I saw his bombs fall and with great joy released my own with a vigorous tug on the release gear. The worthy inhabitants of Zweibrucken did not let us have all our own way and vigorously plastered us with 'Archie' shells but without much effect. As we wheeled round for home I experienced great

satisfaction in seeing flames in various parts of the town where our bombs dropped.[6] *Lieutenant A. S. Keep, 55 Squadron*

The raid had been successful, but the German opposition on that occasion had not been particularly intense. If they survived it was surprising how quickly the pilots and observers got used to the warped routine of the bomber crew. But some targets and some raids could never be routine. One such occurred on 24 March 1918 when 55 Squadron launched a raid on the German poison gas works at Mannheim. When they took off they found themselves flying through clear blue skies with a negligible wind. They reached Mannheim without any problems, but once there their prospects darkened radically. The Germans were more than ready for them.

The sky became black with bursting 'Archie' shells and above the shell bursts we could see the Hun scouts waiting. The feeling was intense. Personally I always found the few minutes preceding a fight the most trying. One's nerves were strung to the highest pitch and it needed no vivid imagination to picture one's machine going down in flames from an enemy's shells or tracer bullet. Once the fight started however all this was forgotten – one saw red and cared for nothing. There was no time to be afraid. The air seemed full of machines circling round each other for position while above the roar of the engines one could hear the crackle of the machine guns and see the smoke trails from the tracer bullets. My observer was blazing away at a Hun while two other machines were doing the same. Suddenly the Hun stalled, turned over and went headlong down at a terrific speed and crashed into the middle of the town. Patey, my observer, was Irish and nothing pleased him more than a winged Hun so he, and I also for that matter, felt the fates had been kind. A few seconds later the formation dropped the bombs and one and a half tons of explosives were spread over Mannheim. In a few minutes the effect was electrical. Huge clouds of grey smoke from the poison gas factory showed that we had hit a container. Other bombs fell on big store sheds along the river dock and the biggest fire it has ever been my lot to see started there. We saw the flames 40 miles away as we crossed the Vosges. The Hun scouts had not been idle during this time and were attacking some of our machines hard. Samson's observer was shot through the heart and Samson himself narrowly escaped the same fate.[7] *Lieutenant A. S. Keep, 55 Squadron*

Eventually they got clear of the scouts, but the Germans had not yet given up the fray. The difference from the tactical raids was that the Germans had plenty of time to organize more than one hot reception on the long flight back. After an inconclusive encounter immediately after crossing the Vosges Mountains, the bombers encountered more serious opposition when they were still about 20 miles from the front lines.

Our tired formation ran into about thirteen Huns and a real hard fight followed. Four Huns were driven down but we also lost two machines, one containing two of our best men. Patey fought well and put in some good shooting.[8] *Lieutenant A. S. Keep, 55 Squadron*

After four stressful hours they landed to discover that the Germans had left their mark on their DH4 in the form of a considerable smattering of bullet damage across their wings, struts and wheels. It had been a close-run thing. Mannheim was a particularly difficult target, but then any raid over Germany was intrinsically dangerous and the pilots and observers of 55 Squadron were being eroded away on a daily basis.

Their courage was officially recognized, of course, with a variety of medals and awards. Above all many of them treasured the memory of a visit by a prominent French general eager to pay tribute to the men striking deep into the homeland of France's enemies. It is sad to say that the august general struck terror of a different kind among the gallant aviators.

There was also a presentation of Croix de Guerres by General Castelnau to four of our fellows. The presentation was duly carried out with appropriate ceremony and the recipients duly kissed on the cheek by the General – much to their disgust and the huge delight of everybody else. As the worthy General was about five feet nothing and Captain Collett, one of the victims, stood 6 feet 4 inches the kissing was worth seeing![9] *Lieutenant A. S. Keep, 55 Squadron*

Day followed day, mission followed mission in a kaleidoscope of new targets and close escapes. On 18 May, 55 Squadron set off on another mission fraught with danger. They were to attack Cologne, deep in Germany, which was considered an ideal place to bring the reality of war home to German civilians. Six machines set off at 06.00 that morning with Lieutenant Keep once again flying with his trusty observer Lieutenant Patey. After a long flight they reached the Rhine and here their troubles began.

> To the west of the river and at about our own height were four Hun scouts approaching us. Some little time before my engine had not been going very well and we were finding it difficult to keep up with the formation. The scouts were beginning to close in by the time we reached Cologne and we began to exchange shots. Cologne was partially obscured by fleecy clouds but not enough to seriously interfere with bombing. Our machine carried the camera for taking photos of the damage. Patey was determined to get his pictures whatever happened and did some splendid work bobbing up and down like a 'Jack in the box'; first taking photos and then up firing a few rounds at two Huns who were trying to close in. Williams the leader fired a white light and down went all the bombs all over Cologne, mostly small 20pdrs which we afterwards learned caused a great number of casualties. The formation wheeled eastwards and lightened of the load started to climb keeping up a running fight with the four Huns. When it came to climbing we were done. Our engine was running all out and could pull no harder so we had the helpless feeling of being left behind as the formation gradually drew away from us and upwards. The leader was doing the right thing as the safety of his formation depended on getting to the greatest possible height on the return trip; they could not risk the others for one machine. It was only a few minutes before two of the attacking scouts discovered we were being left behind and turned their whole attention to us. One swung round behind us right under our tail while the other took up his position to our left and about 50 feet above ready to turn and dive as soon at Patey was busy with the other. The first fellow opened fire – cut two struts nearly through and one landing wire and only a rapid swerve on our part saved worse following. Round came Patey's Lewis gun and he fired a burst at the second one hitting him badly in the radiator. Clouds of steam came out from him and down went his nose to get to earth before

his engine seized up. Very glad we were to see the last of him. This also cooled the ardour of the other, who, much to our relief, turned to see the fate of his companion. By this time we were alone, the formation having left us a mile or more behind. So we were faced with the unpleasant prospect of a flight of 150 miles over enemy territory with a failing engine. As the formation could be of no help to us I decided it was best to keep on a different course as being less likely to attract unwelcome attention. I knew there would be bound to be scouts up waiting for our return. The expectation proved only too true and when we reached Treves away east of us we could see an enemy patrol above us. The bursting 'Archie' gave us away and three scouts detached themselves and started the pursuit. We had about three or four miles start and 60 miles to go. It was intense: mile after mile with the enemy gradually closing in. Suddenly, without warning, came the crackle of machine guns followed by the roar of an engine as a blue painted Albatros dived down past us. We had been so intently watching our pursuers that we had neglected to look for others above us. Fortunately no damage was done, but he was at once followed by a yellow Albatros who swooped down firing as he came and put several holes in the wings. Then there was a splinter of glass as a bullet carried away the top of my windscreen, while two more bullets tore a big hole in the top of the petrol tank and a second afterwards the undercarriage was splintering. Patey could not fire at the fellow as he was obscured by our own tail. That Hun meant business and if we were not going to be shot down we just had to put him out of action. We tried a trick which we had found successful before: stick right back, left bank and left rudder – brought us round and before the Hun realised it we were alongside each other. Patey was waiting and let fly with our last half drum of ammunition catching the Albatros right in the pilot's cockpit. I think he must have riddled him, anyway the machine went up, turned over on its back, spun away and one wing fell off. We made for home and ten minutes later crossed the line. Inside half an hour we were back in our own aerodrome with a very battered aeroplane but feeling lucky to be alive.[10] *Lieutenant A. S. Keep, 55 Squadron*

They had survived to fight another day.

The formation of the Independent Air Force on 6 June 1918 seemed a significant step but in reality nothing much changed. The political fallout of Trenchard's resignation as Chief of Air Staff had reverberated for some time until he had been inveigled into taking command of the new IAF designed to use the fleets of surplus aircraft promised by the Smuts Report. But in fact, although new squadrons did arrive, they never exceeded the number of squadrons Trenchard had requested back in 1916 before the IAF was even dreamed of. The 41st Wing was to be devoted to day bombing with 55, 99 and 104 Squadrons, while 83rd Wing was to carry out the night bombing using 100 and 216 Squadrons. Under the influence of French theories lauding the effects of concentrated bombing, Trenchard had conducted a rethink into the targets tackled by his bombers and some thought was devoted to the possibility of focusing on key German industrial towns and destroying them one by one. The prospect looked attractive but in the end he felt that it was simply not feasible in 1918.

> It was not possible with the forces at my disposal to do sufficient material damage so as to completely destroy the industrial centres in question ... even had the force been larger, it would not have been practical to carry this out unless the war had lasted for at least another four or five years, owing to the limitations imposed on long-range bombing by the weather.[11]
> *Major General Hugh Trenchard, Headquarters, IAF*

Trenchard decided that a scattergun approach to targets was far more effective given the limited forces available at that time.

> By attacking as many centres as could be reached, the morale effect was first of all very much greater, as no town felt safe, and it necessitated continued and thorough defensive measures on the part of the enemy to protect the many different localities over which my force was operating. At present the morale effect of bombing stands undoubtedly to the material effect in a proportion of twenty to one, and therefore it was necessary to create the greatest morale effect possible.[12] *Major General Hugh Trenchard, Headquarters, IAF*

If they were unable to reach their targets then his pilots were to attempt raids on railway stations and the ever obvious blast furnaces. In his mechanistic fashion Trenchard also resolved that the German airfields would have to be attacked in a vicious game of tit-for-tat to prevent the Germans bombing his own airfields out of existence.

From the perspective of the 55 Squadron pilots nothing really changed and few of them make any reference to any change in their status. They were still caught on the treadmill of raids marked by the constant drip of casualties and the haphazard introduction of replacements. Lieutenant Keep lasted four long months before his number was up.

> July 20th proved my last raid and nearly the end of my life. Oberndorf, a munitions centre over the Rhine, was the objective. Our formation reached it without trouble and we did some very destructive bombing. As we left the town our six machines were attacked by nine first-class Hun scouts and we fought as I have never fought before. Almost at once poor Young in the machine next to me went down in flames and his observer jumped out 15,000 feet up, sooner than be burnt alive, and disappeared falling over and over. Another machine piloted by an NCO next went down out of control.[13] *Lieutenant A. S. Keep, 55 Squadron*

The NCO spinning down out of control was Sergeant F. E. Nash who had as his observer Sergeant W. E. Baker.

> Above the roar of the engine I heard a terrific bang forward, water and steam blowing back across my legs, followed by several more crashes and an ominous smell of petrol. I glanced over my shoulder and noticed the twin Lewis guns on the Scarfe ring pointing skyward, and immediately realised that my gunner was out of action. With no defence for my tail, radiator and left main tank gone I knew I was 'for it'. At this juncture I recollect a sledge-hammer blow in the back which I think temporarily knocked me out. I was brought back to my senses by the terrific screaming of the wind through the wires, and noticed the airspeed indicator nearly 'off the map'. I closed the throttle and compensator with difficulty, as my left arm was almost useless, and attempted to pull the nose up, but the stick was immovable. I knew in a flash what had happened, my gunner had forgotten to take his dual control stick out when the scrap started, and after he was hit he collapsed on the floor of his cockpit and pushed the nose down by the weight of his body. By sheer brute force I at last succeeded in pulling

out of that horrible dive at about 7,000 feet.[14] *Sergeant F. E. Nash, 55 Squadron*

Nash eventually managed to make a decent landing behind the German lines. He was a prisoner of war but the unfortunate Sergeant Baker was dead. Meanwhile back in the fast diminishing formation of DH4s Lieutenant Keep was desperately trying to stay alive.

Then came the rattle of a machine gun straight behind us, a splintering sound as the bullets tore through some of the woodwork, then a blow like a terrific kick – my right arm was useless and the machine in a spin. Fortunately I managed to get straight with the left hand and Pollack who was my observer on that trip drove the Hun off and I believe put him down. By this time most of the fighting was finished and the Huns drew off having lost two if not three machines. Then came that awful trip back – 70 miles to go before the line and safety could be reached, one arm out of action and pouring blood. Two tanks draining away through bullet holes and self feeling like nothing. I could not keep with the others in formation and gradually wandered away, a most fatal thing to do. At last we reached the line, but not safety, as coming towards us was a patrol of three hostile scouts, one fortunately in front of the rest. Then the rattle of the machine guns once more with Pollack firing hard. To our joy the shots went home and the Hun lost control, spun earthwards and we afterwards heard from French artillery observers crashed into a tangled heap 14,000 feet below. The other two seeing his fate kept clear but still fate was against us. There was an awful roar and concussion. The machine seemed to go straight up in the air as an 'Archie' shell burst just below us. The steel tank below my seat was crumpled out of shape and undoubtedly saved my life, but poor Pollack had his leg almost severed at the knee by a ragged piece of shell. Somehow we glided over the line and got down in a field beside the French hospital. Stretchers were brought and we were got out of the machine. Poor Pollack was past help and died a few minutes later. I was bundled off to the operating theatre and woke up in bed feeling as if I had returned from another world.[15] *Lieutenant A. S. Keep, 55 Squadron*

The German scouts seemed to be ever more in evidence and casualties were inevitable if the formations were not rigidly maintained. It was thus no real surprise when the one of the worst disasters occurred to an inexperienced batch of pilots from 99 Squadron IAF during a raid launched on Mainz on 31 July. Twelve aircraft set off, but three had already turned back with engine problems before they crossed the lines. As they penetrated into Germany they were attacked by a reported forty German scouts who swirled around them and shot down four of the bombers. The raid on Mainz was abandoned and the five DH9s dropped their bombs on the nearest target, which proved to be Saarbrücken. The German scouts had the bit between their teeth and as the formation fragmented they struck again and again until only two DH9s got back across the lines to safety. The casualty figures were trivial in one sense: five killed and nine languishing as prisoners of war, but the unit had been shredded and was forced to suspend operations until another batch of pilots and observers had not only arrived but had been brought to somewhere near the required minimum standard in formation flying.

In August the IAF received a further reinforcement with the staggered arrival of 97, 215 and 115 Squadrons all flying the Handley Page, and 110 Squadron flying the new improved DH9a which had a slightly more powerful engine. By this stage the high casualties suffered by the IAF were no secret and when new pilots realized where they were to be posted there were entirely understandable reactions. Captain Ewart Garland was a veteran of the skies of 1916 and 1917 but even he could not help worrying when in late August he found he was to be posted to join 104 Squadron on the daylight bombing missions over Germany. Garland was experienced enough to guess the lethal dangers he was about to be exposed to.

> I must admit that I am very depressed, partly because I have been having very happy times in London and also among all the friends when at Amesbury – not to mention girls – and partly because the newspapers report heavy air casualties in the Independent Air Force raiding Germany. I can't shake off the feeling of being condemned to death or imprisonment – it's not cowardice, only that after flying a long time at the front I know the danger only too well. The squadron consists almost all of new pilots and observers, as so many were wiped out recently, hence we must train quite a lot before going over on raids into Germany. I led several formations on

> practice today and the new chaps need it badly.[16] *Captain Ewart Garland, 104 Squadron, IAF*

Garland attempted to screw up his nerve to fighting pitch as they practised the formation flying that could save, or at least prolong, their lives.

> Rumour that we will start on raids in a couple of days' time. The time draws near to say goodbye! Damn me for a frightened fool! But not a coward – it is one thing to be in a funk and yet do your job, and another to shirk because you are frightened.[17] *Captain Ewart Garland, 104 Squadron, IAF*

When they began making raids over Germany they found that one target still stood out from the others for its grim reputation among the day bomber squadrons – Mannheim. On the morning of 7 September the Badische works were to be attacked by a joint force of 104 and 99 Squadrons under the overall command of Major L. A. Pattinson.

> The adjutant gave the target on the phone in a sort of hushed tone: 'Mannheim!' It is like being under sentence of death. But now I am quite calm for some reason and don't mind much, I will trust in God and all that, but at the same time I'll take with me spare socks, a cheque book and my vast pocket Shakespeare![18] *Captain Ewart Garland, 104 Squadron, IAF*

Garland successfully managed to overcome his fears and thereby faced the challenge ahead. And what a challenge it proved to be.

> Hurrah! We have bombed Mannheim and only lost three machines, two of them from my flight. We combined with 99 Squadron, twelve machines each. I led my flight of six, but two turned back with engine failure and two were shot down under control about 20 miles over, so that left Ross and I. Huns got up to us almost as soon as we crossed the lines and we had the little coloured devils at us all the way. Over Mannheim the air became full of them and they got right into us pumping incendiaries till the sky was a mass of smoke. We kept pretty good formation after dropping the bombs and started back attacked all the time – we were about twenty strong. We got back after 4 hours in the air. One observer was wounded and several

machines, including mine, badly shot up and write-offs. However it is considered a good show – maybe – but oooh my head![19] ***Captain Ewart Garland, 104 Squadron, IAF***

For all that tension and suffering the raid had caused little damage and apparently no casualties. But raids on Mannheim were increasing in tempo and soon it was again the turn of the hapless 55 Squadron. Over the month since Lieutenant Keep had been wounded the squadron had lost twenty officers as casualties in action. Pilots were approaching breaking point as they coped with flying a mission most days of the week. On 16 September six of their aircraft were despatched to bomb Mannheim. Among them were Second Lieutenants W. E. Johns and A. E. Amey flying in a DH4. All was well until they got to Savern.

I was watching a string of what appeared to be gaudy butterflies crawling along the ground; now and then the sun flashed on their wings. It was a full squadron of Fokker D.VIIs trailing us, and climbing fast. There was a bit of 'Archie' about, nothing to worry us, but the odd chance came off. There was a terrific explosion almost in my face, and a blast of air and smoke nearly turned my machine over. I tried the controls anxiously and all seemed well, but a stink of petrol filled my nostrils and I glanced down; my cockpit was swimming with the stuff. I switched over to my near main tank – it was empty. A quick glance revealed the Fokkers now about 4,000 feet below and two miles behind. I could not go on with the formation for I had not got enough petrol, but I had just about enough to reach the lines if I could get through. I was about 60 miles from home; my altimeter read 19,500 feet. Pulling my bomb toggle I sent my single 230lb bomb on its last journey; where it fell I do not know, for there were other things I had to attend to. As I swung up into the sun Amey fired a green Very light to let the others know we were leaving the formation, and why the flash did not fire the petrol-soaked machine will always be a mystery. I settled down for the race home hoping the enemy would not see me. What a hope! Within 5 minutes Amey's gun was talking; seven or eight Fokkers had not only caught us, but had height on us. Toying with the compensator I climbed to 21,000 feet, but the coloured gentlemen were still with me. The leader came in with a rush and I touched the rudder-bar to let his tracer go by. A bunch of them came up under my elevators and I kicked out my foot,

slewing Amey round without losing height, to bring his guns to bear. The Fokkers came right in and I give them credit for facing Amey's music. One turned over, a second spun out of it, but another came right in to point-blank range; Amey raked him fore and aft without stopping him. Others came down on us from above. My sky-light was ripped to shreds, the instrument board shed glass and sawdust, a bullet ripped my goggles off and another seared my hip. Wiping the blood out of my eyes I looked back. Poor Amey was sagging slowly on to the floor of his cockpit. Sick with fright and fury I looked round for help, but from horizon to horizon stretched the unbroken blue of the summer sky. Bullets were striking the machine all the time like whip-lashes, so I put her in a steep bank and held her there while I considered the position. For perhaps five minutes we tore round and round, the enemy getting in a burst now and then and me 'browning' the whole bunch of them, but I could not go on indefinitely. My ammunition was running low and I was still over 40 miles from home. Things looked bad. To try to make 40 miles against ten or a dozen enemy machines (several others were joining in the fun) was going to be difficult. In fact, I strongly suspected my time had come. I shot off at a tangent, but they were on me before I had gone a mile, shooting the machine to pieces about me. I think I must have gone crazy then, for I yanked the machine round and went for them like a mad dog. The next few minutes were like a bad dream. Whichever way I looked I saw Fokkers, red, blue, yellow, orange, striped like tigers and spotted like leopards. You will believe me when I say I threw that old 'Four' about like a single-seater, not so much to fight as to try and dodge the hail of lead. How it held together I do not know. If anyone is doubtful about his ability to stunt, the situation I am describing provides an excellent test. There is nothing like a burst of machine-gun bullets to make you shake the tick. We lost height rapidly of course. Eighteen, fifteen, ten, eight thousand, and we were still at it. Wires trailed loose behind me, fabric stripped off, and the centre-section strut splintered at the fuselage junction. At 6,000 feet a striped gentleman put his gun nearly in my ear and sent a stream of lead over my shoulder and into the engine; she cut out dead, a cloud of white petrol vapour trailed aft, and I braced myself for the inevitable flames; I had seen the vapour and what follows it before. That was my worst moment. I switched off and literally flung the machine into a vertical side-slip, but she still smoked as the petrol ran over the hot engine. Suddenly the joystick went loose in my hand as the controls broke somewhere; we spun, half came out, and spun again. With my left hand I tried to wipe the blood and broken goggles off my eyes in order to see where we were going, while with my right I fought to get the machine under control, but it was useless. Below me a man who had been ploughing was running in one direction and his horse in another; bullets were still flicking up the dust around them. Every detail of that field is stamped on my memory with vivid clarity. I knew I was going to crash, but curiously enough, I do not think I was afraid (I have been much more scared on other occasions). I hadn't time to be scared. My brain was whirling at full revs – should I jump as we hit the ground – should I unfasten my belt – and so on, and all the time I was automatically trying to get the machine on even keel. Twice her nose nearly came up of her own accord as she tried to right herself, and it was in this position that we struck. A clump of trees on the edge of the field seemed to rush and meet me. I remember kicking out my foot instinctively, lifting my knees to my chin and covering my eyes. There was a crash like the end of the world. My next recollection is fighting like a madman to get out of the wreck before it fired. I still had the horror of fire on me, and I suppose every pilot would feel the same. When I got out I leaned against the vertically poised fuselage and picked pieces of glass from the instrument dials out of my face. I was bleeding pretty badly, for my nose was broken and my lips smashed to pulp. In that frightful crash my feet had thrust the soles off my flying boots and the 8 inch deep leather safety belt went to pieces like tissue paper, ripping all the clothing and skin off my stomach as cleanly as if it had been cut with a razor. That rattle of a gun made me look up and bullets kicked up the earth around me. The German pilot afterwards told me he did this to drive me away from the machine as he thought I was trying to set fire to it. I tried to get Amey out of the wreckage, but couldn't, so I could not set fire to the machine although I had a Very pistol in the knee pocket of my Sidcot. A long line of grey coated soldiers with an officer at the head came sprinting down the field and I knew that as far as I was concerned the war was over.[20] *Second Lieutenant W. E. Johns, 55 Squadron*

Although he was bruised from head to foot Johns survived to write the copious 'Biggles'[21] series that would inspire many young lads in the post-war years. Amey was far less fortunate as he died that day. They were claimed as victims by Leutnant Georg Weiner of Jasta 3. Once again the damage achieved was minimal and casualties suffered by the bomber crews probably exceeded those they inflicted on the ground.

THE daytime raids were just one side of the IAF operations probing deep into Germany. The 100 and 216 Squadrons were equally hard at work by night. The men of 100 Squadron had been accustomed to flying the aged FE2b as a matter of routine throughout 1917; now they were charged with piloting their sturdy old 'pushers' deep into Germany itself. It sounded ridiculous, but the FE2b, although long obsolete for daytime work on the Western Front, had proved itself a durable, sturdy, robust 'beast of burden' with a reliable engine capable of hauling aloft roughly the same bomb load as the DH4. At night they were far less vulnerable than they had been to the German scouts that had swept them from the skies over Arras in 1917. For over a year 100 Squadron had brought night sweats to Germans. Originally they preyed mainly on German airfields and railways but having been assigned to 41 Wing they were *the* RFC contribution to the night bombing. In a world where flying itself was a relatively new experience, long-range cross-country flying at night where most of the visual clues have been cloaked in darkness was at first a uniquely challenging experience.

> At the start it was very unnatural. You go to bed at night usually! The lack of a horizon to go by – everything was black. Even in your cockpit you couldn't see your instruments. Your feel of balance was quite different to what it was in the daytime and flying was all a question of balance when all's said and done. But after we got used to it, it became quite natural, and we found very little difference between night flying and day flying.[22]
> *Major C. Gordon-Burge, 100 Squadron, IAF*

There were advantages to flying at night however, starting with the contention of meteorologists that the weather was generally better at night, with less wind and cloud. The German anti-aircraft gunners were also severely hampered by the dark, which made the whole prospect safer for the bombers. Their bomb cargo could be dropped from an altitude that would be near suicide during the day and their aircraft would suffer far less damage from repeated close encounters with bursting shells. Many of the day bombers had up to half of their available machines grounded for essential repairs at any one time – not so the night bombers.

The risks were nevertheless considerable. On 24 January 1918 Second Lieutenant Louis Taylor with his observer Lieutenant F. E. Le Fevre embarked with nine other FE2bs of 101 Squadron on the long flight to raid the barracks, Diedenhoten steelworks and the railway station of the German town of Trèves, a round journey of some 200 miles in total. As they dropped their bombs they were hit by anti-aircraft fire that severed their rudder controls. Unable to steer the required course they headed to the south-west and ran into the German barrage balloon defences installed around the town of Esche in Luxembourg. There were thirty-five of these *drachen* balloons hoisted to 4,000 feet and about 50 yards apart with 2-inch thick steel cables dangling below them which were then linked to form a simple mesh net. This was a disaster for a pilot with minimal control over his aircraft.

> To try and get round was worse than useless, so trusting to good luck I kept straight on, hoping to pass through the barrage without hitting a wire. My observer immediately opened fire on the balloon above and straight in front of us, in the vain hope of setting it on fire, and dropping the net, but nothing happened. We were now passing under the balloons and for a moment I had the elated feeling that we must have missed the wires, but suddenly the machine gave a violent lurch and was thrown backwards. I immediately put the nose down, but the speed indicator dial only registered 30mph, and then I knew that I was caught. I wondered why the machine did not stall and plunge to the ground.[23] *Second Lieutenant Louis Taylor, 100 Squadron, IAF*

His ailerons had been severed by the cables and all he could do was use his elevator controls to dive, trying to use the considerable weight of the FE2b to drag down the balloon and hoping against hope that the engine would not stall. It was all but useless and he knew it.

There followed a sickening five minutes, during which I tried to get down to the ground dragging the balloon and net round and round with me, and, thanks to a perfect engine we finally got close to the ground, which was heavily wooded. My observer placed his machine gun to one side, and sat down to await the inevitable crash as calmly as possible, shouting a few encouraging words over his shoulder.[24] *Second Lieutenant Louis Taylor, 100 Squadron, IAF*

Things could have been worse, but the prospect of a crash into splintering trees, with the additional complication of the heavy engine poised immediately behind their cockpit ready to squash them to a pulp on impact, was not for the faint-hearted.

We were only a few feet off the ground, the engine roaring, when I saw directly ahead a small quarry surrounded by a wood. I frantically pulled back the control lever, the machine leapt into the air, hovering over the wood for a second, coming down with a crash in a small field just beyond. We fell on one wing, which crumpled up beneath the weight: I saw the observer leave the machine, when something hit my head and I lost consciousness. I could not have been unconscious for more than a few seconds when I came to my senses and found myself hanging out of the machine, while the wing which was sticking straight up into the air seemed to my dizzy brain to be toppling over on to me bringing the heavy engine with it. I tried to extricate myself from the wreck, and get away from the machine, but was too weak to do so. Eventually a voice roared in my ear, 'All right, old thing, out you come!' and a strong pair of arms went about me, when I was dragged clear.[25] *Second Lieutenant Louis Taylor, 100 Squadron, IAF*

Even then they were not safe as the local German infantry arrived in a state of considerable excitement.

I staggered to my feet to be met by a flash of rifle fire at about 20 yards distance by about ten or more Huns, who were running and shouting like maniacs. I felt my observer grab me by the shoulder and I was flung down on my face, he dropping beside me. The bullets were whistling by and it's a great wonder that neither of us were hit.[26] *Second Lieutenant Louis Taylor, 100 Squadron, IAF*

For them too the war was over.

In late August 1918, 100 Squadron was finally re-equipped with the Handley Pages that had been successfully used by 216 Squadron for most of the last year. The moral questions as to bombing civilian targets from the air were particularly telling, as at night it was usually impossible to see exactly what they were bombing. Pilots and bomb aimers frequently used intuition as much as science in selecting the exact moment to release their bombs. Yet most remained confident that they were free of blame, that they were hitting their targets and not the innocent.

> I don't think anybody deliberately bombed civilian houses or people. So far as my colleagues and myself were concerned we were very, very keen to be on our target. There is no doubt that our raids on German towns – railway stations and factories in those towns – must have been demoralising to some of the civilian inhabitants. In our night bombing it was difficult to see our results – we would see a fire burning or the explosion in a works. But next day the day bombers would be over at dawn and as they passed over our targets they photographed them and within 24 hours we would see pictures of our targets and where perhaps we'd hit, or whether we'd just missed and so forth. So that we were very keen to be on target because our errors were shown up on those photographs – there was no kidding the authorities. I think we were pretty accurate on the whole.[27] *Second Lieutenant Roy Shillinglaw, 100 Squadron, IAF*

The casualties may not have been particularly large – although there must have been incidents that mirrored the massacre of the infants in London – but the effects on civilian morale and general resilience were serious.

> What a terror aeroplanes have been to us lately. Before they come I always say to myself that I will not be afraid, but when they get here I become almost paralysed and then go into a state of collapse. This shows how the raids weaken and exhaust us.[28] *Anon civilian, Stuttgart*

THE IAF had been an anomaly in the history of the air services of Great Britain. Huge expansion programmes had been carefully drawn up on paper to provide for 40 squadrons rising in stages to a fantastical 104 squadrons. Much hard work was also expended in building the new aerodromes and the copious logistical support services that would be required by this aerial armada. And of course a raft of tempting targets in Germany was pinpointed ready for destruction when the moment came. The reality in 1918 was very different as it was belatedly realized that the promised spare fleets of aircraft would not be forthcoming. The plans for the IAF were duly scaled back all the way to the original forty squadrons, yet even this was an utter sham, as the official historian ruefully confessed.

> It will now be revealed that the Independent Bombing Force never came into existence. At the signing of the armistice Major-General Trenchard had under his command nine long-distance bombing squadrons, that is to say, just one squadron short of the number he had asked for in his expansion programme submitted in June 1916, long before an independent force was thought about.[29] *H. A Jones, Official Historian*

As with the tactical bombing on and around the battlefield, the strategic bombing campaign against the German heartland stands revealed as nothing much more than 'work in progress'. The damage caused by bombs could be serious on occasion and the raids certainly forced a huge expenditure of scarce German resources to try to fend off the bombers. But above all the raids caused disruption to production as factories suspended their work during bombing and a fall in civilian morale that far outweighed the physical damage caused by the bombs themselves. Ironically, it was the German air-raid sirens and alarms that did the real damage, not the British bombs. The time of the long-range strategic bombers would surely come, but not in 1918.

Chapter 13

End Game

Although there were hopes that the war might end in 1918 nobody in the Allied High Command was taking anything for granted. The Battle of Amiens had made it clear that their new tactics were a potent brew, but the Germans could still be doughty defensive fighters. It was obvious that there was much hard fighting and many natural obstacles to overcome before they could be pushed back over the Rhine into Germany. To start the ball rolling, Field Marshal Sir Douglas Haig ordered General Sir Julian Byng to throw forward his Third Army. On 21 August Byng drove forward north of the Somme in what would become known as the Battle of Albert. As his men advanced they were encouraged by Field Marshal Ferdinand Foch who pointed the way forward for Haig's generals in unambiguous terms.

> After your brilliant successes of the 8th, 9th and 10th, any timidity on their part would hardly be justified in view of the enemy's situation and the moral ascendancy you have gained over him.[1] *Field Marshal Ferdinand Foch*

Next day, on 22 August, Haig echoed Foch's encouragement in his own orders to his army commanders: Generals Sir Henry Home, Herbert Plumer, Julian Byng, Henry Rawlinson and the new Fifth Army commander William Birdwood. There was no doubt that as far as Haig was concerned caution was to be thrown to the winds.

> To turn the present situation to account, the most resolute offensive is everywhere desirable. Risks, which a month ago would have been criminal to incur, ought now to be incurred as a duty. It is no longer necessary to advance in regular lines and step by step. On the contrary, each division should be given a distant objective which must be reached independently of its neighbour, and even if one's flank is thereby exposed for the time

being. Reinforcements must be directed on the points where our troops are gaining ground, not where they are checked. A vigorous offensive against the sectors where the enemy is weak will cause hostile strongpoints to fall, and in due course our whole army will be able to continue its advance. The situation is most favourable; let each one of us act energetically and without hesitation push forward to our objective.[2] *Field Marshal Sir Douglas Haig, Headquarters, BEF*

From this moment onwards the Third, Fourth and First Armies launched an incredible series of attacks that hammered away at the German lines, constantly switching the point of assault, never letting them rest and constantly moving forward: here, there and everywhere. It was by no means a painless process; warfare never is. The tired divisions of the British Army suffered heavy casualties in the relentless fighting but they succeeded nonetheless in forcing the Germans back step by step across the desert of the old Somme battlefields. In the air this was quite simply the fight to the end: Armageddon could no longer wait. Many of the main aces had already died, but new paragons swiftly emerged, scoring their kills at fantastic rates that reflected both the over-heated pace of fighting and the diminishing standards applied in confirming victories. Who cared: success was all that mattered. New symbols of nationhood were needed and the quicker the better.

One new problem that had to be addressed as a priority by the RAF was that of the German anti-tank guns that had caused such painful casualties among the ranks of the Tank Corps on 8 August and the succeeding days. It had been decided that the normal method of calling up an artillery barrage in support of the tanks was hopelessly slow as tanks tended to be ambushed and disposed of in minutes. In retrospect the answer was obvious: what was needed was a squadron of low-flying, fast, powerful scouts capable of disrupting any German anti-tank battery positions. Sopwith Camels of 73 Squadron were assigned to the role, working alongside the Armstrong Whitworths of 8 Squadron.

The only sound principle was obviously immediate action on the part of the aeroplane with bombs and machine guns, with a view to driving the German gunners from their guns until the tanks had over-run the position. Having decided this, the next question which arose was how best to locate these anti-tank gun positions. It had been possible to gain considerable experience of anti-tank gun positions, by going over the battlefield in front of Amiens. The squadron was acting in close cooperation with tank headquarters staff in this matter, and after the question had been thoroughly discussed, they drew up a map showing the places where the tanks would be most exposed, and the most likely places from which they could be fired at by anti-tank guns.[3] *Major Trafford Leigh-Mallory, 8 Squadron*

The process of second-guessing the Germans was rendered even easier when the British had the good fortune to capture a German document recording in detail the principles of their anti-tank battle dispositions.

The pilot and the observer copied the most likely anti-tank gun positions onto their own maps, in the area over which they were going to fly, each machine only having about 2,000 yards of front to watch. They were to machine gun and bomb periodically all the likely places in their area, whether they were seen active or not, and then when they actually did see a gun firing, to attack it with everything they had got. In this way, by looking at the right sort of places, a great number of anti-tank guns were spotted as soon as they opened fire. As time went on we could reckon on at least 50% of the places so marked actually being active.[4] *Major Trafford Leigh-Mallory, 8 Squadron*

For the low-flying scouts skimming across the battlefield everything was fair game. Ground strafing was now taken for granted as a vital part of harrying the Germans and preventing them from regaining their sense of 'balance'. How could retreating troops rally if they were still under fire? As they became more experienced the pilots developed their own strafing tactics to maximize the effect of attacks. These may have been simple, but carried out well they vastly increased the chaos on the roads already choked to the brim with slow-moving horse transport and the endless columns of marching men.

I used to try and attack them from the front; that is to say from the direction to which they were proceeding. If you could manage to shoot up a couple of transport wagons the whole road was blocked for some time – then they

were just cold meat – you just went along with the Cooper bombs.[5]
Lieutenant James Gascoyne, 92 Squadron

Another task for the scouts acting in support of their ground forces was the continued necessity to somehow shoot down the German observers floating high over the battlefield in their *drachen* kite balloons. As the war drew on this task seemed to get more and more dangerous. The balloons were fixed targets and the Germans could concentrate all the necessary resources, both on the ground and in the air to protect them. The ingredients of the defence did not change; it was the number of anti-aircraft guns and machine guns concentrated below the balloons that increased until attacks became even more fraught with peril. The challenge had brought death to our 'ordinary boy' Lieutenant Edgar Taylor. Yet there was always someone else willing to fling themselves forward to carry on challenging the looming balloons. On 27 August Captain John Middleton found himself in the position where he felt almost obliged to have a go. At first it was just a routine mission when he took off with the SE5s of 'B' Flight of 40 Squadron at 05.30 that morning.

We were to fly at 6,000 feet and look after 208 Squadron who were to shoot down balloons south of Arras. We got to the lines at about 6am and I saw the most wonderful barrage I have ever seen. The shells were bursting in a perfect line on a front of about three miles. It was a fine sight. There seemed to be no Camels in sight and there was a balloon somewhere near Vitry that seemed to be bearing a charmed life; nobody seemed to be taking the slightest notice of it. We waited about for quite a long time but still no Camels turned up. At about 7am I decided to go over and have a shot at it. I went straight for it; there seemed nothing to be gained by manoeuvring about. Just when I was getting within range I saw five Fokkers coming down on me. I was only at about 5,000 feet at the time so I was soon in a mess. They started firing at me right away but I seemed to be dodging the bullets alright. But not for long! With a crack and a bang my engine ceased to function!! I was still about three miles from the lines, so I could not hope to reach them. The chaps in my flight saw what had happened and they drove the Huns away so that I was able to land in peace. I had not much ground to choose a landing ground from, so I came down right into trenches, shell holes, barbed wire and rubbish. I came down about two miles the wrong side of the lines. The long grass etc. bound round my axle and I was pulled up in about ten yards. There was no one in sight but a tremendous noise all around me. Shells were going over my head eastwards by the hundred. I got out, took off my helmet and gloves, put on my panama hat and got into a trench nearby. I remained in that trench for hours – about ten minutes – before anyone came in sight, then I saw three Scotsmen coming towards me. They saw me so I came towards them. They had seen me come down and had expected to find that I had been taken by the Bosch. They were in front of the push! If I had landed a few minutes sooner I should have been behind their front line. When I found this out I decided to get back a bit! I set off and passed lots of our 'Tommies' and a few dead Huns. I picked up a Hun rifle.[6] *Captain John Middleton, 40 Squadron*

He eventually found someone with intact communications back to the rear echelons and 40 Squadron duly sent out a tender and trailer to collect both man and machine.

The scouts were attacking balloons to blind the aerial eyes of the Germans and at the same time the crews of the reconnaissance aircraft had the grinding task of photographing the whole front. These were the eyes of the British. This placed them continually at risk in circumstances that offered little glamour or personal reward, other than the satisfaction of carrying out their duty. For them the war had reached a particularly exhausting phase as the Germans fell back. Photographs were needed to chart every move, every change in the battlefield below. The staff swiftly had to determine where the German artillery batteries were located, which trenches and strongpoints were occupied and where the barbed wire had been erected. Intelligence like this was more than ever crucial to the proper marshalling and conducting of the all-arms battle.

Urgent demands came for photos, and more photos, to see what his next stand was to be. I started now on the most difficult job I have ever succeeded in doing in my life: the photography of the Hindenburg Line from Cambrai to St Quentin. Jerry had his crack squadrons with their finest machines against our front and seemingly intent on preventing photography at all costs. Every day we were at it, Leach being my observer for the most part. On the 13th, 14th and 19th, 22nd and 29th we were attacked, trapped or chased until I began to think of packing my slippers, pyjamas and a toothbrush in the plane for the least pessimistic outcome of these shows landing me in Ruhleben. Time after time we ran the devils out of petrol, sneaked back and stole the photos.[7] *Captain William Grossart, 205 Squadron*

Eventually he was so exhausted that in his last mission, flying from Conteville airfield, he actually dozed off while landing and crashed, happily without fatal consequences.

Through the combined effects of the strain of the last few weeks, of the long shows at high altitude that day and of a confidence in landing born of much experience, I fell asleep to the conscious world around me. My sub-conscious mind sent my right hand mechanically to the incidence wheel low down on the right side of the cockpit and wound it fully back. It also pulled the throttle back and pointed the machine round into the wind against the wind stocking. It probably did everything but land her successfully, for we floated down with a forward speed which could not have been more than 50mph. It was a perfect pancake, sent the undercarriage up, burst the longerons and therefore completely 'wrote off' the machine, but left my observer and me smiling, me a little wanly perhaps for about the whole damn squadron were hanging around sitting on whatever they could find and watching me. I felt very small and uncomfortable.[8] *Captain William Grossart, 205 Squadron*

The commanding officers of the corps and bombing squadrons watched their men slide into exhaustion. Many of them flew missions with their squadrons despite the occasional ineffectual directives issued by RAF Headquarters attempting to ground them. But many other COs who had little or no flying experience grew to feel that their position was untenable for their own peace of mind. They sent young men off to battle, but they did not, in some cases could not, share the risks themselves.

The Major came to me and said that he was completely fed up with watching flights go out, then doing paperwork in his office, which he hated, before

> seeing an often depleted formation return. He added that he feared he could not help much but he wanted to lead the squadron and assist in boosting morale. I replied with absolute certainty and without feeling in the least facetious that he was already doing just that.[9] *Captain Alan Curtis, 103 Squadron*

As a senior flight commander Captain Curtis was one of a very few who were privy to his CO's inner fears and doubts.

> He insisted on coming up with me to see if he could stand our operational height. Deliberately we climbed slowly but at some few hundred feet above 9,000 feet he tapped me on the shoulder, indicating clearly that he was seeing spots and had reached the limits of his physical powers; with our open cockpits it was only a young man's game.[10] *Captain Alan Curtis, 103 Squadron*

The highter altitudes were beyond his CO's slightly more aged body. Such men felt that they were letting their men down, forgetting the value of the stability and continuity they gave to their squadrons as the casualties mounted.

One of the most vital functions for the corps aircraft was monitoring the progress of the fast advancing troops on the ground. Lieutenant George Pargeter of 53 Squadron was on one such infantry contact mission.

> The infantry are out of touch with the guns, so they dare not fire. Coles and I are hurried into the air to demark the position and drop map by message bags at army headquarters so that battle may continue. Flying now at 500 feet and under, call up infantry – 'A', 'A', 'A' on klaxon. The infantry light red flares as if on exercise. Splendid, we carefully plot them, flying up and down over them all the time. Jerry machine guns popping away like a lot of typewriters. Having got a clean plot, signal pilot to go up while I prepare a clean chart for headquarters.[11] *Lieutenant George Pargeter, 53 Squadron*

Sometimes even the most conscientious of pilots and observers could get distracted from their allotted role and Pargeter simply could not resist it when a tempting target popped up in front of them.

Four Germans leave a farm and make their way along a track to sunken road. Tap pilot on head, point and shout in his ear, 'Huns!' He swings over and dives at them firing his gun. Zooming up, then I see hordes of them along the road, so swing round and down on them with the pilot firing, going up, I fire over the tail. Again down, I change drum, turn round and repeat. Machine guns clatter, worse than a typing pool, single optimistic Germans on the knee taking pot shots – some hope! Arriving at north end of area and turning to return, Jerry aims a beautiful burst up through floor between pilot's legs, chews up gun feed, through tank and out through the top wing. We start dripping worse than the old garden watering can. Nowhere below to land and most important – the map! So I must stop the holes – over the side pull away the fabric and cover the holes with my finger tips, telling the pilot, 'Home James and don't spare the horses!' Had to make for our airfield, so could not manage the drop at the headquarters. Just made it and on touching down the engine dies. I called up a despatch motorcyclist; gave him a message bag and said, 'Go like hell to Headquarters!' That evening we got a chit of thanks from the General.[12] *Lieutenant George Pargeter, 53 Squadron*

The complexity of the ground situation meant that low-flying pilots and observers were often unable to determine exactly what was going on around them both on the ground and at higher altitudes. In an effort to coordinate matters a Central Information Bureau was established to collect and then rapidly disseminate information and reports received from observation aircraft. They monitored German air activity, passing the number, height and approximate position to the scout squadrons who would send off scouts as appropriate. Crude arrows were also laid out to guide pilots who were already in the air. As tempting ground targets were identified the designated low-level attack squadrons were duly informed by wireless to ensure a quick response.

Meanwhile, almost every night the Handley Page night bombers of 207 Squadron were engaged in raids on the usual tactical targets behind the German lines. Anything to disrupt the Germans was fair game: billets and camps housing their exhausted troops, railway lines, road junctions, bridges, headquarters and of course their aerodromes. It was cold during the day at high altitudes, but at night the temperatures fell even lower and the bomber crews were swathed in warm clothing.

We had sheepskin boots, leather clothing, fur lined gloves and helmet. I used to wear a silk stocking on my head before I put my helmet on and I had silk gloves underneath the fur lined gloves. They were most effective. We were supposed to have whale oil but we never saw any and I used to put Vaseline on my face.[13] *Gunlayer William Wardrop, 207 Squadron*

Their Handley Pages were imposing beasts of the air and their very size gave the crew a sense of invulnerability. The age of the heavy bomber was fast taking shape.

One felt absolutely confident that the Germans could never bring it down whatever you did. The pilot and the observer sat side by side in the front with the gunlayer at the rear. He had two platforms one higher, one lower with three Lewis guns one at the bottom for firing back underneath the tail and two at the top. The observer had two Lewis guns in the front cockpit and was also responsible for the bomb dropping equipment. He lay almost prone and had five pushes, like bell pushes, with five lights – two red, two green and one white. The white being the centre, the two green meant veer to the right and so on. By this method the pilot was able to see exactly what the observer wanted and try and get lined up on the target.[14] *Gunlayer William Wardrop, 207 Squadron*

One thing that cheered them, as it cheered all the pilots working so hard in such continuous danger, was the visible evidence of Allied success below them. They could see that the troops were making unprecedented progress.

Just recently our troops have been making a tremendous advance. Places which this squadron was bombing a fortnight ago – Bapaume and Peronne – are now in British hands. The troops are still advancing and are only 5 miles from Marquion now on the Arras – Cambrai road. Very interesting sight at night from above when a strafe is going on. To see the shells bursting, ammunition dumps blowing up; then, when the Hun spots us, searchlights, green 'flaming onions' and star shells, streams of tracer bullets coming up and going just in front of one; then bang an 'Archie' on your tail. Zip-zip-zip goes the machine gun at the nearest searchlight which wavers and goes out. Another springs up and then by throwing the machine about and shutting off engines – we are out of the searchlights. See them wavering and searching. One comes closer, closer and closer – will she find us? Yes-no-yes! It flickers across and then passes on; it has passed right over us and not seen us. On we go. The objective is sighted – Boom, Boom – go the sixteen heavy bombs and around we turn to come home as fast as we can, to run through a similar gauntlet as before. After crossing the lines we throttle back and come home on our own. The dummy aerodrome sighted, we signal our code letter which is answered and then the landing 'T' lights up and we land. Another raid over and done. Into the office to make a report, then to the mess for a hot drink and something to eat. Everybody is discussing the raid and finally after the last machine has returned to its lair, we turn in for a well-deserved rest.[15] *Lieutenant L. G. Semple, 207 Squadron*

It was inevitable that the Germans would also launch night bombing raids targeted on the airfields of their tormentors. On the evening of 24/25 August the men of 46 Squadron had received a general warning at their Poulainville airfield that a German bomber raid was expected. Thus it was no surprise when they heard an aircraft somewhere above them.

Listening carefully, we could just make out the slow and unmistakeable throb-throb of a twin-engined machine in the distance. Nearer and nearer it came until we fully expected to see its shape through the branches above our heads, for it was a bright moonlight night. It was at this point that a newly joined pilot took it upon himself to give tongue. This lad was very much 'the Exquisite' – all fur gloves and flatulence – and had transferred from a crack regiment. Nothing was hidden from him in flying matters – he knew for a fact! As the droning bomber passed circling overhead his over-educated bleating was heard, 'Nothing to worry about, chaps, it's only one of our night-flying Camels!' Any terse and pithy comments on this inane remark were utterly lost in the roar of the explosions. The Hun had certainly touched off something to some tune! Our hearing came back to normal, and a pilot piped up from the opposite end of the trench, voicing our unspoken thoughts perfectly, '*There's* your bloody night flying Camel!' It was not our aerodrome that suffered, but the one at Bertangles about a mile away.[16] *Lieutenant Jack Wilkinson, 46 Squadron*

What they had heard was five Gotha bombers coming in fast at a relatively low altitude. They certainly achieved total surprise at the nearby Bertangles airfield, which 48 Squadron shared with 84 Squadron commanded by Major Keith Park and Major Sholto Douglas respectively. The first Gotha dropped three bombs and one of them scored a direct hit on a hangar containing six fully loaded Bristol Fighters, causing a considerable conflagration and lighting up the whole airfield so that soon bombs were raining down accurately on the hangars and huts from the Gothas circling round above them. The bulk of both squadrons and associated guests were ensconced in a converted hangar watching a concert party hosted by 48 Squadron. Luckily they were protected by a substantial 4-foot-high sandbag wall around the hangar, so no-one was hit by flying splinters from the first two bombs.

> The show had been going on for some time when suddenly a bomb exploded slap on another of 48 Squadron's hangars nearby, setting it on fire. A German night bomber had crept over the aerodrome, and the raiders must have seen a chink of light coming from somewhere and aimed at it. The orderly officer came rushing into the hangar and called for the fire party; and just as the audience was giving him a rather rude reply another bomb fell very close by.[17] *Major Sholto Douglas, 84 Squadron, RFC*

Lieutenant C. Thomas, who had only been with the squadron for five days, was the hapless orderly officer on duty that night.

> When a bomb was dropped about half a mile away I thought perhaps I should get out the fire picket, but when I entered the hangar, with a white face as I understand, Captain Steele of 'A' Flight was rude enough to say, 'Sit down, you bloody fool!' which I did. The pianist was playing Rachmaninoff's *Prelude* and on one of the low notes another bomb dropped and put out all the lights.[18] *Lieutenant C. Thomas, 48 Squadron*

Even devoted music lovers like Steele had to tear themselves away from the recital as several more bombs burst across the aerodrome. In a few moments everyone was running for cover.

I was one of those sitting in the front row and I dived under the piano which was standing in front of me, while all the others flung themselves on the floor. But we did not stay there more than a few moments because the fire attracted the attention of other German bombers, and they started unloading their bombs on it and shooting us up. By then the whole place seemed to be erupting, and several of the other wooden hangars were also ablaze. Everybody made a rush to get out, and Charles Steele and I dashed off for some trenches that he said had been dug near the mess about 100 yards away. The fire was blazing and quite out of control, and that was attracting even more attention from the German bombers; and then they started dumping light anti-personnel bombs on us and machine gunning everything they could see. I ran faster than Steele and I managed to get to the trench just before the next load of bombs came down; but, although he threw himself flat on the ground, Steele was hit in three places and had to spend the rest of the war in hospital.[19] *Major Sholto Douglas, 84 Squadron, RFC*

Among the men taking cover in the slit trenches was Second Lieutenant John Pugh.

There was one fellow who dragged himself down there and he had got his leg hanging off at the ankle. He was moaning and this Australian said, 'If there *is* such a thing, you have got a beautiful 'Blighty''![20] *Second Lieutenant John Pugh, 48 Squadron*

Major Keith Park had been slightly injured but threw himself into the task at hand, organizing parties of men to drag Bristol Fighters out of the burning hangars, before they too exploded.

As the officers and men streamed out into the aerodrome, the second bomber was heard approaching. This, coupled with the intense heat of the burning hangars on either side, caused complete panic. Stupidly the crowd stampeded towards the approaching machine and a number of men were hit by two bombs which fell short. Before the panic-stricken crowd, mostly visitors, got clear of the camp a bomb fell in its midst killing several officers and wounding others, also setting the quarters alight. Assisted by my executive officer and a number of Australian privates bivouacked on the edge of the aerodrome, I managed to drag seven machines clear of the burning hangars; all were now on fire. Whilst attempting to get machines into the open the third and fourth bombers dropped more bombs on the hangars and camp, wounding several of the small rescue party.[21] *Major Keith Park, 48 Squadron*

Lieutenant Thomas was one of those assisting in the rescue of the wounded.

I got someone to help me carry a wounded man on to the aerodrome and when I returned the place was as light as day from the blazing hangars. We had a great time pulling out the machines before the fire got to them, and we saved half of them, which was pretty good, considering that the bombs were dropping all the time and all the hangars except two were destroyed. I enjoyed very much watching the tins of petrol going up and listening to the ammunition in the burning machines explode and the continual coughing of the anti-aircraft guns.[22] *Lieutenant C. Thomas, 48 Squadron*

There were thirty-six casualties in all, of whom eight died. One of those fatally wounded was a young observer, Lieutenant Alexander Urinowski, from Wallasey, who was of Russian origin. His fate was strange indeed as he had been due to appear in the role of a female impersonator and consequently when hit he was wearing a long dress and blonde wig. Many of these men had faced their enemies day after day in the skies, but on the ground they had felt safe; they were relaxed and enjoying themselves with their friends. The sudden intrusion of death and maiming had unmanned many of them. When the situation had calmed down some of the pilots and observers, unable to settle, visited their neighbouring squadrons.

Very late that night there came into our mess one of the observers from the bombed aerodrome. He was just about all in. Several of his friends had been killed or wounded, and as he sat with his drink the candle light showed up a face that was still quivering with the horror of what he had seen. It was a 'daisy-cutter' type of bomb he told us, that had laid out so many of his pals; a bomb that seemed to explode before it buried itself in the ground so that bits and pieces flew horizontally in all directions. But, apart from this new form of frightfulness, a number of men had been found dead without a mark on them, killed simply by the force of the explosions.[23] *Lieutenant Jack Wilkinson, 46 Squadron*

With eleven aircraft destroyed or unfit for service and their relatively severe casualties among the pilots and observers it was clear that 48 Squadron was no longer fit for the line. Next day the men were hastily moved out of Bertangles back to Boisdinghem. It was rather unfortunate that, having performed both coolly and practically during his first experience of action that grim night, Lieutenant Thomas then rather blotted his copybook the next morning when his navigation skills let him down.

The squadron was transferred to Boisdinghem near St Omer. The journey took place at night and I was in the second lorry, which lost its way and led the whole convoy into a narrow lane with the result that all the trailers had to be unhooked and the lorries backed for about half a mile before they could be turned round – the language of the equipment officer was very thrilling.[24] *Lieutenant C. Thomas, 48 Squadron*

There were new Bristol Fighters already waiting for them when they arrived at Boisdinghem and the replacement aircrews arrived almost before they knew it. Within days the squadron was back in action although there had been a noticeable impact on overall morale.

The retribution served up next day was on a far greater scale than the hard-pressed German Air Service could possibly match.

Every available aircraft on the Somme-Arras sector should at 6pm that evening rendezvous over the Gotha aerodrome at Mont d'Origny: RE8s were to bomb at 6pm from 2,000 feet; DH9s at 6.03 from 3,000 feet; Bristol Fighters at 6.05 from 5,000; and so through the whole gamut of machines on the front. We set off as late as 5.30 as we had to attain no great height. When we reached our objective the sky was black with British squadrons. We nobly avenged No 48; we blew up an ammunition dump, exploded the petrol store, burnt the hangars and machines, and finally we raked the officers' quarters with machine gun fire. Several German machines attempted to take off, but they were all destroyed and their pilots killed before they could do so. By 6.30pm there was nothing left standing or alive on the aerodrome, which was pocked with bomb craters.[25] *Second Lieutenant George Coles, 107 Squadron*

These huge combined raids on airfields were becoming increasingly common. One series of successful daytime attacks had already been launched by 80th Wing on the Haubourdin and Lomme airfields located in the Lille area.

Why wait for him to come up into the air? – blow him out on the ground! So No.4 Australian and No.2 Australian were ganged up with others from the Wing and they took to the German aerodromes in turn – two names – Lomme and Haubourdin. We went straight in and as far as the SE5s were concerned our fellows carried six 25lb phosphor bombs and six 25lb Cooper high explosive bombs. The phosphor bombs were horrible damn things – when they burst if you got any of that on you then you burnt. The Huns got all their aircraft in the air if they could but they didn't have much to come home to afterwards![26] *Lieutenant Frank Roberts, 2 Squadron, Australian Flying Corps*

RETALIATION was not the only string to the British bow. They had already developed and tested an effective counter-measure to the German night bombers in the concept of 'night-fighters' to secure the air defence of Britain against first the Zeppelins and then the Gothas. As the night bombing increased in size and scope on the Western Front, a specialist night scout unit, 151 Squadron, equipped with Sopwith Camels, was formed and duly proceeded to France on 21 June 1918. The night-fighters had a difficult task, for the art of instrument flying was in its infancy.

We had the enamel basic instruments: a compass, clock, air speed tube and altimeter but there wasn't much else. These weren't electrically lit but had luminous paint on the dials. You could just decipher them when you had to. We had to fly the aeroplane by feel and instinct. It's very funny night flying. You get a very good horizon to fly against and you can see water very clearly underneath you but of course you can't pick out roads or railways or anything like that. The main thing is to keep your eye on the horizon and not find yourself getting into a dive when you don't mean to.

You had to have cat's eyes – you had no aids. You were just up there by yourself, in the dark for two hours on a patrol. One of the things one did was sing, quite unconsciously, and you'd come down absolutely hoarse! Well it's lonely, two hours up there seeing absolutely nothing. The bomber pilot had a crew but you were by yourself.[27] *Lieutenant Archibald Yuille, 151 Squadron*

Once the pilot had taken off there was no way anyone on the ground could communicate with him. In the vast, dark skies the chances of finding a German bomber were negligible. The pilot had to be lucky and it soon became apparent that Lieutenant Yuille had both luck and the skill to capitalize on it. On 23 July Yuille encountered a Gotha flying over Flanders.

I found this bomber up in the searchlights, flak and everything else. I came up behind him as we'd always been taught to do, got pretty close and gave him a burst of fire. He promptly put his nose down. I thought I'd seen a flame coming out of him but I flew into his slip-stream and found myself in a spin. I managed to pull out – it must have been two or three thousand feet lower – and there he was straight in front of me again. A most extraordinary circumstance. I opened fire again and I went on shooting at him until I thought, 'Well, it's time I went home because my petrol is running out!' After I got home I heard that a Hun had come down just about 100 yards behind the British lines somewhere up near Ypres. Three or four were taken prisoner and they turned out to be very senior German officers so they had an unlucky flight. Their story tallied with mine so I was awarded it.[28] *Lieutenant Archibald Yuille, 151 Squadron*

Just a few weeks later on 10 August, Yuille got lucky again. By this time he and his fellow pilots were becoming increasingly accomplished at night flying and had begun to develop a methodology that brought results.

We knew that they would be flying at 8,000 feet so we always flew at about 7,500 so that we could see him against the sky which was always light whereas you could never see him beneath you against the ground which was always dark. We could only tell that there were raiders there by what I call the 'mess', the searchlights and the flak. So we used to fly into that area and switch on our light underneath the aircraft that was to stop the Archie shooting whilst the searchlights went on hunting for the Hun. If we were lucky – and that wasn't very often – we would see the Hun up above us. A black streak going in front of you and you went to try and get behind him. It wasn't very easy but we were faster than he was which let us catch up. This was the whole art of night flying.

The aeroplane throws out a slip-stream from the propellers and we used to come up behind feeling the slip-stream on our top wing which just shook the Camel a little bit. Then you knew you were just underneath the slip-stream coming up straight behind him and he couldn't shoot you because he had no gun actually in his tail. That gave you a narrow angle which got narrower as you got in where you were immune from being hit. If you could control yourself enough to get up little bit by little bit by little bit he couldn't hit you and probably didn't know you were there because he couldn't see you either. Then you opened fire from about 25 yards range if you had the nerve to get in as near as that. If you shot from further away you would probably miss. We had tracer bullets, armour piercing bullets with two machine guns firing through the propeller at 600 rounds a minute each. A pretty good volume of fire, which would go on about two minutes. If you shot straight you only needed one or two short bursts; you could see where the bullets were going because the tracers would tell you. If you were too much to the right or left you adjusted the aeroplane so that you were on target. That really was the whole secret of the thing – to have the patience to get in close after you had been lucky enough to find your Hun – but that was easier said than done.

North of Amiens I found a Hun and I got in behind him, went very close, opened fire and he just went up in flames. I identified myself by shooting a Very pistol out of my Camel then I went down to watch him crash and it turned out afterwards that this Hun was a very special one – one of the Giant aeroplanes that they were using with five engines and eight men in it. It had been making an unusual noise so that the whole of France was watching – including the King, who was visiting.[29] *Lieutenant Archibald Yuille, 151 Squadron*

The drone of the bomber engines, the crash of the bombs, the probing searchlights, the flaming bomber falling from the sky as a funeral pyre for its doomed aircrew. If you were awake, then it was pretty noticeable. Among the witnesses was Lieutenant Thomas Traill.

> On the aerodrome at Vignacourt was No. 151 Squadron whose pilots were flying Camels by night – quite a feat in itself. The German night bombing had become a real nuisance and 151's role was to keep one or two Camels on patrol during the dark hours. They worked in conjunction with the searchlights; when the pilot of a Camel saw two or three searchlights meeting in a cone he would fly over and investigate, and if there was a Gotha caught in the lights, he would come up unseen behind it and shoot it down in flames. I saw them get three in one night. My dog 'Pop' was sick and I was up with him a good deal, and three times I heard 151's mechanics cheering, and each time I was out of the tent in time to see a Gotha falling in flames.[30] *Lieutenant Thomas Traill, 20 Squadron*

Successes like these were rare until 151 Squadron and the anti-aircraft defences changed their tactics. Rather than surrounding the main target areas, the guns and searchlights were moved up closer to the front and tried to pick up the German bombers as they crossed the lines, at which point the night-fighters would strike home. The German bomber airfields had been located and the Camels also launched raids timed to coincide with their return to base, hitting them as they were about to land and at their most vulnerable.

ON the ground the infantry pushed inexorably forward until they retook Bapaume on 29 August. On Ludendorff's orders the Germans fell back to what was optimistically known at the Winter Line, where they would try to stand and fight until the New Year of 1919 might offer some hope of better times. But on the night of 30 August the Australian Corps crashed through determined opposition to take Mont St Quentin overlooking Peronne, which duly fell on 1 September. In just a few days they had advanced right across the old Somme battlefields of 1916, thus mirroring the German successes following the attack of 21 March 1918. To the north, First Army had driven east from Arras with the Canadian Corps leading the way until on 2 September they breached the Drocourt – Queant switch line which effectively guarded the flank of the Hindenburg Line. By this time it was obvious that winter was coming early for the Germans in 1918. That same day, Ludendorff ordered the retreat from the breached Winter Line with his troops forced to seek sanctuary right back where they had started – in the old Hindenburg Line. By now Ludendorff himself was showing severe signs of stress. He was under psychiatric care, with a strict programme of anger management and relaxation prescribed for the grim warlord, which included the quiet contemplative singing of folk songs.

For the German Air Service the situation was increasingly desperate. Their aces had to fling themselves into battle time after time, but it was increasingly obvious that their endeavours were all in vain.

> We fly and fight. Wherever there are cockades to be seen we'll attack them. The numerical superiority of the 'Tommies' has its effect in the air. Their bomber squadrons especially are as busy as bees. This is how they secure the freedom to come and go. Some of them are shot down while doing this. What does it matter? Where one falls, three others pop up and their aircraft are continually better and faster.[31] *Vizefeldwebel Karl Kurt Jentsch, Jasta 2, Jagdgeschwader 3*

One faint hope for the German Air Service was the arrival at the front of the latest Fokker single-seater fighter, the Fokker E.V. This offered a greater speed and manoeuvrability than the Fokker D.VII with an excellent all-round view thanks to its 'parasol' design where the wing was placed above the fuselage. With high hopes, many of the pilots of Jasta 13 gathered to watch an evaluation flight by Leutnant Ernst Riedel of Jasta 19.

> Riedel flew the machine on display for us most brilliantly. He was a wonderful pilot, almost too reckless a pilot. He flew all the figures, but unfortunately at too low an altitude. We could not hide our anxiety. Loops and turns do stress the machine and too much is too much. Suddenly the wing came off. I can see how Riedel tries to jump with his parachute from the falling machine. Already his upper body is out of the fuselage, but the speed of descent, with the engine at full power, is too great. The few hundred metres passed too soon. The impact itself we did not watch, we had already turned

away. But I can still hear the crash and then the complete silence.[32] *Leutnant Hans Besser, Jasta 13*

The Fokker EV was manifestly not ready for service. The wings were indeed faulty and liable to detach due to a combination of faulty design and poor manufacturing standards.

One who was doing well was Leutnant Ernst Udet, but even so he could not but be aware that he and his comrades were fighting a losing battle.

The strain of war increased from day to day. For every one of our machines which took off, five enemy machines started. And should one of them happen to be brought down on our side of the line we pounced upon it, and eagerly seized all instruments and articles of nickel and brass – metals which had long since ceased to exist in Germany. Against the abundant supplies at the disposal of the enemy we had nothing to stake save our sense of duty and four years' fighting experience. Now each start meant a fight, and we started often. Between the 3rd and 25th of August, I shot down twenty opponents.[33] *Leutnant Ernst Udet, Jasta 4, Jagdgeschwader 1*

The German Air Service still had its problem with the lack of fuel, which undermined its ability to put up a coherent resistance and compromised any chances of long-term success.

The question of the supply of fuel had become increasingly serious since the middle of August, and by September rationing was put in practice to a great extent. The quantities allocated for delivery at the front during 1918 had been consumed far more rapidly than we had estimated because of the unexpected large-scale employment of the air units in the heavy offensive and defensive fighting. The Navy needed a large amount in order to carry on submarine warfare. Our reserves began to be exhausted, for the oil wells in Galicia were not sufficient, and we were unable to repair, as quickly as we had expected, the wells in Rumania which had been damaged by the British. The total output of all the available sources was not enough to take care of our requirements. A maximum allowance per day of 250 litres for an observation squadron and 150 litres for pursuit and attack squadrons caused a limitation of aerial activity at a time when our supreme effort was needed.[34] *General Ernest Wilhelm von Hoeppner, German Air Service*

The Germans responded as one might have expected. Their best pilots monopolized the fuel, flying mission after mission to maximize the effectiveness of each Jasta's contribution. Also, to some extent they ignored the stipulations placed upon them and simply overran their fuel allowance. Thus throughout September they could still turn out in force when required. Their forces were dispersed on the ground to avoid the British night bombing, but would gather together in large formations once they took off. Both sides were edging up the size of their formations. As the fighting raged on the ground, so it continued to rage in the sky. The German Army Air Service was no pushover: however hamstrung, its best scout pilots remained excessively dangerous, able to pounce on the slightest misjudgement from their British opponents, who were plentiful but often inexperienced. The Fokker D.VII, especially the later model that was equipped with a 185hp BMW engine, was proving itself deadly in action. It may not have been particularly fast by the standards of late 1918 but it was still a wonderful scout aircraft.

Captain John Doyle certainly found the Germans were still lethal when his 'A' Flight was sent to escort a bombing raid on 5 September to be made by the DH4s of 57 Squadron.

The two-seaters were naturally heavily loaded and I climbed faster than they did all the way to the objective. I knew that when flying light, as they would be on the return home, they would be faster at that altitude than would be my SE5s. So I wanted to have a bit of height up my sleeve, so to speak. When they laid their 'eggs' I was about 4,000 feet above them. They headed west, but I flew on a little way so that when I did turn I could see them over the leading edge of my lower plane. Which meant that I was some way behind them.[35] *Captain John Doyle, 60 Squadron*

Above and behind them, Doyle and his flight were in an ideal position to dive and intervene when they sighted five Fokker D.VIIs approaching the DH4s. Doyle had the opportunity to make a successful defensive interception but the timing would be all-important.

I must not be in too great a hurry. I must wait till they were nibbling at the bait with their attention thus fully occupied. So I closed my radiator shutter and rocked my machine slowly to attract the attention of my patrol. I wound my tail-wheel forward and held the 'bus' up with the stick while I watched the Fokkers' progress with interest. The way they could overhaul empty DH4s was an education. Then I saw some tracer leave the leading Fokker. It was long-range shooting but I knew I could not further delay matters. And at that moment a red Very light curved into the air from one of the DH4s. This was clearly my summons, but I hoped that it would not cause the Huns to look round.[36] ***Captain John Doyle, 60 Squadron***

Unfortunately as he dived to cut out the Fokkers only one of his flight, Lieutenant Bill Rayner, was alert enough to accompany him to the rescue.

Soon we were down behind the Fokkers and rushing at them, we had the two rear machines respectively of that formation of five in our sights. It was essential in this our first dive that we should make certain of our men before the cat was out of the bag. And so we held our fire until the last possible minute, then opening up simultaneously. I can clearly recall being aware that tracer left Rayner's guns at the same instant that I pressed my own triggers. I was also aware of a sheet of flame in the right-hand Fokker cockpit. My own target shot up vertically and stalled. I had to shoot my stick forward to pass below him. I was still travelling very fast and that put me in a dive again. I got the leader in my sight and let go another burst. This time the Fokker did a flick turn and dived in a southerly direction.[37] ***Captain John Doyle, 60 Squadron***

They were now slightly below the level of the DH4s. Raynor had held his position alongside Doyle.

I was flying first on Doyle's right in flight formation when we suddenly spotted five Fokkers creeping under the tails of the bombers. Doyle and I dived to attack from about 2,000 feet above, whilst the remaining three of 'A' Flight apparently maintained station above us. Doyle got two of the Fokkers and I got another two – one in flames and the other out of control and apparently starting to burn. But it seems the fifth Fokker managed to get on Doyle's tail.[38] *Lieutenant Bill Rayner, 60 Squadron*

Intent on his second kill, Doyle still thought that his tail was being guarded by his wingmen as he burst straight through the Fokker formation. Unfortunately he was wrong, for only Rayner was with him as the rest had been left behind.

I got in another burst and held it while I tried to close up, but the only result was my man went into a still deeper dive, always flying straight. So I knew I had got him. But the laugh was on me, for a burst of close range fire smashed into my SE at that moment. I think one's brain works at extra speed on such occasions. The result is a slowing up of the action so I will give my recollections in slow motion. A bullet cracked past just clear of the cockpit; a second went through the instrument board into the tank; the third struck my head just behind the ear and cut the buckle of my chin-strap which fell slowly down. Two more cracks and then a terrific concussion. I was pressed against the side of the cockpit, unable to move while the plane fell headlong, turning on its axis as it did so. Petrol was pouring on to me and I managed to depress the switch.[39] *Captain John Doyle, 60 Squadron*

The tremendous blow he had felt had been a bullet smashing with hammer force into his leg. It was obvious he was going to have to make whatever landing he could manage behind German lines.

I looked up past my tail and got a head-on impression of two Fokkers diving after me. Instinct warned me that there was an ominous meaning in the speed with which they were following me down. They were not, I surmised, solicitous for my welfare! The ground was near but I dived again to maintain my lead and flattening out hurriedly, made a landing of sorts in what appeared to be a park. When the SE had stopped bouncing and come to a rest I threw off my belt and stood on the seat.[40] *Captain John Doyle, 60 Squadron*

His problems were not yet over. One of the Fokker pilots was apparently incensed by the death of his friend and the normal courtesies of warfare were ignored in the heat of the moment.

A burst of lead from the diving Fokker spattered round me, but I was not hit. When this had stopped I jumped to the ground, tried to take a step and of course fell. There was another long burst of firing from above and I lay without moving. Bullets seemed to be smacking into the grass in a circle round my body but again I was not touched. Two German soldiers had approached as near as seemed advisable, and when the firing ceased I got up and hopped over to them. I thought it would be healthier there and it was.[41] *Captain John Doyle, 60 Squadron*

Doyle was made a prisoner of war. His head wound was more of a graze but the leg wound proved serious and gangrene soon made its presence felt. For three days it crept up his leg until there was no option but to amputate. Doyle survived the trauma but only just. The victory claim was put in by Leutnant Egon Koepsch of Jasta 4 who had themselves lost two aircraft in the sharp skirmish.

THE German retreat to the Hindenburg Line was completed on 11 September and there they stood, barring the road to Germany. The Hindenburg Line had been built as an insurance against disaster during the Somme campaign in late 1916 and had been occupied after the tactical withdrawal forced upon them in March 1917. It was an outstandingly strong series of fortifications, but could no longer be considered impregnable, for it had dated since its conception – two years is a long time in war. It had been built in the linear style that dominated defensive thinking prior to the introduction of any real concept of defence in depth. In the south it had been built to a large extent in the valley of the St Quentin Canal which it cunningly utilized as a kind of 40-foot-wide and 50-foot-deep anti-tank ditch. This bonus was however a real point of weakness because it meant that the main line was situated down in a shallow valley and therefore dependent on an extra series of strong fortifications euphemistically known as the Outpost Line running along the ridge in front. If the Allies took this then they would be within easy range, allowing observed artillery fire right down onto the Hindenburg Line itself with all that that entailed.

The honour of launching the next round of offensives on the Germans went to the American First Army which was ready to launch the assault on the St Mihiel salient jutting provocatively into the Allied lines on 12 September. Their Commander-in-Chief General John Pershing was charged with clearing the salient to open the way for further offensives between the Meuse and Moselle rivers. The Americans had decided to plough their own furrow on the Western Front, operating as far as possible alone and to some extent ignoring many of the tactical lessons so painfully learned by the Allies over the previous four years. The American Chief of the Air Service was Colonel William Mitchell who was determined to maximize the use made of his reconnaissance, artillery observation and scout aircraft in the coming battle. By the Battle of St Mihiel on 12 September he could deploy twelve scout squadrons organized in three Pursuit Groups, eleven observation squadrons, one day bomber and fifteen balloon companies. These varied a great deal in experience but the nascent threat was slowly growing into a reality. Nevertheless, to carry out their offensive the Americans were still reliant on assistance from the French and British, particularly in the provision of day and night bombing squadrons. Most ironically of all, they were for the most part flying French and British aircraft as the much vaunted American aviation industry was still a paper tiger.

The best known of the American pilots was probably Captain Edward Rickenbacker who had been born of Swedish emigrant stock on 8 October 1890 in Columbus, Ohio. He had developed a great interest in motorcars and managed to secure a job at a local car manufacturing plant, learned to drive and took every opportunity to race cars in local dirt-track races before graduating to race in the Indianapolis 500 as one of the most successful race drivers with a stupendous income of some $40,000 per year. Nonetheless, as a patriot he had duly enlisted in the American Army in May 1917 and was made an NCO staff driver. By this time Rickenbacker had determined to learn to fly and soon secured a transfer into the US Army Air Corps. After his training he was commissioned and posted to the 94th Aero Pursuit Squadron which had the distinction of being the first all-American air unit to see combat in April 1918. Rickenbacker prospered and duly qualified as an ace. The attack on St Mihiel represented a great 'coming of age' moment for him and the whole of the American forces.

Leaping out of bed I put my head outside the tent. We had received orders to be over the lines at daybreak in large formations. It was an exciting moment in my life as I realized that the great American attack upon which so many hopes had been fastened was actually on. I suppose every American in the world wanted to be in that great attack. The very sound of the guns thrilled one and filled one with excitement. The good reputation of America seemed bound up in the outcome of that attack.[42] *Captain Edward Rickenbacker, 94th Aero Squadron, 2nd Pursuit Group*

He need not have worried. The fighting was painfully hard, but the Americans broke through and began to pinch out the salient. In the morning of the assault it was pouring with rain, but later as he flew over the battlefield he could see that the Germans had been flung into retreat.

We found the Germans in full cry to the rear. One especially attractive target presented itself to us as we flew along this road. A whole battery of Bosche three-inch guns was coming towards us on the double. They covered fully half a mile of the roadway. Dipping down at the head of the column I sprinkled a few bullets over the leading teams. Horses fell right and left. One driver leaped from his seat and started running for the ditch. Halfway across the road he threw up his arms and rolled over, upon his face. He had stepped full in front of my stream of machine-gun bullets! All down the line we continued our fire – now tilting our aeroplanes down for a short burst, then zooming back up for a little altitude in which to repeat the performance. The whole column was thrown into the wildest confusion. Horses plunged and broke away. Some were killed and fell in their tracks. Most of the drivers and gunners had taken to the trees before we reached them.[43] *Captain Edward Rickenbacker, 94th Aero Squadron, 2nd Pursuit Group*

Meanwhile, to the north the increasingly war-weary divisions of the British Third and Fourth Armies were well aware of the trials that still lay before them. By this time many of their battalions were below half-strength. Yet under the new tactical system the firepower they could generate was far more important than their actual manpower. If their morale endured then they could carry on in the front line. There was a reasonable degree of confidence abroad as the British had already comprehensively breached this line during the Battle of Cambrai in 1917 and were increasingly sure that they could do it again. By September 1918 the Royal Artillery had reached a level of dominance that was simply irresistible.

The first stage of the operation was the attack on the Outpost Line, ranged along the ridge above the Hindenburg Line, which went in at 05.20 on 18 September 1918. The British barrage was devastating in its power, suppressing or destroying the German artillery, before a stunningly accurate creeping artillery barrage supplemented by a torrent of machine-gun bullets fired by massed Vickers guns allowed the infantry following close behind to catch the German infantry cowering in their trenches. There were no tanks available on this occasion but the tactics were merely tweaked to compensate for their absence. The attack once again was a success.

The Allies were already planning their next great offensive for late September. This would involve four coordinated assaults. The main British Armies would attack the Hindenburg Line between Cambrai to the north and St Quentin in the south, thrusting towards Maubeuge. Secondly, there would be an offensive in Flanders as the British Second Army under General Herbert Plumer, accompanied by the Belgian Army, attacked towards Ghent. The French would attack in the Argonne, and finally the Americans would bring up the metaphorical rear with an assault in Lorraine. If they succeeded the German front would be hopelessly wrecked and their lines of retreat imperilled on all sides.

As the preparations for the British assault on the Hindenburg Line proceeded apace the photographic reconnaissance was obviously of crucial importance. The Germans would do anything in turn to stop it. On 22 September Captain William Grossart (he had recently been promoted) was on such a mission.

> An Engineer captain arrived as an observer in my flight and I took him up to initiate him as it were. Wright had thought the Engineers a bit tame and thought he would find excitement in the air; and he darned well did! We had taken eighty-six photos of the Hindenburg Line and were just away from St Quentin flying at 22,000 feet when we were suddenly accosted by five Fokkers at our height. I had not been looking out and Wright was

almost frozen behind me, and seemed oblivious to what was happening when I shook him up and pointed hurriedly to Jerry and to the guns sign. It was sheer luck that I ever saw them and they were within 100 yards when I could scarcely believe my eyes at the familiar shape of the Fokker with their camouflage painted canvas, the pilots' heads visible and little spurts of tell-tale smoke issuing from their guns. While Wright swung his guns into position I did a very brave and foolish action in pulling 'Emma' half-left across their bows while I watched Wright's tracer make rings round them as he emptied his two drums. They fortunately allowed too much deflection for a bullet missed my head by the small inch and made a hole in the windscreen, another shattered a bit out of the front left strut and I had had enough. I put 'Emma' down in a merciless stunting full throttle dive and we raced neck and neck almost, for mile after mile, going in a straight death dive until I breathed freely when the 30-odd miles separating us from our own air brought us over the trenches about 4,000 feet up. With Wright it was a case of ignorance is bliss. He was only mildly interested when I pointed out the holes in our plane.[44] *Captain William Grossart, 205 Squadron*

The scouts were constantly in action during late September. After a lull caused by mutual exhaustion and poor weather the pace of aerial fighting seemed to go up another notch from 20 September as both sides jostled for position over the Hindenburg Line. Whatever the German problems with fuel supplies they sensibly concentrated their resources where they were least appreciated by their enemies.

The present policy of the enemy air patrols on this front seems to be to put very strong patrols (twenty to forty machines) into the air at varying periods during the day with a view to making offensive demonstrations and occasionally attacking small patrols of our machines when obviously at a disadvantage. This system makes the work of our small patrols difficult, as either they are not in sufficient strength to attack the enemy or no enemy are found in the air to attack.[45] *Brigadier General C. A. H. Longcroft, III Brigade, RAF*

The usual British tactic of flying squadron patrols with different flights operating at different levels and then joining together only as required was being put under considerable pressure by these tactics. Single flights of four or five aircraft were often being bounced by vastly superior German formations, which could take advantage of the cloudy autumnal skies to achieve surprise. The British answer to these concentrations was inevitable. If the Germans were flying in greater numbers then they would respond in kind. The basic formation had already been edging up in size and it was decided to put up regular offensive patrols of more than one squadron to take on the German scouts immediately above their own airfields, pressing them back; the same tactics as Trenchard had always deployed, but on a greater scale. They would still fly at different heights with massed Sopwith Camels searching out and taking on the German scouts, while the SE5s or Dolphins flew high above them guarding their rear from attack. The patrols were utterly aggressive and if the Germans declined to take them on in the skies then they would launch the Camels hell for leather in low-level attacks on their airfields.

The RAF managed to amass more than 1,000 aircraft as part of the preparations for the attack on the Hindenburg Line on 27 September. To help soften up the Germans a raid was planned for the day before to render their airfield at Lieu St Amand unfit for use. The strike force would be composed of fourteen Camels of 203 Squadron accompanied by eleven SE5s from 40 Squadron with an additional escort of the Bristol Fighters of 22 Squadron. Lieutenant Yvonne Kirkpatrick was obviously worried by the prospects and wrote a muddled letter home that morning which encapsulated his fears and must have worried his family half to death.

> I wish we could get the job done and have it off our minds, but I think we're going to have so many things on our minds in a short time that this particular one won't affect us much. I am sorry I am so vague, but I can't tell you what I mean for obvious reasons. The best thing for you is to hope for the best, and whatever happens be as cheerful as anything. Some people might blame me for putting the wind up you like this, but I think it's much better that you should expect the worst and then be as bucked as anything if I do have the luck to get through. You remember what happened to Stone, I'm sure his people didn't expect it, and it must have come as an awful shock. If I live to tell you how I spent the

hours from 12 noon to 2pm, 26 September 1918, I'm sure they'll be exciting. If I don't, then you have the satisfaction of knowing that at least I was prepared for anything.[46] *Lieutenant Yvonne Kirkpatrick, 203 Squadron*

In 40 Squadron they were equally taken aback at the prospect of the operation. There was little time left for them to prepare. The man designated to lead the raid was Captain John Middleton of 40 Squadron. He was to say the least a worried man.

At 11am the CO sent for all flight commanders and told us that the wing commander had rung up to say that the push was to begin again tomorrow and that the raid had to be done at once! He had ordered the machines to be ready with bombs for noon! The raid was bad enough at dawn, but at noon! Good heavens![47] *Captain John Middleton, 40 Squadron*

The SE5s of 40 Squadron got into the air just before noon. Middleton alone was responsible for leading the assembled squadrons to their target.

After circling round for a few minutes I set off for Izel le Hameau which was No. 203's aerodrome. Before we got there I could see the Camels were in the air. They tacked on behind in their proper places and as they were doing so I looked up and saw the Bristol Fighters up there. I fired a couple of red lights as arranged to show everybody that I was ready to start and off we went at 6,000 feet. I headed straight for Cambrai. There were a lot of big white clouds at 5,000 feet with only a few gaps so it was quite difficult seeing where I was. There is a canal running due east past the north of Cambrai which meets another at right angles about eight miles east of Cambrai. This point was my objective, when I reached that I could easily find the aerodrome because it was about two miles due north of that point. But my trouble now was that I could not see the blessed canal at all![48] *Captain John Middleton, 40 Squadron*

There then came a complication which could have been predicted but which nevertheless posed a whole new set of problems for the harassed Middleton.

When I had got over what I thought ought to be Vis-en-Artois I saw about twenty Fokkers at about 10,000 feet just south of Cambrai! Now what was I to do? We could not attack them from our height and even if we had been high enough we could not do much with four bombs weighing us down. Even if we had had no bombs we were on a special mission and therefore should not stop to fight. It was, however, not a bit of good going past them to the east at a lower altitude, even if we had been coming straight back, but since our job was to go about ten miles east of the lines and then go to within 20 feet of the ground it was quite out of the question. What I was going to do had to be at once, so I fired a red light and flew towards them. I looked back and saw that everyone had turned and was following. I looked up and saw that the Bristol Fighters were heading straight for the Huns, who turned south and flew away from us.[49] *Captain John Middleton, 40 Squadron?*

Middleton's bluff had worked. As the Germans had wisely avoided the superior British formations, he was free to carry out his mission. But another problem arose. His manoeuvring had confused him and he could not but admit to himself that he was lost. Now what?

We followed them past the Somme, then I fired another red light and turned north-east. I looked around and saw that everyone was in their order. I could catch sight of bits of ground at odd moments, and as all the ground round these parts was strange to me, I very soon got lost. If only we had been up by Cambrai it would have been different because I should have seen familiar ground at times. However, I flew on in what I thought to be the correct direction. What a fool I should feel if I had to washout because I had lost the way! What would the CO say? I turned due north because I had been flying north-east for quite a long time. I must have been well east of Lieu St Amand. All this time I had been looking downwards in the hope of seeing something which might have told me where I was, but I had no luck. Then I saw through a gap in the clouds the point where the two canals met! It was well to the west of us. The CO had told me to go down to the aerodrome from the east so it might appear to the chaps I was leading that I had done it on purpose![50] *Captain John Middleton, 40 Squadron*

With serendipity obviously firmly on their side, the SE5s of 40 Squadron dived on the airfield intent on mayhem.

> I shut off my engine, closed my radiator then turned west and glided down. We were at 8,000 feet when we started gliding, the gap in the clouds had moved and past the point I wanted, but I knew more or less where it was. I had to guess where the aerodrome was, and a good guess it turned out to be! The clouds were still at 5,000 feet and I passed over a gap in them at about 5,500 feet. I turned sharply and went straight through this gap and there bang in front of me was the aerodrome! We had all seen aerial photographs of it and it was just as it looked on them. I saw on the aerodrome just outside the hangars a DFW (two-seater). I fired about 50 rounds of Buckingham into it but it did not catch fire. I then flew along the hangars and dropped two of my bombs. I did not see where they dropped. The other chaps came down and I think everyone had a shot at the DFW but I did not see it burst into flames; perhaps its tanks were empty? In a few minutes the hangars were all burning and bombs were dropping all over the place.[51] *Captain John Middleton, 40 Squadron*

In accordance with the hastily made plan, the SE5s had gone in first, dropping their bombs and spraying their machine guns across the German hangars and huts. Then Camels of 203 Squadron tore into action.

> We all broke up the formation and dived on the objective. I dropped my bombs on something which I thought would appreciate them, then I started charging about at 100 feet up, firing my guns at things on the ground till they wouldn't fire any more. Then I decided to come home. The 'Archie' was awful, also machine gun fire from the ground. I was trying to climb up at some of our machines which were going west, when suddenly there was a bang and my engine stopped. Imagine my feelings at the thought of landing about half a mile from where we'd been doing the damage. However I picked a field and was just going to land when I thought I'd try my gravity tank and see if by any chance I could get the engine to start. Fortunately it did, but I hadn't half the power that I would have done if my pressure was working. Well I decided to try and get home.[52] *Lieutenant Yvonne Kirkpatrick, 203 Squadron*

Meanwhile the SE5s of 40 Squadron had dispersed into the area surrounding the airfield firing at anything that attracted their attention. As long as they had some ammunition left they might as well use it. Middleton kept an eye on them rather as a mother hen after her chicks.

> A few of us then left the aerodrome and had a look at the roads nearby. I saw Bruce chasing some Hun soldiers along one road. On the road leading north to Valenciennes, Trubshaw was firing into some transport, they are better things to fire at because they cannot leave the road. I went after Bruce and brought him back, he was getting too far away. The Camels were now enjoying themselves and I saw that one of them had succeeded in setting the DFW on fire. It was blazing away in great form. After chasing some Hun soldiers who had got a machine gun on to us, I fired a red light, which was the signal for home. I set off west. There was no formation to be kept in going home; we just went as hard as we could. The Bristol Fighters stayed until the Camels had finished.[53] *Captain John Middleton, 40 Squadron*

Lieutenant Yvonne Kirkpatrick was struggling back with only the petrol left in his gravity tank. It seemed a long way home.

> I had about 11 miles to go till I got to our lines and there were no more of our machines in sight, so I decided my only hope was to come along so near the ground that 'Archie' wouldn't be able to see me so well. So along I came as best as I could. My engine wasn't going very well and the wind was against me. You should have seen the expression on people's faces. I went over a sunken road and saw two fat old Huns walking calmly along with their hands in their pockets; they simply stared at me with mouths open. Then I saw two Fokkers up above diving at me. I simply tore round trees and churches with them firing at me. After what seemed years, I saw some trees, which I thought I knew were on our side. The machine gun fire got very fierce suddenly, then stopped. I looked over side of the cockpit and saw some Scotsmen waving to me. Oh! Some relief, believe me. I found on landing that I had a bullet through my tank, the petrol was pouring out. We had three people missing. We knew before we went out that we wouldn't all get back and I think we got off lightly.[54] *Lieutenant Yvonne Kirkpatrick, 203 Squadron*

Actually they all turned up unscathed. It had indeed been an extraordinarily lucky escape for Kirkpatrick. Middleton also got back safely. Now he blessed the clouds that had so confused him on the flight out across unfamiliar territory.

> The clouds were very useful; we flew just above them, so that if we had been dived on by some Huns we could have just popped into the clouds. We had no ammunition left, so we were not very anxious to meet any Bosch planes. We crossed the lines between Cambrai and Douai and got home without anything happening. That evening we had a guest night although we had no guests! We heard from 203 that they were attacked just before they left. The Wing Commander came in after mess and made a little speech to which I had to reply. He told me as he was leaving that I should hear more of the raid in a week or so. I wonder! We kept the party going well into the next day.[55] *Captain John Middleton, 40 Squadron*

In all they had dropped eighty-eight bombs between the two squadrons and managed to set fire to the airfield hangars and huts, destroyed a DFW on the ground and caused numerous casualties to surrounding troops during the haphazard strafing of nearby roads. Additional claims were made for five German aircraft destroyed during the course of the operations.

Next day, 27 September, was the Battle of the Canal du Nord when the British First and Third Armies finally assaulted the Hindenburg Line on a 13-mile front between Ecourt St Quentin and Gouzeaucourt. The usual crushing barrages would be followed by the infantry assault at the appointed Zero Hour of 05.30. As the weather was initially good, the air component of the plan could operate in perfect harmony with the rest of the 'all-arms orchestra'. On the First Army front 40 and 203 Squadrons were just part of massed scout attacks launched on various key tactical objectives.

> We were all called at dawn. The orders for the day were to proceed to No. 203's aerodrome where we should meet the Wing Commander and all the scout squadrons in the wing. We should receive all flying orders there. We landed at Izel le Hameau soon after six in the morning. The first job we had to do was to drop four bombs each on the bridges over the Sensee Canal

due north of Cambrai. There would be no escort for us! We set off at about ten o'clock. When we got as far as Arras we could see sights that made it obvious that the Bosch was going back. Dumps were burning all over the place and Cambrai was in flames. It was a great sight. We were flying at about 4,000 feet and east of Cambrai there were some Huns. I messed about for nearly half an hour hoping they would go. It would be rotten flying up the canal at 3,000 feet with six Huns diving on us. The Huns did not go so there was nothing for it but to ignore them. They did not come for us at first and I began to think they had not seen us! We did our best with our bombs and then turned to come home. We were east of the Huns now. As soon as they saw we were going home they came for us, diving on us from the west. We flew for it as hard as we could. The leader picked me out and came for me and he was the last Hun I got to my credit! The 'Archie' people saw him crash. I looked back and saw that Drinkwater was all right, he was quite near to me. I saw Bruce with a Hun on his tail, he suddenly dived vertically and with the engine full on he flew from 3,000 feet smack into the earth on the outskirts of Cambrai. It was a rotten sight.[56] *Captain John Middleton, 40 Squadron*

Further to the south the scout squadrons of III Brigade were used differently. All but one of the squadrons would fly in pairs strafing and getting rid of their bombs on ground targets before gaining altitude to carry out normal offensive patrols searching out German aircraft. The exception was 201 Squadron whose Camel pilots were to devote themselves just to ground strafing, weaving low across the battlefield seizing on targets of opportunity. Among them was Lieutenant Ronald Sykes.

I went over early in the morning at about 1,000 feet over the Hindenburg Line which was south west from Cambrai. At that instant a shell burst below me and within a second the whole of the ground seemed to be turning over, boiling up in brown earth that had been thrown up and smoke from the bursting shells. I thought, 'Well nobody can live down there and I don't think I'm going to live long if I stay over the top of it!' So I went straight to the clear air over the German support areas. There I found the sunken roads were full of German troops – within seconds they all vanished into the grass verges so I strafed the verges. I got rid of three of my four little bombs.

Then four Fokkers came down from above and attacked me. I saw them coming and I'd had quite a lot of practice at taking evasive action so I went down to ground level round the trees and zig-zagged back keeping out of their way. We'd been told to attack troops and not go in for aerial combat as other squadrons were up above to do that. As I got back into the battle smoke they broke away to the east and left me. I went back to the German infantry and got rid of my last bomb. Then the smoke over the battle area was clearing and I could see the trenches. I spotted one advance trench with some Germans. I dived on it, fired, pulled up and did what I call a cartwheel over the far end and down again. I didn't shoot because they were running and seemed to have their hands up as I got close to them – I pulled up again. Some British troops were just arriving and the Germans started to climb over the parapet going off west as prisoners. Then I went back to our advance landing ground to rearm and refuel.[57] *Lieutenant Ronald Sykes, 201 Squadron RAF*

As the RAF pilots could clearly see, the operations were a success. The troops successfully breached the Canal du Nord defences and surged forwards to such effect that by the next day they were surrounding the town of Cambrai itself. Although the weather closed in many of the ground support scouts were run ragged on their countless missions strafing the German troops. And of course, as they concentrated on the events proceeding apace on the ground, so the German Air Service was grimly concentrating on them.

This morning we got a pretty warm reception. We went out bombing this morning. We dropped our bombs and started to come back, when umpteen Fokkers appeared from nowhere. I picked up the other two Camels and we came out hell for leather. They had us in a rather tight corner because there was a strong wind blowing us into Hunland the whole time. Wherever I looked round the sky was thick with Fokkers. We dived right down to the ground and they followed us. I looked round and saw a Camel with a Fokker on its tail. The Camel went round trees, over hedges, everywhere the Fokker followed him. If my engine hadn't had that tired feeling, I'd have turned round and taken a pot at him, but it felt as if it was going to seize, so I thought I'd better get home. How it was I never hit anything on the ground I don't know. I was watching my tail more than where I was going.

> Anyhow it's much harder to hit you from the ground when you're so low, and much harder for the Fokker, because he has to look where he was going as well as where I was. Anyhow, somebody shot the Fokker down that was chasing us. Several of our pilots had some holes in their machines, but we all got back except a sergeant pilot, who, we hope, has landed this side somewhere. It's raining now, and personally I don't mind if it continues for a bit. Things are rather too exciting now.[58] *Lieutenant Yvonne Kirkpatrick, 203 Squadron*

They were often flying through intensive ground fire and there was an additional very real peril from the shells of their own artillery as they rained down to burst within the German lines.

> The machine gun fire from the ground is pretty awful. You see the old Huns crouching in trenches and they 'Crack-Crack-Crack!' away at you for all they're worth. Then the sight of our Tommies relieves you and you know you're out of Hunland. It's quite exciting with field guns going off underneath and shells bursting all around. One seemed to burst right under me. I got an awful surprise, but one doesn't mind these little things. When we've dropped our bombs we career about the battlefield. It's awfully interesting and I really enjoy it. You see all sorts of things: burnt out tanks, Huns hanging up to dry in barbed wire etc. The best of it is you can't smell anything![59] *Lieutenant Yvonne Kirkpatrick, 203 Squadron*

At 05.30 on 28 September the next stage of the overall Allied offensive was launched as the British Second Army, assisted by the Belgian Army and the French, attacked on a wide front between Dixmude to the north and St Eloi in the south. This encompassed the old Ypres battlefields but the situation was very different from the grim days of Passchendaele in 1917. The German divisions in the area were now well under strength, progressively denuded of artillery and men as Ludendorff strove to hold the line further south. But the Allies were now strong everywhere. They had no need to move their units up and down the line; they had enough troops, aircraft, tanks and, most important of all, artillery so that the German High Command could have no real idea as to where the next blow would fall. It only knew that it would be soon and that there was very little it could do about it. When the attack came in

Flanders they could not resist and the troops surged forwards, blasting their way across the old 1917 battlefields in just one day.

Next day, before dawn, the Headquarters of 11th Wing telephoned orders to 206 Squadron to carry out a special low-level reconnaissance to try to determine the exact positions of the advance troops. This task was given to Second Lieutenant John Blanford, who was acting as observer to Captain Rupert Atkinson. They would take off at 06.00 although sunrise was not due until about 07.00.

We crossed the pre-attack front line at about 5,000 feet and continued at about that height during the reconnaissance. It was a bright sunny morning with good visibility when we crossed the lines, but there was a thin ground mist covering all the low-lying devastated area between Ypres and Passchendaele, which was a morass of water-filled shell craters. We could see a good many shell bursts popping through the mist, German as it proved, for beyond the misty area we could see our infantry patrols and some tanks probing forward and in action against the German rearguards in open country, all along the front. We knew then that the Second Army had broken clean through all the German defences, and that here was open warfare again after four long years! A great moment, believe me.[60] *Second Lieutenant John Blanford, 206 Squadron*

The British troops were well beyond the Passchendaele Ridge of accursed memory, while to their left the Belgian troops cleared the brooding Houthulst Forest. All seemed to be going well but then the men of 206 Squadron were given a task where failure was not a considered option.

About 5pm we received orders from Eleventh Wing to bomb Menin station despite the weather, as some of our fighters who had been ground strafing along the Menin Road reported heavy German reinforcements, probably a division, detraining at Menin and it was expected they were preparing a counter-attack. It would have been suicidal to fly in formation from our airfield at Alquines to Menin, some 45 miles, with cloud down to ground level in places; so it was decided we should take off independently at short intervals, and fly at a set speed and height on a compass course, and after a calculated time come down low until we could locate Ypres and the straight road from there to Menin. When we could see the target we could use our own judgement in regard to bombing height according to the visibility there. Atkinson and I took off first, followed by the others in turn; all our available aircraft – fifteen – had been laid on. Atkinson and I found Ypres on schedule and flew low along the Menin Road just above the clouds. As we neared Menin we suddenly ran into a clear area, like a dome over the target with the ceiling about 3,000 feet or so. We climbed to about 1,500 feet for our bombing run, dropped our 12 x 25lb bombs and machine gunned the station area, which was full of rolling stock with German troops all over the place unloading and forming up.

As we turned away we saw the next one of our machines arrive and repeat the act, followed at regular intervals by all the others in turn; bombing from about 3,000 feet. Atkinson and I had achieved complete surprise and were not fired at during our attack, but by now every 'Archie' gun and machine gun in the Menin area seemed to be pooping off at our machines; we could see clearly the gunners in their emplacements. However 1,500 to 3,000 feet was reckoned a pretty safe height in those days, too high for effective ground machine gun fire and too low for the guns – they just could not swing their guns fast enough to follow their target, and all their shells were bursting 400 yards astern. None of us were hit and after our last machine had bombed and shot up the station I fired the signal to break off combat and return home. By now, however, we must have used up our ration of luck for two of our pilots lost their way on the homeward run through the still thick clouds. Both of them crash-landed, though not too badly, and none of the crews were hurt. We learned next day that we had so disrupted the detrainment and deployment of the German division that the expected counterattack never materialised.[61] *Second Lieutenant John Blanford, 206 Squadron*

Second Army captured the town of Menin just two days later and the 206 Squadron raid was generally considered to have had a real impact on the course of the battle. In the succeeding days the pace of the Allied advance in Flanders was so great that the bombers found themselves occasionally given the far more congenial task of dropping food to elements of the advanced British, Belgian and French troops who had outrun the overstretched supply arrangements. In all some 13 tons of food were dropped in this manner. One can only speculate how many poor soldiers were injured as this manna from heaven crashed down all around them. A similar exercise occurred when two tons of bully beef and biscuits were dropped for the townspeople of Le Cateau.

Meanwhile 29 September had also been marked by an attack made by Fourth Army on the Hindenburg Line, after a two-day bombardment intended to soften up the formidable German defences. The attack was hard going with mixed results, although the 46th Division was able to breach the line and over the next few days the Germans were gradually turfed out of their 'impregnable' defences along the Canal du Nord.

THAT day, 29 September, saw the death of one of the wilder aces of the whole war. Lieutenant Frank Luke was born on 19 May 1897 in Phoenix, Arizona, to a large and prosperous family of Catholic German immigrants. He grew up as a bit of a handful, but excelled at school sports and spent much time hunting in the hills. He enlisted in September 1917 and manoeuvred his way into pilot's training, qualified and was duly commissioned as a second lieutenant on 23 January 1918. He received his advanced flying training at the Issoudun airfield in France where he first met another German-American flyer, Lieutenant Joe Wehner. He and Wehner were finally posted to 27 Aero Squadron at Saints on 26 July. In the first few weeks the casualty rates were appalling as the Germans routinely milked the squadron dry but slowly they gained experience and after teething troubles grew to appreciate the sturdy qualities of the Spad XIII. On 16 August Luke claimed to have shot down a German aircraft. Unfortunately his subsequent report was badly confused and many of the squadron simply disbelieved the brash young man.

> My machine was not ready, so left an hour after formation expecting to pick them up on the lines, but could not find formation. Saw Hun formation and followed, getting above, into the sun. The formation was strung out leaving one machine way in the rear. Being way above the formation, I cut my motor and dove down on the rear man, keeping the sun directly behind. Opened fire at about 100 feet, keeping both guns on him until within a few feet, then zoomed away. When I next saw him he was on his back, but looked as though he was going to come out of it, so I dove again, holding

both guns on him. Instead of coming out of it he side-slipped off the opposite side, much like a falling leaf, and went down on his back. My last dive carried me out of reach of another machine that had turned about. They gave chase for about five minutes, then turned back, for I was leading them. My last look at the plane shot down convinced me that he struck the ground, for he was still on his back about 1,500 metres below. The machine was brought down northeast of Soissons in the vicinity of Jouy and Vailly. Do not know the exact location as, this being my first combat, did not notice closely, but know that it was some distance within German territory, for 'Archies' followed me for about ten minutes on my way back.[62]
Lieutenant Frank Luke, 27 Aero Squadron, 1st Pursuit Group

His claim was rejected and this seems to have lit a slow-burning fuse within Luke over the following weeks. His relationship with authority was further undermined by his new commanding officer, Captain Alfred Grant – a strict disciplinarian. Over the next few days Luke seems to have withdrawn into his shell and become slightly obsessive about practising his marksmanship. Finally on 12 September he went up determined to score a kill and had resolved that he would shoot down a German kite balloon.

Saw enemy balloon at Marieulles. Destroyed it after three passes at it. Each within a few yards of the balloon. The third pass was made when the balloon was very near the ground. Both guns stopped, so pulled off to one side. Fixed left gun and turned about to make one final effort to burn it. The next instant it burst into great flames and dropped on the winch, destroying it. There was a good field near our balloons, so landed for confirmation. The observer, Joseph M. Fox, who saw the burning, said he thought several were killed when it burst into flames so near the ground.[63]
Lieutenant Frank Luke, 27 Aero Squadron, 1st Pursuit Group

His insistence on landing to seek confirmation of his destruction in writing was a sign of his burning resentment at the previous failure to confirm his claim. But this was just the start. Luke went on an almost unprecedented trail of destruction. He shot down several more balloons and he soon began flying with Lieutenant Joe Wehner who was charged with protecting the balloon-buster from the unwelcome attentions of German scouts.

There is no doubt that Luke's personality was an acquired taste that could easily sour, and certainly he seems to have been regarded within his squadron as unduly boastful. Time and time again he and Wehner raced into action: defying death was the least of it; these two defied everyone and everything. In one three-day period Luke shot down six German balloons while the equally remarkable Wehner claimed two in addition to three German scouts. They discovered that their best chance came at dusk and demonstrated their ability to target balloons successfully in front of a distant audience of senior officers on 16 September.

> Patrol to strafe balloons. Flew north-east passing over Verdun and attacked balloon in vicinity of Reville with Lieutenant Luke at 19.05. We each fired one burst when I observed that it instantly caught fire. The observer jumped but was burned to death by the flaming balloon before reaching the ground. I headed towards the Meuse river trying to pick up another balloon; could not locate one so headed towards Verdun. On the way back saw a fire in the vicinity of Romagne which evidently was Lieutenant Luke's second balloon. While waiting for Lieutenant Luke near Verdun saw red flare over Mangiennes. Thinking it our prearranged signal from Lieutenant Luke, I headed in that direction. Saw balloon just above the tree tops near Mangiennes and brought it down in flames with one burst at 19.35. Anti-aircraft very active.[64] *Lieutenant Joe Wehner, 27 Aero Squadron, 1st Pursuit Group*

They had shot down three balloons in the one evening. It simply couldn't last and on 18 September, right in the middle of a chaotic rampage which saw him shoot down two balloons and three aircraft, Luke lost his partner in chaos.

> Lieutenant Wehner and I left the airdrome at 16.00 to spot enemy balloons. Over St. Mihiel we saw two German balloons near Labeuville. Manoeuvred in the clouds and dropped down, burning both. We were then attacked by a number of enemy aircraft, the main formation attacking Lieutenant Wehner, who was above and on one side. I started climbing to join the fight when two EA attacked me from the rear. I turned on them, opening both

> guns on the leader. We came head on until within a few yards of each other when my opponent turned to one side in a nose dive and I saw him crash to the ground. I then turned on the second, shot a short burst, and he turned and went into a dive. I saw a number of EA above but could not find Lieutenant Wehner, so turned and made for our lines. The above fight occurred in the vicinity of St. Hilaire. On reaching our balloon line, flew east. Saw Archie on our side, flew toward it, and found an enemy observation machine. I gave chase with some other Spads and got him off from his lines. After a short encounter he crashed within our lines, southeast of Verdun. Lieutenant Wehner is entitled to share in the victories over both the balloons.[65] *Lieutenant Frank Luke, 27 Aero Squadron, 1st Pursuit Group*

This amazing sequence of victories left Frank Luke the leading American ace with fourteen victories (four aircraft and ten balloons), leaving Captain Eddie Rickenbacker trailing some five victories behind him. Luke reacted badly to the loss of his friend Joe Wehner and was sent on leave to Paris both to console him and hopefully calm him down. He wrote a letter to his mother which seems wilfully deceptive.

> Now, mother, remember that I have passed the dangerous stage of being a new hand at the game, so don't worry, for I now know how to take care of myself.[66] *Lieutenant Frank Luke, 27 Aero Squadron, 1st Pursuit Group*

On his return to active service on 26 September, flying with a new partner in Lieutenant Ivan Roberts, he once again tasted success, but Roberts too was killed. It was evidently a suicidal business watching Luke's back. He seems to have responded by deciding to go on a new killing spree – this time on his own. By now, despite his burgeoning reputation, his personal animosity to authority had become so pronounced that he was increasingly falling foul of his commanding officer, Major Grant. The last straw seems to have been when Luke flew from the airfield to spend time with a nearby French unit on the evening of 28 September. Grant was incandescent and demanded that his errant ace be arrested and brought under proper military control, or, failing that, be sent back for punishment.

On 29 September the brief tragedy reached its final act. Ignoring direct orders grounding him, Luke took off alone late that afternoon. As he flew over an American balloon company he dropped a note reading, 'Watch three Hun balloons on the Meuse. Luke.' This final fight was the stuff of legend, and like most legends is now enshrouded in myth. He certainly attacked three balloons flying high above the Meuse which he duly shot down after being engaged by up to ten Fokker D.VIIs. There are unconfirmed reports that he shot down two of these before being wounded in the shoulder by ground fire which led to a forced landing near the village of Murvaux. While coming down he is reported to have strafed a group of German infantry. He then seems to have staggered from his machine to a nearby stream for a last cooling drink before suicidally engaging an approaching German patrol. The villagers later provided an affidavit as to what they saw.

> The undersigned, living in the town of Murvaux, Department of the Meuse, certify to have seen on the twenty-ninth day of September, 1918, toward evening, an American aviator, followed by an escadrille of Germans, in the direction of Liny, near Dun, descend suddenly and vertically toward the earth, then straighten out close to the ground and fly in the direction of the Briere Farm, near Doulcon, where he found a captive balloon, which he burned. Following this he flew toward Milly, where he found another balloon, which he also burned, in spite of an incessant fire directed against his machine. There he was apparently wounded by a shot fired from rapid-fire cannon. From there he came back over Murvaux, and with his machine gun killed six German soldiers and wounded many more. Following this he landed and got out of his machine, undoubtedly to quench his thirst at a near-by stream. He had gone some fifty yards, when, seeing the Germans come toward him, he still had strength to draw his revolver to defend himself, and a moment after fell dead, following a serious wound received in the chest. Certify equally to having seen the German commandant of the village refuse to have straw placed in the cart carrying the dead aviator to the village cemetery. This same officer drove away some women bringing a sheet to serve as a shroud for the hero, and said, kicking the body: 'Get that out of my way as quickly as possible.' The next day the Germans took away the aeroplane, and the inhabitants also saw another American aviator fly very low over the town, apparently looking for the disappeared aviator.[67]

Frank Luke received the Congressional Medal of Honor and whatever really happened during his brief burst of heroic insanity above the Meuse he has never been forgotten.

BY 1 October, all along the Western Front the Germans were being given no chance to organize an effective counter-attack or to consolidate any kind of coherent defensive line. The attacks upon them were ceaseless, hammering at their front here, there and everywhere without warning. In the north Lille was under threat, Cambrai was all but surrounded, St Quentin was safely back in British hands and the Hindenburg Line was but a memory. That was just the British. In the south the French and Americans were also tearing huge chunks out of the German line. It had long been clear that the Allies would eventually win the war; the question was when? Since the tide had turned in mid-July the Allies had captured around 4,000 guns, 25,000 machine guns and 250,000 German soldiers. No army on earth could withstand the earth-shattering blows raining on them from all sides and the answer was increasingly obvious. If the Allies could only keep up their frenetic assaults the war would end in 1918. This was the culmination of four years of murderous hard graft, allied to very considerable ingenuity and innovation to solve one of the most intractable problems ever posed in the history of warfare. These are deeds of war that should be remembered as a tremendous Allied victory.

The German Army was at the end of its tether: the collapse wrongly predicted on the Somme in 1916 and at Passchendaele in 1917 had finally come to fruition. With increasing desperation the German High Command pressed its politicians to seek peace. There was no way that the situation could be stabilized; only military defeat lay ahead. The new Imperial Chancellor, Prince Max von Baden, was a makeweight, with little experience of any value. He duly made approaches to the American President, Woodrow Wilson, requesting an immediate armistice based on Wilson's much vaunted 'Fourteen Points'.

In the meantime it is fair to say that General Paul von Hindenburg was not a natural peacemaker; even as he pleaded for peace he was planning for a possible resumption of war. He saw the armistice as a military necessity but also as a means of gaining time for Germany to regain its strength before returning to the battle. The Allied war leaders were not fools. The conditions they sought for an armistice would preclude any possibility of Germany restarting the war. When this became apparent Hindenburg and Ludendorff resorted to mere posturing. After having first called for an armistice, they now jockeyed for position, trying to evade responsibility for defeat by presenting the army as having being 'stabbed in the back' by civilian politicians. While the German High Command prevaricated its troops fell back towards their borders; day by day their military situation worsened.

In the air the German tactics were changing. Desperately outnumbered and short of fuel, they were increasingly concentrating on withstanding the attacks from the RAF day bombers that threatened to cut the German divisions off, not only from their reinforcements and supplies but from any feasible avenues of retreat. As such the bomber squadrons found that their already formidable task was made notably harder. One example of these additional dangers occurred on 5 October, when the DH9s of 206 Squadron launched a concerted raid on Courtrai. They flew in two formations of five aircraft, led Captain Rupert Atkinson with Second Lieutenant John Blanford as his observer. They were to fly well to the north and past Courtrai, before turning back to drop their bombs on the homeward run, attacking the target from the rear from a height of 10,000 feet. Courtrai was a notable centre for German anti-aircraft batteries.

> As soon as we in the front formation had made our turn and were beginning our bombing run, I had to stop looking astern because I had to watch for Atkinson's signal to pull off bombs as soon as his bomb-sight was on target. During the last two or thee minutes of the run-in we began to be 'Archied' heavily and accurately, and becoming increasingly so every minute. We were flying through the middle of 'crumps' and black smoke and our aircraft were being bumped about more than on any other raid.[68] *Second Lieutenant John Blanford, 206 Squadron*

Luck was on their side and all five escaped unscathed and the camera record seemed to indicate twenty-nine effective hits on their target. As they moved away Blanford looked back at the rear formation.

> They should have been closed up about 100 yards behind us, but to my dismay I saw that they were at least 400 yards astern, and not only that, there were at least a dozen Fokker D.VIIs beginning to dive on them from the south-east and about 1,000 yards higher. I told Atkinson and fired a red Very light to warn the rest of our formation in case they had not already spotted the Huns. Atkinson shouted back to me, 'I'm going to throttle back to give 'B' Flight the chance to catch up with us.' I gave the customary 'slow down' arm signal to the two aircraft flying just behind us and saw their observers pass the signal on to our two rear aircraft.[69] *Second Lieutenant John Blanford, 206 Squadron*

This manoeuvre left them flying at only about 85mph rather than the more usual 120mph nose-down and hell-for-leather speed used in these circumstances. Unfortunately they were still far too close for comfort to the anti-aircraft batteries at Courtrai.

> We became sitting ducks for the German gunners who took immediate advantage of the target we presented. Within a minute there was an almighty bang right underneath our aircraft which was tossed upwards and then fell like an express lift. Recovering from the shock, I looked round and saw that Atkinson seemed to be OK, then took a quick look round for damage. There were countless holes in the fabric of the wings and fuselage, not necessarily dangerous, and several of the inter-wing straining wires were cut – but they must have been merely landing wires, not flying wires, as the wings showed no signs of collapsing. Far more serious was water coming out from a hole near the top of our radiator, and a thin stream of petrol coming back above our heads from a small hole in the gravity tank set in the top of our centre section. The petrol was pumped up into this tank by a small air screw operated pump, passing by gravity into the engine. I also looked round for the rest of our formation, could not see them at first, then looked up to find them a good 1,000 feet above us. I reported to Atkinson, whom I saw was straining like mad at the control column. He yelled, 'The bloody stick's jammed, I can't move it!'[70] *Second Lieutenant John Blanford, 206 Squadron*

Their DH9 was already listing badly to the left and it was inevitable that they would soon fall into a spin. The only chance was for Blanford to correct the balance by hanging over the right-hand side of the cockpit, leaning out as far as he could while clinging on to his Scarfe gun ring. He knew that if this failed he would have to climb past the pilot and walk out onto the starboard wing.

> Slowly our aircraft got back on to an even keel and remained that way, possibly the drag on my body leaning over the side contributed something to this, apart from the combined weight of the guns and my body. Having got back on an even keel, our immediate problem was to maintain enough altitude to enable us to cross the line and it was Atkinson's superb skill as a pilot that achieved this. We were about 8 miles from our lines at an altitude of under 8,000 feet. In a normal glide a DH9 could travel roughly 1 mile in still air for every 1,000 feet of altitude, so it was obvious that we would have to flatten our gliding angle considerably to make sure of getting back to friendly territory, this entailed using an overheating engine with petrol escaping overhead. Atkinson therefore kept opening and closing the throttle at short intervals, just sufficiently to decrease our loss of height without putting too much strain on the engine.[71] *Second Lieutenant John Blanford, 206 Squadron*

The rest of the formation kept station above them until they were safely back on the British side of the lines. But the scars of four years of trench warfare were everywhere and there seemed nowhere safe to land. For Blanford, half in and half out of his cockpit, the situation was precarious in the extreme.

> When we went down to about 500 feet, Atkinson yelled to me, 'I'm going to try to make a belly landing. To get the nose up, we shall have to land at flying speed, so hold tight when I open full throttle.' When we were almost down, he suddenly opened up the engine and after a few seconds cut the ignition. There was a moment of silence, and I hastily hopped back into my cockpit and held on like grim death. Then came a sudden crash, the aircraft swung violently to starboard, followed by a succession of crashing and splintering noises and bumps under the fuselage. I was aware of the wings folding up backwards on each side of us – and suddenly we pulled up with a crunch. We had made it, against all the odds![72] *Second Lieutenant John Blanford, 206 Squadron*

With extraordinary luck they had managed to land on a rare shell-free stretch of pavé road near St Jean, in one of the very worst shell-holed sectors of the Ypres salient.

Another spectacular incident occurred for Captain Ronald Ivelaw-Chapman of 10 Squadron, based at Abeele, who with his observer Lieutenant Fletcher was ordered to carry out a routine artillery observation mission in their Armstrong Whitworth. As usual, they were carrying a number of Cooper bombs to drop on a target before they started work with the guns.

> As we were gathering speed over the airfield, my engine spluttered rather badly, it picked up again, but I hit a pile of stones at the edge of the airfield. I felt a little bit of a lurch, however we staggered into the air and we were going alright. I guessed that I had crashed the undercarriage, but I thought, 'Well it will be much better to get rid of the bomb that I had on the rack under my seat before I came back to the airfield for the inevitable crash!' So off I went, I got rid of my bombs and finished my two hour stint. On the way back, I don't know what prompted it but it suddenly struck me that I would like to make quite certain that all of these four 20lb Cooper bombs had in point of fact fallen clear of the undercarriage. So I asked Fletcher to put his head through the camera hole to make quite sure they had all gone. Well after a moment or so he came back with his face as white as a sheet and passed me a note to say that three of them had gone alright, but the fourth one was lodged in the V-strut of what was now just a dangling undercarriage just below the bottom of the fuselage.[73] *Captain Ronald Ivelaw-Chapman, 8 Squadron*

Their peril was obvious. The bomb detonator was such that once it had fallen off the rack it had a small propeller that wound up with the motion of the air and turned a disc in the bomb so that two holes were brought opposite each other. When the bomb struck the ground, or any other really sharp shock such as was inevitable in landing, it would cause the plunger to pass through the holes and thereby explode the bomb – with disastrous consequences for the two men setting immediately above it. Ivelaw-Chapman decided to try to drop the whole assembly in the North Sea, but as he passed over Zillebeke Lake, by Ypres, he conceived an alternative plan.

I saw this big expanse of water and I thought, 'Well this is the chance to try and get rid of it!' I set the aircraft on course and I handed over control to my observer who had some primitive form of control with two hand grips on the two rudder bars. I got out on to the wing and laid along the lower plane holding onto a strut in the hope of being able to reach the bomb and push it off. I hadn't been on it for very long before I realised two things. First of all, the bomb was well out of my reach, and secondly that the aeroplane had got into a rather peculiar attitude. I clambered back into the cockpit only to discover that the observer, through no fault of his own, had got us into a fairly nice spin and we were spinning down towards the ground.[74] *Captain Ronald Ivelaw-Chapman, 8 Squadron*

Having brought the Armstrong Whitworth out of the spin, he perforce had to come up with another plan. To land as they were would blow them to bits; something had to be done.

Then the thought struck me that maybe I could get this bomb off by gravity. So I pulled it up in a normal loop, but instead of completing the loop I hung on my back for quite a long time. We both were naturally at that time hanging on to our straps, because we were in inverted flight. Then I felt the very thing I had been hoping for: a dull thud on my backside when the bomb fell off the broken strut, onto the fuselage just below me and slithered off. I righted the aircraft and looked down. There to my wild delight I found the waters of Zillebeke Lake in a wild eruption and the bomb had found its home quite peacefully.[75] *Captain Ronald Ivelaw-Chapman, 8 Squadron*

Now all he had to do was land the aircraft without an undercarriage. Somehow this seemed a formality after what they had been through.

I flew low over the airfield to start with to signify that they were going to have a crash on their hands. They got quite excited; started waving wheels about in the air to show that I had got a damaged undercarriage – a point I already knew! There then followed the inescapable belly landing with no terrible ill effects.[76] *Captain Ronald Ivelaw-Chapman, 8 Squadron*

They had been very lucky indeed.

THE American squadrons were still full of inexperienced pilots and the tactics they employed were sometimes a little rigid, mirroring the problems their infantry were suffering on the ground. The occasionally unnecessary casualties were exacerbated and magnified by problems of reliability with both the aircraft and the men flying them.

> The 1st Pursuit Group was ordered by Mitchell to patrol at less than 2,000 feet, and any pilot above that altitude would be court martialled. We were to strafe the infantry, we were to protect our balloons and our troops. The 2nd Pursuit Group would be flying at 2,000 – 4,000 feet and the 3rd Pursuit Group above 12,000 feet. He had us in what he called echelons. This didn't work for the reason that the 2nd Pursuit Group were never out there and the 3rd Pursuit Group was on paper. So the Germans were having a holiday. In groups as big as thirty they were coming down on us, firing their guns and pulling up above 2,000 feet where they were safe from attack. I'd take out my flight and a lot of these 'brave boys' all had 'engine trouble' and dropped out. Some actually did because motors were extremely unreliable, very frequently conking out, or missing and malfunctioning, giving our pilots a darned good excuse for not being out there. On many a patrol did I wind up flying with one pilot only, or flying alone. After a few weeks of this it led to a nervous breakdown: shaking and in tears, cursing like hell, tears of anger not fear – until the doctor ordered me to take a rest. I was ordered back.[77] *Lieutenant Ralph O'Neill, 147 Aero Squadron, 2nd Pursuit Group*

One dramatic incident occurred during a major operation by 2nd Pursuit Group on 10 October 1918. Captain Eddie Rickenbacker commanding 94th Aero Squadron took off with fourteen Spads at 15.30 that afternoon to be joined by a further eight Spads led by Lieutenant Wilbert White of 147 Aero Squadron and yet another seven from 27 Aero Squadron. They were on a mission to destroy a German balloon tethered above Dun-sur-Meuse. The 147 Aero Squadron Spads led, but they had drifted out about a mile to the right of Rickenbacker when eleven Fokker D.VIIs were sighted from the direction of Stenay. At this stage Lieutenant Wilbert White was accompanied only by Lieutenants James Meissner and Charles Cox, for they had been covering Lieutenant William Brotherton as he dived to shoot down the balloon. It was to be White's last flight before being withdrawn from the line.

Evidently the Fokker leader scorned to take notice of me, as his scouts passed under me and plunged ahead towards White's formation. I let them pass, dipped over sharply and with accumulated speed bore down upon the tail of the last man in the Fokker formation. It was an easy shot and I could not have missed. I was agreeably surprised, however, to see that my first shots had set fire to the Hun's fuel tank and that the machine was doomed. I was almost equally gratified the next second to see the German pilot level off his blazing machine and with a sudden leap overboard into space let the Fokker slide safely away without him. Attached to his back and sides was a rope which immediately pulled a dainty parachute from the bottom of his seat. The umbrella opened within a fifty-foot drop and settled him gradually to earth within his own lines.[78] *Captain Edward Rickenbacker, 94th Aero Squadron, 2nd Pursuit Group*

Meanwhile a general dogfight was beginning to break out as the Fokkers attacked White, Cox and Meissner.

Their leader dove on a new pilot in our formation of three. 'Whitey' leading, instantly turned in his tracks to drive the Hun off and save the new pilot, naturally excited and apt to lose his head when he heard bullets crack around.[79] *Captain James Meissner, 147 Aero Squadron, 2nd Pursuit Group*

The new pilot was Lieutenant Charles Cox and as his flight commander White was aware, a natural rawness was not by any means his only problem.

He knew I had a bad motor and was inexperienced at the front and all the way to the lines he kept close and waved his arm occasionally to cheer me. Brotherton went down and was hit from the ground as he dived. White turned to the left, back towards our lines, when a Hun came down directly behind me and about 400 yards back. White turned back and as he passed opposite me I turned. The float in my carburettor flipped up and my motor cut out an instant slowing me up. I saw White and the Hun going directly at each other, the former climbing a little.[80] *Lieutenant Charles Cox, 147 Aero Squadron, 2nd Pursuit Group*

Meissner was close behind but too far away to intervene.

I turned back too, but was further away and could just watch what happened. The Fokker kept diving on Cox as White raced back, head on at it, firing without effect. He must have realised that Cox would be shot down unless he put the Bosche out of the fight, so he never swerved. I watched them come together, thought for a moment they would just pass side by side, but the next instant off came a wing of each plane amid a cloud of splinters and shreds of fabric and down they went spinning like tops.[81]
Captain James Meissner, 147 Aero Squadron, 2nd Pursuit Group

The grim sight of the two splintering, shattered aircraft would haunt Rickenbacker's dreams for years.

White rammed the Fokker head on while the two machines were approaching each other at the rate of 250 miles per hour! It was a horrible yet thrilling sight. The two machines actually telescoped each other, so violent was the impact. Wings went through wings and at first glance both the Fokker and Spad seemed to disintegrate. Fragments filled the air for a moment, then the two broken fuselages, bound together by the terrific collision, fell swiftly down and landed in one heap on the bank of the Meuse![82] *Captain Edward Rickenbacker, 94th Aero Squadron, 2nd Pursuit Group*

It was believed by everyone who saw the incident that this was no accident and that Wilbert White had deliberately sacrificed himself to save Cox. In the circumstances it is instructive to remember White's earlier words in a letter home.

In this war it is either a case of get or be gotten, and I choose the former if ever there is a choice in the matter.[83] *Lieutenant Wilbert White, 147 Aero Squadron, 2nd Pursuit Group*

When his helpless comrade was in imminent danger there was apparently no choice for Wilbert White. His comrades in 147 Aero Squadron were stunned at the extent of his personal sacrifice.

It was sickening to fly then to the spot where they had collided and think what their thoughts must have been the last instant before they met –

Spartans both. White was married, had two children, was to have received orders returning him to the States in a few days and he knew it. But he never hesitated when he saw his duty cut out, which makes his act all the more heroic.[84] *Lieutenant James Meisssner, 147 Aero Squadron, 2nd Pursuit Group*

AS the Allies advanced on all fronts there was a pressing need for reconnaissance missions to probe deep behind the German lines to record the movements of German trains in and out of the major rail centres. This information would enable the High Command to judge the German strengths and weaknesses as it launched its next attack. Late in October, Lieutenant F. C. Pargeter of 53 Squadron was sent on one such mission.

Jerry crumbling. The 'big wigs' ask us to find trains, trains and more trains. Skipper calls Dunlop and me, who are for pre-dawn flight take off so as to be over at first light. He says we have not found as many trains as the squadrons to the right and left. I reply if I see a train and report, 'Waterloo to Clapham Junction', I do not also report it at Vauxhall and Queens Road. But we take off in the dark, rather piqued and in a, 'If they want trains they shall have them mood!' The result was we glued ourselves to the railways, found every train, engine, etc. and forgot all else. So we were too far, too low, too light and we touch Jerry in a tender spot for up comes the kitchen sink and everything else. Shells, red tracers, flaming onions – a pretty display from outside but rather different inside. We dodge madly about. I watch pieces of airplane blown off, control wires cut, bracing wires snapped and we ponder on the least possible amount of plane that will keep us airborne. In defiance I keep on giving odd bursts, a sort of snap of the fingers, 'We are still here!' but kept plenty of ammo in case on way back the fighters were up.[85] *Lieutenant F. C. Pargeter, 53 Squadron*

As the troops advanced they needed to know what lay ahead of them. The freedom of open warfare had seemed desirable when faced with the relentless muck and blood of the trenches, but the combination of modern weapons and quickly dug defensive positions had not got any less deadly. There was a real chance of severe casualties if ambushed by running into a series of unsuspected machine-gun posts. But at the localized tactical level, low cloud or the sheer speed of the advance could render photographic survey inappropriate. Thus it was that the 'Mark I Eyeball' once again became a valid method of observation. Fast scouts were increasingly being used for low-level reconnaissance and Major Sholto Douglas of 84 Squadron took this to its absolute limit, descending as low as 20 feet on occasion.

> Visibility was only about 400 yards, and the cloud base was down to about 300 feet. I took off and flew just above the tree tops down the long, straight road that ran from north of St Quentin to Le Cateau. There were three or four roads running out of Le Cateau to the east, and I flew along each of these in turn until I found myself shot at from the ground, at which point I rapidly turned around. After marking on my map the spot where I had been fired at I made my way back to Le Cateau and repeated the process along the other roads. Having collected this information I then groped my way back to my own aerodrome by contour-chasing with my map on my knee. When I got there and gave the information to our intelligence people they were able to join up the points that I had marked, and through that they were able to gain quite a fair picture of the location of the German front line.[86] *Major Sholto Douglas, 84 Squadron*

As the infantry pressed ahead on all fronts so the squadrons were frequently forced to move their airfields forward in order to remain close enough to the ever-advancing front lines. This was administratively complicated for it was not just a matter of moving the pilots, observers and their aircraft; all the ground crew, support staff, equipment, MT, accommodation and hangars had to be moved or sorted out anew. All this without interrupting the number of missions flown by the squadron.

> We all flew over to the new aerodrome here. It is in a ghastly position. Not a house is standing within 30 miles. Nearest occupied town is Amiens which is a 2 hour ride in a tender. The country all round is desolate. Full of shell holes and trenches full of water owing to the recent rains. Houses and villages, even towns simply blasted to the ground, nothing but piles of bricks and the sad sight of little white crosses sticking up by the roadside

to mark the lonely grave of some poor lad who fought for his country.[87] *Lieutenant L. G. Semple, 207 Squadron*

Sometimes the pace of the advance had increased to such an extent that when the aircraft flew in to occupy their new airfield it was glaringly obvious that the recent German occupants had only just left.

When our squadron finally took possession of Linselles aerodrome the following afternoon, we learnt that the enemy had vacated it only that morning. We had been warned to beware of booby traps, but the enemy appeared to have left in a hurry. Flowers had been left on the table in the officers' mess and in the evening we had our first meal on ex-enemy territory. In the middle of the meal the ticking of some mechanical device became noticeable and we quickly cleared out of the mess – only to discover that the ticking had emanated from an alarm clock which an unknown hand had placed against the side of the hut.[88] *Recording Officer Lieutenant B. H. Rook, 206 Squadron*

For many of the pilots and observers it seemed strange to be occupying an airfield that just a few days ago they had been bombing.

We are right up near the war now, billeted in a village which ten days ago the Huns had. The civilians are still here and have been for the last four years. Naturally they are very bucked to be rid of the Hun. There don't seem to have been any of the awful atrocities here, they've simply been bullied. The Huns commandeered everything and when they left they took everything, all the animals, hens, goats, etc. We arrived yesterday by air, but our kit didn't come till the night, with the result that we spent a pretty awful night. Four of us were stretched out on the floor on a mattress. However *c'est la* blooming *guerre!*[89] *Lieutenant Yvonne Kirkpatrick, 203 Squadron*

As they moved forward, as they occupied areas once deep behind the German line, they could not help wondering if the war would soon be over. Yet in many squadron messes there was no relaxation either of effort or of grim intent. Human nature being what it was, some pilots undoubtedly saw the possibility of imminent peace as a threat to their all-consuming ambition to qualify as an ace with the requisite five victories. For the last few weeks one young American pilot, Lieutenant Lancing Holden, 95th Pursuit Squadron, had been absolutely desperate to claw his way through to become an ace. Although attacking balloons was excessively dangerous, they were relatively easy to find and hit, and could in a sense therefore be seen as a temptingly easy way to progress without having to shoot down five agile, dodging Fokker D.VIIs.

> I flew around waiting till it got darker, then made for five German balloons all in a row. If I could get all five. . . . I picked the end one, which proved to be a fake with no basket. It didn't burn and both my guns jammed. I fixed them on my way to the next one, and oh, the barrage they put up all the time, looked like the Fourth of July. Not many 'Archies' but millions of flaming onions and incendiary bullets. The second one, the observers jumped from, but that didn't burn either and the guns jammed again. The third I attacked twice. They had pulled them all down – this one was about 50 metres up – again the guns jammed, but as I turned away two little red holes like bloodshot eyes were burning on the side. Slowly the fire spread then up she went. Gee I felt good, but my dream of five didn't pan out. It is certain to be confirmed and that will make three – two official – three more and I am an official ace. That is my dream and I swear I shall accomplish it.[90] *Lieutenant Lancing Holden, 95th Pursuit Squadron, 1st Pursuit Group*

Within a few days Holden was back. He certainly knew the risks; he was personally scared, but in truth he was a man in the grip of a dangerous obsession – one that had drawn many such young men to their early deaths over the last three years.

> Last night I dodged over the clouds and burned the balloon just as the observer jumped. Poor devil, the whole burning mass of balloon must have fallen on his parachute. I am getting this job down pretty fine now – the balloon burned after one burst of thirty shots. Tonight Al Weatherhead, Sumner Sewell and I went over. They were to protect me. I went down and burned mine. They can pull those balloons down at 30mph. I didn't catch it till it was on the ground. It is more fun to see them burn up in the air, but it burned and fell on all its machine gunners, which must have been

annoying. If there is any one class of human beings I heartily detest it is the German 'flaming onion' shooters. At last, at last! I am an ace! I burned another balloon last night and one tonight. That makes five official balloons and one official plane. Ted Curtis and myself are the only men with six official victories in the squadron.[91] *Lieutenant Lancing Holden, 95th Aero Squadron, United States Air Force*

One strange incident occurred on 27 October when Major William Barker, who was temporarily attached to 201 Squadron, was reported to have engaged in a tussle with a truly astonishing number of German aircraft while flying one of the new Sopwith Snipes. Barker was an experienced aviator: he had first served as both observer then pilot in 1916 and 1917; then a tour of duty had taken him to the backwaters of the Italian front where he had prospered to the extent that he had forty-six claimed victories before returning to England. In October 1918 he was back on the Western Front attached to 201 Squadron on the excuse of needing a practical refresher course in current aerial tactics before taking up an appointment to command an Air Fighting School in England. Poor weather meant that most of his stay was uneventful, yet his last flight on his way back to the Aircraft Supply Depot would be the stuff of legend. As he took off in his Snipe, Barker was determined to add to his victory score and saw this as his last opportunity for a while. In doing so he was directly ignoring the prevailing advice that lone-wolf missions were no longer feasible in the crowded skies of late 1918.

After crossing the lines Barker seems to have engaged a two-seater over Mormal Woods, which he duly shot down, but while distracted he was raked by a Fokker D.VII and badly wounded in the right thigh. He spun down and as he evened out found himself being assailed by several more Fokkers. The number of these varies from sixty in newspaper accounts, through fifty, via a feasible fifteen, to the hard-boiled cynics who consider it to be all the doing of the original Fokker that had then followed him down. Whatever the truth of it, Barker seems to have fought gallantly and indeed claimed to have shot down three aircraft in flames, despite being wounded twice more, in the left hip and the left elbow, wounds that finally rendered him almost helpless and only semi-conscious. The Snipe crashed to the ground close to a

British kite balloon where only prompt medical assistance saved his life. This dramatic dogfight is often referred to as having been seen by thousands of front line troops, but there is a noticeable dearth of credible eyewitnesses[92] and William Barker himself always kept his own counsel, other than to brief the officer who completed his original combat report for him. In public all he ever seems to have said was the memorably terse summary, 'I was severely wounded and shot down.' What is certain is that, whatever the numbers involved, Barker had indeed been in a battle for his very life and, as he was unconscious for several days, he probably had little or no idea what had really happened. Happily, Barker survived and was awarded a Victoria Cross, but of course he had no chance of recovering from his wounds in time to fly again. Another ace had fought his last battle of the war.

While the scout pilots sought glory in carrying out their duties, the less glamorous day bombers were still pushing deep into the German-held territory, attacking their infrastructure. Their missions were designed to prevent the movements of German reinforcements, and stop their efforts to reorganize and stabilize their front; they also served a third function in harassing their retreat. The last few days of October assuredly saw the heaviest air fighting in the war so far. The Germans continued their policy of concentrating their shrinking scout resources, flying in large formations and desperately trying to protect the remaining rail and road junctions that represented their only realistic hope of an orderly retreat. If these were destroyed the retreating troops would be cut off and forced to surrender *en masse*. They therefore focused on stopping the day raids carried out by the assuredly inadequate DH9s, on the sensible grounds that this was the best way to make a difference.

The single worst day was 30 October 1918: a day no longer remembered, but it was one of appalling casualties for both sides. On this day alone the British claimed to have shot down 67 German aircraft while 41 British aircraft were shot down. Losses like this made 'Bloody April' look like a mere taster of real war.

One notable event that day was the raid by 80th Wing, led personally by Lieutenant Colonel Louis Strange, on Rebaix airfield, north of Ath. A reconnaissance flight early that morning had spotted that the airfield was being used by a dangerous collection of German scouts. Retribution was on a biblical scale as Strange led sixty-two assorted aircraft from his wing into a low-level raid which scored direct hits to destroy most of the hangars and raked aircraft standing on the airfield. Peculiarly, Strange also seems to have shot down a Fokker D.VII without even realizing it. The old campaigner had been one of the first to take a machine gun aloft in August 1914; now he was fighting in another world of multi-gun purpose-built scouts.

> To show how little one knows of what happens in an air fight, I may say that until I got back I was blissfully unaware that I had shot down a Fokker. An observer in one of the DH9s who recognised the machine I flew, reported and confirmed that I had got this enemy when he was sitting on the DH9's tail. Personally, I had no idea this Hun had crashed, although I thought I got a good burst on him; but I was more worried about the question whether I had any undercarriage left, because I hit the Fokker's wing hard with my wheels when I pulled out of my dive having left.[93] *Lieutenant Colonel Louis Strange, Headquarters 80th Wing*

Many of the men of the German Air Service were clearly intent on fighting to the end. They may have been hampered by a shortage of petrol; by the gnawing realization that it was all hopeless. But they had been brought up and trained to fight, and fight on they would. Certainly Lieutenant Yvonne Kirkpatrick noticed that the Germans were still game enough when he ran into them on 3 November.

> We're having a pretty exciting time nowadays. Every time we go up we meet these blooming Huns, about forty of them. They're very cautious and try to lure us over to their side where they could deal with us fairly comfortably. We sort of hare round and they chase us, and we turn round and chase them back again. Today we had a sort of scrap. The clouds were at about 10,000 feet, at least one layer was. When we crossed the lines just below these clouds we saw about fifteen of them climbing and going south, so we went towards them, but they went east, then we did a turn to the left and went north and they chased us. This sort of thing went on for ages and no real dogfight developed. The Huns wanted to have it all their own way and we didn't see why they should. One came fairly close and I took a shot at him. Then we turned and one came down and took a shot at me. I tore the sky up with some colossal turns and he left us. I had

a sort of feeling that if we went over after them that we'd have all the German Air Service down on us from above the clouds, and I was right because somebody who'd been above the clouds had seen a whole crowd more of them. The war news is good, but the Huns on this front, the aerial ones anyway, don't seem to be thinking about stopping fighting.[94]

Lieutenant Yvonne Kirkpatrick, 203 Squadron

Yet although the German Air Service could concentrate their resources for special efforts they could not face the sheer ubiquity of the swarms of Allied aircraft that pressed deep into their territory.

On 4 November the final Allied offensives were launched. It was barely possible to distinguish an offensive from a routine advance to contact by this stage of the war. The British First, Third and Fourth Armies all lunged forward. Above them the men of the RAF could see their relentless advance and the scouts harassed the retreating Germans every inch of the way. There was certainly no concept of magnanimity in victory. Sometimes the attacks on the near-helpless German columns took on the semblance of a killing frenzy. An American pilot serving with 46 Squadron recalled one such attack on 10 November.

We went out on a squadron sweep and found a long straight road filled with retreating German supply trains. We saw horse drawn artillery, motor trucks, infantry and other military equipment of one kind or another. We formed a big circle and as we went down this road, we fired our machine guns and dropped our 25lb bombs. When we got through with that road it was one unbelievable scene of chaos, with dead horses, lorries and dead soldiers all over the road. As I went down the last time to use up what was left of my ammunition and bombs, the two planes in front of me collided.[95]

Lieutenant Richmond Viall, 46 Squadron

The victims were Second Lieutenants George Dowler and William Coulthurst. Killed trying to kill in the very last hours of the Great War, these men were two of the last RAF fatal casualties of war.

As the exhausted, harassed Germans fell back, they evacuated the Belgian town of Mons; the very town where it had all begun for the British Army at the Battle of Mons on 23 August 1914.

At the end of an offensive patrol, we flew low over Mons from which town the Germans had now retreated more than four years after the famous British retreat from the same town. Flags were flying from every house and the people in the streets waved to us with great enthusiasm as we skimmed over the housetops.[96] ***Captain Leonard Rochford, 203 Squadron, RAF***

By a strange coincidence Mons was actually formally 'liberated' only with the arrival of Canadian troops at dawn on 11 November, the very day the war would end.

IF any part of the war was futile it was the last month. The Germans had lost: it was just a matter of negotiating the surrender. Ludendorff had adopted an intransigent attitude towards the armistice conditions proposed by the Allies, which he characterized as unconditional surrender. In this he was of course correct; the question was whether Germany had any remaining option. The Allies were fast approaching its frontiers and it was evident that invasion was nigh. Ludendorff had convinced himself that the frontiers could be defended, but this was more wish fulfilment than generalship. After a spectacular argument with Kaiser Wilhelm, his resignation had been accepted on 26 October. His replacement as Hindenburg's Chief of Staff was General Wilhelm Groener who quickly assessed the situation and duly found it hopeless. It was not just on the Western Front that defeat stared Germany in the face. The Turks, Austro-Hungarians and Bulgarians were also suing for peace. On 4 November the High Seas Fleet, penned into its Wilhelmshaven bolt hole for so long, mutinied rather than emerge to fight the Royal Navy. The war was over in all but name and thousands of men were falling victim to German intransigence.

Each day they prevaricated the Allies' stance grew harder. When the Germans finally began armistice negotiations in early November they were told that they must do so with Marshal Ferdinand Foch himself; no inviting prospect. With their country imploding into revolution, their army and navy falling apart and in a state of mutiny, they had no leg to stand on. By the time the armistice conditions imposed by the Allies were accepted all the 'guilty men' had gone, the Kaiser had abdicated and a socialist Chancellor, Friedrich Ebert, had picked up the reins of power.

And what conditions they were. There was no doubt who had won: Belgium, France and Alsace-Lorraine were to be immediately cleared of German troops and the means of war – some 5,000 guns, 30,000 machine guns, 3,000 trench mortars and 2,000 aircraft – were to be handed over. The left bank of the Rhine was to be evacuated and occupied by the Allies, while there would be a neutral zone established on the right bank. The rest of the conditions were equally stringent – and all this for an armistice theoretically of just thirty days. The Allies were making absolutely sure that there could be no chance of the Germans taking a short breather and then resuming the fight.

TOWARDS the end of 10 November the first rumour of an armistice to commence at eleven o'clock on 11 November 1918 began to circulate at the front and in the airfields up and down the Western Front. But the imminence of peace did not stop planned air raids on that last night of the war.

> Raid carried out on Namur. Owing to dud engines I was late in starting and consequently bombed 1½ hours after everybody else. Very good shooting obtained, but hundreds of 'flaming onions' all around me. Gave my observer, Boshier, control on the way home. He was quite good. Went to bed at about 11pm and at 1 am news came via the wireless that the Armistice had been signed and cessation of hostilities from 11am today. Beautiful news. Lighted a tin of petrol and we kicked it all round the camp. This morning we all had a jolly good drink. Sent somebody to Rouen to buy as much as possible. Have discovered that I was the last pilot to drop bombs on enemy territory during this war. Very good.[97] *Lieutenant L. G. Semple, 207 Squadron*

As the rumours spread there were spontaneous outbreaks of slightly premature celebrations, which in turn spread the news further. What else could anybody be celebrating so vigorously in the fifth year of the Great War?

> We were all sitting in the anteroom when somebody said they were ringing bells and blowing sirens in the town. We went outside and sure enough they were. The searchlights were swinging about all over the sky and

thousands of Very lights going up from all the aerodromes and infantry and artillery people right up to the front line. We guessed what the news was and later confirmed it through our wireless. Then all the sergeants came up and proceeded to lap up our drink. 'Grid' Caldwell brought his lot across and we had a jollification until all our drink had gone. Then we all went down to the aerodrome but all the Very lights had been fired off. Next we trooped into Courtrai and assisted at the bonfire – even furniture was fed into it. Finally we got to bed at 2am. Jolly good ending to the war.[98] *Major Charlie Dixon, 29 Squadron, RFC*

Lieutenant Yvonne Kirkpatrick was still not sure what was happening. Could it really be true that the killing had stopped?

Rumour has it this blinking war's over. Supposed to stop at 11am this morning. I'm blowed if I know whether to believe it or not. Anyway we've got orders to do our patrols a mile this side of the lines which is rather nice. Now we want to know what we're going to do. I expect as the Huns evacuated Belgium we'll follow them up and do sort of police patrols to see that they clear out all right. All the military bands in the place are playing. I lost five francs. I bet somebody last night five to one that there wouldn't be an armistice, but I don't mind paying more than that for the blooming war to stop.[99] *Lieutenant Yvonne Kirkpatrick, 203 Squadron*

Captain Ronald Ivelaw-Chapman decided to celebrate in a unique manner reminiscent of Captain Wilfred Neville's use of footballs to encourage the men of the 8th East Surreys over the top on the Somme on 1 July 1916.

I put myself on the patrol that was due to take place over the front line at that time. Sure enough when 11 o'clock came along, all our troops all halted at the positions that they had reached. I had persuaded some of the mechanics in my flight to give me a football and I had taken it up in the air with me. At 11 o'clock I swooped down pretty low on our front line troops and they waved at me; thereupon I dropped this football amongst them. It was quite a pleasure to watch them kicking it round having dropped their rifles on the ground.[100] *Lieutenant Ronald Ivelaw-Chapman, 8 Squadron*

Back in England, Major Harold Balfour, a veteran ace although forced back from the front at just 20 years old, decided to express himself by wild stunt flying as eleven o'clock tolled.

> Caught up in the enthusiasm of the moment, but, looking back, with really very little foundation for this enthusiasm, I jumped into a Sopwith Pup and proceeded to go about as near killing myself in a stupid and senseless way by low stunting as I suppose I have ever done in my flying career.[101] *Major Harold Balfour, No.3 Air Fighting School*

Human nature reacted to staggering news in many different ways. Some seemed almost stunned. But for most there soon blossomed the urge to let rip in the mother and father of all parties.

> It was a wonderful night in Amiens. Many shell wrecked houses, but flags all along the streets, tied to every cart or car, and even carried by the crowd. We did a little shopping and ordered dinner in the Godbert Restaurant. An Australian band then marched through the streets with swarms of civilians following it. They stopped opposite a group of German prisoners and played the 'Marseillaise'. When it got dark Chinese lanterns were carried about, people fired off red rockets and there was a general noise of singing and shouting. We then went to have dinner. The place was absolutely crowded. It was a very quiet dinner, but towards the end a little humming was heard and then the whole room broke out with 'Tipperary'. A French colonel then got up and sang a French song; a little more talking and then the whole room sang the 'Marseillaise' – a few minutes 'God Save the King'. After that there was a general mixture of singing and talking during which the 94 Squadron gave its cry of 'Big White Chief'. Practically the whole room after that marched round and round the room singing hard.[102] *Captain Francis Cave, 94 Squadron*

Some had not been able to bring themselves to celebrate until the news was made official. Only then did one gnarled veteran of three years of war trust himself to cast off the cloak of war and reflect on what it all meant, what it all might mean.

> So! It's over!! I can scarce realise the stupendous event. Cease hostilities! Good Lord is it really true! I am writing this at noon having heard it officially

and have just paraded the men to tell them – everyone has taken it very quietly, just as a Britisher would! I was acting officer commanding of the squadron and I felt the 'history' of the occasion, standing there addressing all these men, the majority much older than I, and quietly asking them to behave 'properly' when celebrating – I was 21 years old![103] *Captain Ewart Garland, 104 Squadron, IAF*

THE GREAT WAR was indeed over at last. Empires had fallen and the world had changed for ever. Millions of men had died; millions more were crippled or maimed. The war had flared right across the globe, reached under the seas and up to the heavens. The young men who had survived the modern Armageddon knew they were lucky, but their lives had been irrevocably changed. The pilots and observers of the RAF who had survived found that few of them were unmarked by what they had endured. Whether aces or journeymen they had experienced thrills that their ancestors could only dream of; they had flown like birds high in the sky, soared like eagles. At the same time they had faced the screaming nightmares of flensing bullets and burning aircraft; of bubbling flesh and the last leap tumbling to eternity. But the war was over. After all they had seen and done what were they going to do now?

Chapter 14

When the Show is Over

In the end the armistice was an anticlimax. It was inevitable. Men had invested so much in the concept of 'peace in our time', that they were bound to be disappointed when it arrived on 11 November 1918. For peace could be dull; especially if one had been a scout pilot, an ace engaged in the 'great game'. In civilian life how and where could the reconnaissance and artillery observation crews achieve anything that made a difference to the extent that their work on the Western Front had? Where was the mission accomplished that could compare with a successful bombing raid over German cities? A life of boredom beckoned: a life of mundane jobs and minimal responsibility.

The war was over. Not formally – for that they would have to wait until the Treaty of Versailles in 1919 – but it was soon obvious that fighting would not recommence. Men who had had their every waking hour regulated by the demands of life-or-death missions found that time began to hang heavy on their hands. Some looked forward to peacetime flying – the chance to try out the German aircraft in the air; to see exactly what they could do, how good they really were.

> Goodness only knows what we're going to do when we get to Tournai. There's a lot of talk about ferrying Hun machines, which I hope is true. I'm full out to fly as many 'buses' as I can, specially the nimble Fokker.[1]
>
> *Lieutenant Yvonne Kirkpatrick, 203 Squadron*

The problem with bored young pilots is that once wartime dangers have been removed they soon generate their own perils. Many pilots actively sought to recreate the thrills and spills of combat by bouts of extreme low-level stunting.

It was silly, mad. People who had risked their lives, prayed that they lived – no sooner were they free of war then they did the most curious things in the air. Contour chasing was following the contours of the ground, going across towards a farm house and just zooming up over the top missing the chimney pots by a few feet. The cows would run with their tails stiff out behind them! The chickens would fly as though they were trying to take off going at a rate of knots running. Old ladies came to the door and shook their fists as you came along. We got amusement from that! This was sport. It struck me then that it was extraordinary what a kick one could get out of other people's uncomfortableness – these old ladies were infuriated with us – but it was rather fun.[2] *Lieutenant T. E. Rogers, 22 Squadron*

They had the imagined invulnerability of the young. After all, nothing could happen to them, they were safe – the war was over and they had survived. Unfortunately, stunt flying was in itself intrinsically dangerous and accidents were frequent.

One of our fairly new pilots went and brought himself to a sticky end the other day, diving on some soldiers he hit a telegraph pole when he was doing about 150mph. Jolly bad luck as he'd been right through the war with the infantry. Hedge-hopping is like drink: it's absolutely fascinating and a very hard habit to get rid of, but I hereby register a vow to stop it for at least a week.[3] *Lieutenant Yvonne Kirkpatrick, 203 Squadron*

The old hatreds had not died with the onset of peace. When Major Wilfred Snow visited a German cemetery he pondered on the graves of men who could well have been killed by the air raids carried out by his squadron in the previous months. His comments make uncompromising reading; feelings were still red raw and real reconciliation seemed inconceivable.

The squadron did in a few Huns there I am glad to say. It is quite an amusing sensation really to wander in these Hun cemeteries and read the name on the crosses and say to oneself, 'I wonder if I killed you?' and rather hoping that you did. I am glad to know that I did my share all right, and rid the earth of quite a few of the vermin. For that is all you regard them as – just vermin – to be stamped out as you would kill a bug, and the mere fact that they were human beings didn't interest you at the time. And when you have seen hundreds of thousands of our own graves it makes you regret very much that you haven't done far more.[4] *Major Wilfred Snow, 2 Squadron, RAF*

As the German Army retreated the Allies moved forward with the British Army of Occupation earmarked to occupy Cologne. One of the squadrons chosen to accompany the troops was 206 Squadron. It is distressing to note that they marked their entry into German territory in a crude, but to the modern eye strangely familiar manner.

Some of us travelled with the CO in his car during the last stage of the road journey to Cologne and when we had crossed the frontier into Germany at Aix-la-Chapelle, we got out of the car and relieved ourselves with 'military precision' at the roadside in full view of the passengers on a German tram.[5] *Recording Officer Lieutenant B. H. Rook, 206 Squadron*

There was obviously going to be no question of winning hearts and minds, but rather of rubbing the faces of the Germans into the figurative dirt. In this the young men were mirroring the attitudes of the Allied governments. There was no real rapprochement with the German people, as was clearly shown by the behaviour of pilots following a special mess guest night organized to commemorate the departure next day of 4 Squadron, Australian Flying Corps.

It developed into a wild party which reached its climax when the Australians decided to paint Kaiser Bill's gigantic equestrian statue, nearly opposite our mess, with white aircraft fabric dope. The Kaiser's charger, twice as large as life, was a stallion and the sculptor, with true Teutonic thoroughness, had faithfully reproduced every detail of the animal's anatomy to scale. After the Aussies had finished the job, the stallion possessed zebra stripes and huge white bollocks! To crown all (literally) they borrowed our CO's enamel chamber pot and wired it on top of the Kaiser's head. Like Queen Victoria, the Germans were definitely *not* amused when they beheld this ribald spectacle next morning, Furious protests were made, but the culprits were by then well on their way home. For several days afterwards the Germans had a party of charwomen with buckets of water and scrubbing brushes at work trying to clean up the statue. Alas, the white dope was both water and petrol resistant and when I myself left Cologne the zebra stripes still showed up faintly despite all the efforts of the 'Seven maids with seven mops'![6] *Second Lieutenant John Blanford, 206 Squadron*

As a result of the armistice conditions, the German Air Service ceased to exist as a meaningful weapon of war.

The ignominious conditions of the Armistice of Compiègne demanded the immediate delivery of 2,000 pursuit and bombardment airplanes. In this way, any future continuance of aerial warfare would be impossible, and there could be no basis on which the German nation could resist to the limit of its strength. It was impossible for us to turn over the desired number of planes, for there were not that many in all the pursuit and bombardment units along the entire front, not even if they had been at full strength. The clearly thought-out dictates of the Entente showed how much emphasis they placed on the value of aerial warfare and their over-estimate of our strength showed how highly the enemy esteemed our performances.[7] *General Ernest Wilhelm von Hoeppner, German Air Service*

For the defeated Germans it was just one insult after another. Their proud country was in ruins, racked by revolutions on every side. It seemed as if the whole spectrum of political extremism was up in arms. Bands of nationalist Freikorps stalked the cities, but for many of the German officers it was the spectre of the Communists and their burgeoning revolution that was most distressing.

On 1 December I decided to make our farewell flight to Gotha with my faithful 'Emil' Franz Jessen. Here we had our first experience with the communist crews. We had already removed the axle from the undercarriage of our aircraft. The aircraft itself, our uniforms and remaining equipment had to be handed over in exchange for a worthless receipt. I had to take the train to reach my home in Berlin. Four years of war experience: first in the infantry and then as an aviation observer lay behind me; an uncertain future lay ahead.[8] *Leutnant Fritz Kampfenkel, Flieger Abteilung (A) 240, Imperial German Air Force*

One man certainly kicked against the traces. Rudolf Berthold was not a man designed to live in a peaceful world. During the war he had craved peace to give him time to heal his smashed body; yet the end of the war brought him nothing but renewed conflict. An ardent German nationalist, he formed and led a strong Freikorps detachment known among other things as 'Berthold's Iron Band'. He fought on and on, fighting for a culture and society that were already doomed, until he was eventually killed by Communists on 15 March 1920. The rumour spread swiftly that he had been strangled with his own Pour le Mérite ribbon. The story may be apocryphal but there is no doubt that he was a man who truly fought to the death in the cause of peace.

Lothar von Richthofen had, despite his own best efforts, survived the war. He eventually became a pilot for a German commercial air service flying on the Hamburg to Berlin route. It was on 4 July 1922 that, in a sense, he finally broke his 'curse of thirteen', the 'curse' that had seen him shot down or crash on the thirteenth of the month on three separate occasions. There was not a thirteen in sight when the engine of his converted LVG CVI failed him. His passengers, the American film starlet Fern Andra and her manager, were injured in the resulting crash, but Lothar von Richthofen was killed outright.

The highest-scoring surviving German ace, Ernst Udet, seemed to have it all in the post-war years: adventures roaming about lost in the African desert, flying lunatic stunts for actors gallivanting about in cinematic romps set in the Alps. Unfortunately he was then persuaded to join the Luftwaffe in 1935. The cheerfully slapdash Udet was not suited to the vicious infighting that typified the Nazi war machine and finally shot himself in 1941. His charming associates then announced he had been killed on a test flight. All they had really valued of Ernst Udet was his glittering reputation as the top surviving German ace.

AFTER the war there was plenty of wild speculation as to what would be the future of the RAF. No-one at a junior level had any idea of what was really happening, but they generally believed what they wanted to believe: that they still had a valid role and a prospective career in the RAF.

> There's absolutely no talk about demobilising us, as far as I can make out they're going to keep an enormous standing Air Force. All the bombing machines are going to be used for mail carrying, that I know for certain, but what they'll do with the scouts I don't know. Personally I think they've got it all planned out what they're going to do with us, and I think it'll be pretty hard to get out of the RAF.[9] *Lieutenant Yvonne Kirkpatrick, 203 Squadron*

Other pilots seemed to regard the armistice as far more of a full stop in their lives. Perhaps sensibly they recognized that there was simply no future for them in flying; it was just too crowded and too dangerous a playing field.

> I refused a permanent commission immediately after the Armistice and never piloted an aeroplane again as long as I lived. Strangely enough, I lost interest completely the moment the war was over.[10] *Captain Ewart Garland, 104 Squadron, IAF*

The reality, of course, was that the RAF would be cut to the very bone in the peacetime years. Slowly the ordinary young pilots began to realize that their options were severely limited in the brave new world after the war.

> What on earth am I going to do? I certainly don't want to go to Oxford, or Cambridge, or any other place like that. In the first place it'll take them years to get those places going again, after all the Cadet Schools have cleared out. Two years ago I'd have enjoyed that sort of life, but now I'm afraid it would bore me stiff. I don't want to learn Latin or any of those funny sorts of things again. I don't enjoy playing games so much that I should want to play football all day. I really haven't the foggiest idea what I do want to do and I haven't met anybody else out here who does.[11] *Lieutenant Yvonne Kirkpatrick, 203 Squadron*

As they were demobilized in their thousands many continued to clutch at dreams that they might be able to forge a career in civilian aviation, or at the very least continue to fly in a private capacity. Two pilots who had flown two-seaters in action attended a war surplus sale of aircraft at Hendon airfield with real ambition in their hearts.

> We both thought it would be lovely to buy an SE5a, which were on sale for £5. We agreed to the price: he bought one; I bought one. We had them filled up with petrol and oil, tested them there and then for engine efficiency against the chocks, then took our aircraft up and flew around Hendon for about half an hour. We landed within five minutes of one another, stopped out props, climbed out and shouted to one another in joy at having enjoyed such a wonderful flight.[12] *Philip Townshend*

Once back on the ground and their natural euphoria had died down, the grim reality set in. Neither of them had a job or private means – how could they possibly own such an expensive luxury item as a scout aircraft that needed a certificate of airworthiness, constant mechanical attention and some kind of year-in year-out hangar accommodation? The answer was obvious – they could not – it was all a dream.

> Both of us became very dejected at having to realise that we couldn't possibly afford them. We'd no hangar, no reason to believe that we had any place at home where we could even house the aircraft. So we talked to the air mechanics and we agreed to sell them back for £4-10s. It took us I should think half an hour in silent tears to walk away from Hendon aerodrome realising that we had been defeated in our objective of being civil flyers.[13]
> *Philip Townshend*

In a sense they were lucky. The world, even at peace, was a dangerous place. Lieutenant John Blanford's former pilot with whom he had shared a tent, Captain Rupert Atkinson, did not long survive the war. Atkinson was a brave man, a brilliant pilot and also an amateur poet. Way back in 1917 he had mused in verse on his possible death in battle and the chances of joining some celestial Round Table.

> O! Spirits, who for ever fly,
> Banish the fears that terrify,
> Stifle the horror of being afraid,
> Still the conscience that would upbraid.
> Give me no chance to hesitate,
> Let me go out and meet my fate,

As all men do, so I may be,
One of your knightly company.[14]
Captain Rupert Atkinson

After four and a half years of war service, during which he completed more than 1,000 hours of combat flying, Rupert Atkinson had somehow avoided his anticipated wartime death. Yet he was to be dead within six months of the armistice. He fell victim to the killer that dwarfed even war: the influenza pandemic that seemed to prey on the young, weakened as they undoubtedly were by the awful trials they had undergone. His long-time observer had owed Atkinson his life several times over and he could hardly believe that he was dead.

> Atkinson went home on leave for which he was considerably overdue. He did not turn up on 7 March, the day he was due back, and the following day the sad news reached us that he had died the previous day of pneumonia following an attack of Spanish flu. This was a shattering blow to all of us, for we had thought the world of him. And especially to myself as his observer.[15] *Second Lieutenant John Blanford, 206 Squadron*

Families back at home were slowly realizing that their hopes, somewhat cruelly raised by optimistic letters from the front when their sons and lovers were originally shot down or lost in action, were to be doomed to disappointment. The New Year brought an end to the hopes of many, including the family of Edgar Taylor, the 'ordinary' but gallant young American who had been shot down trying to increase his fast growing tally of balloons destroyed.

> I have made enquiries about your son, but have not got any satisfactory answer to them so far. I am very sorry to say that this lack of news looks rather ominous, though until one hears otherwise one will continue to hope that he may be alive. I have lost both of my brothers during the war and can therefore have a rough idea of how you must feel about your son. Though I am afraid it is rather cold comfort to offer you in your distress, you can rest assured that everything possible is being done in the matter and both I and my squadron tender you our heartfelt sympathy.[16] *Major Anthony Arnold, 79 Squadron*

There has been some recent speculation that Edgar Taylor *did* make a safe landing, but was then shot out of hand by the Germans for using incendiary ammunition – despite a copy of the orders from his commanding officer that he always carried to prevent just such an eventuality. These claims seem to have originated in the vacuum of information as to his fate and should perhaps be ignored until some hard evidence emerges.

The war was over but the suffering of such families never really ended. The men knew the risks they were taking. But for their parents, wives and children these were dark times indeed. Lieutenant Edward Lee had written a poignant little letter to be delivered to his wife and children in the event he was killed. He tried to explain why he was doing what he was doing; tried to say goodbye as best he could.

> My very dear wife,
>
> You will only read this if I am killed or reported missing. If not the former you must hope on and be certain that I shall escape if it is at all possible. If I am killed, I know how you love me and it is not possible to put on paper what you are to me. I think you know, dear, without any extravagant language from me. It will be poor consolation, but perhaps some consolation, to know that I still think there is no death I would prefer to dying for my country and I know my darlings will be brought up in that belief. You have to bear the burden, but I am perfectly convinced that our souls do not die. So try hard and be cheerful and brave so that when you meet me again in the spirit world, which we all feel must exist, there may be no regrets. Remember I leave you something better than money – two precious children whom together with you I love more than anything that this world has to give. In material things I feel certain that Ingle will help you. And now I don't know how to say goodbye. Give my darlings kisses from me and always remember that you have made my life as happy as it has been and it is now your hard duty to live for our darling children, Your loving husband,
>
> Teddie[17]

The postman would deliver this tragic letter just a few days before the end of the war. Lieutenant Edward 'Teddie' Lee and many of his comrades had been killed while returning from a bombing raid with 98 Squadron on 30 October 1918. His family would have the rest of their lives to think about his sacrifice and their loss.

A proud but grieving American father managed to visit the site of his son's rough grave in person. There had never been much doubt as to the fate of Wilbert White, who had been killed when apparently deliberately ramming a Fokker threatening to shoot down one of his young comrades on 10 October. His father merely sought some kind of personal closure by discovering exactly where the body of his hero son was lying so he could arrange a proper funeral.

> After four days of careful searching, we found the ragged remnants of his machine on the other side of the river along the road toward Milly, near Dun. We were led to the spot by a shining substance which proved to be an aluminium part of the fuselage. Far across the ploughed field from where the machine lay, we found the unidentified grave under a heap of wire. Five days later, on May 1st, which was his thirtieth birthday, we placed his body in the great National Cemetery at Romagne. For me, that was a hard lonely funeral.[18] *Reverend Dr Wilbert White*

For many the New Year brought nothing at all. Lieutenant Thomas Hughes was a remarkably cynical observer throughout the war. His comments were occasionally misguided, always forthright to the point of rudeness, but sometimes in his more prescient moments he seemed to hit the nail right on the head. What was it all for? What had been achieved in the Great War, the 'War to end Wars'?

> What a moment for improving reflections. Let us look back upon the achievements which have justified the slight sacrifices which we have all so gladly made. What are the achievements? Well, we have – er – er – we have – er – held our own against the – er – numerically and morally inferior hordes of our assailants. We have – er – shown the whole world that Britain is fighting as she has always fought – in India, Ireland, South Africa and elsewhere – to uphold the rights of the smaller nationalities to determine their own destinies and forms of government, and to redress the wrongs of the weak. We have from time to time set before ourselves many nobler aims, modified from time to time by our inability to carry them out or by our realisation of their unprofitable nature. We will never sheath the sword until we have finally crushed Prussian militarism and even then we won't sheath

> it much, as we intend to starve the German nation, men, women and children, by an economic boycott for ever and ever and ever, as a means of removing the causes of war and of paving the way to everlasting peace. Germany will presumably sit contrite and humbled in sackcloth and ashes, joyfully expiating the sins of her rulers; without thought of revenge, without hope of prosperity; just as we should, of course, do if we were so humbled.[19]
>
> *Lieutenant Thomas Hughes, 53 Squadron, RFC*

But this was no voice marked by the effects of disappointment, boredom and disillusionment in the post-war period. For Hughes had died in action on 5 February 1918 and these thoughts were as recorded in his diary for 1 January 1918 now preserved in the Imperial War Museum. Thomas Hughes never had the chance to grow old; to join us armchair historians with our perfect 20-20 vision into past-futures. His predictions of German reactions to defeat were opinions born of his personal depression and pessimism right in the very heart of the war. His opinions, sadly, were to be more than vindicated by the course of events over the next twenty years.

Acknowledgements

In writing this book I am fully aware that I am not the 'real' author. The hundreds of personal experience accounts that I quote are the real heart of this book and I have merely linked them together with a narrative to explain what was happening around them. The veterans' original words have an immediacy and power that I could never duplicate. Nevertheless it is important to note that these original quotations have been very lightly edited for readability as necessary. Thus punctuation and spellings have been largely standardized, material has occasionally been re-ordered and irrelevant material has been omitted without any indication in the text. However, changes in the actual words in original sources have been avoided. I have tried to contact the original copyright owners wherever possible and I hope that those I failed to find will be tolerant. I thank you *all* for your kind permissions and indulgence.

I owe a great debt to the Trustees of the Imperial War Museum who have been kind enough to employ me as an oral historian for twenty-five years and still counting! Though I may be biased, the Sound Archive at the IWM is simply *sans pareil*. The Keeper, Margaret Brooks, has patiently helped me at every stage over the long years and I must also thank my colleagues Richard Hughes, Richard McDonough and John Stopford-Pickering. The Sound Archive is an amazing collection, laid down in the early 1970s by David Lance and added to every year since, until its collection of detailed and unsentimental interviews is genuinely second-to-none. I began interviewing First World War veterans when they were in their late eighties and nineties; now I'm interviewing 20-year-olds just back from service in Iraq and Afghanistan. Oh well . . .

The IWM Department of Documents is also the stuff of legend to Great War researchers. Under the ever vigilant eye of their Keeper Rod Suddaby, his staff bestride the world of archivists like *colossi*, combining efficiency with a cheery tolerance. I am as ever particularly grateful to the wonderful Tony Richards. It is the sheer breadth and stunning quality of their collection that takes the breath away. I would also like to thank the Photographic Archive for their assistance in supplying the photographs. As ever Dr Bryn Hammond, one of the finest historians employed by the IWM, has been a positive shower of advice and encouragement. I am particularly indebted to him for sharing his expertise in air/tank cooperation in 1918, and look forward to his book *Cambrai, 1917*, to be published by Weidenfeld & Nicolson in 2007.

I also owe an enormous debt of gratitude to the splendid staff of 'DORIS' at the RAF Museum, Hendon. Like the Royal Flying Corps they do not believe in the ace system, preferring to fly into action on behalf of their visitors wreathed in anonymity. But they were all extremely helpful and friendly. I am also very grateful to the hard-working staff of the Special Collections Section of Brotherton Library at the University of Leeds.

The air historians of the Great War have my heartfelt admiration and gratitude. Men like Chaz Bowyer, Christopher Cole, Norman Franks, Floyd Gibbons, Hal Giblin, Trevor Henshaw, Alex Imrie, Peter Kilduff, Peter Liddle, Alex Revell and Greg Van Wyngarden and so many more who have devoted their lives and blazed a trail for others to follow. Different styles, different methodologies, but all have worked long and hard over the years to document and explain the course of the aerial fighting as it developed during the war. The *Cross & Cockade* and *Over the Front* magazines have also informed and entertained in equal measure. When I was about 16 years old I read Christopher Cole's *McCudden VC* and was spellbound, almost moved to tears at the incongruous fate of the great ace. It triggered my first interest in the subject; I'm still fascinated and I still think it's a great book nearly forty years later. I want to thank the air historians, one and all. If you buy and read any of their books you can't go far wrong and you are in for a thorough treat.

On a personal level I would thank my lovely Polly, Lily and Ruby in descending order of age and ascending order of nuisance. They are *all* my favourites. I would also like to thank my old chum John Paylor who was kind enough to read an early copy of this manuscript and point out many errors in an amusing fashion. Also Alex Revell and his wife Linda, who were kind enough to proof read the manuscript and whose input was invaluable in every respect.

And finally, first things last, I really must thank my editor, Keith Lowe. I think of him as a veritable dynamo of creative energy at the very centre of the cultural whirlpool that is the mighty Weidenfeld & Nicolson publishing empire. I dread to think what foul crimes he committed in past lives to deserve his current status as my editor, but I'm glad to have him all the same. Also his entire editorial and production team who all seem to be very tolerant and exceptionally talented human beings.

Notes to the Text

PREFACE

1 IWM DOCS: W. F. J. Harvey, Edited manuscript letter, 20/7/1918

CHAPTER 1: WHERE ARE WE?

1 E. Ludendorff, *Ludendorff's Own Story*, Vol. II (New York and London: Harper & Brothers, 1919), p.221
2 D. Haig, quoted in G. Sheffield and J. Bourne, *Douglas Haig: War Diaries and Letters, 1914–1918* (London: Weidenfeld & Nicolson, 2005), p.440
3 E. W. von Hoeppner, translated by J. Hawley Larned, *Germany's War in the Air*, (Nashville, US, 1994), p.133
4 H. A. Jones, *The War in the Air*, Vol. IV, Appendix XIV (London: Naval and Military Press, 2006), p.444
5 Ibid., pp.444–5
6 Ibid., p.445
7 Ibid., p.446

CHAPTER 2: SO MUCH TO LEARN

1 IWM DOCS: J. McDonald, Manuscript letter, 16/11/1917
2 RAF MUSEUM: J. C. F. Wilkinson, Typescript memoir, pp.174–5
3 Ibid., pp.176–7
4 Ibid., pp.178–81
5 Ibid., p.181
6 Ibid., pp.191–2
7 IWM SOUND: H. Andrews, AC 984, Reel 1
8 RAF MUSEUM: J. C. F. Wilkinson, Typescript memoir, pp.195–7
9 Ibid., pp.198–9
10 IWM DOCS: T. C. Traill, Typescript account, p.41
11 IWM DOCS: W. Grossart, Typescript letter, 17/9/1936
12 Ibid.
13 IWM SOUND: L. Field, AC 11376, Reel 7 and 8
14 RAF MUSEUM: J. C. F. Wilkinson, Typescript memoir, pp.199–200
15 IWM DOCS: H. G. R. Williams, Microfilm typescript, pp.345–6
16 RAF MUSEUM: J. C. F. Wilkinson, Typescript memoir, p.211
17 Ibid., p.203
18 Ralph O'Neill, quoted in N. Shirley, 'An Interview with Ralph O'Neill', *Over the Front*, Vol. 2, No. 2, p.117

19 RAF MUSEUM: J. C. F. Wilkinson, Typescript memoir, pp. 219–21
20 B. Rogers, quoted in J. H. Morrow and E. Rogers, *A Yankee Ace in the RAF* (Kansas: Kansas University Press, 1996), p.91
21 Smith-Barry, quoted in K. Jopp, 'Gosport', *Popular Flying*, 8/1936, p.251
22 IWM DOCS: E. Garland, Typescript diary, 2/7/1918
23 IWM SOUND: A. B. Yuille, AC 320, Reel 1
24 IWM DOCS: E. Taylor, Transcript letter, 12/1/1918
25 Ibid., 30/3/1918
26 IWM SOUND: A. B. Yuille, AC 320, Reel 2
27 IWM SOUND: R. Sykes, AC 301, Reel 11
28 S. Douglas, *Years of Combat* (London: Collins, 1963), pp.244–5
29 H. H. Balfour, *An Airman Marches* (London: Hutchinson, 1933), pp.126–7
30 IWM DOCS: E. Taylor, Transcript letter, 3/4/1918
31 Ibid., 8/2/1918

CHAPTER 3: ACES RISING

1 A. E. Woodbridge, quoted in F. Gibbons, *The Red Knight of Germany* (New York: Garden City Publishing, 1927), p.292
2 M. von Richthofen, translated by P. Kilduff, *The Red Baron* (Folkestone: Bailey Brothers & Swinfen, 1974), pp.99–100
3 M. von Richthofen, translated by S. T. Lawson, 'Dicta-Richthofen: The Last Will and Testament', *Cross & Cockade*, Vol. 23, No. 2, p.68
4 Ibid., p.70
5 Ibid., p.66
6 Ibid., p.67
7 Ibid.
8 Ibid., p.69
9 Ibid., p.71
10 E. Udet, *Ace of the Black Cross* (London: Newnes, 1937), pp. 91–2
11 M. von Richthofen, quoted in 'Vigilant', *Richthofen: the Red Knight of the Air* (London: John Hamilton Ltd, 1934), p.221
12 IWM SOUND: G. Lewis, AC 11308, Reel 3
13 W. Douglas, quoted in J. M. Dudgeon, *Mick: The Story of Major Edward Mannock* (London: Robert Hale, 1993), p.112
14 F. Gilbert, *McElroy of Forty* (privately published)
15 Ira Jones, *King of Air Fighters* (London: Greenhill Books, 1989), p.195
16 Ibid.
17 Ibid.
18 K. Caldwell, Letter, 22/3/1977, quoted in 'Fighting High Up and Far Over: Caldwell and Lewis Exchange Views', *Over the Front*, Vol. 3, No. 1, p.21
19 RAF MUSEUM: A. H. Cobby, Typescript article, 'Aerial Fighting', p.63
20 E. Mannock, quoted in I. Jones, *King of Air Fighters: Biography of Major 'Mick' Mannock, VC, DSO, MC* (London: Ivor Nicholson & Watson, 1935), p.161
21 RAF MUSEUM: A. H. Cobby, Typescript article, 'Aerial Fighting', p.60
22 IWM DOCS: W. F. J. Harvey, Manuscript letter, 5/3/1918
23 S. Douglas, *Years of Combat*, pp.246–7
24 IWM SOUND: J. C. F. Hopkins, AC 47, Reel 6
25 IWM SOUND: H. N. Charles, AC 4060, Reel 1
26 IWM SOUND: T. Isbell, AC 4017, Reel 1
27 J. T. B. McCudden, *Five Years in the Royal Flying Corps:* (London: *The 'Aeroplane' and General Publishing Co. Ltd. 1918*), p.235

28 S. Douglas, *Years of Combat*, p.247
29 J. T. B. McCudden, quoted in *A Short History of the Royal Air Force* (Air Historical Branch, Air Ministry, 1929), pp.208–9
30 McCudden, *Five Years in the Royal Flying Corps*, p.242
31 IWM SOUND: Gwilym Lewis, AC 11308, Reel 4
32 IWM DOCS: T. C. Traill, Typescript account, p.55
33 RAF MUSEUM: A. H. Cobby, Typescript article, 'Aerial Fighting', p.63
34 L. H. Rochford, *I Chose the Sky* (London: William Kimber, 1977), pp.133–4
35 S. Douglas, *Years of Combat* p.278
36 Ibid., p.290
37 A. W. Beauchamp-Proctor, quoted in F. K. Mitchell and A. Blake, 'The Little Man with the Guts of a Lion', *Kommando*, 1/1964), p.37
38 H. O. MacDonald, quoted in Mitchell and Blake, 'The Little Man with the Guts of a Lion', p.37

CHAPTER 4: IMPENDING STORM

1 IWM DOCS: C. Dixon, Microfilm typescript diary, 1/1/1918
2 E. W. von Hoeppner, *Germany's War in the Air*, p.135
3 Ibid., p. 140
4 F. Kampfenkel, translated by P. Kilduff, 'Flieger Abteilung (A) 240', *Over the Front*, Vol. 2, No. 3, p.196
5 von Hoeppner, *Germany's War in the Air*, pp. 143-4
6 Kampfenkel, 'Flieger Abteilung (A) 240' pp. 196–7
7 RAF MUSEUM: J. T. B. McCudden, *Five Years in the Royal Flying Corps*, Original manuscript, p.148
8 Ibid., p.161
9 Ibid., p.172
10 Ibid., pp.173–4
11 Ibid., p.178a
12 IWM DOCS: T. C. Traill, Typescript account, p.49
13 IWM DOCS: F. C. Ransley, Typescript account
14 Ibid.
15 IWM DOCS: T. Hughes, Transcript diary, 1/1/1918
16 IWM DOCS: Walter Giffard, Edited as a collage of typescript diary entries, 12/1917–2/1918
17 IWM SOUND A. F. Behrend, AC 4017, Reel 1
18 Ibid.
19 Ibid.
20 Ibid.
21 E. Löwenhardt, translated by S. T. Lawson, 'Dicta-Richthofen: The Last Will and Testament', *Cross & Cockade*, Vol. 23, No. 2, p. 73
22 IWM DOCS: Walter Giffard, Edited typescript diary entries, 28/12/1917
23 Ibid., 3/1/1918
24 Ibid., 2/4/1918
25 Ibid., 4/3/1918
26 Balfour, *An Airman Marches*, pp.135–6
27 IWM DOCS: F. C. Ransley, Typescript account
28 Ibid.
29 Ibid.
30 NATIONAL ARCHIVES: AIR/1/2389/228/11/101, N. H. Anderson, *War Experiences*

31 IWM DOCS: W. Grossart, Typescript letter, 29/9/1936
32 IWM DOCS: J. B. Heppel, Typescript account in papers of J. S. Blanford
33 C. H. Latimer-Needham, 'Observer's Story', *Cross & Cockade*, Vol. 5, No. 2, p.64
34 K. Bodenschatz, translated by J. Hayzlett, *Hunting with Richthofen: The Bodenschatz Diaries* (London: Grub Street, 1998), p.59
35 C.P.O. Bartlett, *Bomber Pilot, 1916-1918* (London: Ian Allen Ltd, 1974), p.142
36 M. von Richthofen, quoted in S. Wise, *Canadian Airmen and the First World War: The Official History of the Royal Canadian Air Force*, Vol. I (Canada: Ministry of Supply and Services, 1980) p.487
37 Bartlett, *Bomber Pilot, 1916–1918* p.143
38 Ibid.
39 Bodenschatz, *Hunting with Richthofen*, pp.63–4
40 von Hoeppner, *Germany's War in the Air*, p.140
41 IWM SOUND: H. Pohlmann, AC 4197, Reel 1
42 F. Nagel, *Fritz: The World War I Memoirs of a German Leutnant* (Huntingdon, West Virginia: Der Angriff Publications, 1981), pp.74–5

CHAPTER 5: GÖTTERDÄMMERUNG ON THE SOMME

1 Bodenschatz, pp.65–6
2 S. Douglas, *Years of Combat*, p.262
3 IWM DOCS: E. E. Stock, Manuscript diary account, 21/3/1918
4 NATIONAL ARCHIVES: AIR/1/2388/228/228/11/80, T. Leigh-Mallory
5 IWM DOCS: E. E. Stock, Manuscript diary account, 21/3/1918
6 RAF MUSEUM: C. R. Outen, quoted in *Experiences of RFC Ground Wireless Operators on the Western Front during 1918* (Old Comrades Association: *c.* 1965), p.21
7 IWM DOCS: E. E. Stock, Manuscript diary account, 21/3/1918
8 Ibid.
9 S. Douglas, *Years of Combat*, p.263
10 Nagel, *Fritz*, p.77
11 Kampfenkel, 'Flieger Abteilung (A) 240', pp.201–3
12 IWM SOUND ARCHIVE: G. Lachman, AC 4151, Reel 1. He is referenced elsewhere as being wounded on 22 March 1918 but he states it was the day before
13 Rochford, *I Chose the Sky*, p.142
14 Ibid., pp.142–3
15 RAF MUSEUM: C. R. Outen, quoted in *Experiences of RFC Ground Wireless Operators on the Western Front during 1918*, p.22
16 von Hoeppner, *Germany's War in the Air*, pp.147–8
17 IWM DOCS: E. E. Stock, Manuscript diary account, 22/3/1918
18 S. Douglas, *Years of Combat*, pp.266–7
19 IWM DOCS: E. E. Stock, Manuscript diary account, 22/3/1918
20 S. Douglas, *Years of Combat*, p.280
21 von Hoeppner, *Germany's War in the Air*, p.148
22 R. W. Mackenzie, 'My Most Thrilling Flight: An Encounter with Richthofen', *Popular Flying*, 6/1934 p.134
23 S. Douglas, *Years of Combat*, p.279
24 IWM DOCS: F. C. Ransley, Typescript account
25 RAF MUSEUM: M. Pocock, quoted in *Experiences of RFC Ground Wireless Operators on the Western Front during 1918*, p.25
26 M. von Richthofen quoted in Bodenschatz, *Hunting with Richthofen*, p.67
27 IWM DOCS: E. E. Stock, Manuscript diary account, 24/3/1918

28 Ibid.
29 J. M. Salmond, quoted in S. Wise, *Canadian Airmen and the First World War*, p.500
30 Nagel, *Fritz*, p.77
31 Ibid., p.78
32 IWM SOUND: J. C. F. Hopkins, AC 47, Reel 4
33 IWM SOUND: J. C. F. Hopkins, AC 47, Reel 1
34 G. W. Higgs, 'My Most Thrilling Flight', *Popular Flying*, 2/1936, pp.608–9
35 J. M. Salmond, quoted in Jones, *The War in the Air*, Vol. IV p.320
36 IWM DOCS: E. E. Stock, Manuscript diary account, 25/3/1918
37 RAF MUSEUM: J. Baker, Edited from manuscript copies of two letters, 26/3/1918
38 M. von Richthofen, quoted in Bodenschatz, *Hunting with Richthofen*, p.67
39 Rochford, *I Chose the Sky*, p.145
40 Ibid., p.147
41 von Hoeppner, *Germany's War in the Air*, pp.148–9
42 M. von Richthofen, quoted in Bodenschatz, *Hunting with Richthofen* p.67
43 IWM DOCS: E. E. Stock, Manuscript diary account, 26/3/1918
44 Ibid.
45 Ibid.
46 NATIONAL ARCHIVES: AIR/10/973, B. E. Smithies, *Experiences during the War, 1914–1918*
47 IWM DOCS: E. E. Stock, Manuscript diary account, 26/3/1918
48 Ibid., 27/3/1918
49 Ibid.
50 Nagel, *Fritz*, p.89
51 Ibid., p.78
52 RAF MUSEUM: W. M. Butler, Typescript diary, 28/3/1918
53 Udet, *Ace of the Black Cross*, pp.94–5
54 Ibid., pp.95–6
55 E. Ludendorff, *Ludendorff's Own Story: August 1914–November 1918*, Vol. II (New York: Harper & Brothers, 1919), p.231
56 H. von Kuhl, quoted in Wise, *Canadian Airmen and the First World War*, p.509
57 G. H. Lewis, *Wings over the Somme, 1916–1918* (Wrexham: Bridge Books, 1994), p.121
58 IWM DOCS: E. E. Stock, Manuscript diary account, 28/3/1918
59 Ibid.
60 Ibid.
61 NATIONAL ARCHIVES: AIR/1/2391/228/11/148, G. M. Knocker, *War Experiences*

CHAPTER 6: THE BATTLE FOR FLANDERS

1 H. Trenchard, quoted in A. Boyle, *Trenchard: Man of Vision* (London: Collins, 1962), p.232
2 D. Haig, quoted in Boyle, *Trenchard* p.230
3 IWM SOUND: T. Thomson, AC 309, Reel 6
4 IWM DOCS: C. Dixon, Microfilm typescript letter, 17/4/1918
5 Jones, *The War in the Air*, Vol. IV, Appendix XVIII, p.458
6 Ibid., p.457
7 Kampfenkel, 'Flieger Abteilung (A) 240', *Over the Front*, Vol. 2, No. 3, pp.203–4
8 IWM DOCS: R. A. Archer, Manuscript memoir
9 IWM DOCS: H. A. Blundell, Typescript diary, 9/4/1918
10 IWM DOCS: R. A. Archer, Manuscript memoir

11 C. Draper, quoted in Anon, *Naval Eight: A History of No. 8 Squadron, RNAS* (London: Signal Press, 1931), p.51
12 Ibid., p.52
13 Ibid.
14 Ibid., p.53
15 J. H. Weingarth, quoted in G. Weingarth, 'Camel Pilot', *Cross & Cockage*, Vol. 27, No. l, p.8
16 IWM DOCS: R. A. Archer, Manuscript memoir
17 Ibid.
18 Ibid.
19 Ibid.
20 Ibid.
21 D. Haig, quoted in Sheffield and Bourne, *Douglas Haig*, p.402
22 A. H. Cobby, *High Adventure* (Melbourne: Kookaburra Technical Publications, 1981), p.57
23 Ira Jones, *King of Air Fighters*, p.180. Jones says that it is from the diary of a pilot named VanIra but it is a pseudonym
24 E. Mannock, quoted in Ira Jones, *King of Air Fighters*, p.183
25 Ira Jones, *King of Air Fighters*, p.180
26 G. H. Lewis, *Wings over the Somme*, p.125
27 Rochford, *I Chose the Sky*, p.157
28 C. Draper, quoted in Anon, *Naval Eight*, pp.65–6
29 IWM DOCS: W. Grossart, Typescript letter, 9/10/1936
30 R. Compston, quoted in Anon, *Naval Eight*, p.79
31 IWM DOCS: C. Dixon, Microfilm typescript diary, 25/12/1917
32 Ibid., 4/4/1918
33 Ira Jones, *King of Air Fighters*, pp.208–9
34 R.S. Dallas, quoted in A. Hellwig, *Australian Hawk over the Western Front: A Biography of Major R. S. Dallas* (London: Grub Street, 2006), pp.156–7
35 C. Usher, quoted in Hellwig, *Australian Hawk over the Western Front*, p.149
36 IWM DOCS: H. W. Williams, Typescript account in papers of J. S. Blanford
37 IWM DOCS: P. R. Hampton, Manuscript and typescript copy of letters, 5/1918
38 IWM DOCS: A. H. Curtis, Microfilm typescript account, p.93
39 RAF MUSEUM: J. Baker, Manuscript copy of letter, 30/2/1918
40 IWM DOCS: T. C. Traill, Typescript account, p.54
41 IWM DOCS: W. Grossart, Typescript letter, 29/9/1936
42 S. Douglas, *Years of Combat*, pp.277–8
43 IWM DOCS: A. H. Curtis, Microfilm typescript account, pp.149–50
44 Balfour, *An Airman Marches*, pp.144–5
45 NATIONAL ARCHIVES: AIR/10/973, K. R. Park, *Experiences during the War, 1914–1918*

46 C. Usher, quoted in Hellwig, *Australian Hawk over the Western Front*, p.153

CHAPTER 7: THE DEATH OF RICHTHOFEN

1 D. G. Lewis, 'My Most Thrilling Flight: An Encounter with Richthofen', *Popular Flying*, 5/1938, p.75
2 M. von Richthofen, quoted in N. Franks et al., *Under the Guns of the Red Baron: The Complete Record of von Richthofen's Victories and Victims* (London: Grub Street, 2000), p.202
3 D. G. Lewis, 'My Most Thrilling Flight: An Encounter with Richthofen', p.76

4 Ibid.
5 H. J. Wolff, quoted in Kilduff, *Richthofen: Beyond the Legend of the Red Baron* (London: Arms and Armour, 1993), p. 199
6 RAF MUSEUM: R. M. Foster, Typescript account, 'von Richthofen 21st April 1918'
7 W. May, 'Lieutenant Wilfred "Wop" May's Account', *Cross & Cockade*; Vol. 23, No. 2, p.112
8 H. J. Wolff, quoted in Kilduff, Richthofen, p.201
9 R. Brown, quoted in F. R. McGuire, 'Documents Relating to Richthofen's Last Battle', *Over the Top*, Vol. 2, No. 2, p.168
10 May, 'Lieutenant Wilfred "Wop" May's Account', p.112
11 C. Popkin, quoted in M. G. Miller, 'The Death of Manfred von Richthofen: Who Fired the Fatal Shot?', *Sabretache*, Vol. 29, No.2, 1998
12 D. L. Fraser, quoted in F. R. McGuire, 'Documents Relating to Richthofen's Last Battle', *Over the Top*, Vol. 2, No. 2, p.165
13 Ibid.
14 W. May, 'Lieutenant Wilfred "Wop" May's Account', p.112
15 R. Buie, quoted in Miller, 'The Death of Manfred von Richthofen'
16 C. Popkin, quoted in Miller, 'The Death of Manfred von Richthofen'
17 F. J. W. Mellersh, quoted in McGuire, 'Documents Relating to Richthofen's Last Battle', p.165
18 G. M. Travers, quoted in McGuire, 'Documents Relating to Richthofen's Last Battle', p.166
19 R. Buie, quoted in Miller, 'The Death of Manfred von Richthofen'
20 P. Markham, 'The Events of 21 April 1918', *Over the Front*, Vol. 8, No. 2, pp. 127–8
21 S. Douglas, *Years of Combat*, p. 305
22 H. J. Wolff, quoted in Kilduff, *Richthofen*, p.201
23 Ibid.
24 Bodenschatz, *Hunting with Richthofen*, p.59
25 Lothar von Richthofen, quoted in Kilduff, *Richthofen*, p.201
26 RAF MUSEUM: H. S. P. Walmsley, Manuscript letter, 23/4/1918
27 RAF MUSEUM: J. Middleton, Typescript diary, 17/8/1918

CHAPTER 8: FADING HOPES

1 NATIONAL ARCHIVES: AIR/1/2392/228/22/185, W. E. Theak, *Service Experiences*
2 Bodenschatz, *Hunting with Richthofen*, p.93
3 NATIONAL ARCHIVES: AIR/1/2392/228/22/185, W. E. Theak, *Service Experiences*
4 Ibid.
5 Ibid.
6 von Hoeppner, *Germany's War in the Air*, pp.154–5
7 G. H. Lewis, *Wings over the Somme*, pp.134–5
8 G. H. Glasspoole, 'My Most Thrilling Flight', *Popular Flying*, 3/1937, p.624
9 Ibid., p. 625
10 J. Salmond, quoted in H. A. Jones, *The War in the Air*, Vol. VI, p.405
11 R. Berthold, quoted in N. Franks and G. Van Wyngarden, *Fokker D.VII Aces of World War I, Part I* (Wellingborough: Osprey Publishing: Aircraft of the Aces, N. 53), p. 51
12 Ibid., p.52
13 Ibid.
14 E. Udet, quoted by A. van Ishoven, edited by C. Bowyer, *The Fall of an Eagle: The Life of Fighter Ace Ernst Udet* (London: William Kimber, 1977), pp.63–4

15 IWM DOCS: T. C. Traill, Typescript account, p.55
16 Ibid., p.46
17 Ibid., p.55
18 Ralph O'Neill, quoted in Shirley, 'An Interview with Ralph O'Neill', p.131
19 W. White, quoted in J. Parks, 'No Greater Love: The Story of Lieutenant Wilbert W. White', '*Over the Front*, Vol. 1, No. 1, p.49

CHAPTER 9: FALLING ACES

1 E. Mannock, quoted in P. Vansittart, *Voices from the Great War* (London: Penguin Books, 1963), p.230
2 Ira Jones, *King of Air Fighters*, p.202
3 E. Mannock, quoted in Ira Jones, *King of Air Fighters*, p.207
4 McCudden, *Five Years in the Royal Flying Corps*, p.258
5 J. T. B. McCudden, quoted in C. Cole, *McCudden VC* (London: William Kimber, 1967), p.189
6 L. M. Fenelon, quoted in Cole, *McCudden VC* pp.191–2
7 Ira Jones, *King of Air Fighters*, p.180
8 E. Mannock, quoted in Ira Jones, *King of Air Fighters*, p.232
9 J. Eyles, quoted in Dudgeon, *Mick*, p.154
10 L. Callahan, quoted in S. Douglas, *Years of Combat*, p.310
11 IWM SOUND: G. Lewis, AC 11308, Reel 3
12 L. Callahan quoted in S. Douglas, *Years of Combat*, p.311
13 D. Inglis, quoted in Ira Jones, *King of Air Fighters*, p.248–9
14 RAF MUSEUM: E. Naulls, Letter to editor of *Strand* magazine, 1/11/1943
15 D. Inglis, quoted in Ira Jones, *King of Air Fighters*, p.249
16 Sergeant John, quoted in D. Whetton, *Mannock, Patrol Leader Supreme* (Falls Church, USA: Ajay Enterprises, 1977), p.34
17 Ira Jones, *King of Air Fighters*, p.251

CHAPTER 10: A BLACK DAY

1 von Hoeppner, *Germany's War in the Air*, pp.165–6
2 Ibid., p.166
3 IWM DOCS: W. Grossart, Typescript letter, 9/10/1936
4 Ibid.
5 Ibid.
6 Ibid.
7 NATIONAL ARCHIVES: AIR/1/2388/228/228/11/80, T. Leigh-Mallory
8 LEEDS UNIVERSITY: Special Collections, Brotherton Library, Peter Liddle Personal Experience Archive: F. M. F. West, AIR 339, Recording transcript
9 LEEDS UNIVERSITY: Special Collections, Brotherton Library, Peter Liddle Personal Experience Archive: J. A. G. Haslam, AIR 150, Recording transcript
10 IWM DOCS: W. Grossart, Typescript letter, 9/10/1936
11 Ibid.
12 IWM DOCS: G. T. Coles, Manuscript diary, 8/8/1918
13 von Hoeppner, *Germany's War in the Air*, p.167
14 L. von Richthofen, translated by J. Hayzlett, 'My Last Time at the Front', *Over the Front*, Vol. 14, No. 3, p.237
15 IWM DOCS: W. Grossart, Typescript letter, 9/10/1936

16 R. Sykes, 'Serving with 201 Squadron', *Cross & Cockade*, Vol. 2, No. 2, p.34
17 IWM DOCS: W. Grossart, Typescript letter, 9/10/1936
18 Ibid.
19 Ibid., 29/9/1936. This excerpt refers to an earlier raid but conjures up the effect so well I have used it here without changing the overall concept
20 Ibid., 9/10/1936
21 Ibid.
22 IWM DOCS: G. T. Coles, Manuscript diary, 9/8/1918
23 LEEDS UNIVERSITY: Special Collections, Brotherton Library, Peter Liddle Personal Experience Archive: J. A. G. Haslam, AIR 150, Recording transcript
24 Ibid., Recording transcript
25 F. M. F. West, quoted in P. Reid, *Winged Diplomat: The Life Story of Air Commodore Freddie West* (London: Chatto & Windus, 1962), p.95
26 LEEDS UNIVERSITY: Special Collections, Brotherton Library, Peter Liddle Personal Experience Archive: J. A. G. Haslam, AIR 150, Recording transcript
27 LEEDS UNIVERSITY: Special Collections, Brotherton Library, Peter Liddle Personal Experience Archive: F. M. F. West, AIR 339, Recording transcript
28 F. M. F. West quoted in Reid, *Winged Diplomat*, p.95
29 Ibid.
30 LEEDS UNIVERSITY: Special Collections, Brotherton Library, Peter Liddle Personal Experience Archive: J. A. G. Haslam, AIR 150, Recording transcript
31 F. M. F. West, quoted in Reid, *Winged Diplomat*, p.96
32 LEEDS UNIVERSITY: Special Collections, Brotherton Library, Peter Liddle Personal Experience Archive: F. M. F. West, AIR 339, Recording transcript
33 LEEDS UNIVERSITY: Special Collections, Brotherton Library, Peter Liddle Personal Experience Archive: J. A. G. Haslam, AIR 150, Recording transcript
34 L. von Richthofen, 'My Last Time at the Front', p.238
35 Ibid.
36 A. Wenz, quoted in Bodenschatz, *Hunting with Richthofen*, p.115
37 Ibid., pp.115–16
38 Ibid., p.116
39 Ibid.
40 Ibid., p.117
41 L. von Richthofen, 'My Last Time at the Front', p.240
42 Ibid.
43 Ludendorff, *Ludendorff's Own Story*, Vol. II, pp.330–31

CHAPTER 11: ORDINARY BOYS

1 RAF MUSEUM: J. C. F. Wilkinson, Typescript memoir, p.277
2 IWM DOCS: E. Taylor, Transcript letter, 7/5/1918
3 Ibid., 14/5/1918
4 Ibid., 15/5/1918
5 Ibid., 21/5/1918
6 Ibid., 1/6/1918
7 Ibid., 30/5/1918
8 Ibid., 1/6/1918
9 Ibid., 23/6/1918 and 26/6/1918
10 Ibid., 29/6/1918 and 1/7/1918
11 Ibid., 21/6/1918
12 Ibid., 9/7/1918
13 Ibid., 20/7/1918

14 Ibid., 2/8/1918
15 Ibid., 5/8/1918
16 RAF MUSEUM: J. C. F. Wilkinson, Typescript memoir, pp.272–3
17 Ibid., pp.240–41
18 Ibid., pp.246–9
19 Ibid., pp.258-9
20 Ibid., p.249
21 Ibid., pp.249–51
22 Ibid., pp.252–3
23 Ibid., pp.256–7
24 Ibid., p.258
25 Ibid., p.263–6
26 IWM DOCS: E. Taylor, Transcript letter, 2/8/1918
27 RAF MUSEUM: J. C. F. Wilkinson, Typescript memoir, pp.269–72
28 IWM DOCS: E. Taylor, Transcript letter, 17/8/1918
29 Ibid.
30 Ibid., 20/7/1918
31 Ibid., 15/8/1918 and 16/8/1918
32 Ibid., 23/8/1918
33 Ibid.
34 IWM DOCS: A. R. Arnold, Transcript letter, 3/9/1918, in papers of E. Taylor
35 IWM DOCS: M. Munden, Transcript letter, 25/8/1918, in papers of E. Taylor
36 RAF MUSEUM: J. C. F. Wilkinson, Typescript memoir, pp.287–8

CHAPTER 12: BOMBERS OVER GERMANY

1 D. Haig quoted in H.A. Jones, *The War in the Air*, Vol. VI, p.125
2 RAF MUSEUM: O. L. Beater, Typescript dairy, 5/12/1918
3 IWM DOCS: A. S. Keep, Manuscript account
4 Ibid.
5 Ibid.
6 Ibid.
7 Ibid.
8 Ibid.
9 Ibid.
10 Ibid.
11 H. Trenchard, quoted in H.A. Jones, *The War in the Air*, Vol. VI, p.136
12 Ibid.
13 IWM DOCS: A. S. Keep, Manuscript account
14 F. E. Nash, 'My Most Thrilling Flight', *Popular Flying*, 8/1935, pp.272–3
15 IWM DOCS: A. S. Keep, Manuscript account
16 IWM DOCS: E. Garland, Typescript diary, 23/8/1918 and 27/8/1918
17 Ibid., 31/8/1918
18 Ibid., 4/9/1918
19 Ibid., 7/9/1918
20 W. E. Johns, 'My Most Thrilling Flight', *Popular Flying*, 6/1932, pp.142–3
21 Particularly recommended by my editor, who has a penchant for this kind of literature, is the truly awesome adventure that is *Biggles Takes it Rough* (London: Children's Book Club, 1963)
22 IWM SOUND: C. Gordon-Burge, SR 19, Reel 4
23 L. G. Taylor, quoted in C. Gordon-Burge, *The Annals of 100 Squadron* (London: Herbert Reiach, 1919) p.140

24 Ibid.
25 Ibid., pp.140–41
26 Ibid., p.141
27 IWM SOUND: R. Shillinglaw, SR 4224, Reel 1
28 Report of the British Commission, 1/1920, p.36
29 H.A. Jones, *The War in the Air*, Vol. VI, p.164

CHAPTER 13: END GAME

1 F. Foch quoted in J. E. Edmonds, *Military Operations, France and Belgium, 1918*, Vol. IV, (Nashville: The Battery Press, 1993), p.173
2 D. Haig, quoted in Edmonds, *Military Operations, France and Belgium, 1918*, Vol. IV Appendix XX, p.588
3 NATIONAL ARCHIVES: T. Leigh-Mallory, *Cooperation of Aeroplane and Tanks*, pp.9–10
4 Ibid., p.10
5 IWM SOUND: J. Gascoyne, SR 16, Reel 3
6 RAF MUSEUM: J. Middleton, Typescript diary, 27/8/1918
7 IWM DOCS: W. Grossart, Typescript letter, 9/10/1936
8 Ibid.
9 IWM DOCS: A. H. Curtis, Microfilm typescript account, p.145
10 Ibid., pp.145–6
11 IWM DOCS: G. L. Pargeter, Typescript account, pp.2–3
12 Ibid.
13 IWM SOUND: AC 29, W. E. D. Wardrop, Reel 6
14 IWM SOUND: AC 29, W. E. D. Wardrop, Reel 3, 4 and 5
15 IWM DOCS: L. G. Semple, Typescript diary, 2/9/1918
16 RAF MUSEUM: J. C. F. Wilkinson, Typescript memoir, pp.285–7
17 S. Douglas, *Years of Combat*, p.300
18 C. Thomas, 'Under the Windstocking Letter', *Popular Flying*, 1/1937, p.536
19 S. Douglas, *Years of Combat*, pp.300–301
20 LEEDS UNIVERSITY: Special Collections, Brotherton Library, Peter Liddle Personal Experience Archive: J. Pugh, AIR 252, Recording transcript
21 NATIONAL ARCHIVES: AIR/10/973, K. R. Park, *Experiences during the War, 1914–1918*
22 C. Thomas, 'Under the Windstocking Letter', p.536
23 RAF MUSEUM: J. C. F. Wilkinson, Typescript memoir, pp.285–7
24 C. Thomas, 'Under the Windstocking Letter', p.536
25 IWM DOCS: G. T. Coles, Manuscript diary, 22/8/1918–3/9/1918
26 IWM SOUND: F. Roberts, AC 9466, Reel 1
27 IWM SOUND: A. B. Yuille, AC 320, Reel 2 and 4
28 IWM SOUND: A. B. Yuille, AC 320, Reel 3
29 Ibid.
30 IWM DOCS: T. P. Traill, Typescript account, p.61
31 K. K. K. Jentsch, translated by O'Brien Browne, 'Jagdstaffel Boelcke / Jagdgeschwader III', *Cross & Cockade*, Summer, 2005, p.126
32 H. Besser, quoted in R. Duivan, '*Das Königliche Preussiche Jagdgeschwader Nr. II*, Part II', *Over the Front*, Vol. 9, No. 4, pp. 244–5
33 Udet, *Ace of the Black Cross*, p.144
34 von Hoeppner, *Germany's War in the Air*, p.167
35 J. E. Doyle, 'My Most Thrilling Flight', *Popular Flying*, 4/1936 p.18
36 Ibid., pp.18–19

37 Ibid., p.19
38 LEEDS UNIVERSITY: Special Collections, Brotherton Library, Peter Liddle Personal Experience Archive: J. W. Rayner, AIR 257, Recording transcript
39 Doyle, 'My Most Thrilling Flight', p.19
40 Ibid.
41 Ibid.
42 E. Rickenbacker *Fighting the Flying Circus* (New York: Frederich Stokes Company 1919) p.232
43 Ibid. p.233–4
44 IWM DOCS: W. Grossart, Typescript letter, 11/11/1936
45 C. A. H. Longcroft, quoted in H.A. Jones, *The War in the Air, 1918*, Vol. VI, p.506
46 IWM DOCS: Y. Kirkpatrick, Typescript copy of letters, 26/9/1918
47 RAF MUSEUM: J. Middleton, Typescript diary, 26/8/1918
48 Ibid.
49 Ibid.
50 Ibid.
51 Ibid.
52 IWM DOCS: Y. Kirkpatrick, Typescript copy of letters, 26/9/1918
53 RAF MUSEUM: J. Middleton, Typescript diary, 26/8/1918
54 IWM DOCS: Y. Kirkpatrick, Typescript copy of letters, 26/9/1918
55 RAF MUSEUM: J. Middleton, Typescript diary, 26/8/1918
56 Ibid., 27/8/1918
57 IWM SOUND: R. Sykes, AC 301, Reel 5
58 IWM DOCS: Y. Kirkpatrick, Typescript copy of letters, 28/9/1918
59 Ibid., 29/9/1918
60 IWM DOCS: J. S. Blanford, Typescript manuscript, *Sans Escort*, p.16
61 Ibid., pp.16–17
62 F. Luke, Combat report, 16/8/1918
63 Ibid., 12/9/1918
64 J. F. Wehner, Combat report, 16/9/1918
65 F. Luke, Combat report, 19/1918
66 Internet source: http://www.acepilots.com/wwi/us_luke.html
67 Ibid.
68 IWM DOCS: J. S. Blanford, Typescript manuscript, *Sans Escort*, p.21
69 Ibid.
70 Ibid., pp.21–2
71 Ibid., pp.22–3
72 Ibid., p.23
73 LEEDS UNIVERSITY: Special Collections, Brotherton Library, Peter Liddle Personal Experience Archive: R. Ivelaw-Chapman, AIR 174, Recording transcript
74 Ibid., AIR 174, Recording transcript
75 Ibid., AIR 174, Recording transcript
76 Ibid., AIR 174, Recording transcript
77 Ralph O'Neill, quoted in Shirley, 'An Interview with Ralph O'Neill', p.137
78 E. Rickenbacker
79 J. Meissner, quoted in Parks, 'No Greater Love', p.54
80 C. Cox, quoted in Parks, 'No Greater Love', p.57
81 J. Meissner, quoted in Parks, 'No Greater Love', p.53
82 E. Rickenbacker:
83 W. White, quoted in Parks, 'No Greater Love', p.49
84 J. Meissner quoted in Parks, 'No Greater Love', p.52
85 IWM DOCS: G. L. Pargeter, Typescript account, pp.4–5
86 S. Douglas, *Years of Combat*, p.334

87 IWM DOCS: L. G. Semple, Typescript diary, 26/10/1918
88 IWM DOCS: B. H. Rook, Typescript account in papers of J. S. Blanford
89 IWM DOCS: Y. Kirkpatrick, Typescript copy of letters, 24/10/1918
90 L. C. Holden, quoted in N. Franks, *Dogfight: Aerial Tactics of the Aces of World War I* (London: Greenhill Books, 2003), p.231
91 Ibid., pp.231–2
92 W. Ralph, *Barker VC: The Life, Death and Legend of Canada's Most Decorated War Hero* (London: Grub Street, 1997)
93 L. Strange, *Recollections of an Airman* (London: The Aviation Book Club, 1940), p.199
94 IWM DOCS: Y. Kirkpatrick, Typescript copy of letters, 3/11/1918
95 R. Viall, quoted in A. J. Lynch, 'An Interview with Lieutenant Richmond Viall', *Cross & Cockade*, Vol. II, Autumn 1961, pp.248–9
96 Rochford, *I Chose the Sky*, p.196
97 IWM DOCS: L. G. Semple, Typescript diary, 10/11/1918–11/11/1918
98 IWM DOCS: C. Dixon, Microfilm typescript diary, 10/11/1918
99 IWM DOCS: Y. Kirkpatrick, Typescript copy of letters, 11/11/1918
100 LEEDS UNIVERSITY: Special Collections, Brotherton Library, Peter Liddle Personal Experience Archive: R. Ivelaw-Chapman, AIR 174, Recording transcript
101 Balfour, *An Airman Marches*, p.151
102 IWM DOCS: F. O. Cave, Manuscript Diary, 11/11/1918
103 IWM DOCS: E. Garland, Typescript Diary, 11/11/1918

CHAPTER 14: WHEN THE SHOW IS OVER

1 IWM DOCS: Y. Kirkpatrick, Typescript copy of letters, 23/11/1918
2 IWM SOUND: T. E. Rogers, AC 171, Reel 7
3 IWM DOCS: Y. Kirkpatrick, Typescript copy of letters, 13/12/1918
4 RAF MUSEUM: W. Snow, Manuscript letter, 13/7/1919
5 IWM DOCS: B. H. Rook, Typescript account in papers of J. S. Blanford
6 IWM DOCS: J. S. Blanford, Typescript manuscript, *Sans Escort*, Appendix D, pp.40A–40B
7 von Hoeppner, *Germany's War in the Air*, p.169
8 Kampfenkel, 'Flieger Abteilung (A) 240', p.212
9 IWM DOCS: Y. Kirkpatrick, Typescript copy of letters, 23/11/1918
10 IWM DOCS: E. Garland, Typescript diary and subsequent note, 15/6/1918
11 IWM DOCS: Y. Kirkpatrick, Typescript copy of letters, 23/11/1918
12 IWM SOUND: P. Townshend, AC 14910, Reel 1
13 Ibid.
14 IWM DOCS: R. N. G. Atkinson poem quoted in J. S. Blanford, Typescript manuscript, *Sans Escort*, p.52
15 IWM DOCS: J. S. Blanford, Typescript manuscript, *Sans Escort*, Appendix D, p.48
16 IWM DOCS: A. R. Arnold, Transcript letter, 2/1/1919, in papers of E. Taylor
17 RAF MUSEUM: E. A. R. Lee, Manuscript letter, 29/10/1918
18 W. W. White, quoted in Parks, 'No Greater Love', p.52
19 IWM DOCS: T. Hughes, Transcript diary, 1/1/1918

Index

INDEX